Poesis in Extremis

COMPARATIVE JEWISH LITERATURES

Bloomsbury's **Comparative Jewish Literatures** series creates a new venue for scholarship and debate both in Jewish Studies and Comparative Literature as it showcases the diversity of a nascent field with unique interdisciplinary footprints. It offers both a new way of looking at Jewish writing as well as insights into how Jewish literature is looked at by scholars indifferent to or sympathetic with these texts. Through its focus on the diversity of these groups' perspectives, the series suggests that disciplinary location informs how comparative Jewish literatures are understood theoretically, and it establishes new sectors that abut and intersect with the field in the twenty-first century.

Series Editor
Kitty Millet, San Francisco State University, USA

Advisory Board
Agata Bielik-Robson, University of Nottingham, UK
Sarah Phillips Casteel, Carleton University, Canada
Bryan Cheyette, University of Reading, UK
Nan Goodman, University of Colorado at Boulder, USA
Vivian Liska, University of Antwerp, Belgium
Orly Lubin, Tel Aviv University, Israel
Susan McReynolds, Northwestern University, USA
Paul Mendes-Flohr, University of Chicago, USA
Anna Parkinson, Northwestern University, USA
Na'ama Rokem, University of Chicago, USA
Maurice Samuels, Yale University, USA
Axel Stähler, University of Bern, Switzerland
Ilan Stavans, Amherst College, USA

Volumes in the Series:
Jewish Imaginaries of the Spanish Civil War: In Search of Poetic Justice,
edited by Cynthia Gabbay
Derrida's Marrano Passover: Exile, Survival, Betrayal, and the Metaphysics of Non-Identity, by Agata Bielik-Robson
Holocaust Literature and Representation: Their Lives, Our Words,
edited by Phyllis Lassner and Judith Tydor Baumel-Schwartz
Poesis in Extremis: Literature Witnessing the Holocaust, by
Daniel Feldman and Efraim Sicher
Kabbalah and Literature, by Kitty Millet

Poesis in Extremis

Literature Witnessing the Holocaust

Daniel Feldman and Efraim Sicher

BLOOMSBURY ACADEMIC
NEW YORK • LONDON • OXFORD • NEW DELHI • SYDNEY

BLOOMSBURY ACADEMIC

Bloomsbury Publishing Inc, 1359 Broadway, New York, NY 10018, USA
Bloomsbury Publishing Plc, 50 Bedford Square, London, WC1B 3DP, UK
Bloomsbury Publishing Ireland, 29 Earlsfort Terrace, Dublin 2, D02 AY28, Ireland

BLOOMSBURY, BLOOMSBURY ACADEMIC and the Diana logo are
trademarks of Bloomsbury Publishing Plc

First published in the United States of America 2024
Paperback edition published 2025

Copyright © Daniel Feldman and Efraim Sicher, 2024

For legal purposes the Acknowledgments on pp. ix–xi constitute an
extension of this copyright page.

Cover design by Eleanor Rose
Cover image: *Death March* (Czechowice-Bielsko, January 1945)
by Jan Hartman, 1945 © Imperial War Museums, UK

All rights reserved. No part of this publication may be: i) reproduced or transmitted in any form, electronic or mechanical, including photocopying, recording or by means of any information storage or retrieval system without prior permission in writing from the publishers; or ii) used or reproduced in any way for the training, development or operation of artificial intelligence (AI) technologies, including generative AI technologies. The rights holders expressly reserve this publication from the text and data mining exception as per Article 4(3) of the Digital Single Market Directive (EU) 2019/790.

Bloomsbury Publishing Inc does not have any control over, or responsibility for, any third-party websites referred to or in this book. All internet addresses given in this book were correct at the time of going to press. The author and publisher regret any inconvenience caused if addresses have changed or sites have ceased to exist, but can accept no responsibility for any such changes.

Library of Congress Cataloging-in-Publication Data
Names: Feldman, Daniel, author. | Sicher, Efraim, author.
Title: Poesis in extremis : literature witnessing the Holocaust /
Daniel Feldman and Efraim Sicher.
Description: New York : Bloomsbury Academic, 2024. |
Series: Comparative Jewish literatures | Includes bibliographical references and index. |
Summary: "This innovative study asks how genocide can be witnessed
through imaginative literature and affect readers who were
not there"– Provided by publisher.
Identifiers: LCCN 2023029671 (print) | LCCN 2023029672 (ebook) |
ISBN 9798765100189 (hardback) | ISBN 9798765100226 (paperback) |
ISBN 9798765100202 (pdf) | ISBN 9798765100196 (epub) | ISBN 9798765100219
Subjects: LCSH: Holocaust, Jewish (1939-1945), in literature. | Holocaust, Jewish
(1939–1945)–Psychological aspects. Classification: LCC PN56.H55 F45 2024 (print) |
LCC PN56.H55 (ebook) | DDC 809/.93358405318–dc23/eng/20230927
LC record available at https://lccn.loc.gov/2023029671
LC ebook record available at https://lccn.loc.gov/2023029672

ISBN:	HB:	979-8-7651-0018-9
	PB:	979-8-7651-0022-6
	ePDF:	979-8-7651-0020-2
	eBook:	979-8-7651-0019-6

Series: Comparative Jewish Literatures

Typeset by Integra Software Services Pvt. Ltd.

For product safety related questions contact productsafety@bloomsbury.com.

To find out more about our authors and books visit www.bloomsbury.com
and sign up for our newsletters.

CONTENTS

Acknowledgments ix

Introduction *Daniel Feldman and Efraim Sicher* 1

Part One

1 Elie Wiesel's *Night:* Literature as Testimony *Efraim Sicher* 25

Part Two

2 A Poetics of the Holocaust?: Celan, Sutzkever, Miłosz *Efraim Sicher* 43

3 Writing Nothing: Negation and Subjectivity in the Holocaust Poetry of Paul Celan and Dan Pagis *Daniel Feldman* 79

4 Miklós Radnóti: Postcards from a Death March *Efraim Sicher* 107

5 Władysław Szlengel's Ghetto Poems: Writing to the Dead *Daniel Feldman* 131

6 "Poem in a Bottle": Itzhak Katzenelson's *Song of the Murdered Jewish People* *Daniel Feldman* 157

Part Three

7 Translating Oral Memory in Ida Fink's "Traces" *Daniel Feldman* 177

Postscript *Daniel Feldman and Efraim Sicher* 197

Notes 204
Bibliography 245
Index 250

ACKNOWLEDGMENTS

The authors wish to express their deep gratitude to David G. Roskies, Vivian Liska, and Hannah Pollin-Galay for their invaluable guidance, as well as their exemplary scholarship. John Felstiner was a special source of inspiration and friendship before his untimely death. Leona Toker generously read the manuscript and made useful suggestions.

Thanks to Tsiviya Frank-Wygoda, a collocutor in David Roskies and Amos Goldberg's reading group in Holocaust literature at the Hebrew University of Jerusalem and a constant colleague.

Thanks to Neta for initial bibliographical research and to Michael for reformatting, as well as to Paulette for indexing and to Kate for legal advice.

We thank Amy Martin, Hali Han, and all the team at Bloomsbury for their dedication and efficiency.

Earlier versions of passages in Chapter 2 first appeared in Efraim Sicher, "Is There a Poetics of the Holocaust? Three Exemplary Poets," *Narracje o Zagładzie* 6 (2020): 343–71.

An earlier version of Chapter 3 appeared as Daniel Feldman, "Writing Nothing: Negation and Subjectivity in the Holocaust Poetry of Paul Celan and Dan Pagis," *Comparative Literature* 66, no. 4 (2014): 438–58.

An earlier version of Chapter 7 appeared as Daniel Feldman, "Translating Oral Memory and Visual Media in Ida Fink's 'Traces,'" in *Translated Memories: Transgenerational Perspectives on the Holocaust*. Edited by Bettina Hofmann and Ursula Reuter, 31–49. Lanham, MD: Lexington Books, 2020.

Excerpts from Paul Celan, "Todesfuge," from Paul Celan, *Mohn und Gedächtnis* © 1952, Deutsche Verlags-Anstalt, München, Penguin Random House Verlagsgruppe GmbH.

Excerpts from Paul Celan, "Nähe der Gräber," "Winter," "Schwarze Flocken," "Niemand," "Einmal," and "Aschenglorie," published by Surhrkamp. Taken from: Paul Celan, *Die Gedichte*. Neue kommentierte Gesamtausgabe. Mit 25 Radierungen von Gisèle Celan-Lestrange. Herausgegeben von Barbara Wiedemann. © Suhrkamp Verlag, Berlin, 2018.

Excerpts from Paul Celan: "Mandorla," "Einfühlung," "Psalm," "Soviel Gestirne," in *Die Niemandsrose/Sprachgitter* © S. Fischer Verlag GmbH, Frankfurt am Main, 1959. All rights reserved by S. Fischer Verlag GmbH. (ISBN: 978-3-596-52145-6).

Excerpts from Paul Celan, "Winter," "Black Flakes," "Nearness of Graves," "Deathfugue," "Psalm," "Stretto," and "Mandorla," from *Selected Poems and Prose of Paul Celan* by Paul Celan, translated by John Felstiner. Copyright © 2001 by John Felstiner. Used by permission of W. W. Norton & Company, Inc.

Excerpts from Zuzanna Ginczanka, "Non omnis moriar" with kind permission of Nancy Kasell.

Excerpt from Friedrich Hölderlin, "Mnemosyne," translated by Michael Hamburger, in *Poems and Fragments,* with kind permission of Cambridge University Press through PLSclear.

Excerpts from Czesław Miłosz, "Biedny chrześcijanin patrzy na Getto," "Campo di Fiori," and "Przedmowa" © 2023, Estate of Czesław Miłosz, used by permission of The Wylie Agency (UK) Limited.

Excerpts from Czesław Miłosz, "A Poor Christian Looks at the Ghetto," "Campo di Fiori," and "Dedication," *The Collected Poems, 1931–1987,* translated by the author with R. Hass and others (New York: Ecco, 1988), used with permission of HarperCollins © Estate of Czesław Miłosz, 1988.

Excerpts from Dan Pagis, *Kol hashirim* (Jerusalem: Hakibbutz Hameukhad, 1991), with kind permission of Hakibbutz hameukhad and Ada Pagis © estate of Dan Pagis.

Excerpts from Dan Pagis, "Written in Pencil in the Sealed Railway Car," "Roll Call," "Testimony," and "Footprints," translated by Stephen Mitchell, *The Selected Poetry of Dan Pagis* (Berkeley: University of California Press, 1996) with permission of University of California Press, conveyed through Copyright Clearance Center © 1996.

Excerpts from Miklós Radnóti, *The Complete Poetry in Hungarian and English*, trans. Gábor Barabás (Jefferson, NC: McFarland, 2014), with permission of Gábor Barabás, English translations © 2014.

Excerpts from Władysław Szlengel, "Telephone," "Things," "What I Read to the Dead," "The Little Railway Station at Treblinka," "A Window onto the Other Side," and "A Page from the 'Aktion' Diary," translated by John and Bogdana Carpenter, *The Manhattan Review*, 15, no. 2; 16, no. 1; 17, 2. From the Ringelblum Archive ŻIH, with kind permission of John and Bogdana Carpenter.

Excerpts from Władysław Szlengel, "Counterattack," translated by John and Bogdana Carpenter, *Chicago Review*, 52, no. 3–4 (2006), 287–91. From the Ringelblum Archive ŻIH, with kind permission of John and Bogdana Carpenter.

Excerpts from Wladyslaw Szlengel, "Co czytałem umarłym," trans. Frieda Aaron, in *Bearing the Unbearable: Yiddish and Polish Poetry in the Ghettos and Concentration Camps,* by Frieda Aaron (Albany: State University of New York Press, 1990), with permission of State University of New York Press © 1990.

ACKNOWLEDGMENTS

Excerpts from Avrom Sutzkever, *Zingt alts nokh mayn vort/Still My Word Sings: Lider/Poems*, trans. and ed. Heather Valencia, bilingual edition (Dusseldorf: Dusseldorf University Press, 2017) © 2017, 2021 by permission of De Gruyter publishers conveyed through Copyright Clearance Center.

Excerpts from Avrom Sutzkever, "Mira the Teacher," in *The Last Lullaby: Poetry from the Holocaust*, ed. and trans. Aaron Kremer, by permission of Syracuse University Press © 1998.

Introduction
Daniel Feldman and Efraim Sicher

Literature as Testimony

It seems as if the systematic persecution and extermination of the Jewish people from 1933 to 1945 left no possibility for the human spirit, let alone literature. Yet there was no period in Jewish culture more productive than the Holocaust.[1] All over occupied Europe, anyone who could find pen and paper or drawing materials recorded the unprecedented horror for posterity, often at great personal risk.[2] Before he was murdered by the Nazis, the elderly historian Simon Dubnow was said by witnesses in German-occupied Riga to have exhorted his fellow Jews, "Yidn, shraybt un farshraybt" ("Jews! Write and record!").[3] Yehiel Szeintuch remarks that "in no other period was so much written in a limited number of years by so many authors,"[4] and David Roskies estimates that there were "over three hundred writers in Yiddish and Hebrew alone, who spanned the entire arena of Nazi domination with a full range of literary expression."[5] They wrote diaries, letters, stories, poems, songs, reportage, sermons, and chronicles in all the languages of occupied Europe, which they smuggled out to safety or hid in the slim hope someone somewhere would find and read them.

The best-known example is Emanuel Ringelblum's secret *Oyneg Shabbos* archive of written testimonies and all kinds of other writing, a collective history of the Jews' suffering but also of their heroic spiritual and cultural resistance. The archive was partly recovered after the war in the original milk cans in which it was hidden under the Warsaw Ghetto.[6] Separately from the official record kept by the *Judenrat* in Łódź, which was toned down out of fear of discovery, a putative encyclopedia of the ghetto attempted to record every detail of daily life for the postwar Yiddish reader.[7] Also in Łódź, Isaiah Spiegel buried his stories of ghetto life, only some of which he was able to recover after liberation, while Simkha Bunim Shayevich composed two unforgettable poems, "Lekh-lekho" and "Friling 1942" ("Spring 1942"), which recorded the raw emotion of witnessing the starvation of children and the deportations. In Vilna, Abraham (Avrom) Sutzkever served as bard of the ghetto and participated in the rescue of valuable cultural treasures from the hands of the Nazis before joining the partisans in the forest, without ceasing to write poetry. In Auschwitz itself, Zalman Gradowski left a horrendous record of the crematoria before dying in the revolt of the *Sonderkommando* on October 7, 1944. The urgency and immediacy of events as they were happening or shortly afterward give writing during the Holocaust a heightened affect and importance, driven by a sacred duty to tell the story to future generations, as well as by faith that the Germans would one day be defeated and that their crimes would be exposed.

Much was lost, and many of the authors were killed or died of starvation and disease. They wanted the world to know. They wanted retribution or justice after their deaths. They wanted to prevent the erasure of their memory. They clung to the desperate hope that at least something might be left of the writer's life. Above all, writing it down preserved a modicum of human dignity in an inhuman, surreal existence amid the total destruction of everything that was familiar to them, including the loss of their families and loved ones. "Their use," writes Milton Teichman, "of words as weapons during the Holocaust is further evidence repudiating the notion that the Jewish response to the Nazi terror was passivity, paralysis, submission. The response of numerous Jewish writers was one of courageous resistance under the most difficult conditions."[8]

What remains is an incredible collective document attesting to the greatest inhumanity the world has ever known, but also a literary testimony of enduring worth. *Poesis in Extremis* shows how very different authors responded to what they experienced in language that strained its limits. We are not just asking whether the unrepresentable can be represented, but to what extent the use of existing traditions and conventions in describing daily atrocity in these unparalleled circumstances undermines the assumptions we usually make about literature. Atrocities of unprecedented scale and scope dictated new strategies of writing alongside reliance on traditional forms such as the epic or lament. But can we speak of a Holocaust poetics? That is a question which the literary theorist Geoffrey Hartman considers apposite when the limits of the human have been broached and tragedy can no longer encompass the unbelievable evil that was perpetrated, but which must not be allowed to slide into clichés and kitsch, into the stereotyped thinking which the Nazis themselves used to demonize the Jews. Perhaps, he suggests, there ought to be a generic shift as there apparently was for Aristotle and for Nietzsche (in *The Birth of Tragedy*).[9] Our study of *poesis in extremis* in the Holocaust investigates the constraints that the everyday experience of Nazi genocide of European Jewry imposed on existing romantic and modernist conventions in Polish, German, Yiddish, Hebrew, and Hungarian, especially the aesthetics of death when the figural smoke of charred corpses from chimneys became literal. Contrary to the assumption noted by James E. Young that literary testimony of the Holocaust privileged documentary realism, we will see that any juxtaposition of *mimesis* to *poesis* might prove fallacious.[10]

The war on the Jews threw religious and secular Jews alike back to Jewish resources. The existing literature of destruction, the Jewish canon of lament and mourning with its message of faith and consolation, was reread in the ghettos, and, as we will see in Chapter 6, poets wrote back to it. David Roskies declares that Bialik's epic poem on the Kishinev pogrom, "Be'ir haharega" ("In the City of Slaughter," 1903), was never so relevant and meaningful as when it was read in the ghettos. If Bialik in his outrage at the extent of the massacre found it difficult to accept conventional forms of lament such as the 'a*qeda* (binding of Isaac), how much more so did the enormity of what was happening in the Nazi ghettos challenge diary writers like Abraham Lewin in Warsaw who concluded, "We have lost the ability to use words."[11] Lewin's attempt to resort to archetypes such as Cain to describe the evil that Nazis were perpetrating breaks down when he considers the enormity of what the Jews were going through; he can only point to Bialik's poem as a measure of the impossibility of the expression of feelings and the resulting breakdown of language that must nonetheless be expressed in words. As traumatic violence becomes daily routine, any linear narrative disintegrates, leading to either impotent rage or numbness and apathy that could only be worked through in writing.[12] The 1903 Kishinev pogrom paled in comparison with the present catastrophe, yet Bialik's poem nevertheless inspired ghetto intellectuals who looked for a poet who would voice the tragedy of this unprecedented national disaster, this new *khurbn*.[13] In his diary, Chaim Kaplan commented that Bialik's elegy for the pogrom victims was just as much part of the religious poetry that transmitted Jewish history from one generation to another: "A poet who clothes adversity in poetic form immortalizes it in an everlasting monument. And this monument provides historic material from which future generations are nourished."[14] Kaplan calls for a national poet worthy of the tradition of the medieval *piyutim* (liturgical poems) which lamented massacres or the burning of the Talmud and looks back to a literature of destruction which recorded (as the midrash relates) the tears that God kept in a vial in memory of the Jewish people's suffering: "Who will write of our troubles and who will immortalize them? Where is the folk poet of Polish Jewry who will gather all the tragedy in our lives and perpetuate and guard it in the reliquary of his tears?"[15] The enormity of that suffering, Kaplan writes, now defied any newspaper report. A poet of exceptional talent was required.

Historical memory acquired new meaning as writers and educators drew on archetypes to voice lament and bereavement but also commemoration and solidarity. The stories of the heroism of the Maccabees or of medieval martyrdom endowed the ghetto children with pride and determination, but, alongside the Jeremiah of *Lamentations,* Job served as a strong archetype since so many shared his suffering in the loss of family and all they had. Katzenelson, whose translation into Yiddish of Bialik's "City of Slaughter" appeared in the 1940 issue of the underground periodical *Dror,* wrote a verse play *Iyev* (Job), the only sole-authored book published in the Warsaw Ghetto, on the day of the German invasion of the Soviet Union on June 22, 1941.[16] Leona Toker has, in fact, pointed to the paradigmatic importance of Katzenelson's play for her reading of Elie Wiesel's *Night* as a parable of Job, the universal figure of human suffering, so often invoked by ghetto and concentration camp inmates as their contemporary.[17]

Seeking a radical outlet for their wrath, poets reread literary classics and used diverse models from Jewish religious texts, but for some, such as German Jewish poet Gertrud Kolmar or Mieczysław Jastrun, Christian tropes of suffering spoke more loudly. Kolmar (born Chodziesner), who was banned in 1938 from publishing under her pseudonym and could only appear in Jewish publications, felt so at home in German that anything Jewish was strange to her (she was deported to Auschwitz where she was murdered in March 1943). Kolmar recorded her estrangement of self in a poem "Die Jüdin" ("The Jewess," 1936), finding herself a foreigner in a strangely unfamiliar mythical landscape of the biblical past, which she had to explore for the first time. Still, many writers who documented the incredible events through which they were living drew on a long Jewish tradition of the *kinah* (lament) and archetypes from Jewish history, but also adapted the modernist traditions of Polish and other European cultures they had adopted as their own.

The popular folk poet Mordecai Gebirtig's prewar song "Undzer shtetl brent" ("Our Shtetl is Burning," 1938), written in response to Polish pogroms, became an anthem of resistance. Gebirtig wrote poems of despair and hope, defiance and retribution in the Kraków Ghetto before being shot dead there in 1942.[18] Gebirtig's poetry, less well known than his songs, is included alongside Hirsh Glick's partisan anthem "Zog nit kaynmol" ("Never Say This is Your Last Road") in anthologies which canonized the commemoration of the Holocaust in terms of heroism, faith, and mourning and which connected it to a continuum of lamentation for past catastrophes and to biblical accounts of destruction.[19] In the camps and ghettos, songs such as Kaczerginski's "Shtile, shtile" ("Quiet, Quiet"), about the deportations to the killing pits of Ponar, bonded all Jews in a common fate, creating a defiant communal identity. In countless satirical or ironical adaptations of well-known songs and poems, familiar words and lyrics took on new meanings, such as the folksong *Ofn pripetchik* ("On the Hearth"), adapted by poet Avrom Akselrod in the Kovno ghetto to lament new sorrows of Jewish history.[20] In 1942, a small boy in the Kraków Ghetto reread Julian Tuwim's famous onomatopoeic Polish poem "Lokomotywa" ("The Train Engine," 1936) in a sinister version of his own now that the train engine was puffing and blowing relentlessly as it dragged cattle cars crammed with Jews to their deaths in Auschwitz.[21] This was one way to cope with the abnormality of the extreme, or rather the normalization of mass murder, and still maintain some kind of cultural identity and some semblance of sanity.

Poets did not stop writing—on the contrary, they applied their craft and aesthetics to an unprecedented reality. The poems collected in Ringelblum's *Oyneg Shabbos* archive include, besides songs of resistance and poems of faith and doubt, nature poems extoling the joy and power of nature. But Simkha Shayevich's "Balade fun der vayser nakht" ("Ballad of the White Night") turns any romantic idea of night knocking on a young woman's window into a nightmare of the terrors lying outside the ghetto.[22] We will see how Avrom Sutzkever welcomes spring in the Vilna Ghetto with a cruel irony. Poetry was written about hunger and death in extreme conditions that usually numbed thought and paralyzed creativity but sometimes elicited a spontaneous response that could more easily be recorded orally or on an easily hidden scrap of paper. Recitation of poetry in ghettos and camps helped preserve the will to live.

Writing Trauma

Writing prose fiction or diaries—and especially poetry—requires a subject position. As Amos Goldberg argues in his seminal analysis of ghetto diaries, a narrative voice presumes formation of identity.[23] Yet in Nazi-occupied Europe, Jews knew their existence was limited to slave labor and a starvation diet which were meant to exterminate them, if they were not gassed and incinerated in the death camps. Even those who were not taken in by the elaborate and systematic Nazi deceit and camouflage designed to give false hope and expedite the efficient roundup and extermination procedures knew that precious few options (if any) were left open to them. Therefore, the self who writes under erasure is claiming an identity that has already been annihilated. As we will see repeatedly, genocide denies subjecthood, and writing resists annihilation of the author. On the other hand, the act of writing itself establishes a voice only too aware that to speak is an attempt at continuity in a state of complete rupture from the past and in isolation from the outside world. This voice struggles with the traumatizing effects of dehumanization by addressing the alienation of self and body and exposing the blurring of the distinction between life and death.[24]

What then is this speaking I, whose speech is banned and secret? In his analysis of testimonies of Holocaust survivors, Lawrence Langer ponders the splitting of self that enabled the victims to carry on despite horrific ordeals that threatened to reduce them to unfeeling creatures whose emotions and moral judgment were stifled. He suggests in his reading of Holocaust testimony that one way of surviving was to adapt to the normality of an oxymoronically impossible reality that beggared credulity.[25] Language requires a mythical or metaphysical structure to describe what the victims went through, yet the systematic dehumanization and extermination process defied any such structure and neutralized any response except for unthinking submission and obedience. Of course, we should be cautious in drawing conclusions from single readings of such a disparate range of memoirs, testimony, and fiction; nor should we run away with the idea that everyone in the ghettos and camps descended to the bestial level of minimal existence, of the Zombie-like *Musselman*, or the desperate fugitive on the run hiding for months in dug-out pits. People starved and suffered, but also sang and danced, loved, and even, against all odds, had children. The best-known example is Warsaw's teeming Jewish mini-republic with its own police and postal service, but also an underground press and a vigorous cultural life, including clandestine and semi-legal literary readings and theatrical performances before the deportations brought them to an end, much of it recorded in Ringelblum's *Oyneg Shabbos* archive. The cultural and armed resistance of Sutzkever, Shmerke Kaczerginski, and Abba Kovner in the Vilna Ghetto, however, followed the slaughter of sixty thousand Vilna Jews, which left a dwindling remnant trapped in the ghetto, yet there were schools, yeshivas, and a theater, although there was criticism of cultural activities as "dancing in a graveyard" and increasingly the choice was between bread and entertainment. Life nevertheless went on with Ponar down the road. Poems by Kaczerginski were set to music and sung in the Vilna ghetto, while Sutzkever was admired as the ghetto bard.[26]

Cultural activity and musical performances in Theresienstadt continued, even as the performers or their families were facing transportation to Auschwitz. Viktor Ullmann and Peter Kien wrote the opera *The Emperor of Atlantis* in Theresienstadt as a victory of the human spirit when death was the sole salvation (the opera was not performed because Ullman and members of the cast and orchestra were deported to Auschwitz in October 1944, at which time cultural activity in the camp was suppressed; the libretto was first produced in 1975). Ullmann, an Austrian-Czech composer who produced his greatest works in captivity in 1942–3, was not exceptional in discovering Jewish and Zionist music in the cramped quarters of the ghetto but more than anyone else he understood the appalling enormity of Hitler's war against humanity and its significance for world culture. Ullmann remarked how prolific he was in Theresienstadt, where imprisonment and malnutrition freed him from the habitual comforts of the outside world. Like Schiller, Ullman concluded, they were forced to annihilate matter through form; here, where there was a shortage of paper and pianos, he could focus on an aesthetic vision inspired by Goethe's saying that one must live the present moment to live eternity. Ullman declared that he bloomed in musical growth and did not feel his creativity was at all inhibited: he felt that "in no way whatsoever we sat down to weep on the banks of the waters of Babylon, and that our effort to serve the Arts respectfully was proportionate to our will to live, in spite of everything."[27] To create was a dire need. And the coming together of Jewish and European traditions resulted in a unique if doomed resurgence of culture under the sign of a common death. Writing was for Jews in Nazi-ruled Europe an act of resistance to their own erasure from existence and from history. Eric Sundquist summarizes his reading of wartime diaries and memoirs of the camps and ghettos: "At extremity, writing might have to stand in for a self that was being slowly annihilated."[28]

Only literary expression could bridge the gulf separating the mythical past from the unthinkable present. Langer cites the "Canto of Ulysses" episode in Dante's *Inferno* which Primo Levi introduces in *If This Is a Man* as a subtext for the radical shift in meaning when translated into the present-tense of Auschwitz.[29] Literary devices and metaphors, Langer realizes, distinguish the retrospective, constructed view of Holocaust survivors[30] from their recollection of spontaneous witnessing as it happened, though that is surely filtered also through the foreknowledge of survival and the shifting perspectives of post-Holocaust memory. Yet it is precisely through literary intertexts that Otto Dov Kulka frames his memoir of his Kafkaesque experiences in Auschwitz, *Landscapes of the Metropolis of Death* (2013), where as a boy he first learned about Dostoevsky from an older inmate.[31] One can readily agree with Langer that the failure of aesthetic responses to the horror indicates the inadequacy of any representation of the experience of the Holocaust.[32] This surely can be said of much atrocity literature, except that Dante's foregrounding of the difficulty in conveying the transcendental experience of the *Inferno* at least assumed a shared set of references that would enable his readers to access it.[33] However, to regard the gates of Auschwitz with their cynical motto "Arbeit macht frei" as the entrance to Dante's hell is to risk either understatement or cliché; if anything, it foregrounds the inadequacy of the comparison it invokes. The German Jewish writer H. G. Adler remarked of his imprisonment in Theresienstadt, where he lectured on Kafka and other literary topics, that Kafka's K. was for him a symbol of inescapable human suffering. Yet Adler, who himself wrote poetry in the camp, felt that in Theresienstadt one might live in illusions, whereas in Auschwitz there was no denying reality; Dostoevsky's *House of the Dead*, he wrote after liberation, was not comparable.[34] As George Steiner showed in *Language and Silence* (1967), the Nazis' systematic and unrelenting state genocide seemed to push language beyond any capability of human sympathy in its use of German for murderous purposes. It undermined the purpose of culture to humanize.[35] Steiner's call for the poet to respect silence has nevertheless, like Woodrow Wilson's moral call to defend democracy, become a commonplace of the twentieth century and one that has been emptied of meaning.

Poetic Testimony

Much has been written about Holocaust novels.[36] There has been less discussion of the aesthetic, ethical, and hermeneutic issues that Holocaust poetry shares with testimony but also sets it apart from diaries and prose fiction. Poetry claims an exalted status in neo-romantic views of it as sacred and true to passion, but also as a safeguard of the word itself in times of authoritarian oppression. Broad claims for the truth value of poetry, however, do not fully engage with the issues underlying the status and concept of poetry as testimony, which has generally been assumed to be a characteristically prose genre, as if only prose could be representational and only the representational could testify. Shoshana Felman and Dori Laub, however, have called for poetry and literature in general to be read as testimony.[37]

"Poetry of witness" is a generic tag for writing that describes experience of war, imprisonment, torture, and slavery; it has been applied, sometimes uncritically and indiscriminately, to include poetry about the Nazi genocide.[38] Antony Rowland has remarked on the lack of attention to testimonial poetry, especially surprising in view of the fact that that with mass conscription in the First World War poets found themselves on the front line in a position of witnessing extreme events. Rowland understands testimony here in a judicial sense, requiring the reader to bear witness in what he calls "hyper-attentiveness." "Poetry of witness" expresses the feelings of the survivor and the ephemeral or sublime aspects of trauma in ways that prose cannot do.[39] The assumption here of an ethical contract with the reader makes testimonial poetry more than merely performative or an act of political protest. It calls on the reader to imagine what it was like in the Nazi and Soviet camps not just as an act of emotive solidarity but as an experiential engagement with the reader. Taking her cue from Emmanuel Levinas, Carolyn Forché explains:

> The word "extremity" (*extremus*) is the superlative correlative of the word "exterior" (*exterus*). Extremity suggests "utmost," "exceedingly great," and also "outermost," "farthest," implying intense suffering and even world-death; a suffering without knowledge of its own end. Ethical reading of such works does not inhere in assessing their truth value or efficacy as "representation," but rather in recognizing their evidentiary nature: here language is a life-form, marked by human experience, and is also itself material evidence of *that-which occurred*. This evidence continues to mark human consciousness. The *Aftermath* is a region of devastated consciousness of barbarism and the human capacity for cruelty and complicity with evil. In this aftermath, we are able to read—in the scarred landscape of battlefields, in bomb craters and unreconstructed ruins, in oral and written testimony *and* its extension in literary art—the mark or trace of extremity.[40]

One can object that the abnormal need not typify the human condition and that intersubjective identification with victims does not guarantee activism for the prevention of further atrocities. But first-hand literary testimony bears witness to the truth which we might, in our comfortable complacency, otherwise ignore.

The poet and literary critic Michał (Michel) Borwicz (born Maksymilian Boruchowicz), who escaped from the notorious Janowska camp near Lvov (Lwów) and joined the Polish partisans, pleads in his book *Ecrits des condamnés à mort sous l'occupation nazie, 1939–45* (Writings of Those Condemned to Death under the Nazi Occupation, 1939–45), for the testimonial value of the poetry written spontaneously by both unpracticed and professional authors in immediate response to events in the ghettos and camps, so that they will not be forgotten. From the moment of the German invasion of Poland, the victims attempted to commit their thoughts and experiences to writing in order to make sense of what was happening to them and appeal to the conscience of the world. Their spontaneous reactions dictated the choice of poetry or diary, driven by the exigencies of terror and the urgency of the moment.[41] In the concentration camps poetry circulated illicitly along with news of the war and personal messages that buoyed morale and gave hope.[42] In her introduction to poetry in the ghettos and camps, which includes her own personal memoir as a camp survivor, Frieda W. Aaron engages with the power of the poetic word not only to affirm life and document the horror, to give name to hunger and pain, but also to prevent its domination over the human spirit.[43] The poetic element that brings out the density and texture of expression can be identified in both prose and poetry and is distinct from narrative form, but poetry lends itself to eyewitness testimony, easily remembered, like the songs that were spontaneously composed or adapted in the ghettos and camps. Rachmil Bryks risked being sent to the gas chambers for reading out his poem *Geto Fabrik 76*, an exposure of the exploitation of factory workers in the Łódź Ghetto, and later recalled how he read it again in a German labor camp, where song and poetry kept up the inmates' spirits.[44]

Some poems were written in immediate response to ongoing events without it being possible to know if the author would survive or whether the addressee would read the poem; Celan refers to that uncertainty as a built-in risk of poetry in his speech on receipt of the 1958 Bremen literature prize when he talks of the poem as always headed somewhere in search of an addressee, in search of a firm reality: "Das Gedichte kann, da es ja eine Erscheinungsform der Sprache und damit seinem Wesen nach dialogisch ist, eine Flaschenpost sein, aufgegeben in dem—gewiss nicht immer hoffnungsstarken—Glauben, sie könnte irgendwo und irgendwann an Land gespült werden, an Herzland vielleicht" ("A poem, as a manifestation of language, hence essentially dialogue, may be a letter in a bottle, thrown out to sea with the—surely not always strong—hope that it may somehow wash up somewhere, perhaps on a shoreline of the heart").[45] How much more true is this of poems written in camps or ghettos in the hope that the message in a bottle ("Flaschenpost") would find an addressee in a free land, that they would find an unknown interlocutor in a heartland ("Herzland"). In a different sense, we find the "message in a bottle" trope in a poem of that title by the popular Hungarian writer Tamás Emőd warning European civilization as it stood on the brink of shipwreck in 1938 that the shore will never be reached.[46]

Poetry provided the earliest literary response to the Holocaust. Unlike prose, poetry more readily foregrounds emotional density and reference that call attention to the difficulty of finding a language to convey trauma. Rather than fulfill a communicative, constative, or informative purpose, poetry is necessarily oriented toward aesthetic expression; poetry is primarily concerned not with what to say but with how to say it. Poetry, moreover, displaces the usual boundaries that divide the metaphorical and figural from the literal. This blurring of lines between the imaginary and the real produces a lyrical and often-associative semantics or, alternatively, a graphically stark realism that shocks the reader into accepting the truth of the incredibly surreal reality of the Holocaust. The poetic compression of affect and experience into the density of verse thus makes poetry a test case for the immediate literary response of witnesses to the Holocaust. Szlengel, Radnóti, Celan, Sutzkever, Miłosz, and Katzenelson, like Pagis after the war, are all probing the limits of what language can and cannot say. After the liquidation of the Warsaw Ghetto and before he was murdered, Katzenelson wrote his *Song of the Murdered Jewish People*, whose diction and language contrast with the undermining of conventional metaphor and imagery in Celan and Sutzkever. Szlengel, who did not survive, was writing original Polish verse within occupied Poland and witnessed unspeakable horror in real time, which he recorded with the urgency of immediate testimony. These works illustrate the importance and peril of writing poetry amid the catastrophe itself.

Of all the writers we discuss, Miklós Radnóti perhaps came closest to writing in real time: he left "picture postcards" when he was killed on a death march in 1944. Another example of writing *in extremis* and of a poetic message in a bottle, Radnóti was writing to the readers who would come after his death, whereas Sutzkever, Szlengel, and Katzenelson were writing to the living dead and the dead of the ghetto, hoping against hope there would be someone left to read their works. Celan addressed his murdered mother, as did Sutzkever, who prophesied the ignominious death of the ghetto Jews brought by their own apathy and passivity. We will ask what it means to write to the dead when the poet has witnessed the death of the readers and can barely imagine a future when it will be possible to read poetry.

Poetry can achieve epiphany, and as Robert Antelme remarked on reading poems by the political prisoner Maurice Honel about survival in a

Nazi prison camp, it can affect the reader more than the false objectivity of prose or photographs and it resists the denial or burying of testimony which Antelme observed immediately after the liberation:

> Poetry did not, surely, run so great a risk of creating that naked, "objective" testimony, that kind of abstract accusation, that photograph that only frightens us without explicitly teaching anything. It could, on the contrary, risk fleeing the reality of the camps, letting that reality be glimpsed only through a melodic counterpoint, through themes of nostalgia that surround but never penetrate this reality of fog and words—the sun, laughter, color, and so on.[47]

Poets who served as conscripts in regular army units were forced witnesses of total destruction; concentration camp inmates, by contrast, were forced to witness their own dehumanization and imminent annihilation, so that each word they breathed and wrote was an act of survival. Referring to Celan's "Meridian" speech on acceptance of the 1960 Georg Büchner Prize, Alvin Rosenfeld has termed the aesthetics of such Holocaust poets as Celan and Nelly Sachs in their representation of death a "poetics of expiration,"[48] not in the sense of an inversion of Romantic inspiration but as the language of life that has become death, the bare breath of words which we will discuss in Chapter 3. That basic achievement of breathing words means that Holocaust writing speaks in a language of negativity to convey the impossibility of speaking. In doing so it testifies.

Poetry, no less than fiction, speaks to us as testimony, but its poetic form is especially apt for collective memory. In the Bible, poetry serves as a testimony which Moses bequeaths to the people of Israel in chapter 32 of the Book of Deuteronomy ("*shirat haazinu*"). The Holocaust has similarly left a legacy of responsibility for testimony to witness beyond the six million dead, beyond the generation of survivors. As Elie Wiesel remarked, his generation invented a new literary genre, testimony.[49] Testimony grants agency to the witness, even though in fact the witness was often totally powerless. The witness, Shoshana Felman writes, has become a key figure who personifies the ethical drive of the literary text. The writing of testimony, Felman notes, is a discursive practice; as opposed to pure theory: "To testify—to *vow to tell*, to *promise* and *produce* one's own speech as material evidence for truth—is to accomplish *a speech act* [....] As a performative speech act, testimony in effect addresses what in history is *action* that exceeds any substantialized significance."[50] To put it a little differently, testimony is a literary form that, in its moral obligation to tell the truth, speaks the unspeakable and tells what is impossible to tell. This approach enables Felman to read Camus and Dostoevsky, as well as the poetry of Celan and the taped witnessing of survivors, as testimony, thus removing the generic barrier between fiction and document. There is a crisis of hermeneutics and epistemology when the readers are made witnesses to the witness who challenges their safe assumptions of normality. Readers are made privy to a terrible knowledge that would be inconceivable if it were not being narrated as a lived experience. Language in all these texts claims the truth of an unthinkable reality of death as the writer-witness creates a new anti-aesthetics which makes room for an "I-you" eliminated by the law of genocide.[51] This is what elevates an act of survival to the level of "poetic testimony."

The poetic element that brings out the density and texture of expression can be identified in both prose and poetry and is distinct from the narrative form of diaries. These terms are not measurable or commensurable, but they are essential to our argument and are reflected in our readings of the texts. However, truth value in fiction and poetry cannot be reduced to the documentary value of verifiable facts and therefore the texts must be allowed to speak for themselves. We read them as works of art that confront the extreme. Criteria of "good" or 'bad" writing do not apply. They are not, in George Steiner's phrase, for review.[52]

What Is Holocaust Poetry?

In reflecting on the paucity of critical attention to Holocaust poetry, Joy Ladin wonders whether there is an ethical problem stemming from a reluctance to judge poems about the Holocaust, or perhaps the lack of tools to do so. It is not a matter of representability, Ladin believes, rather we are easily tempted into clichés or the satisfaction that we have said the right words. And yet Ladin makes little distinction between the poets who were there and those who wrote afterwards, in knowledge of what would have been their fate, like Irena Klepfisz in "Death Camp" (1975), who imagines being gassed and burnt in a crematorium.[53] And that is just the point: unlike the victims who tried to understand that history was happening to them, post-Holocaust poets such as Charles Reznikoff are writing in order to understand a history which they come after.[54] Paul Celan wrote in metaphors and metonyms of the collective and universal experience, not just what he himself experienced, but with the unmistakable traumatic knowledge of what it was to be there, in the abyss of death. When he talks of digging in "Todesfuge" ("Death Fugue") or "Es war Erde in ihnen" ("There Was Earth Inside Them") the poet knows what digging meant in a forced labor brigade. Post-Holocaust poets do not have that personal knowledge as an existential experience, nor can they do more than imagine its memory.

Literary critics have rarely delved deeply into the question of a Holocaust poetics, though Michał Borwicz (himself a survivor who wrote poems in the camps) has noted the unprecedented novelty of the surreal settings of an incredible reality. Frieda W. Aaron (also a survivor) declares that Holocaust poets drew on existing forms to deal with the new situation in which they found themselves.⁵⁵ Yet, surprisingly, the question of categorizing a Holocaust poetics has not been discussed in a comparative context, although the issue has been broached by David Roskies in relation to Yiddish poets Sutzkever and Katzenelson.⁵⁶ The breakdown of social organization, the destruction of cultural institutions, and the clandestine nature of literary production in abnormal wartime conditions make it difficult to apply conventional tools of analysis, while the diversity of languages and circumstances complicates any attempt at generalization. Moreover, the sheer quantity of thousands of poems in the archives, some unsigned or by unknown authors, defies attempts to decide on criteria of classification.⁵⁷

Susan Gubar has pointed to the paradox of Holocaust poetry caught in a vise between the inadequacy of minimalism that blocks testimony and verbosity that impedes aestheticism.⁵⁸ She proposes that poetry can nevertheless be testimonial in ways that show the inadequacy of language to testify: "Verse is the most unrealistic of languages, [...] and thus it produces a posthumous facsimile of a living voice."⁵⁹ Gubar's promotion of "Holocaust poetry," or more precisely post-Holocaust poetry in English which excludes wartime writing, derives from her anxiety that memory of the genocide is "dying" with the last survivors; it rests on her conviction that poetic imagery can prevent foreclosure of memory of an event which in many ways resisted narration and can prevent it slipping into cultural amnesia.⁶⁰ Antony Rowland and Robert Eaglestone in their edited special issue of *Critical Survey* entitled "Holocaust Poetry" and Rowland in his book of that title similarly look at poetry written mainly in English after 1945 as representing poetry "after Auschwitz" that is characterized by an "awkward poetics."⁶¹ The translator Jean Boase-Beier does make distinctions between poetry written by victims in the camps or ghettos and those who came after (though she avoids distinguishing between Jews and non-Jews out of concern for a racialized, exclusionary category). However, her claim for Holocaust poetry as testimony that calls attention to the truth of the poet's experience could be applied to much poetics as a cognitive pact with the reader who would otherwise be unable to imagine such inhumanity.⁶²

This is not a book about translations, although, as Boase-Beier has demonstrated, the translator's perspective can offer precious insights into the texts, and translation from one culture and language into another can throw light on context and difference in the original.⁶³ Translation is foregrounded in the form and substance of several texts in our discussion. Wiesel's *Night* is a work of auto-translation that converts his earlier Yiddish memoir into a French text modeled on the *nouveau roman*. Fink's stories frequently raise questions of translation, which shaped the reception of her work, and portray surviving witnesses who negotiate the challenge of making their anguished memory communicable to readers far removed from that "other planet" (as Ka-Tsetnik called Auschwitz).

All-inclusive definitions of "Holocaust poetry" obscure the fact that much of the poetry by victims and survivors (including Celan and Sutzkever) does not deal with the Holocaust, although there is no doubt that everything they wrote after the Holocaust was informed by their personal and collective experience, which necessarily shaped their conception of poetry and of history, not least their awareness of a changed existential situation, and increased their wariness about the inadequacies of language, especially if they wrote, as Celan did, in German. Saul Noam Zaritt, writing about Sutzkever, urges us not to overdetermine "Holocaust literature" to include anything and everything Holocaust victims wrote and not to ignore the context of their prewar writing.[64] Furthermore, Alan Udoff has placed a number of qualifications on the historical and ontological meanings of situating Celan as a "Holocaust poet," or in relation to the Holocaust.[65] All too often Celan and other poet survivors are detached from their work as a whole or from the collections in which their "Holocaust poems" first appeared. For good or bad, anthologies of Holocaust poets tend to keep to a canon that all too often downplays the poets' early lives and gives prominence to the names of those who are familiar in English translation.[66] Exceptionally, Aaron Kremer's volume *The Last Lullaby: Poetry from the Holocaust* (1998) focuses on poetry about suffering in the camps and ghettos by lesser known as well as major poets, and Boase-Beier and Marian de Vooght have produced an anthology, *Poetry of the Holocaust* (2019), which is devoted entirely to poetry about the experiences of victims during the Holocaust in various languages, but unfortunately does not distinguish between what was written *during* from what was written *after* the Holocaust and does not distinguish between those who lived or died under the Nazis and those who came later. Moreover, the categories of "Holocaust literature" in Anglo-American scholarship do not always accommodate poetry written in the Theresienstadt ghetto or by prisoners in concentration camps.[67]

There is, in fact, no consensus on what should be included in a corpus of Holocaust poetry. David G. Roskies includes ten ghetto poets in his important anthology of Jewish literature through the centuries, *Literature of Destruction* (1989),[68] but Edward Alexander considers both writers who were there and those who wrote elsewhere in the aftermath in Yiddish and Hebrew.[69] Several anthologies of contemporary poems go further afield and include the witnessing of war and political protest in general or "bearing witness" vicariously to genocide.[70] Gubar justifiably speaks of the impermeable gap between writing during or shortly after the Holocaust and in the aftermath:

> [W]hat one can sense about the shape of the past as it is rendered in verse, however, is a pause or gap between, on the one hand, the literature composed primarily in Yiddish, German, Hungarian, Romanian, and Polish during and directly after the war and, on the other, that

by English-speaking writers who, emerging in the 1960s, developed a tradition that evolved through the turn of the century.[71]

Our study goes back before that gap and focuses on writers who were in danger of their lives because they were Jews, even if some thought of themselves writing as Poles or Hungarians. Mieczysław Jastrun (born Moshe Agatstein), for example, survived on the Aryan side of Warsaw and published poems together with Miłosz, Jan Kott, and Maksymilian Boruchowicz (who changed his name after the war to Michał Borwicz), in an underground anthology of poetry *Z otchłani: Poezja* (Out of the Depths: Poetry, 1944), which was smuggled abroad in the naive belief that poetry could stir the conscience of the free West. Then there were those who held on to a dual identity, like the Polish-Jewish writer Julian Tuwim, whose famous essay, *My, Żydzi polscy* (We, the Polish Jews), written in the safety of American exile in 1944, expressed solidarity with the persecuted Jews. Many Hungarian Jews remained loyal to their country despite the anti-Jewish laws, and we will see that the prominent Hungarian poet Miklós Radnóti clung to his patriotism to the end. We will turn to the vexed question of the identity of German Jewish writers in our discussion of Celan.

In the aftermath of the Holocaust, a veritable industry of memoirs and literature emerged as survivors gave early testimony and rescued what remained of pre-Holocaust east European Jewish culture in *yizker-bukher* (memorial books of destroyed Jewish communities). Yiddish was not dead, as Jan Schwarz shows in *Survivors and Exiles: Yiddish Culture after the Holocaust*, but Ashkenazic culture redefined itself largely in relation to the *drite khurbn* (the Third Destruction).[72] The Nazi genocide killed a third of world Jewry and it also destroyed the centers of Jewish culture in Europe, systematically eradicating Jewish books and the Yiddish language. Yechiel Szeintuch reminds us how this loss overshadowed memory of Jewish eastern Europe and directed attention to the horrors perpetrated in the ghettos and forests of Poland and Ukraine; as a result, the creativity during the Holocaust that desperately sought to witness and to sustain the victims was neglected.[73] If this book can do a little to redress that neglect, it will have achieved its aims.

Plan of the Book

Not only did individual experiences differ during the Holocaust, but circumstances varied from one location to another. We cannot ascribe a uniform style to writers whose responses differed not just from one language and culture or from one situation to another, but from person to person, although the same Final Solution awaited them all. We have therefore chosen major authors (though perhaps not all as well-known as they should be) but have not included, among many others, Abba Kovner, who wrote in Hebrew after the Holocaust, and Nelly Sachs, who wrote on the verge of insanity in Swedish exile. Since our focus is on the poetics of Holocaust writing, many issues deserving attention have receded into the background. The chapters in this book can be read independently, yet they all are informed by our central argument for reading Holocaust literature as literary testimony. More crucially, we consider how its literary value is constituted and how that literary value interacts with—indeed, enhances—testimony. Each chapter takes up these issues in the common focus on language and silence, the continuity or subversion of poetic traditions, and the witnessing of unimaginable horror as an immediate reality.

The book falls into three parts: literature as testimony, the poetics of wartime poetry, and translating testimony into fiction. We frame the discussion with *Night* as an exemplary transformation of factual memoir to literary form. One of the most searing testimonies written by a Holocaust survivor, Elie Wiesel's *La Nuit* (1958; *Night*, 1960) was based on his memoir published in Yiddish in Buenos Aires under the title *…Un di velt hot geshvigen* ("…And the World Was Silent," 1956). In this chapter, Efraim Sicher rereads Wiesel's classic as a literary text to demonstrate that literature can bear witness but also to interrogate what it means to cross the boundary between memoir and novel. We might say that the conventional generic boundaries do not hold. Wiesel's bestseller joins a long line of novels and other fictional works written about historical events that tell the truth more starkly and more credibly than memoirs or historical documentaries. Yet the Holocaust seems to defy imagination. *Night* is written as Wiesel's life story and has been read as autobiography. However, its literary, some might say poetic, qualities make *Night* different from Wiesel's Yiddish memoir, on which it is based. This chapter explains what these literary qualities are and why it bears witness all the more powerfully as a work of literature. The recognition of *Night* (the first part of a trilogy) as a great work of literature removes it from a strict test of facticity or historical accuracy, but its testimonial value is all the greater for its power to bring the reader into the unimaginable horror it describes as lived experience. The issues of truth in representation and the poetics of a lived extreme experience are at the core of the following chapters.

The main part of the book is devoted to case studies of major poets in the ghettos and camps, singling out the way in which their writing confronts the Holocaust as they experience it in real time, though we will also compare some post-Holocaust verse. Chapter 2, "A Poetics of the Holocaust? Celan, Sutzkever, Miłosz," by Efraim Sicher circumvents Adorno's much-cited and often-misquoted dictum on poetry after Auschwitz and challenges the binary of either "Holocaust poetry is barbaric and impossible" or "art is uplifting and unaffected by the Holocaust." Poetry itself is being challenged. This chapter analyzes three individual cases of Holocaust poetry as a means of both survival and testimony during the Holocaust—not seen retrospectively or imagined by poets who were not there. Aesthetic and ethical issues are central to a writing *in extremis* well before Adorno and the critical theory that followed in his wake. In a comparison of Celan (who wrote 75 poems in labor camps), Sutzkever's ghetto poems, and Miłosz's two canonical poems witnessing the burning of the Warsaw Ghetto, we can see their desperate attempt to write a poetry that meets the challenge of the historical moment, for all the differences between them in their cultural backgrounds, language traditions, and literary influences.

Celan is caught between his immersion in a German modernist tradition and his calling as a German-Jewish poet, on the one hand, and his anguish over the loss of his mother and his own suffering as a Jew in a labor camp whose poetic identity has been denied, on the other: *Muttersprache* (mother tongue) has become *Mördersprache* (the language of murder). Sutzkever's poems are dated and located in the Vilna Ghetto or in the forests, a precision of time and place which makes his poetry a form of immediate testimony alongside the diaries written in the ghetto. Sutzkever uses poetic form and language with disturbing effects: the simple rhyme scheme, for example, brings home the contrasting violence that is destroying lives and words but also evokes the martyrdom of an entire people and resists the elimination of poetry itself. The Polish poet Czesław Miłosz was not himself a victim but, as a Gentile bystander, he was deeply affected by what he witnessed. Scholars and critics have read these poets separately; we study them as part of a phenomenon of grappling with an unprecedented horror in all its historical dimensions and outcome. We also take into account their use of sources and antecedents in forging a "Holocaust poetics" that would convey something of the inadequacy of language and the failure of the imagination in representing the unspeakable, which they personally experienced on a day-to-day basis.

A different perspective on Celan is offered in the next chapter, "Writing Nothing: Negation and Subjectivity in the Holocaust Poetry of Paul Celan and Dan Pagis," by Daniel Feldman, which addresses the pervasive negation and articulation of "nothing" by the two poets. In their post-Holocaust poetry, their expression of nothingness reflects a model of negative subjectivity that underlies the writing self of survivors. By contrast to metaphorical readings of absence in the poetry of the Holocaust, this chapter reads Celan and Pagis's frequent statements of nothing as literal rather than as solely figural and argues that they give voice to a "nothing" in an apophatic mode of subjectivity that grants existence to "nothing." This negative subjectivity, expressed by Celan as "nothing I am" and by Pagis as "I am not," stretches logic, transgresses syntax, and posits the existence of its negativity, affirming nothing as a substantive presence. In linking literary statements of nothing to survivor subjectivity, the chapter challenges critical consensus by emphasizing how Celan and Pagis inscribe "nothing" in terms of an eccentric ontology that represents a traumatic experience of survival of one's own death and annihilation. An excursus on Celan's challenge to Heideggerian ontology juxtaposes Celan's notion of how negation negates itself in producing substantive nothing against Heidegger's theory of "nothing" as a nihilating void. Celan and Pagis in their similar technique of negative poetics turn verse into an exacting medium of writing nothing that tests the readers' hypersensitivity to the absences, erasures, and silences which circumscribe the Holocaust.

The book does not proceed chronologically, but takes in labor camps, ghettos, deportation, and death marches in consideration of widely different authors from various backgrounds whose responses to extreme conditions offer contrasts in aesthetics and poetics. Not all authors, even if they agreed something unprecedented was happening to human civilization, understood the Holocaust as a cataclysmic event in Jewish history. An outstanding Hungarian poet, Miklós Radnóti (1909–44) published his first book in 1930. His second book was accused of indecency and banned. His *Cartes Postales* (Postcards from France, 1937) anticipated darker images of war in *Razglednicák* (Picture Postcards), as well as a poet's martyrdom. From 1940, Radnóti was conscripted to various labor brigades and in 1944 was doing forced labor near Bor in Serbia when the camp was evacuated due to the advance of the Red Army. Radnóti joined a forced march in which he perished; when the prisoners reached Abda, near Gyor in north-west Hungary, those who could not go on any further were shot. Radnóti's last poems were found on his body in a mass grave, literally messages from the dead. In the chapter "Miklós Radnóti: Postcards from a Death March," Efraim Sicher asks what these camp poems say about poetic witnessing when the poet's homeland rejected the poet, making him wonder if he had a readership. This chapter examines the poetics of Radnóti's representation of the extreme reality of facing a gruesome death, which he had long foreseen and which became real when he witnessed the shooting of a fellow-prisoner. Unlike Celan, Radnóti was not conflicted by his assimilated personal and artistic identity, and his use of the hexameter continues his prewar efforts, in a Hungarian tradition of the oppositional national bard, to resist tyranny and persecution. His premonitions of his martyrdom as a poet (rather than as a Jew) recur in several collections of prewar verse that combine modernist practices and confessional tones of a poetic voice seeking immortality in nature. Radnóti serves as an example of a poet who, to the last, continued to write in the traditions of Hungarian poetry and saw the extreme horror he experienced though his already-formed apocalyptic vision of the world. There is good reason to think that he would not have accepted the label of "Holocaust poet."

In the following chapter, "Władysław Szlengel's Ghetto Poems: Writing to the Dead," Daniel Feldman reads Szlengel's Warsaw Ghetto poetry as an early example of literary testimony of the Holocaust. Szlengel's Polish-language poetry circulated widely in the ghetto, where he cultivated ties with both avant-garde salon artists associated with the Café Sztuka and distinguished communal leaders, such as Janusz Korczak, who heroically stood by the children in his orphanage and accompanied them on their deportation to the death camps. Szlengel's poems were written between the devastating *Grossaktion* in summer 1942, when most of the ghetto was liquidated and its inhabitants murdered, and the spring 1943 Warsaw Ghetto Uprising, when Szlengel was killed. These poems combine caustic, sometimes-acerbic satire with elegiac eyewitness accounts of unfathomable events transpiring in real time. The concatenation of poems such as "Mała stacja Treblinki" ("Little Station of Treblinka"), "Pomnik" ("A Monument"), and "Kartka z dziennika 'akcji'" ("A Page from the *Aktion* Diary") reflect a nascent but already-clear comprehension of the scale and character of the unfolding catastrophe. Szlengel seeks a literary idiom in which to articulate his rage, loss, solitude, and sense of responsibility to the dead and to his readers—groups that merge in the poet's imagination in his final poems before his murder in May 1943. This chapter analyzes Szlengel's poetic legacy as a pioneering literary form of eyewitness lamentation and elegiac report. He sees a world disappearing before his eyes and draws on irony, comparison, and metonymy in order to give expression to what his imagination can hardly fathom. In sharing his poems with ghetto inhabitants, Szlengel sought to assuage and explain, to protest and warn. His work offers valuable early evidence of how writers searched for a language that could accommodate their immediate experiences of extreme violence and systematic genocide. The chapter argues that for Szlengel and later poets of the Holocaust, the pen was the first and often the only means of response and resistance.

In Chapter 6, "'Poem in a Bottle': Itzhak Katzenelson's *Song of the Murdered Jewish People*," Daniel Feldman follows the perilous peregrinations of the manuscript of Itzhak Katzenelson's 1944 epic *Dos lid fun oysgehargetn yiddishn folk* (*Song of the Murdered Jewish People*) which reflect the extreme difficulties of writing during the Holocaust. Three bottles were sealed and buried in a detention camp, while another copy was folded and sown into the suitcase handle of a released prisoner heading to Palestine. A celebrated Hebrew and Yiddish poet, educator, dramatist, and communal leader, Katzenelson was a seasoned and respected author, who became an active participant in the ghetto resistance, teaching and writing in the clandestine press. His wartime writing constitutes a seminal landmark in testimonial poetry written during the Holocaust by its Jewish victims. Katzenelson's poems about Jewish resistance to adversity, written in Yiddish for maximum dissemination, were widely read in the Warsaw Ghetto. His wife and two sons were deported to the Treblinka extermination camp during the *Grossaktion* of 1942. After the fall of the ghetto, Katzenelson and his surviving son were interned in Vittel, France, where Katzenelson wrote a Hebrew-language memoir, *Pinkas Vittel* (*The Vittel Diary*), in which he recorded his memories of the ghetto and his fears of encroaching insanity. Here he wrote *Song of the Murdered Jewish People* in late 1943 and early 1944, which shows a remarkably complete awareness of the Holocaust and its historic consequences. It names sites of extermination, describes the machinery of death, and connects Katzenelson's personal grief with anguish over the destruction of European Jewry. Crucially, the poem addresses (well before Adorno) the impossibility of writing poetry after witnessing the horrors of the Holocaust. This literary masterpiece of bereavement, protest, testimony, and literary intertextuality forms one of the most important works of wartime writing written by a victim and witness at the time of the Holocaust. Katzenelson was murdered in Auschwitz in 1944. Although Katzenelson was a major figure in early Israeli memory of the Holocaust (Ghetto Fighters' House in Israel was named in his honor), his work is less read today. This chapter attempts a reassessment of his poetic achievement in his wartime writing, but also examines the breakdown of time in the overwhelming succession of traumatizing violent events that tore apart Katzenelson's world and challenged his beliefs. Like Celan, he developed a paradoxical theodicy but, unlike Wiesel, he could not maintain the traditional faith of his religious and literary sources. Like other Holocaust writers, he smuggled out and hid his manuscripts as messages in a bottle in the hope that they would one day reach a reader, but he was essentially writing, like Szlengel, to the dead.

In the third, final part, we move from poetic practice to consideration of translatability and transmission. Ida Fink's stylized and self-reflexive understanding of literature as testimony is the subject of a chapter by Daniel Feldman, "Translating Oral Memory in Ida Fink's 'Traces,'" which asks how testimony can be translated into prose fiction. The chapter questions whether the story can be told. An Israeli-Polish author whose autobiographical short fiction about the Holocaust is written in Polish but widely read in translation, Fink capitalized on the power of literature to "translate" unimaginable history into language comprehensible to contemporary readers. The translation is both literal and figural. Her short story "Traces" ("Ślad") meditates on an older survivor's struggle to transmit clotted memories that are visual, polyglot, and traumatic to a video-testimony interview team guided by vastly different visual, linguistic, and historical coordinates. The story's protagonist is asked by the film crew to convey orally the ineffable backstory behind a disturbing wartime photo which encodes the traumatized memory of Polish Jewish children who defied a German command in order to save their parents. The mixing of media, the crossing of generational assumptions, and the bridging of a linguistic divide make the story a rich site for exploring the central themes of "translated memories." This chapter considers Fink's intellectual investment in the culture of memory as a parallel idiom in the intergenerational transmission of the Holocaust, but also explores the significance of translating memories across linguistic and cultural borders.

Summoning the traumatic memory of the Holocaust in lucid prose after the act of witnessing raises issues of translation and translatability. A survivor who writes in Polish, Ida Fink is an example of how language meets the challenge of witnessing the Holocaust through the literary imagination. With their emphasis on quiet scenes of pain, Fink's short stories eschew graphic horror and collective trauma in favor of individual accounts of ordinary people—parents, neighbors, lovers, and children—who had to cope with a bewildering and sudden terror. Instead of dramatic narratives of heroic resistance and collective struggle, Fink creates discreet, interior portraits of private agony. Her work stages the Holocaust as a series of intimate crises, domestic catastrophes, and individual moments of pathos and loss. This depiction of the Holocaust as a local and human tragedy, rather than as a national or global watershed, makes her an exemplar of contemporary trends toward individuation in Holocaust literature, historiography, education, and commemoration. Fink's place in the canon of Holocaust literature is contested: Neither completely Polish nor Israeli, neither a memoirist nor a fabulist, Fink produces a translational aesthetics of memory that speaks across the margins of time, place, and medium.

We end with a postscript that contemplates the mass loss of lives and of manuscripts in the Holocaust. With the passing of the last witnesses, we must move on from witnessing to mourning and transmission of loss. The loss must be incorporated into our knowledge, aware that we who were not there can never fully know what the victims knew, even if not all of them could imagine the simultaneous events that were destroying Jewish life all over occupied Europe or if some imagined they were the last Jews on earth. Theirs is a knowledge which we can access, albeit imperfectly, only through their writing. Despite the efforts of Steven Spielberg (in *Schindler's List*) and Claude Lanzmann (in *Shoah*) to give the viewer the feeling of being *there*, nothing can surpass the words of the victims, many of whom came to realize the inadequacy of language.[74] It seems that we come close to silence when we ask how we can speak in such knowledge, but then, how can we not speak?

The challenge of excess to literature is hardly new. From Terence's *Homo sum, humani nihil a me alienum puto* through the Baroque and the Gothic to postmodern provocations by George Bataille and others, writers and artists have stretched the boundaries of what can be said. Chroniclers of Khmelnitsky's massacres of thousands of Jews in Ukraine in 1648 and the pogroms of 1918–20 certainly did not flinch from graphic details of mass rape and disemboweling of pregnant women. However, leaving aside the question of the exceptionality of the Holocaust which brings in the politics of memory and historiographic discourses,[75] it seems to us that the wartime literary responses to the Holocaust pose aesthetic and ethical questions of a different order. This book aims to change the way we think about the boundaries of Holocaust literature but also to provoke debate over the question of the limits of representation. We ask what kind of aesthetic effect extreme horror has when it goes beyond anything we may enjoy or appreciate in the literary description of terror or the sadistic hardcore genre of popular fantasy. The unspeakable horror of the Holocaust, by contrast shocks us because it is only too unbelievably real in a systematic process of industrialized genocide.[76] Yet it takes a great poet to find words to describe it that are not trite or cliché and that show how inadequate literary conventions are in representing the unimaginable reality of what in his 1946 book of that title David Rousset called the *univers concentrationnaire* ("concentrationary universe").

PART ONE

1

Elie Wiesel's *Night*: Literature as Testimony

Efraim Sicher

One of the most searing testimonies written by a Holocaust survivor, Elie Wiesel's *Night* first appeared in Yiddish in Buenos Aires under the title *...Un di velt hot geshvigen* ("... And the World was Silent," 1956). Abridged and adapted by Jérôme Linden, an editor at Editions de Minuit (the wartime underground press), the French version appeared in 1958 as *La Nuit* (*Night*); it was translated into English by Stella Rodway as *Night* in 1960. Later, Wiesel returned to the French text in a new English translation by his wife Marion Wiesel, which appeared in 2006.[1]

By way of framing the discussion in this book about writing the Holocaust, this chapter sets out underlying issues in literary representation of the Nazi genocide and the poetics it employed. One of those issues is the question of whether authors who lived through the trauma of the camps and ghettos are bound by the division governing the rules of verisimilitude between memoir and fiction, documentation and literature. I will argue that however we label *Night*, it is a masterpiece that uses literary devices to call on the reader's imagination to believe in what defies the limits of human experience. The reliability or credibility of Wiesel's testimony does not depend on the quibbles over factual inaccuracies or discrepancies between the versions in his memoir, *Night*, and the first volume of his autobiography, *Tous les fleuves vont á la mer* (1994; *All Rivers Run to the Sea*, 1995).[2] Those debates indicate how the critical reception of *Night* has reflected and to some extent determined its reading as a memoir or as a novel. The literary critic Phyllis Franklin, for example, writes that *Night* has been tagged so often as a novel that it cannot be an ambassador for the "infallibility" of a memoir.³ She prefaces her summary of the critical debate over *Night* with an epigraph from Wiesel's introduction to *Legends of Our Time* (1968), where he foregrounds the storyteller's fusion of truth and fiction by telling the Hasidic rebbe that he invents true stories about events that did not occur.⁴ Veracity, Wiesel seems to be saying, is not canceled out by the literary genre of a work. The literary qualities of *Night* have certainly not gone unnoticed, but the canonical status of *Night* has acerbated a debate in which the stakes are high both for those who hold Holocaust memory sacred and for Holocaust deniers or relativists. Naomi Seidman claims that Wiesel played down the rage of the original Yiddish memoir, yet the angry denouncement of the Jews' blind faith which lulled them into a false sense of security is there from the first line of the French version, as is the questioning of Divine justice.⁵ What is different is the adaptation of a standard survivor memoir in a series aimed at the Yiddish survivor community around the world, which relied on their shared understanding of ironic references in Yiddish and Hebrew to biblical verses and Jewish practices, as well as the rhetorical devices of Yiddish literature, to a concise work of literature that appeals to the conscience and aesthetic tastes of French readers.⁶ The 2006 re-translation in turn addressed an American audience which was familiar with the conventions of Holocaust literature and appreciated tales of survival and endurance. By then Wiesel was a bestselling Nobel Prize winner and the spokesperson of Holocaust survivors. Moreover, Holocaust memory had achieved an importance he did not imagine at the time of the publication of the first French translation, a time when the Holocaust was still largely absent from public consciousness in Europe and after a hiatus of about a decade since the first testimonies appeared—this was two years after the release of Alain Resnais's film *Nuit et brouillard* (*Night and Fog*) in 1956 and the year when Einaudi finally issued the complete edition of Primo Levi's *Se questo e un uomo* (*If This Is a Man*).⁷

Wiesel once said that Holocaust literature inaugurated a new genre, testimony.⁸ This chapter rereads Wiesel's *Night* as a literary testimony and one that is all the more powerful when we consider the gap between the hurried notes of a young camp survivor turned into a 245-page memoir and the accomplished literary work less than half that length of a budding twenty-five-year-old writer making his debut in French literature. That gap is already anticipated in the memoir, when Wiesel contemplates the distance of ten years since he found himself in a cattle-car with his father on the way to Buchenwald witnessing the animal depravity to which the prisoners had been reduced by their ordeal as they scrambled for morsels of bread thrown by German passers-by: "Strange, even while jotting down these words, the event seems incredible to me. I seem to be writing a horror novel—a novel that should not be read at night. It is hard to believe that what I set down in writing is really true, has actually happened to me" ("Modne: shreybndik di dozike shuros, gloybt es zikh epes mir nisht, mir aleyn. S'dukht zikh: ikh shreyb a shrek-roman, a roman velkhen m'darf nisht leynen beynakht. S'ken zikh nisht gloybn, az dos alts vos ikh shreyb—iz take geshen, mit mir aleyn gesheyn").⁹ In order to bridge that gap and achieve the clarity of vision after ten years, only the literary imagination would do.

I will argue that the conventional dichotomy between fact and fiction is not helpful here. Lawrence Langer notes how:

> Wiesel's account is ballasted with the freight of fiction: scenic organization, characterization through dialogue, periodic climaxes, elimination of superflouous or repetitive episodes, and especially an ability to arouse the empathy of his readers, which is an elusive ideal of the writer bound by fidelity to fact.[10]

Similarly, Bronislava Volková notes how Wiesel "compels the reader to become a witness to the unthinkable and absorb it inwardly. *Night* is not a novel, and it is not exactly a memoir either. It has a hybrid form, which balances fidelity to events and literariness."[11] In an effort to explain how a work of literature can document so powerfully what lies beyond any aesthetic criteria and defies metaphor, she declares that Wiesel's "memoir is a genuine artistic achievement, and as such it is naturally not simply a literal description of facts but also austerely poetic."[12]

None of this adequately explains how Wiesel bridges the incredulity of living through unspeakable horror by telling a convincing life story with a plot and a central protagonist. As in many coming-of-age stories, we share the loss of innocence of a child confronted by a totally strange and incomprehensible world. We are introduced to the unbelievable scene of babies being thrown into the flames through the naïve eyes of a child walking with his father for the first time into the camps; we follow him as he is berated by the *kapos* for not understanding that they are all destined to be burnt in the crematoria. By the end, he has been transformed into a figure whom he cannot recognize in a mirror. The memoir did not end with this split between the camp inmate and Wiesel's former self, but on a pessimistic note (consistent with the memoir's title) that the world still remained silent and will remain silent.[13]

Before we explore in the following chapters how poetry documents the most extreme situations, we must understand what literary testimony is. We might say that the conventional generic boundaries no longer hold when fiction claims historical truth, and autobiography uses literary artifice. Just think of the numerous novels and other fictional works written about historical events that tell the truth more starkly and more credibly than memoirs or historical documentaries. The police line between history and a novel won't hold. Defoe's *Journal of a Plague Year* is a fictional account of mass death and bereavement that uses the devices of documentation and diaries to give the convincing effect of a lived experience but also envisions

London as Jeremiah's Jerusalem after destruction. However, since the author was aged only five when the events took place, he could not possibly have witnessed what the narrator presents as testimony. Similarly, Tolstoy's novel *War and Peace* shapes the events to fit the author's religious and political views, yet gives the illusion that history is being witnessed. In both cases, the events are historically true, although the author was not present and did not participate in them. It is a fallacy to say that if it is a document, it is testimony, and if a story is being told, it is fiction. History is also a story. Indeed, Hayden White has shown how historians use emplotment to tell a story that is not entirely objective, although they conventionally make claims for its truth value.[14]

As for the claims of authenticity, there are few foolproof tests to safeguard against fake memoirs such as Binjamin Wilkomirski's *Fragments*, except for the unmasking of the author's true identity, but even then, the author might say that a fake memoir also tells the truth about what really happened to others.[15] It is, however, not only about being there and seeing it with one's own eyes. The "truth" told in Jerzy Kosinski's novel *A Painted Bird* can be questioned, not just because Kosinski spent the war under false identities and none of this happened to him, but because Kosinski manipulated the story to fit his programmatic view that inhuman cruelty and sadistic bestiality are universal, not primarily a product of Nazi genocide. Wiesel initially welcomed the "authenticity" of Kosinski's novel, before the scandal erupted over plagiarism and the truth emerged about Kosinski's real experiences during the Holocaust, as well as the shocking revelations about his personal life.[16]

By contrast, Wiesel was there and lived to testify to the truth of what he described. Nevertheless, *Night* fits the novel form. Wiesel more than once declared that a novel about Majdanek was either not a novel or not about Majdanek.[17] Yet most of the books he wrote (apart from his memoirs, collected essays, and collections of Hasidic stories) are novels that are unquestionably fictional. Wiesel himself is on record denying that *Night* is a novel, though he admitted its literary qualities, on the grounds of its veracity, since he and the other protagonists were there, not imagined in someone else's story.[18] Yet, however justifiable is Wiesel's struggle to maintain the truth of what happened in the Holocaust in the face of denial and revisionism, this simplistic distinction does not help us understand *Night* as literary testimony.

Night is written as Wiesel's life story and has been read invariably as autobiography. It has the salient features of Lejeune's "autobiographical pact," in which the author's experience is lived in the flesh, not imagined or invented.[19] However, there is a cognitive gap between the boy Eliezer and the I-narrator Elie Wiesel who recounts his experiences. Moreover, its undisputable literary (I would say poetic) qualities distinguish *Night* from Wiesel's Yiddish memoir, on which it is based. I argue that the literary qualities of *Night* bear witness all the more strongly in its use of such tropes as the journey, the *aqeda* (binding of Isaac), the testing of God, and the conflicted feelings about the father in the boy's struggle to maintain basic Jewish and human values of honoring parents without succumbing to the systematic dehumanization and starvation. The highly structured narrative, which proceeds from deportation and incarceration to liberation, raises it from the documentary to the literary genre of a novel (it was the first part of a trilogy, of which *Dawn* and *The Accident* cannot be read other than as fiction). *Night* has won recognition from some scholars as a great work of literature, and its power to tell the truth cannot be measured by facticity or historical accuracy, but, as I will show, its testimonial value is all the greater because of Wiesel's ability to bring the reader into the unimaginable horror it describes.[20]

François Mauriac, in his preface to the first French edition of *Night*, relates that Elie Wiesel vowed not to speak of his experiences in the camp, but in an interview which Wiesel conducted with him for the Israeli daily newspaper *Yedi'ot akhronot* in 1955, the prominent French writer encouraged him to tell the story. There is no mention here of a preexisting memoir, published in Argentina in 1956. Instead, Mauriac proposes a Christian interpretation of Wiesel's unforgettable tale of surviving Auschwitz as the story of a suffering victim of evil. Mauriac recalled the story of the Jewish children who had been assembled at Austerlitz railway station in Paris and sent off to their deaths during the German Occupation of France. For the Catholic Mauriac, sensitive to France's wartime record of collaboration, references to which were then still taboo, Wiesel's testimony was clear evidence of the suffering of the innocent lambs. It confirmed Mauriac's faith in the God of love and the workings of grace through belief in the crucified Jesus, also a Jew. Mauriac acknowledged, "Did I affirm that the stumbling block to his faith was the cornerstone of mine, and that the conformity between the Cross and the suffering of men was in my eyes the key to that impenetrable mystery whereon the faith of his childhood had perished?" ("lui ai-je affirmé que ce qui fut pour lui pierre d'achoppement est devenu pierre d'angle pour moi et que la conformité entre la croix et la souffrance des hommes demeure à mes yeux la clef de ce mystère insondable ou sa foi d'enfant s'est perdue?").[21] An extreme version of that view of the suffering of children is presented by the Jesuit priest Paneloux in Camus's *La Peste* (*The Plague*, 1947), which Camus was writing during the war as the Jewish children were being rounded up by French police and deported to Auschwitz. Critics who see Christian references in *Night* pay no attention to Mauriac's admission of passivity in his report (at second hand) of the deportations, an admission made at a time when the official French narrative of the war emphasized heroic resistance to the occupation and de Gaulle's triumphal liberation of France.

Readings of *Night* as a work of literature nevertheless take up Mauriac's "Lazarean" interpretation in his foreword to the novel. In Christian scriptures (John 11), Lazarus rose from the dead, and, in Mauriac's view, so did Eliezer Wiesel. In remarking that the "stumbling block" of Wiesel's faith was the "cornerstone" of his, Mauriac reveals a theological bias that debars Jews from true faith because of their refusal to recognize Jesus as a messiah. Yet, as Ellen Fine has noted in her reading of Wiesel's trilogy,[22] the figure of Lazarus served as an early attempt to create a poetics of camp literature in Jean Cayrol's two essays of 1950, "Lazare parmi nous" ("Lazarus among Us") and "Pour un romanesque lazaréen" ("Lazarean Literature").[23] For Cayrol, Lazarus, in his secular reincarnation, is a figure of the living dead, who has seen death and can never be free of the terror of the camps. His scars are the "stigmata" that will never fade, but his spirit lives on among the frivolity of modern life that seeks to forget the recent past. The consciousness of the camps has seeped into the human condition, Cayrol writes, and claims its place in literature and art. What divides the modern Lazarus from other humans is the knowledge of death. However, Cayrol, who wrote the screenplay for Alain Resnais's *Night and Fog*, was a political prisoner, not a Jew slated for extermination, and Resnais's film in fact almost avoids mentioning that the Jews were singled out for genocide. Certainly, in Buchenwald prisoners were systematically dehumanized, yet it was not necessarily the bottom rung of hell or the last stop before the gas chamber. Far from the message Mauriac proposed in the foreword to Wiesel's book, this story of a young man's test of faith contains a mystical idea rooted in Hasidism, though couched in the literary style of the *nouveau roman* and expressed in the language of a universal questioning of evil. Wiesel is therefore in the company of Camus and Sartre in asking fundamental questions about the human condition, about evil, and about God, but he does not subscribe to their existential philosophy.[24]

As a Jew, Wiesel could never accept Mauriac's Christian view that faith was based on suffering. From the opening of *Night*, Wiesel writes from within the ancient Jewish literature of destruction and within a theology that goes back to the suffering of Job, not Jesus. Wiesel's theodicy relates, moreover, to arguments with God from Rabbi Levi-Yitskhak of Berdichev, who composed a *kaddish* which challenged God to remember His side of the covenant with Israel and to have pity on His oppressed people, to Zvi Kolitz's legendary story, "Yosl Rakover Talks to God" (1946). Wiesel begins the Yiddish version of his memoir, ...*Un di velt hot geshvigen*, with the keynote of his tale,

> In anheyb iz geven di emunoh, di narishe emunoh; un der bitokhon, der puster bitokhon; un di illuziye, di geferlekhe iluziye.
>
> In the beginning there was faith, a foolish faith; and there was trust, a foolish trust; and there was an illusion, a terrible illusion.[25]

These opening words signal the underlying theme of religious faith which is tested but never abandoned. However, instead of the "beginning" of a new era, the phrase relates the passing of an old world with its false illusions and naïve ideals and an awakening to the truth of a stark reality of inhuman destruction. Wiesel states at the outset that the illusion of the "holy spark" of faith emanating from the Divine Presence ("a haylike funk fun fayer fun der shekhinoh") and misguided trust in man were the source, "if not the cause," of their misfortunes ("dos iz geven der kval—oyb nisht de siboh—fun ale undzere umglikn").[26]

Turning now to *Night,* we can trace this crisis of faith, but it develops rather differently. The evocation of the devout traditional East European Jewish way of life in the opening of *Night* might have inspired the Yiddish storyteller Sholem Aleichem, except that in reality Sighet was a bustling town under Romanian rule and later Hungarian occupation with a vibrant modern Jewish culture and a Yiddish press. One fictional work in particular that came out in Sighet in 1940, Yechezkel Ring's *Oyfen himel a yarid* (A Turmoil in Heaven), recounted the Devil's rebellion against God and stirred a turmoil, not only among the town's strictly religious Jews.[27] That too is a trial of God, albeit before the full horror of the Holocaust was revealed. However, Wiesel's purpose is different, to create the impression of a sudden break in the continuity of a religious community that could not foresee its end.

The French adaptation and its English translation begin by introducing Moshe the synagogue beadle, a clownish, reticent figure, who elicits the sympathy of all. Here I will mention "Monsieur Chouchani" (born Hillel Perlman, in Brisk in 1895), an enigmatic and elusive mystic, with whom Wiesel studied between 1947 and 1952, as did the philosopher Emmanuel Levinas. The influence of Chouchani can be traced in the figure of the boy's mystical mentor at the beginning of *Night.* Moshe the beadle acts as seer and oracle amid the general innocence of the local Jews, the boy among them, who deny their coming doom. Moshe is a symbolic figure who voices the warning of history to the Hungarian Jews (Daniel R. Schwarz calls him a metaphysical extension of the narrator).[28] After Moshe survives the deportation of foreign-born Jews and escapes from a massacre in Nazi-occupied Poland, he returns to warn the Jews of their imminent murder, an act of self-sacrifice taken for granted, but not explained in *Night,* though the informed reader realizes there were very few options at this point for escape from Europe. Moshe is a messenger from the dead who is not heeded by the Jews of Sighet, Eliezer included.

Although undoubtedly based on a real person,[29] Moshe is one of Wiesel's mystics and madmen who people his fictional universe, including "Moshe the Madman," the cantor who led the first deportation of Sighet Jews dancing and singing to the cattle cars, a figure who haunts Wiesel in *Legends of Our Time.*[30] Menachem Keren-Kratz draws attention to a remarkable similarity with the synagogue beadle Simon in Ring's debut novel *Farblondgeter nigen* (The Lost Melody, 1937), who also risks his sanity in study of the Kabbalah, among other similarities with *Night.*

Keren-Kratz dispels the impression Wiesel gives that as a young teenager he led a strictly religious life secluded from the outside world but does not consider the possibility that Wiesel may have become familiar with prewar Sighet literary authors as a budding journalist and writer in Paris after liberation.[31] The boy Eliezer gives us to understand that Moshe has mystic knowledge beyond mortal understanding: the snatches of song or chanting he hears "told of the suffering of the divinity, of the Exile of Providence, who according to cabbala, awaits his deliverance in that of man" (15; "de la souffrance de la divinité, de l'Exil de la Providence, qui, selon la Kabbale, attendrait sa délivrance dans celle de l'homme" [13]). According to Kabbalah, the *shekhinah*, or Divine Presence, is in exile together with the people of Israel. Their yearning for the return to Zion of the *shekhinah* will bring redemption. In that future redemption the original cosmic rupture in Eden will be repaired, so that, according to the Zohar, "the redemption of Israel is one with the redemption of God Himself from His mystic Exile."[32] Moshe the Beadle teaches the boy that asking questions brings one nearer to God, but he adds that we do not understand the answers which God gives. He assures the boy, "you will find the true answers, Eliezer, only within yourself!" (16; "Les vrais réponses, Eliezer, tu ne les trouveras qu'en toi" [17]). Eliezer looks forward to the future messianic times when question and answer will be one.

Mauriac, however, true to Christian eschatology, ties the resurrection of "Elie" to the resurrection of the Jewish nation, which has risen from the ashes of the crematoria. The "suffering of the divinity" cannot refer to the crucifixion, as a Christian reader would understand these words, but refers to the familiar Jewish teaching that the *Shekhinah* is in exile with the Jewish people, and the tears which God sheds for the Jewish people's suffering will bring redemption.

The opening of *Night* sets the scene not just for the chronicle of the destruction of an entire way of life and the destruction of hope in humanity, but also for the boy's struggle with his faith in a God of salvation. It is, from the outset, a redemptive narrative in which any chance of rescue, assistance, or Divine intervention seems to be dashed by the trials of torture and death that undermine assumptions about social and human norms. The story of how the boy faces those trials and survives to tell the tale forms the plot of an anti-Bildungsroman, an education in death, where everyday survival is a slow and agonizing dying.[33]

The fate of Sighet's Jews was sealed much later than that of the rest of European Jewry. Under the Vienna Awards of August 30, 1940, Romania ceded Transylvania to Hungary, and the Jews of Sighet fell victim to the anti-Jewish violence and policies of the Horthy regime. There were deportations of stateless Jews, yet these ceased in March 1942 with the succession of the Kallay government, which expropriated Jewish property and conscripted Jews for forced labor but generally resisted German demands to hand over Jews for deportation to concentration camps in Poland. However, in March 1944 Germany occupied Hungary, and Eichmann arrived in Budapest to implement the Final Solution of Hungarian Jewry. The incredulity of Sighet Jews described by Wiesel in response to the unbelievable news that seeped out from Polish ghettos and concentration camps (known from 1942 to Hungarian Jewish leaders, who largely kept silent) was not just a result of German deception and ruses to gain the compliance of the Jews.[34] It was a willing self-delusion that they would be spared, a deluded faith in humanity that would soon be disappointed. On the seventh day of Passover, the Jewish festival of redemption from Egyptian slavery, the Jewish communal leaders are arrested. From then on everything happens quickly: "The race toward death had begun" (21; "La course vers la mort a commencé" [26]). Then starts the inexorable road to deportation and death for all the Jews of Sighet. The boy's initiation into Auschwitz is a journey, no less existential for being real, in search of truth, a truth which will change the boy forever.

Wiesel used to paraphrase the saying that after Auschwitz there can be no questions for the faithful and no answers for the unbelievers.[35] However, on reaching Auschwitz the questions seem unanswerable. In the cattle car on the way to Auschwitz-Birkenau, which Wiesel presents as a trope for the hermetically sealed trap in which they are caught, Madame Schächter goes crazy and imagines a fire outside the cattle-truck window. When they arrive at the concentration camp, the fire is real, belching out of the pit of dying babies and the crematorium chimney. The boundary between the insane and the normal has been breached. We enter a world impervious to metaphor, where the unbelievable is a matter of fact.

This is a *rite de passage* into a world that is a never-ending night. The initiation tests the boy's faith in God and his hold on human dignity. When confronted by the pits where babies are being burned, the boy asks how the world can stand by in silence when they are burning children? His father answers that now anything could happen, that humanity is not concerned with them (42). As they approach the flames, someone recites the *kaddish*, the mourner's prayer which exalts God. The boy revolts at God's apparent silence, wondering why he should express praise and thanks, but, as the prisoners step nearer their own deaths, he too whispers the words of the *kaddish*.

> Jamais je n'oublierai cette nuit, la première nuit de camp qui a fait de ma vie une nuit longue et sept fois verrouillée.
> Jamais je n'oublierai cette fumée.
> Jamais je n'oublierai les petits visages des enfants dont j'avais vu les corps se transformer en volutes sous un azur muet.
> Jamais je n'oublierai ces flammes qui consumèrent pour toujours ma Foi.
> Jamais je n'oublierai ce silence nocturne qui m'a privé pour l'éternité du désir du vivre.

> Jamais je n'oublierai ces instants qui assassinèrent mon Dieu et mon âme, et mes rêves qui prirent le visage du désert.
> Jamais je n'oublierai cela, même si j'étais condamné à vivre aussi longtemps que Dieu lui-même. Jamais. (60)

> Never shall I forget that night, the first night in camp, which has turned my life into one long night, seven times cursed and seven times sealed. [...] Never shall I forget those moments which murdered my God and my soul and turned my dreams to dust. Never shall I forget these things, even if I am condemned to live as long as God Himself. Never. (43–4)

The litany of "never" lends force to the boy's oath never to forget when night became no longer a metaphor but a permanent state of being. Blunted by blows, the naked men lose their concern for their families, they lose their pride and their own sense of self-preservation. They enter the antechamber of hell, where it seemed they "were damned souls wandering in the half-world, souls condemned to wander through space till the generations of man came to an end, seeking their redemption, seeking oblivion—without hope of finding it" (45; "des âmes condamnés à errer à travers les espaces jusqu'à la fin des générations, à la recherche de leur rédemption, en quête de l'oubli—sans espoir de le trouver" [63]).

In this Jobian quest, the boy does not entirely lose faith. When a *kapo* demands that new shoes be given up, he thanks God for creating the mud that covers his and conceals them from the *kapo*. The testing of faith bears out Moshe the Beadle's admonition that questions bring a person closer to God, although we might not understand the answers. These are questions from within faith, questions of faith in the God of justice, as when Abraham questioned the justice of the punishment of Sodom or when Job sought understanding of his suffering. For Wiesel it would be heretical *not* to ask where is God in Auschwitz.[36]

The greatest test of faith takes place within the boy. Throughout the narrative, the narrator's attitude is severely judgmental toward his younger self, toward the spoiled child who would not at first eat the soup given them on their transfer from Birkenau to Auschwitz. Such distancing deepens our moral recoil at the depths to which the prisoners are plunged. Yet even in the degradation into the debased condition of all concentration camp inmates, the boy is struggling not to lose faith. The words of welcome by the Polish prisoner in charge of their block are not without significance for that struggle: their only hope is if they believe in liberation and stick together (50).

As the prisoners sing Hasidic tunes and talk of God's mysterious ways, or of their future deliverance, a fellow-prisoner, Akiva Drumer, tells them that God is testing them and that His punishments are signs of love for

His people. From the Kabbalistic perspective, the coming of messiah is supposed to be a time of war and atrocity. In one Talmudic tradition, the rabbis were terrified at the prospect of living in the days leading to messianic times; another tradition, however, has it that they would be happy to smell the dung of the messiah's donkey.[37] The prisoners have no right, just as the Polish orderly told them, to despair. Yet the boy notes that he has ceased to pray, "How I sympathized with Job! I did not deny God's existence, but I doubted His absolute justice" (53; "Comme j'étais avec Job! Je n'avais pas renié Son existence, mais je doutais de Sa justice" [76]). It is as if the boy is putting God on trial, as in Hasidic stories of a *din torah* (litigation) against God. A covenantal dialogue can only be conducted on the basis that there is a God with whom one can engage. Moreover, the Kabbalistic notion of *hester panim* (Divine concealment) insists that God's presence in history is not always visible—for example, in the story of the attempted genocide of the Jews by Haman in the Book of Esther the name of God is not mentioned once.

When a small boy with the face of an angel is hanged after a sabotage attempt, the prisoners are made to watch him die on the gallows. Someone behind Eliezer asks, "Where is God now?" A voice within him answers, "Where is He? Here He is—He is hanging here on [these] gallows" (71; "'Où donc est Dieu?' Et je sentais en moi une voix qui lui répondait: 'Où il est ? Le voici—il est pendu ici, à cette potence'" [105]). Is this the answer within himself that Moshe the Beadle predicted? Christian readers, like Mauriac, might understand this to refer to the crucifixion, others to a Nietzschean death of God, or, as for Alfred Kazin, a darkening of divine revelation.[38] By contrast, the Jewish thinker Emil Fackenheim has placed this passage in the midrashic context of the promise of redemption precisely when there exists either absolute evil or absolute righteousness.[39]

Wiesel has said that he never claimed that God was dead and that this passage in *Night* was taken out of context.[40] Although Wiesel has occasionally spoken of the impression that God died in the deported children at Buchenwald, the simple meaning would appear to be that what has been murdered is the divine image in which man was created; a biblical commandment in fact prohibits leaving a condemned man on the gallows for this reason, because the divine image resides even in the most wicked. Wiesel has said that the question is not where was God in Auschwitz, but where was man. For humanity has been murdered, and with it the divine image, a murder of God who created man in His image. Wiesel places himself firmly within Jewish tradition when defending against Nietzschean readings of this passage: "I have never renounced my faith in God. I have risen against His justice, protested His silence and sometimes His absence, but my anger rises up within faith, not outside it."[41] Moreover, in contrast to Mauriac's reading of this passage, He is also there, suffering with His people in exile, a common Kabbalistic belief. Jewish tradition describes

God shedding tears—over marital strife, or over the exile of His people, and collects these tears for the moment of redemption. Citing the well-known midrash that God follows Israel into exile and suffers with them and quoting the Zohar's statement that there is no place without God, Wiesel comments that this offers no consolation but leaves another question, why did not man listen to God's tears? The onus is on man who has failed to live up to the divine image. The boy's question in *Night* is not whether there is a God who could allow such cruelty, but rather why God, who entered into a covenant with the people of Israel, should torment them like this without apparent mercy or justice. Wiesel has told the story elsewhere of the trial of God he witnessed in Auschwitz, in which inmates pronounced God guilty of abandoning His people, but afterward they went to pray. In other words, in bringing God to trial, the inmates are not denying His existence—on the contrary—but questioning the *tsiduk hadin*, the justification of His ways, with which midrashic and Talmudic writing, as well as centuries of *kinot,* usually conclude the story of destruction and exile.[42] This fits the plot line of grappling with God's mysterious ways which was introduced at the beginning of the story. After previous hangings Eliezer had found the soup tasty, but this evening it tasted of corpses.

The Jewish New Year (Rosh Hashanah) is the Day of Judgment when God remembers the deeds of every person, and on that day a thousand camp inmates bless God in their evening prayers, acknowledging the Creator of the universe. However, the boy sees no reason to bless the Creator as he feels he is the stronger one, he is the accuser. Job was not more sorely tested! The public prayer meeting is exceptional, given the severe punishment for anyone caught observing Jewish religious practices (the Nazis allowed public prayer meetings in camps and ghettos only to suit their purposes, such as preliminary to roundups and selections, which were sometimes timed deliberately on Jewish holidays in order to further demoralize the inmates). It is a set scene for metaphysical conflict. The boy stands alone in a world that appears to him to be without God and without man. After the service, he finds his father bowed down, defeated; the look they exchange reveals mutual understanding. On Yom Kippur, the Day of Atonement, the holiest day in the Jewish calendar and the closure of the ten days of repentance that begin with the New Year, his father makes him promise not to fast (since fasting was life-endangering for camp inmates on a starvation diet and therefore not permitted by Jewish law). But Eliezer refuses to accept God's silence and turns his bowl of soup into an act of revolt. Yet he concludes significantly, "In the depths of my heart, I felt a great void" (75; "Au fond de mon cœur, je sentais qu'il s'était un grand vide" [111]). Having been reduced by starvation to constant hunger, to mere bones and stomach, the boy nevertheless feels lost without faith.[43]

The Jewish New Year is cynically chosen by the Germans to carry out a selection that will determine who is too weak to work and must die.

Eliezer passes the selection, but his father has not been so lucky, yet is later reprieved in a second selection. The days of selection—a mockery of their significance in the Jewish calendar, when Jews await judgment who will live and who will die—are a further test of faith: Akiva Drumer despairs and a learned rabbi loses his belief in divine mercy. If only, muses the boy, Akiva Drumer had sustained his belief, he would have continued to live. Sadly, numbed by hunger and blows, his comrades forget they promised to say *kaddish* for him. Thus, we see that, against all odds, Eliezer's faith is tested but wins out in the end.

Through centuries of Jewish martyrology, the paradigm was of Abraham who was commanded to bring his beloved son Isaac to be bound for an offering, one of Abraham's ten trials of faith. Abraham proves his pure faith in a Creator who has promised that he will be blessed with many descendants who will inherit the land of Israel and yet he is being asked to sacrifice his only son, born to Sarah at an advanced age, without whom there will be no descendants, except through Ishmael, whom God discounted as a worthy heir. An angel stays Abraham's hand, and Abraham brings a ram as a sacrifice. Ellen Fine suggests that in *Night* Wiesel takes up, as he does in *Messengers of God*, the focus in the midrashic retelling of this story on the father and son facing the altar *together*, "'victims together,' bound by their communal offering."[44] Over the centuries, particularly during the medieval massacres by the Crusaders, Jewish fathers sacrificed their Isaacs for their faith, and the Hebrew poets recorded their martyrdom in the *'aqeda* liturgy of Yom Kippur and the fast of the Ninth of Av. In the Holocaust, it was often the father who was sacrificed in front of the son. As Wiesel recalls in his memoir, *All Rivers Run to the Sea*, the Germans killed sons in front of their fathers, and the shooting of his cousin in front of his Uncle Mendel makes him think of the compassion implicit in the biblical injunction not to slaughter the ox and its calf on the same day.[45] The Holocaust, inevitably, has given a cruel twist to this *topos* of Hebrew lamentation poetry, for it would be obscenely blasphemous to seek sanctity or divine command in such a sacrifice when it is not stayed by an angel's hand and is carried out, moreover, in a fiendish plan to wipe out God's people in gas chambers. As André Neher has averred, the *aqeda* has been reversed and Isaac leads the aged Abraham on a forced march, prodded by SS whips, to the sacrifice, yet Abraham asks no questions. It is again Job who questions the silence of God, a testing of faith that does not receive an answer.[46] The *aqedah* has become the trial of Isaac as much as of Abraham, the son's test when he sees his father sacrificed. The boy's sticking to his father through thick and thin in *Night*, despite the temptation to be free of this burden and despite the examples of sons who mistreat or abandon their fathers, is true to the paradigm in its terrible dénouement in the Holocaust.

The evacuation from Buna in winter 1944–5 provides a further trial of faith and tests his love for his father: hospitalized for treatment of an infected foot wound, the boy must choose whether to stay in the ward, amid rumors the camp will be destroyed by the retreating Germans, or to be evacuated from the camp with his father and the other prisoners. The boy wraps his bleeding foot in a blanket and sets off on a death march to an uncertain destination and an uncertain fate. On the march, the boy and his father prevent each other from falling asleep in the snow and freezing to death. Rabbi Eliahou, a prophetic figure like Elijah, for whom he is evidently named, comes looking for his son, who has let the old man lag behind, wishing to be free of the burden of his father and thus improve his chances of survival. Eliezer prays to the God whose justice he doubts not to let him become like Rabbi Eliahou's son and abandon his father. The fourth commandment, to honor one's father and mother, is the mainstay of the Jewish family and its guarantee of continuity. Here the son must cope with a merciless world which does not honor fathers or mothers, where the son may have to choose between his life and his father's.

In *Night*, the boy's love for his father is repeatedly tested—when the foreman hits his father at Buna the son only wishes to get farther away so that he will not be hurt too. Trying to fend off Franek's demand that his father hand over his gold crown tooth, he tries to get his father to march better to avoid Franek's vindictive blows. There is no place for loving one's father in a concentration camp. A *pipel* (child kept by a homosexual officer or orderly) strikes his own father mercilessly. Yet Eliezer is determined not to abandon his father. Again, during the selection at Gleiwitz, where they stop for three days before being sent on trains into Germany, Eliezer instinctively runs after his father who is directed with the weaker men to the left, and in the ensuing confusion they both manage to return to the column being marched out of the camp. Yet, faced by sons who abandon their fathers' corpses without a tear, how long can he withstand this test? The metaphorical and real night of the book's title was "long and never ending" (100; "La nuit se faisait longue, longue à n'en plus finir" [153]). Desperately he wakes his father who is taken for dead and almost thrown out of the train. Later, it is his father who raises the alarm when Eliezer is almost strangled by an unknown assailant.

In the train, the boy witnesses how a son snatches bread from a dying father. Yet he is still determined to hold on to his father. On arrival at Buchenwald, he loses his father during an air raid alert and catches himself wishing for a moment that he will not find him and then he too will be free of this burden. The thought shames him and, although he does not succumb, the thought stands accusingly in his memory: he remembers how almost grudgingly he gave his father the soup which revived him. He nevertheless manages to change beds to be with his dying father, who is sick with dysentery. As he lies on his bunk, his father is powerless to avoid being beaten and robbed of his bread. He begs his son for water, which Eliezer knows he must not have, and asks his son to have mercy on him: "Have mercy on him! I, his only son!" (111; "Avoir pitié de lui! Moi, son fils unique!" [171]).

A week passes and the head of the block advises the boy not to give his father his soup or bread ration; nobody can help his father—he should be looking after himself. He should be having his father's ration, now of little use to him. "Here, every man has to fight for himself and not think of anyone else. Even of his father. Here, there are no fathers, no brothers, no friends" (111; "Ici, chacun doit lutter pour lui-même et ne pas penser aux autres, même pas à son père. Ici, il n'y a pas de père qui tienne, pas de frère, pas d'ami" [172]). This call to break one of the holiest commandments, to honor one's father, is a test that the boy cannot easily withstand; his heart tells him the man is right and he should be eating his father's rations as well as his own. It is a momentary fall, but he feels guilty for it. He does not abandon his father but runs to bring him soup and pretends to be ill himself so as to stay with him. When an SS officer deals his father a violent blow because he is making a noise with his call for water, he cannot do anything. The next morning his father is no longer there. He has been taken away to the crematorium. Had he been able to search his weakened conscience, he comments, he might have found something like "free at last" (113; "enfin libre" [174]). This scene is missing in other accounts that Wiesel wrote of his father's death. However, the reader understands that Eliezer is not indifferent to his father's death and has not betrayed the filial duty written in the Ten Commandments: on arrival at Auschwitz he risked his life to bring his father water and now he is tormented by the thought that his father's last words may have been his name, a last summons to which he failed to respond. This is the highest form of spiritual resistance to an inhuman brutality which does everything to crush basic human feelings and needs. Eliezer reports that after his father's death nothing more could touch him. He is transferred to the children's block.

In a last-ditch act of resistance, some of the prisoners rebel as the SS are about to liquidate the camp. They take over the camp until the Americans arrive at Buchenwald in the evening of April 11, 1945. But it is too late to regain the loss of innocence, or the loss of humanity. After recovering from food poisoning following a life and death struggle, Eliezer looks at himself in a mirror. A corpse looks back at him, "The look in his eyes, as they stared into mine, has never left me" (116; "son regard dans mes yeux ne me quitte plus" [178]). The mimetic reflection of what he has become records the distance between the innocent boy at the beginning of the journey and the haunting eyes of the concentration camp survivor at its end. By contrast, in the Yiddish memoir, Eliezer smashes the mirror with its image of a skeleton awaiting death, detaching himself from the dehumanized concentration camp prisoner, and recovers his will to live, as well as to write this memoir of survival.[47] In the literary adaptation, however, Eliezer remains forever changed by his experience, so that the reader too must confront the harrowing look of the camp inmate's eyes which accompanies the survivor in the present, ten years later, after a decade of silence and of reflection, as well as immersion in contemporary philosophy and literature.

This embodied witnessing does not follow the strict chronology and circumstantial verification of a memoir or historical account but tracks the Jewish religious calendar of redemption and judgment as the boy grapples with his faith in God in the madness of mass murder. It provides a harrowing account of the human condition when night has thrown its dark shadow over the soul. Step by step, the boy descends into the cauldron of his spiritual and physical trial. He has become reduced to a stomach, unable to think of anything but staving off his hunger. Yet the narrative proves that all is not despair, as when a French Jewess, passing for Aryan, supports the boy after he is punished by whipping in the Buna labor camp, comforting him with some words in German, which could have cost her life. The prisoners gain hope even from the encouragement shouted by their persecutors on the death march. Yet apart from the physical struggle to survive there is an urgent moral call to humanity, not to avenge the deaths of so many and not to hate the perpetrators (as in Lengyel's *Five Chimneys*), or to despise fascism (as in Rousset's *The Holocaust Kingdom*), but to learn a lesson in ethical behavior. When, some years later, Wiesel sees a Parisienne throwing money to children in Aden, he thinks of how German workmen enjoyed the spectacle of the camp inmates freezing in cattle-trucks who fought to the death over the bread which they threw them. Here lies Wiesel's message—not of endurance, but of remaining, despite almost total despair, a moral being.

PART TWO

2

A Poetics of the Holocaust?: Celan, Sutzkever, Miłosz

Efraim Sicher

Introduction

Scholars and critics often talk about poetry "after Auschwitz." That, properly speaking, is a question of the politics of memory, of how we read and how poets write after the Holocaust. This chapter looks at poetry written *during*, not *after*, the Holocaust in order to consider whether one can speak of a "Holocaust poetics." I ask what are the implications of this question for our reading of Celan, Sutzkever, and other poets who wrote in the uncertainty and instability of a war that was not over and before the full horror was known. They wrote before the Holocaust entered public consciousness, before it was hypermediated through postwar politics and ideologically framed discourses. Celan's postwar verse will be discussed in the next chapter, and we will deal separately with Miklós Radnóti, whose last poems were found when his body was exhumed from a mass grave, and ghetto poets who perished, such as Władysław Szlengel and Itzhak Katzenelson.[1] Their poems are, as Sue Vice has remarked, literally messages in a bottle,[2] left for posterity in the uncertain hope that someone might read them or written as letters that would never reach an addressee. Their writing may

---

I am grateful to Vivian Liska for sharing her insights into Celan in her Axel Springer lecture, Hebrew University of Jerusalem, December 24, 2014, as well as to David Roskies, Daniel Feldman, and Hannah Pollin-Galay for their inspiration and helpful comments.

be considered early testimony, produced under extraordinary conditions of duress and lack of adequate food or sometimes basic writing materials.

Unlike *post*-Holocaust poetry, poetry composed during the Holocaust by those who were there and as it was happening is a writing *in extremis* that forces us to accept that artifice and experience are not contradictory. On the contrary, the force of truth comes across in artistic form in ways that are shocking, disturbing, and affective. And yet, as I will show, these poets did not emerge out of a vacuum and worked in established traditions of romantic or modernist poetry; nevertheless they were conscious of the strain on poetic language of unprecedented and unspeakable horror. If Aristotle maintained that the difference between the historian and the poet was that the historian described what happened and the poet imagined what might possibly or necessarily happen, we run up against a mental block when what really happened is beyond imagination.

The Israeli critic Sidra Dekoven Ezrahi quotes the Yiddish poet and Holocaust survivor, Mendel Mann (1916–75), speaking of poetry written in the ghettos, "This was in most cases a desperate poetry, but passionate and sacred. [...] I admired not so much their literary form, but their faith, their confidence in the Jewish word."[3] Unlike the writing of bystanders or other persecuted groups, these poets knew that at stake was the future of Jewish culture and the existence of the Jewish people, both slated for extinction by the Nazi state. This chapter asks whether during the Holocaust poets found an adequate voice in existing forms or whether the unprecedented and overwhelming reality strained language and required a new poetics.

Poetry before Adorno

The question "is there a Holocaust poetics?" might have no definitive answer, but it is a question we must ask if we want to know to what extent poets who wrote in and about the Holocaust were able to find a new poetic language for what they experienced and to what extent they adapted existing conventions to an ironic mode or to a new and shocking meaning. The question undermines our assumptions about the purpose and value of literature. Yet discussion of Holocaust poetry and Holocaust literature in general has been overshadowed by criticism after Adorno. Before offering a reading of Holocaust poetry that was written and read before critical theory quoted or misquoted Adorno and made him the measure of judgment, I wish to set the record straight.

In discussion on literature "after Auschwitz," the starting point is invariably Theodor Adorno's statement, made in his essay "Kulturkritik und Gessellschaft" ("Cultural Criticism and Society," 1949), that to write poetry after Auschwitz is barbaric: "Nach Auschwitz ein Gedicht zu schreiben ist barbarisch" ("To write a poem after Auschwitz is barbaric").[4] Yet it is often forgotten that this was said in the immediate postwar period, when some German intellectuals wished to make a new start and put the Hitler period behind them, while others saw that the destruction of humane values represented by "Auschwitz" had irrevocably damaged the possibility of carrying on writing the same way as before.[5] Adorno was defending cultural criticism from the reification of a totalizing society in which it faced the final stage of the dialectic of culture and barbarism. Adorno's moral imperative that culture take cognizance of what had happened marked not so much a break from the past as a condition for continuity. Therefore, we should think of the term "after Auschwitz" not only in historical terms but also in the philosophical framework of the Frankfurt School's investment of hope in culture to help bring about a better world. For Adorno, Auschwitz was an epistemological as well as ontological break, an "earthquake" that shook the foundations of Western philosophy.[6] Every philosophical term, everything we think about the human condition had to be reexamined in order to understand the conditions of the cultural criticism.[7]

Adorno's dichotomy of "culture" and "barbarism" is one which George Steiner questioned in his collection of essays *Language and Silence* (1967) when he remarked that the SS officer may very well have gone home to his wife and family after gassing Jews and spent the evening reading Rilke. This showed, to Steiner's mind, how culture and barbarity lay cheek by jowl. Weimar and Buchenwald, where "Goethe's Oak" stood, were adjacent. Freedom meant nothing more than the mocking sign over the gates of Auschwitz-Birkenau and several other camps, "Arbeit macht frei." The belief that the humanities necessarily humanize was placed in doubt by the bestiality of the twentieth century. Literature and sadism can coexist:

> Literary values and the utmost of hideous inhumanity could coexist in the same community, in the same individual sensibility; and let us not take the easy way out and say "the man who did these things in a concentration camp just said he was reading Rilke. He was not reading him well." That is an evasion. He may have been reading him very well indeed.[8]

Nonetheless, Steiner believes the critic's role after Auschwitz, in the age of bestiality, is to preserve the values of humane liberalism by showing what to read and how to read it. The possibility of humaneness, Steiner asserted, lies in the cathartic power of literature. Yet it might be objected that we cannot know whether the SS officer was reading Rilke "properly," as the Nazis put literature and language to their own purposes to suit their ideological and racist vision. Or it may be that Western culture was itself contaminated by barbarity, if not complicit through silence. Western civilization's linguistic and philosophical assumptions of a common humanity were an illusion dispelled by the Nazis' race laws. Indeed, they may have been an illusion well before the mass book-burnings on May 10, 1933. Walter Benjamin warned historical materialists that the treasures of culture could not be contemplated without horror considering their origin: "Es ist niemals ein Dokument der Kultur, ohne zugleich ein solches der Barbarei zu sein" ("There is no document of civilization which is not at the same time a document of barbarism").[9]

Adorno's famous declaration (usually quoted incomplete and out of context) did not, however, cancel the possibility of writing "after Auschwitz" so much as question its status and mode in conditions of total reification. In remarks directed at Jean-Paul Sartre's avowal of literary *engagement*, Adorno conceded in 1961, "Den Satz, nach Auschwitz noch Lyrik zu schreiben, sei barbarisch, möchte ich nicht mildern; negativ ist darin der Impuls ausgesprochen, der die engagierte Dichtung beseelt" ("I do not want to soften my statement that it is barbaric to continue to write poetry after Auschwitz; it expresses, negatively, the impulse that animates committed literature").[10] If the aim of art was to give aesthetic pleasure, what pleasure could be squeezed out of the screams of the victims? To derive aesthetic pleasure from depiction of the victims seemed to Adorno to trivialize and distort their experience. Yet suffering had its right to expression, Adorno wrote in *Negative Dialectics* (1966):

> Das perennierende Leiden hat so viel Recht auf Ausdruck wie der Gemarterte zu brüllen; darum mag falsch gewesen sein, nach Auschwitz ließe kein Gedicht mehr sich schreiben. Nicht falsch aber ist die minder kulturelle Frage, ob nach Auschwitz noch sich leben lasse, ob vollends es dürfe, wer zufällig entrann und rechtens hätte umgebracht werden müssen. Sein Weiterleben bedarf schöner Kälte, des Grundprinzips der bürgerlichen Subjektivität, ohne das Auschwitz nicht möglichgewesen wäre: drastische Schuld des Verschonten.

> Perennial suffering has as much right to expression as a tortured man has to scream; hence it may have been wrong to say that after Auschwitz you could no longer write poems. But it is not wrong to raise the less cultural question whether after Auschwitz you can go on living—especially whether one who escaped by accident, one who by rights should have been killed, may go on living. His mere survival calls for the coldness, the basic principle of bourgeois subjectivity, without which there could have been no Auschwitz; this is the drastic guilt put on him who was spared.[11]

It was not wrong to question living after Auschwitz when life was daunted by the survivor's guilt at having been spared and by the absolute negativity in the "destruction of nonidentity," now "ideologically lurking."[12]

However, in order to write poetry, one had to free it from a culture that was complicit with what had happened and that ignored how fascism corrupted Goethe and the German poetic tradition.

Muttersprache and *Mördersprache*

Not only was poetry possible, Sartre remarked immediately after the war, it was necessary in a world that can do without literature and even better without mankind.[13] This leaves unresolved the paradox of Adorno's conviction that to subscribe to the "garbage" of post-Auschwitz culture amounted to the same barbarism which destroyed culture under the Nazis. Rather, as Jean-François Lyotard has proposed in his critique of *Negative Dialectics*, we need to resist the "amnesia" in the concealment that comes with utterance in all art, especially in a technological age of production.[14] When Adorno said that it would be barbaric to write a poem ("ein Gedicht") after Auschwitz, it was lyricism which Adorno apparently felt to be a betrayal of the victims. In Celan's poetry the lyricism disturbs because its subversion of poetic language invokes familiar conventions in a cruel irony that mocks and undermines our basic definitions of life and death. In that regard, Celan's disturbing lyricism might not be so far from Adorno's position,[15] though Celan, for his part, was angered by Adorno's statement, which seemed to him to reflect a misunderstanding of poetry.[16] We will turn to Celan's poetry of negativity and its bearing on Adorno's statement in a later chapter, but first we must consider the conditions in which Celan grew up and became a German-language poet before we read his wartime writing.

Paul Antschel (as Celan was called before he took his more familiar and appropriate penname) grew up under Romanian rule in Czernowitz (Romanian Cernăuți, today Chernivtsi in Ukraine), the regional capital of Bukovina. He experienced persistent anti-Semitism at school and in society at large which prevented him from being anything other than a Jew. The brief Soviet occupation in 1940 dispelled any illusions Celan had about communism. The Soviets took over every aspect of life, enforced Russian and Ukrainian as official languages, and deported 3,800 men (mostly Jews) to Siberia. When Antonescu seized power, the notorious Iron Guard began massacring Jews in the annexed territories of Bukovina, Bessarabia, and Transnistria. Then, in July 1941 Romania joined the Axis powers in invading Ukraine. The Einsatzgruppen killing units reached Czernowitz on July 4–5, 1941, and Romanian police helped round up the Jews. Thousands of Jews were deported to Transnistria where they were incarcerated in make-shift labor camps or massacred. The traumatic experience of roundups and a short stay in an overcrowded ghetto did not deter Celan from writing poetry imbued with German romanticism but with surreal effects ("Finsternis" ["Darkness"] and "Notturno" ["Nocturne"]). Celan was requisitioned to clear debris and confiscate Russian books, but his family survived a wave of deportations thanks to authorization permits issued by the mayor Tristan Popovici. However, these soon became worthless, and in June 1942 the deportations resumed.[17]

Celan evidently felt much guilt after his parents were taken away while he was out of the house on June 27, 1942. He was in a hiding place where they apparently refused to join him over a Saturday night, when the German Einsatzgruppen and Romanian fascists routinely conducted their raids on Jewish homes. Celan's parents were deported to the Ukrainian work camps on the other side of the Dniester, a five-day journey in cattle cars. There Jews were lodged in stables and had to do arduous labor in gravel pits. Celan's father died of typhus in fall 1942; in late 1942 or early 1943. Celan heard from a relative that his mother had been shot. Celan managed to stay in Czernowitz but was drafted into the Romanian labor battalions, administered by the military authorities, which required Jewish men to report for construction work and, in the winter, snow clearing. The Romanian labor battalions were brutal, though not as sadistic and lethal as the Hungarian labor brigades we will meet in Chapter 4, and their administrators and commanders were often corrupt or incompetent.[18] Celan was assigned to physical labor shoveling rocks and building roads, first in Tăbărești, four hundred kilometers south of Czernowitz, later in other camps, making a total of nineteen months doing forced labor. Those who met him at this time reported that he was taciturn, with a gallows humor, and he later remained reticent about his experiences in the camps; on the brief furloughs in Czernowitz he answered friends who asked what he was doing that he was "shoveling." Even in the labor camps he continued to write verse and collected what he had written so far, bequeathing to his close friend Ruth Lackner, an actress in the Yiddish theater, his poetic legacy in expectation of his demise.[19]

Celan's first mature poems date from the period 1938–41, and others were composed in the Czernowitz ghetto and in forced labor camps in the period between July 1942 and around February 1944, altogether two collections of verse, one typewritten (spring 1944), the other written out by hand, dating from fall 1944 to spring 1945. In the most dismal conditions, sometimes in hiding, he wrote neo-romantic poems of love and flowers, as well as studying symbolist poets and translating Shakespeare, not so much escaping from reality as testing the endurance of poetic language when love and flowers were nowhere in sight. Yet he does not lose sight of the Jews' suffering and universal destruction, as in "Dornenkranz" ("Crown of Thorns").[20] Celan wrote to a friend that he was writing poetry in an effort to maintain his humaneness, his *Menschlichkeit,* in a brutalizing regime of persecution and back-breaking labor that was meant to destroy the body and the spirit.[21]

In "Festland, oder Die Geisterstunde" ("The Witching Hour," 1942) the poet addresses his mother's spirit, white in the darkness, and asks when this surrealist dream will end. The poet's agonized questions pierce the essence of nature and question the possibility of voicing the splintering of self from home, from this wondrously indifferent and violent universe.[22] The poem "Winter" responds in rhymed quatrains to news of his mother's death and imagines her presence in a real landscape of snow in a distant Ukraine that makes the surreal mythology of the conventional poetic universe disturbingly present and near:

> Es fällt nun, Mutter, Schnee in der Ukraine:
> Das Heilands Kranz aus tausend Körnchen Kummer ....
> Von meinen Tränen hier erreicht dich keine,
> Von frühern Winken nur ein stolzer stummer... [23]
> It's falling, Mother, snow in the Ukraine:
> The Savior's crown a thousand grains of grief.
> Here all my tears reach out to you in vain.
> One proud mute glance is all of my relief...[24]

The reference to the Christian Passion is somehow dislocated from any sense of redemption, as the poet stands alone, cut off from his mother, and unable to convey his love. The poet doubts whether, if he remains in his forlorn darkness, time will bring healing or sharp pangs of loss; he closes the poem wondering what would be if he sank into the Ukrainian snowdrift with his mother, wounded or awakening, in oblivion or consciousness.

> Was wär es, Mutter: Wachstum oder Wunde—
> versänk ich mit ihm Schneewehen der Ukraine?[25]
> What would come, Mother: wakening or wound—
> if I too sank in the snows of the Ukraine?[26]

A paradoxical question strikes at the heart of Celan's identity as a poet and as a Jew in the midst of the Holocaust: to join his mother in death is to resign himself to silence, but to live and write is to suffer pain and loss as central tenets of his poetics, a peculiarly modernist self-image after the First World War of the suffering poet.

The loss of the poet's mother stands at the center of "Schwarze Flocken" ("Black Flakes," 1943), originally called "Mutter" ("Mother"), in which the poet recalls receiving a letter from her telling him of his father's death and imagines a conversation with her.[27] The poem is built around the trope of a shawl which the poet weaves to warm her in the cold Ukrainian winter and which he weaves into a poem, a conventional trope of text/texture derived from Latin *texere,* "to weave" (the image of the shawl later served as inspiration for Cynthia Ozick's novella "The Shawl"). As the seasons turn to deathly, permanent winter, the poet imagines his mother begging him for

> „Ein Tuch, ein Tüchlein nur schmal, dass ich wahre
> nun, da zu weinen du lernst, mir zur Seite

die Enge der Welt, die nie grünt, mein Kind, deinem Kinde!"[28]
"A shawl, just a thin little shawl, so I keep
by my side, now you're learning to weep, this anguish,
this world that will never turn green, my child, for your child."[29]

In the mother's imagined appeal, as she lies dying in Ukrainian snow, she calls on Jewish historical memory: the Hetman's troops who perpetrated pogroms under Khmelnitsky in the seventeenth century and under Petliura just over twenty years previously. Now the snow sifts (or scatters) the poet's father's bones. Voicing a Jewish historical perspective of martyrdom—"Jaakobs himmlisches Blut" (the patriarch Jacob's heavenly blood)—the mother in the poem refers to the continuity of Jewish suffering. Death in time and space runs counter to the Christian eschatology with which the poem began. As in "Winter," the conventional images of Christian redemption are blocked out by the unremitting red torrents of ice that represent the poet's inescapable Jewish fate. In the mother's reference to the song crushed under the heels of the perpetrators, "das Lied von der Zeder," an allusion to the popular late-nineteenth-century German-Jewish song "Dort, wo die Zeder," which competed for some years with *Hatikvah* as the Zionist national anthem, there are complex feelings toward the father, of whose death in a forced labor camp Celan was informed in a letter that somehow reached him from his mother. The first stanza of "Dort, wo die Zeder," like Celan's poem, evokes Jewish martyrdom and the father's bones:

Dort, wo die Ceder [*sic!*] schlank die Wolke küßt,
und wo die schnelle Jordans welle fließt,
dort, wo die Asche meiner Väter ruht,
das Feld getränkt hat Makkabäer Blut—
dies heh're Reich am blauen Meeresstrand,
es ist mein liebes, trautes Vaterland!
There, where the cedar kisses the thick clouds,
and where the rapid current of the Jordan flows,
there where the ashes of my father rest,
the field is drenched with the blood of the Maccabees—
this kingdom by the blue seashore,
it is my beloved fatherland.[30]

Celan's troubled feelings toward his Jewish identity here can be traced to his rejection of his father's Zionism and of his fervent hopes of immigrating to the Land of Israel; moreover, Celan harbored uneasy memories of his father's harsh discipline during his childhood.[31]

In writing this poem, during his grueling service in labor camps which allowed only brief periods of leave, Celan is able to weave for his mother the shawl she asks for, which is his poem:

> Blutete, Mutter, der Herbst mir hinweg, brannte der Schnee mich:
> sucht ich mein Herz, daß es weine, fand ich den Hauch, ach des
>   Sommers,
> war er wie du.
> Kam mir die Träne. Webt ich das Tüchlein. [32]
> Autumn bled all away, Mother, snow burned me through:
> I sought out my heart so it might weep, I found—oh the summer's
>   breath.
> it was like you.
> Then came my tears. I wove the shawl.[33]

Only when he learns to mourn, to accept his murdered mother's tears, can the poet pour out his heart and commune with her so that autumn's blood can be assuaged and in the burning snow he can see the summer—the warm memory of his mother. Yet there is no vision here of a future, for the poet remains frozen in pain and loss. Celan's biographer and translator John Felstiner comments that "Black Flakes" "holds in a single moment the European Jewish catastrophe," as well as the poet's "private loss" and his calling as a poet. When in the poem his mother asks for a shawl to keep warm in the Ukrainian winter, his poem restores "to her something at least in the mother tongue."[34]

German is the poet's mother tongue, yet how can he relate to a language and culture that denied him existence? And what future was there for a Jewish poet in German? When the *Muttersprache* (mother tongue) becomes a *Mördersprache* (the language of murder), the writer faces a dilemma of finding words that do not deny a subject position. Celan was not the only German Jewish writer to experience this linguistic alienation. H. G. Adler in Theresienstadt or Nelly Sachs and Else Lasker-Schüler in exile reacted in different ways. Viktor Klemperer, who lived under Hitler in Dresden, noted in *Lingua Tertii Imperii: Notizbuch eines Philologen* (1947; *The Language of the Third Reich: LTI, Lingua Tertii Imperii*, 2000) how the Nazis changed the German language for the purpose of annihilating the Jews, creating an ethical and ontological double bind. Additionally, they conscripted the German poetic tradition, which formed an essential component in the identity of assimilated German-speaking Jews, and expunged Jews from it. As is well known, Hannah Arendt disagreed and in a 1964 interview with Gunther Gaus ("What Remains? The Language Remains") declared that her mother tongue was what remained unharmed, and she could not translate its poetry and idioms into English, her adopted language of exile.[35] In his Bremen speech, after the war, Celan spoke of the survival of language "secure against loss"; language was all that was left after the disaster to help orient him "en route" in his search for cultural identity, to chart his reality: "Aber sie musste nun hindurchgehen durch ihre eigenen Antwortlosigkeiten, hindurchgehen durch furchtbares Verstummen, hindurchgehen durch die tausend Finsternisse todbringender Rede. Sie ging hindurch und gab keine Worte her für das, was geschah, aber sie ging durch dieses Geschehen und durfte wieder zutage treten, 'angereichert von all dem'" ("But it had to go through its own lack of answers, through terrifying silence, through the thousand darknesses of murderous speech. It went through. It gave me no words for what was happening, but went through and could resurface, 'enriched' by it all").[36]

Celan continued to write in German, a language which tied him to his mother and to the assimilated German Jewish world in which he lived before the Holocaust, although after liberation his use of German became imbued with the contrary influences of Romanian folk elegies and surrealism.[37] Language was the home denied to the Bukovina Jewish poets. Rose Ausländer, a friend of Celan from Bukovina who survived with her mother, later wrote: "Schreiben war Leben. Überleben [...] während wir den Tod erwarteten, wohnten manche von uns in Traumworten—unser traumatisches Heim in der Heimatlosigkeit" ("To write was to live. To survive [...] while we were waiting for death, some of us inhabited dream-words—a home in our trauma, our homelessness").[38] For both poets, the mother figure was intrinsic to their writing of trauma and for each of them German was their mother tongue, although, significantly, Ausländer switched to English for ten years after her mother died. Only in her later years did she learn from Celan how to innovatively reconfigure her habitual metaphors in German and resolve the conflict between the mother-tongue and the language of the murderers.[39]

Celan emerged out of a tradition of German-speaking poets from Bukovina, which enjoyed a multicultural cosmopolitanism in German, Yiddish, and Romanian under the Austro-Hungarian Empire, but was subject to rival ethnic tensions under Romanian rule following the First World War and during anti-Semitic measures in the 1930s.[40] Bukovina enjoyed an exceptional history of multilingual coexistence as an Austrian crown province before the First World War, where Jews were recognized as an ethnic group. Ukrainian, Romanian, and even Yiddish writers (such as Itzik Manger) published their early works in German. Aharon Appelfeld and Dan Pagis grew up as children in Bukovina, survived the Holocaust, and immigrated to Israel; both adopted Hebrew as their mother tongue. Faced with growing Romanian and Ukrainian nationalism, German-speaking Jews under Romanian rule identified as assimilated Jews with the local German culture and opted for Austrian citizenship.[41] His native Bukovina, as Celan later noted in his Bremen speech, was a vanished land whose language lived on in his memory and poetry, although unknown and unnamable for his listeners.[42] Amy D. Colin summarizes the dilemma of the Bukovina poets writing in the language of their murderers and their diverse responses:

> Poetry of the Holocaust written in German uncovers a deep fissure between the language it uses and the experience it attempts to convey.

[...] Paul Celan destroys the traditional syntactic and semantic structure of his native German tongue. Out of the residues he creates an innovative poetic idiom that bears his testimony of the Jewish persecution as an urn bears ashes. But Celan's Bukovina contemporaries—Alfred Margul-Sperber, Moses Rosenkranz, David Goldfeld, Isaac Schreyer, Alfred Kittner, Rose Ausländer, Immanuel Weißglas, and Alfred Gong—often used traditional poetic devices and a classicist German style to utter the unspeakable.[43]

The reason for this conservatism, explains Colin, lies in their various beliefs in the power of language as a bulwark against tyranny and in their false hopes in the purity of German poetry, in Goethe's German, which they sought to reclaim from the Nazis as an abiding force of their own cultural identity, even when writing poetry inside the ghettos and the camps of Transnistria, or on forced marches, amid typhus and death.[44]

The Music of Death

Given this context, it is easier to understand why the putative poetics of "Black Flakes" resists pastoral elegy and adopts an estranged position in its presentation of the cozy winter scenes of German folk songs. The underlying contradiction becomes explicit in a poem written shortly after Celan returned as an orphan to liberated Czernowitz in early 1944, "Nähe der Gräber" ("Nearness of Graves"), also addressed to the poet's mother, which ends:

> Und duldest du, Mutter, wie einst, ach, daheim,
> den leisen, den deutschen, den schmerzlichen Reim.[45]
> And can you bear, Mother, as once on a time,
> The gentle, the German, the pain-laden rhyme?[46]

Here the cloth from which the poem is sewn forces rhymes that scream with the violence done, which nature cannot hide. The poem is modeled on the repetition and symmetry of the Romanian folk *doină* in its modulation of the natural landscape (the river Bug, the meadows and aspen trees) with images of the beloved's suffering and death, as in Celan's earlier poem "Espenbaum" ("Aspen Tree"), challenging the innocence of language in the lament for his mother, murdered amid the beauty of nature in Ukraine.[47] As Felstiner notes, when Celan met his old friends from Bukovina again and discovered the extent of the loss in the Holocaust, he sought a poetic form that would be free from the Nazi corruption of the German language and culture, so he turned to the *Nibelungenlied*. However, in his poem "Russischer Frühling" ("Russian Spring") Celan fused the idyll of the High

German with the singing of Soviet Katyusha rockets as the front drew nearer. Again he turned to the Jewish patriarch and evoked Jacob's struggle with the angel, the wrestling of a lone Jew with his heritage and identity, but also with the poetic tradition in which he is writing.[48]

That tension, present already in modernism, between poetic language and the unbearable reality which it represents grows into a more complex response to death in "Todesfuge" ("Death Fugue," 1944):

> Schwarze Milch der Frühe wir trinken sie abends
> wir trinken sie mittags und morgens wir trinken sie nachts
> wir trinken und trinken.[49]
> Black milk of daybreak we drink it at evening
> we drink it at midday and morning we drink it at night
> we drink and we drink.[50]

This well-known opening of Celan's poem erases any remaining romantic idea of harmony with nature. The tension with the conventional lyrical associations of metaphor cannot fail to unsettle the reader.

Celan's "Death Fugue" sounded to Adorno incongruously and even obscenely lyrical, yet the abrasive, almost manic rhythm mocks any lyricism when the repetition literally represents the unremitting brutality, the dehumanization of the prisoners, and the starvation diet, all rendered in the present tense. The ballad-like repetition ("wir trinken sie mittags und morgens wir trinken sie nachts wir trinken und trinken") reminds Felstiner of a German beer-hall song, but also of the refrain of Heine's protest song, "Die schlesischen Weber" ("The Silesian Weavers," 1844), except that the mind-deadening labor of the prisoners is weaving *their* death, not, as in Heine's poem, the doom of Germany, "the false fatherland."[51]

Rose Ausländer, who met Celan after the dissolution of the camps in her native Czernowitz in 1944 and again in Bucharest in 1946, told Israel Chalfen in 1970 that Celan took the metaphor "schwarze Milch" from her poem, "Ins Leben" ("Into Life," 1925), first published in a local magazine *Literari* in 1939 and included in her first collection of verse *Der Regenbogen* (The Rainbow, 1939), a copy of which she later sent to Celan.[52] However, besides the familiar trope, in Jeremiah's description of the destruction of Jerusalem, of drinking Divine wrath (25:15-38; see Isaiah 51), the phrase recalls Arthur Rimbaud's nostalgia for his mother's breasts, when he returned in memory to his parents' country home and to an erotic infatuation with a servant, which brought him to tears in a general nostalgia for a bygone age: "Moi, j'étais abandonné, dans cette maison de campagne sans fin: lisant dans la cuisine, séchant la boue de mes habits devant les hôtes, aux conversations du salon: ennui jusqu'à la mort par la murmure du lait du matin et de la nuit du siècle dernier" ("As for me, I was abandoned, in this endless country house: reading in the kitchen, drying my muddy clothes in front of the guests, in drawing-room conversations, bored to death by the murmur of the milk of morning and the night of the previous century").⁵³ Celan's poem is indeed another memorial to his murdered mother, yet Celan's phrasing "*black* milk of morning" can only be taken literally as an expression of the physical blackness of starvation and forced labor in the camp. The "black milk of morning" is a literal representation of the morning coffee, or what passes for coffee, which the prisoners routinely drank before being forced out to work at the crack of dawn.⁵⁴ The "black milk" does not nurture anything but death; it is a literal imbibing of death yet also a denaturing image. The oxymoron is aligned asyntactically in the poem with death. Shoshana Felman's psychoanalytic interpretation of a thirsting child does not take account of that undoing of metaphor.⁵⁵

The dark humor of a "grave in the air" similarly defers figurality since the smoke in the sky from the crematoria was quite literal and did release victims from the living death cramped in the barracks; Mieczysław Jastrun uses the phrase in his wartime poem "Pogrzeb" (Funeral), published clandestinely in *Z otchłani* (Out of the Depths), and it was presumably in common use.⁵⁶ The forced grave-digging mockingly releases the Jews to a celestial freedom in a parody of Nazi cynicism: "wir schaufeln ein Grab in den Lüften da liegt man nicht eng" ("We shovel a grave in the air/where you won't lie too cramped").⁵⁷ The clash of figurality and literalness surfaces in the Nazis' cruel cynicism in ordering an orchestra to play while prisoners are marched out to the daily labor that is slowly killing them or to play while graves are dug and prisoners are being executed. The SS officer in Celan's poem orders the Jews to dance to the music in a perverse *danse macabre*. He shouts at the Jews to play death more sweetly, reminding Felstiner of Bach's "Komm süßer Tod," ("Come, Sweet Death"),⁵⁸ for Death is the blue-eyed "Meister" from Germany:

> Er ruft spielt süßer den Tod der Tod ist ein Meister aus Deutschland⁵⁹
> He shouts play death more sweetly this Death is a master from Deutschland⁶⁰

The music of death has been normalized as a literal and unpoetic reality. The "we" of the narrator's point of view, however, who are the objects of annihilation, are claiming poetic subjectivity when they have been assigned to death, to nonexistence, to silence.

Paradoxically, the speaking voice has no subjecthood because it is slated for extermination, but its speech act resists its own extinction. From the first line of "Death Fugue" the poem focalizes the Jews who are intimately familiar with the "black milk" (addressed familiarly as "dich") and who are dehumanized below the level of the SS officer's dogs, whom he whistles to attention. Indeed, the poet identifies with the Jewish collective and gives voice to the disembodiment of the Jews who have no right to human existence and who shovel their graves to order. The dehumanized "we" is juxtaposed with a "man" who lives in a house, for whom these are "seine Juden" ("his Jews")—a relation of master and slave seen ironically from the abject position of the victims. The irony is deepened by the composition of the poet's "death-fugue" of the poem's title (which is, significantly, not given a definite or indefinite article). This contrapuntal poetics, as we will see, subverts the musical and literary tradition in which Celan writes.

The SS officer is identified as the Master from Germany—the master of death, who writes to his lover Margarete, a Faustian figure of love and an emblem for all that Goethe represented, the humane culture which—to return to Steiner—can coexist comfortably with unspeakable inhumanity. The Jews, on the other hand, apostrophize Shulamit from Song of Songs, the antitype of the Aryan woman, who is assigned to the crematorium, to ash, which gives the epithet of her ashen hair. Of course, Goethe's Margarete is not an ideal figure of German beauty but a morally compromised character who unwittingly killed her mother and her child after being abandoned by Faust; she is nevertheless redeemed, as is Faust, but remains divided between earthly desire and heavenly ideals. Shulamit, on the other hand, is the sensuous biblical figure who no longer exists in the German imagination, banished from literature and exterminated, though both figures have an ambivalent history in German art; among the German "Nazarenes," Franz Pforr tried to reconcile Judaism and Christianity, Italy and Germany, in his *Shulamite and Maria* (1811).[61] The juxtaposition of the two female lovers alerts us to a larger movement of Celan's poem that does not so much cut off or erase the poetics of the past as audaciously answer and rewrite it. The poet is asking how the poetry that was the backbone of German civilization could be read with knowledge of the death camps. The poet has not rejected Goethe and the German literary tradition in which he is writing. Rather, he is showing its dislocation in a reality of death that is far from the beautiful ideal of European music and poetry. He is playing a counter-fugue to that of the other master of death, Meister Johann Sebastian Bach, undermining the aesthetics of death in his music. As Lawrence Langer points out, Celan's poem has the opposite effect to the "Liebestod" in the finale of Richard Wagner's 1859 opera *Tristan and Isolde,* in which love is consummated in death.[62] The resulting dissonance, audible in Celan's recorded reading of his poem, undermines the aesthetics of death in European culture.[63]

On closer analysis, Celan's "Death Fugue" seems to be in dialog with much romantic and modernist poetry in German. Closely familiar with French surrealism in the interwar years, Celan was well-versed in Rilke and Mallarmé, Rimbaud and Verlaine, Stefan George and Georg Trakl. Trakl was the leading avant-garde Austrian poet who ended his days watching shell-shocked soldiers in a psychiatric ward committing suicide before putting an end to his own life—"Grodek" describes that surreal landscape of the First World War in which the evening sky is transformed into a universal death.

In "Psalm" (second version), Trakl rendered an exotic paradise as a sinister hallucination of a mental hospital inmate, writing:

> Und die Schatten der Verdammten steigen zu den seufzenden Wassern nieder.
> In seinem Grab spielt der weiße Magier mit seinen Schlangen.[64]
> And the shades of the damned go down to the sighing waters.
> In his grave the white magician plays with his serpents.[65]

Trakl concludes, "Schweigsam über der Schädelstätte öffnen sich Gottes goldene Augen" ("Silently, above Golgotha, God's golden eyes open").[66] In "Death Fugue" Celan writes: "er spielt mit den Schlangen und träumet der Tod ist ein Meister aus Deutschland," as if completing Trakl's thought not with the golden eyes of a malevolent god watching over a damned world but with the Master of Death from Germany (which Felstiner leaves untranslated for the force of its sinister associations of a darkening vision of *Deutschland* of the Master Race).[67] Celan wrote in 1960 to the German critic Walter Jens, who cited the Trakl line in his defense of Celan against charges of plagiarizing Yvonne Goll, that he was an old metaphor peddler and Trakl's snakes were archetypal.[68] The "snakes" are the literal whips with which the SS officer is playing to make the Jews dig faster. However, in the context of the Holocaust, the snake-whips, like the grave in the air, break free of metaphor and become only too surreal.

Celan could have learned this use of Trakl from a poem remarkably similar to "Death Fugue" entitled "Er" ("He") by Immanuel Weißglas, another Bukovina poet, who wrote poems in the camps. Weißglas was a schoolmate and close friend of Celan, with whom he translated poetry before the war and whom he met regularly after liberation at the home of Rose Ausländer in Czernowitz. If Celan read "Death Fugue" to his friends in spring 1944, as Kittner testifies, then his poem probably preceded the one by Weißglas, which was apparently written in 1944 but first published without his knowledge in 1970. The coincidence of language and imagery is striking, and critics were quick to accuse Celan of yet another instance of plagiarism, though the two friends' shared affinities and cultural background can easily explain the similarities. In any case, the conventional form of Weißglas's poem is quite different from Celan's iconoclastic use of language.[69]

At this stage in his writing career, Celan sounds ambivalent about the possibility of poetry "after Auschwitz" but certainly rejects any romantic ideal as out of touch with reality. In this he connects with other contemporary German poets who were cynical about the relevance of Friedrich Hölderlin in a war-torn devastated world. For example, Günther Eich in his poem "Latrine" (published in 1946) did not share Hölderlin's faith in poetry when the snowy clouds were reflected in a pool of urine in occupied France in 1940; there is a double irony in referring to Hölderlin's "Andenken" "Remembrance," written in occupied southern France at a time when Hölderlin was conscripted as a national poet by the Nazis.[70] Celan would nevertheless have been able to empathize with Hölderlin's question in "Mnemosyne" (third version) about whether the past can be put to rest when loyalty and silence are required so that the Muses can sing undisturbed. Historical memory, ordained by the gods, can be disrupted by the crooked paths of what we remember, yet we need to somehow balance sorrow over the loss of friends and dear ones with the need to live in the present:

> Vorwärts aber und rückwärts wollen wir
> Nicht sehn. Uns wiegen lassen, wie
> Auf schwankem Kahne der See.[71]
> Forward, however, and back we will
> Not look. Be lulled and rocked as
> On a swaying skiff of the sea.[72]

Celan could reject the way Hölderlin had been conscripted by the Nazis, but he could not ignore his own inner conflicts. It is surely no coincidence that, instead of a suicide note, before drowning himself in the Seine Celan left on his writing desk a biography of Hölderlin open to a page with the underlined phrase by Clemens Brentano, "Sometimes this genius goes dark and sinks down in the bitter well of his heart."[73]

Felstiner calls "Death Fugue" the "benchmark of 'poetry after Auschwitz.'" Its reading and interpretation have been determined largely by its reception after 1952 and by its anthologization into a canonic poem—to the poet's chagrin in view of its reading as part of the German attempt to rework the past after it first appeared in German in Celan's debut collection *Der Sand aus den Urnen* (*The Sand from the Urns,* 1948). Yet "Death Fugue" does not witness something that Celan personally experienced. However unbearable the brutal conditions, Jews in Romanian labor battalions were not generally sent to Auschwitz. Celan probably wrote the poem in 1944 after liberation from the camps and his return to Czernowitz, which again came under Soviet rule, when refugee survivors of the death camps were arriving and telling their stories of Nazi genocide. They probably included former prisoners familiar with the extermination process and with digging graves at mass executions (rather different from Celan's experience of shoveling). Celan apparently knew a Soviet propaganda pamphlet by the Russian writer Konstantin Simonov, which described the Lublin (Maijdanek) concentration camp and recounted that tangos and foxtrots were played as the condemned victims were murdered. Felstiner surmises that Celan was familiar with this source from an editorial note to the first publication of Celan's poem in a Romanian translation in May 1947 by his friend Petre Solomon under the title "Tangoul Morții" ("Death Tango"). As Felstiner notes, the "Death Tango," presumably the popular "Tango de la Muerte," which Celan would have heard before the war in Paris, was played at the notorious Janowska Road camp near Lvov (Lwów) as graves were dug and inmates were tortured to death, but it was also a name given to whatever music was played in other camps to smother the screams of the victims and to enforce a regime of sadistic cruelty.[74] This would also explain the otherwise-incongruous mention of a dance in Celan's poem.

However, it is not any historical or biographical authenticity that gives the poem its force of immediacy but its disruptive diction and rhythm that work against the unsettling lyricism. The obscenity is thus deflected onto the aesthetics of European conventions of death music, which gives pleasure and produces affect. The poem's mimicry of the death fugue challenges the tradition to which it discursively refers and exacerbates this disturbing irony in an insoluble dilemma of how we can possibly derive pleasure from Holocaust poetry.[75] The familiarity of the intertextual allusions and conventions disturbs us into asking the question Celan posed at the end of "Nearness of Graves" (which I discussed earlier): how painful this all now sounds in German.[76]

Celan's much-discussed poetics of negativity (to which we will return in the next chapter) creates a new language and does so in German, a language, as George Steiner astutely noted, that was sanitized and neutered by the Nazis and put to work to dispossess the Jews, process them for resettlement (deportation), then *Sonderbehandlung* (special treatment), and finally *Vernichtung* (annihilation).[77] Answering a questionnaire from a Paris bookstore about his work in progress in 1958, Celan explained that the terrible thing which had happened changed German poetry in ways that did not affect French poetry. He asserted that German poetry "can no longer speak the language which many willing ears seem to expect. Its language has become more sober, more factual. [...] a language which wants to locate even its 'musicality' in such a way that it has nothing in common with the 'euphony' which more or less blithely continued to sound alongside the greatest horrors."[78] Celan adds, "It does not transfigure or render 'poetical'; it names, it posits, it tries to measure the area of the given and the possible."[79] Eric Kligerman concludes that in this "critical description of poetry after Auschwitz, where the euphony sounds alongside the most terrible things ('einhertönte'), one hears Adorno's reflections on art after Auschwitz in his *Meditationen zur Metaphysik* (*Meditations on Metaphysics*), where he describes how the SS drowned out (*übertönen*) the cries of their victims with *Begleitmusik* (accompanying music)."[80]

At the same time, dislocation of language reflects a dislocation of the poet, who must retrace his steps, given the contradiction, evident in "Death Fugue," between his German cultural identity and the Nazi state's denial of his existence. Kligerman explains that Celan refers to the event which cannot be named: "The name of the disaster [*Unheil*] can only be spoken silently."[81] In *Aesthetic Theory* Adorno commented on Celan's poems that they showed the shame of art in the face of experience of suffering and wanted "to speak of the most extreme horror through silence. Their truth content itself becomes negative."[82] The disaster or "Unheil" is "conveyed not through images, photographs, or other art forms that gesture toward authentic depictions of historical catastrophe, but through a language that has been radically altered and struggles with its silences and paratactic disturbances." Celan seems after all not so far from Adorno's position on poetry after Auschwitz.[83]

In his Bremen speech, as mentioned in the introduction to this book, Celan took the notion of a poem as a message in a bottle from Osip Mandelstam's 1913 essay "O sobesednike" ("On the Interlocutor"). Mandelstam was discussing the construction of the reader in Symbolist poetry and likened the poet's ideal addressee to the unknown finder of the message sealed in a bottle by a shipwrecked sailor, which binds the finder to the testimony of what happened to the sailor. However, when the poet writes to posterity in a labor camp without any idea of whether someone will find the bottle, we can understand that the poet's endangered or deceased "I" is seeking a "thou" that will call his reality into existence when words themselves have been canceled along with the poet's right to existence. The "topography" which Celan sketches in his address at the prize ceremony in Bremen takes him back to the Hasidic tales of his native (unnamed) Bukovina, to people and books that were wiped out by the Nazis. Hence, the "Sprache" (language) of the message in the bottle might not be a language shared by his audience, if understood by them at all.[84] Yet we should remember that, given the dialogical nature of Celan's poetry, the interlocutor is always present in the text.

Poetry as Resistance

Scholars who maintain that Holocaust poetry marks a break from anything previously written ignore the prehistory of Holocaust poets and their literary context. As Roskies has noted, writers came to the ghettos with a cultural baggage of neo-romanticism and modernism in all its forms, from surrealism to futurism, and the years preceding the Holocaust saw a new secularized interest in the bible and traditional Jewish sources as one way of expressing a newfound solidarity in the face of adversity—economic distress and violent anti-Semitism. Moreover, the violence of the years of war, revolution, and pogroms in 1918–21 provided a stock of apocalyptic imagery and modernist responses to mass killing, rape, and destruction of whole communities. When read in the ghettos, as noted in the Introduction above, Y. L. Peretz or Haim Nahman Bialik, as well as Job and Isaiah, gave new meaning to what was literally happening.[85] In the ghettos, a traumatized collective memory met an incommensurate situation which seemed to many like the final days of apocalypse, without their knowing how much worse it was to become. In every language that Jews spoke, they sang new songs about their despair and misery to prewar tunes (such as *Papirosen*) and wrote diaries, documentary journalism, fiction, and poetry to give hope and consolation when there seemed to be none, but also to record for posterity, to warn against this ever happening again. In the relatively short span of time when cultural life could be maintained in the larger ghettos, writers sought paradigms to express the unprecedented scale of daily deportations and starvation in a fast-changing reality. However, as Roskies comments, when the full intent and extent of the Nazi Final Solution became clear, "What had begun as a retrospective act of consolation ended as a prophecy of utter doom. The most modern of destructions finally made sense only on the most archetypal level of meaning."[86] To write was a sacred task, in the hope that the martyrdom of the Jewish people would not be forgotten.

Unlike Celan, who had to subvert his native tongue which was the language of the perpetrators, the modernist Yiddish poet Abraham (Avrom) Sutzkever wrote in the language of the victims, the vernacular Yiddish that carried the memory of Jewish literary responses to catastrophe. Sutzkever was unexpectedly catapulted into the role of the bard of the Vilna Ghetto where he participated in cultural resistance, though occasionally racked by inner qualms over his preoccupation with poetry instead of fighting.[87] Sutzkever was already a well-known poet and public figure before the German invasion of Lithuania in June 1941 and had established a reputation in the interwar years for his experimental nature poetry, which followed the neo-romanticism of Cyprian Norwid, to whom Sutzkever devoted a poem.[88] That did not initially endear him to the avant-garde Yiddish poets of *Yunge Vilna* (Young Vilna), who believed that poetry should be engaged in political struggles. However, the modernist innovations of his poetry, its exuberance of living life, soon made him a leading Vilna poet.[89] The poems Sutzkever wrote in the ghetto were later completed and collected in *Di festung* (The Fortress, 1945) and *Lider fun geto* (Poems from the Ghetto, 1947). They were composed without knowing what the next day would bring, in inhuman conditions of total physical and psychological devastation. Hannah Pollin-Galay writes: "One theme that arises throughout his diverse ghetto poetry concerns the Jewish capacity to speak, to become cognizant of one's suffering, and to convey it aloud."[90] After the war his epic account of survival in Vilna's sewers in *Geheymshtot* (Secret City, 1948) was hailed as "a centerpiece to that new entity called 'Holocaust poetry.'"[91]

Sutzkever devoted his life to bearing witness to the Vilna Ghetto and salvaging Yiddish culture from the ruins.[92] His poems record the daily death which the ghetto Jews lived through and reflect his sense of responsibility until the day he fled to join the partisans in the forests.[93] Sutzkever held a highly romanticized ideal of the mission of the poet which demanded faith in the exalted task of poetry: he fervently believed in "the power and the wonder of poetry and of the Yiddish language."[94] The moment of his own execution could inspire poetry. When he was once ordered to dig his own grave, he cut a worm in two and marveled at the worm's stubborn rebirth and insistence on living, a lesson he turned into a poem.[95]

In his memoirs, Sutzkever later described the sheer terror, from July 1941, of constant public humiliation, random shootings, imprisonment, dispossession, extortion, and confiscation of valuables. One day Sutzkever was caught by a German soldier and forced at gunpoint to undress and dance naked with an elderly rabbi and a young boy around burning Torah scrolls; this harrowing experience too gave birth to a poem, "Der tsirk" ("The Circus," dated July 1941, published after the war, and later revised as "Before My Burning").[96] Sutzkever literally wrote in extreme conditions, such as hiding in a narrow space under a burning hot tin roof. In a hideout with barely any light seeping through the roof he found himself next to a naked corpse. Sutzkever recalls Turgenev writing about the surgeon's knife that cut his body during an operation and speaks of writing a poem on the dead body to metaphorically inscribe the pain of mass death in the ghetto as a corporeal experience.[97] Somatic writing incorporates the poetics of the Holocaust in the body of the poet.

Once Sutzkever hid in a coffin, which became a literal expression of his death-in-life existence fleeing from German soldiers and Jew-catchers who roamed the city in search of Jews whom they hauled off to be murdered. He writes in a poem, "I Lie in a Coffin," dated Vilna Ghetto, August 30, 1941:

> Ikh lig in an aron
> vi in hiltserne klayder,
> ikh lig.
> zol zeyn, s'iz a shifl
> oyf shturmishe kvalies,
> zol zeyn, s'iz a vig.
> I lie in a coffin
> as in clothes made of wood, here I lie.
> Let it be a small boat
> on wild stormy waves,
> let it be a cradle.[98]

This poem does more than document the poet's decision to hide at the *Khevra Kadisha* (Burial Society), when he opted for sleeping in a coffin instead of going home to a certain death: the choice to lie down in a coffin with the dead is here the only means to live among the condemned to die. The metaphors of boat and cradle are deceptively simple images of lulling a child to sleep or sailing on a lake, a fantasy of normality and safety. The coffin is, in fact, a portal to the other world that grants the poet a glimpse of his sister who died in Siberia and enables him to speak to the dead. Yet he has not joined them, for there is unaccountably a living body moving in the coffin, now, in the present of this world. The poem concludes: "zingt alts nokh mayn vort" ("and still my voice sings").[99] In this death-in-life, the poet's *vort* (literally, word), that is, his poetry, still speaks.

The gruesome, stark reality was that of confinement in the overcrowded ghetto, in danger of being condemned to the notorious Lukishki prison or taken away to be executed in the killing pits at Ponar. The Jews were at all times subject to new and seemingly arbitrary regulations designed to reduce the population of the ghetto and keep them unaware of what was intended for them, while using the work permit (*lebns-shayn*) to deceive them into the delusion that obedience would give them a chance of survival. Any existence outside the ghetto was precarious and perilous. Lithuanian Jew-catchers stalked their prey, and the Einsatzgruppen were massacring Jews by the thousands all over Lithuania. A local Pole might turn out to be a rescuer or a denouncer. It was out of his almost-religious sense of speaking for the ghetto Jews and saving the Yiddish language, but also out of his personal anguish, that Sutzkever created his aesthetics of poetry *in extremis*.

Sutzkever lost his mother, as well as his newborn son, who was murdered by soldiers carrying out the edict that prohibited Jewish children being born. Although attempts were made to hide the babies, German soldiers came to the hospital and killed them; at the Nuremberg trials, Sutzkever testified that his wife described how she saw a German smear a blue substance on her newborn's mouth, laughing as he threw down the dead child.[100] Addressing the dead child on the first anniversary of its murder, the poet asks:

> Far vos hostu fartunkelt dem bashaf,
> mit dem vos du host tsugemakht di oygn
> un gelozt mikh betlerdik in droysn
> tsuzamen mit velt an oisgeshnayter,
> vos du host opgevorfen oyf tsurik?
> Why have you darkened all Creation
> By closing your eyes
> And leaving me outside, a beggar,
> Together with a snowed-up world,
> Which you have cast behind you?[101]

The child is the third person in the conjugal union and his absence leaves the poet incomplete, a beggar in a desolate world, shut out from the child's death. But he cannot live as the boy's tomb and releases the dead child to the snow, to nature which had previously filled Sutzkever's early poetry with joy and splendor, but which is now frozen.

In conventional poetic idiom, spring could renew nature through the poet's creativity, but in the ghetto it was one form of resistance to systematic dehumanization. In Sutzkever's ghetto poem "A bliml" ("A Little Flower," Vilna Ghetto, May 29, 1943), the poet tells the story of the poet's neighbor who was punished with seven lashes for smuggling a little flower into the ghetto; spring was painfully inscribed on his body, but he thought it not too high a price to pay. The language in which this deceptively simple anecdotal message about beauty amid death is conveyed, Yiddish, is itself straining against its own extinction no less than the poor ghetto dweller's hope of spring.

Sutzkever's poem "Di lererin Mire" ("Mira the Teacher," Vilna Ghetto, May 10, 1943), about a teacher who led her charges when Vilna's Jews were herded into the ghetto, does more than merely record the heroism of Mira Bernshteyn (1908–43), a principal of the Real Gymnasium in Vilna, who was active in social welfare, education, and theater in the ghetto; for health reasons, she was unable to escape to join the partisans and was deported to Majdanek. Mira reads the children a story by Sholem Aleikchem or tells them about the courage of Hirsh Lekert, the revolutionary hero who was hanged for his attempt to assassinate Vilna's Russian governor in 1902. The rhyming Yiddish of a folk legend belies the sinister fact that the children are being taken away and fewer and fewer are left.

> Ven zon hot di bluntn getrikt, hot Mire
> bahangen mit grins de faryesomte diroh.
> When sun dried the blood, Mira silently hung
> Her orphaned apartment with bits of spirit.[102]

Another teacher Gerstein (presumably Yankev Gerstein, the cultural activist who died in September 1942) rallies her to carry on so that their song will be heard beyond the ghetto gates, a song of their belief that spring is not far off. After the number of children dwindles from one hundred and thirty to only forty, Mira has them put on a show to celebrate the coming holiday. Even though the sun and the brook are only fictional scenery on the stage, they create a hope for the future. Yet that hope is cruelly cut down and by dawn only Mira and seven children are still alive.

> Azoy, biz di hak tseshploytn dem tsinen
> iz Mire a blum un di kinderlekh—binen.
> Shoyn gro iz di blum un farvelkt ire glider
> Nor morgen in toy vet zi oyfbliyen vider.
> And so, till her senses were split by the blade,
> the children were—bees, and their teacher—a flower.
> The flower's gone gray and her limbs have decayed,
> But tall in the dew of the dawn she will tower![103]

The metonym of the children as bees and the teacher as a flower is a pedagogical figure of speech that barely conceals a reality in which there is very little chance of the children living to pollinate and transmit their knowledge. The poem with its ballad-like quatrain works against the annihilation that is destroying the delusion of spring and joy which Mira has created and the violence of the ax cleaving the senses (*tsinen*), threatening the children (*binen*), a rhyme that screams out in muffled silence the mind-boggling horror of the situation. Yet the conceit of creating spring and a future in the children's minds is itself a victory against the Nazis and a poetic achievement in its fusing of life and death—the orphaned woman who has gone suddenly gray, this wilted flower, has achieved a heroic stature and has bequeathed life, metaphorically. Indeed, the poem has created its own afterlife in the song that will penetrate hearts beyond the deaths of those who sing it, which, as Frieda Aaron points out in her close reading of the poem, calls for a communal response (in Northrop Frye's term) just when the collective is facing its decimation.[104] We might apply the Russian notion of "civic poetry" (*grazhdanskaia poeziia*) and recall that Sutzkever was calling in his poetry for open resistance before the Jews were ordered into the ghetto. The fact that the Scouts, *Di binen* (The Bees), of which at seventeen Sutzkever had been a member, swore allegiance to nature and to its worker-bees lends poignancy to the simile of children and bees. However, it is difficult to accept the simile at face value, given the poet's anger and despair after his mother's hiding place was discovered and she was taken away. That is also the imminent fate of these children.[105] Unlike the liturgical poem "Eleh ezkera," commemorating the Ten Martyrs executed by the Romans, which is recited on the Day of Atonement, the holiest day of the Jewish calendar at the height of the devotional service describing the sacrifices in the Temple, Sutzkever is writing here, as in his poem "Kol Nidre," of a martyrdom not of individuals who sacrificed their lives for the Torah, but of a martyred people.

A sentimental reading of "Mira the Teacher," moreover, does not take account of the poem's intertext, Y. L. Peretz's short story "Di dray matonos" ("The Three Gifts"). Peretz tells how a *shtetl* fiddler redeems his soul after death with three testimonials of pure virtue to Jewish martyrdom—a bag of soil from the Holy Land which a plundered Jew clings to, a cap worn by a rabbi who refuses to go bareheaded when tormented by Cossacks, and a bloody pin from the hem of the dress of a Jewish maiden who preserves her modesty when condemned to be tied by the hair to horses and dragged through the streets until she dies. This tale of multiple Jewish martyrdom is the secular Yiddish heritage of Peretz which sustains the children, but it is also itself a narrative of martyrdom, or *mesirut nefesh* (self-sacrifice), to which the poem testifies in its story of Mira, who sacrifices herself for the sake of Jewish children. This, remarks the poet, is the third gift of pure virtue in the Peretz story, but catastrophe strikes, not redemption, and the

Jewish narrative of martyrdom for the sacred cause repeats itself in what seems a final act of mass killing. Significantly, the Peretz story was thought so appropriate to the destruction of European Jewry in the Holocaust that it was dramatized on the stage in 1945 in London's bombed-out Yiddish theater with a cast of refugee and survivor actors, as well as (in a translation by Maurice Schwartz and Melech Ravitch) in New York's Yiddish Art Theater. In acting out the martyrdom narrative, the poet confirms its historical meaning and its alignment with Peretz's secular culture yet, ironically, gives no assurance of a redemptive ending.

Sutzkever believed that he literally owed his survival to poetry as he chronicled daily life in the ghetto. He saw himself defending not just a Jewish but a Western poetic tradition: "Am I the last poet in Europe?" ("der letster poet in eyrope"), Sutzkever asked himself in "Gezang fun a yidishn dikhter in 1943" ("Song of a Jewish Poet in 1943," Vilna Ghetto, June 22, 1943). Addressing the passive ghetto Jews who did not rebel against their fate, the poet writes, "Tsi zing ikh far mesim, tsi zing ikh far kroyen?" ("Do I sing for the dead, do I sing for the crows?"). His answer is that he is trapped by "yellow-badged time"—the ghetto time of doom awaiting death—but, as the embodiment of the dead, hiding the *khurbn* (destruction of the Temples) in his heart, it is his task to be the repository of their song, to sing it so that their bones will hear it. To abandon the ghetto is to turn his back not just on the dead but on his living readers, the fellow Jews who need him for moral support. As the "last poet in Europe" his was a voice in a void, threatened by extinction.[106] Sutzkever implicitly questions the epistemology of his craft and its purpose when overwhelmed by the merciless forces of darkness.

Resistance meant saving as much of Jewish culture as possible. Sutzkever participated in the so-called "Paper Brigade" (the Rosenberg Task Force) ordered to sort and destroy Vilna's libraries, but which smuggled precious books and manuscripts to safety under the noses of the SS, at great personal risk, in a literal rescue of the word. Sutzkever described this daring secret operation in a poem with the symbolic title "Kerndelekh vayts" ("Grains of Wheat," Vilna Ghetto, March 1943).[107] The books and papers he smuggles are grains which he buries wherever he can in order to preserve the soul of Yiddish, in the belief that, like the grain in the storehouses of the Egyptian Pharaoh, they will sprout and bloom at some future time, nourishing the survivors with these precious words. In another poem, after the organization of armed Jewish resistance in the ghetto, "Di blayene platn fun roms drukeray" ("The Lead Plates of Romm's Printing House," Vilna Ghetto, September 12, 1943), the poet extends the analogy of the word and the soul of the people in the (imagined) story of how fighters of the Jewish underground broke in to the Romm press, famous for its editions of the Talmud, in order to use the lead type as bullets. There was some truth in Sutzkever's poetic metaphor in that a few members of the Paper Brigade did assist the underground armed resistance of the ghetto, the FPO, first in smuggling a Soviet arms manual and later in smuggling weapons into the ghetto, using the YIVO building for liaison and concealment; they also arranged for Jewish ritual objects to be smelted down and sold on the black market to buy arms.[108] In his invented legend of lead plates, which Roskies calls "a midrash on Jewish heroism,"[109] Sutzkever literally forged a chain in Jewish cultural and national history by bringing together the Jewish word from east and west, religious and secular, just when a new vocabulary had to be invented for the unprecedented destruction of both Jewish life and word. That destruction could only be resisted, given the lack of arms that were difficult to smuggle into the ghetto, if words were melted down into bullets:

> dos blay hot geloykhtn baym oysgisn koyln
> makhshovos—tsegangen an oys nokh an oys
> a shuroh fun bovel, a shuroh fun poylin.
> gezoten, geflaytst in der zelbiker mos.
> di yidishe gevuroh in verter farhoyln,
> muz oyfraysn itster di velt mit a shos!
> The lead shone as from it we poured the bullets,
> Thoughts melted together—letter by letter.
> One line from Babylon, one line from Poland
> Seethed, flooded into identical moulds.
> And now Jewish valor, concealed in these words
> Must with a gunshot tear open the world![110]

In this startling smelting together of *safra veseyfa* (book and sword), the fire that consumed the word in the Nazis' burning of Jewish culture enrages the poet into a call for resistance.

However, in "Farbrente perl" ("Burnt Pearls," Vilna Ghetto, July 28, 1943) what moves him most is the sight of the dying pyre, where the "froy in flam gevashn" ("a woman washed in flames") is unrecognizable in the "grofarbrente perl in di ashn—" ("grey-burnt pearls in the ashes ... ")—one of several examples of ironic rhyme in Sutzkever's poetry.[111] The oxymoronic "washed in flames" suggests a baptism of fire, while the burnt pearls are all that are left of the poet's Yiddish culture, the words with which to create poetry. Sutzkever's oxymora, Frieda Aaron notes, were a way to show that it was possible to live in a surreal reality in which the poet was trapped, which exceeded any literary metaphor or anything Dante imagined in *The Inferno*, though Dante also feared he would not be able to describe the full horror.[112]

If in "I Lie in a Coffin" Sutzkever imagined himself talking to the dead, he was now facing a diminishing readership of Jews who were consigned soon to join them. A threshold was crossed when the Gestapo caught Liza Magun, an underground courier and liaison officer for the Jewish United Partisan Organization (*Fareynikte Partizaner Organizatsye*), and she was killed at Ponar on February 17, 1943. Sutzkever declaimed his poem "Lid tsu di letste" ("Song for the Last Ones," Vilna Ghetto, March 16, 1943) at her memorial meeting and lashed out at the ghetto Jews who did nothing to resist but seemed resigned to join the dead. They were weaker than moths, in the words of the poet, who did not spare his anger for the disgusting self-hate and apathetic cowardice of the last of the Jewish people. They allowed the trap to close in around them and licked their enemies' spittle in anticipation of their kindness in allowing them to live. They were condemned to perish, and the poet could find no words of consolation. The opening stanza echoes Bialik's prophetic poem, "Akhen khatsir ha'am" ("Surely, the People Is Grass," 1897), which takes up the verse in Isaiah (40:7) that likens the people to dry grass awaiting their revival (a chapter usually read as one of consolation and hope):

> Akhen khatsir ha'am, yavesh hayah ka'ets
> Akhen khalal ha'am, khalal kaved eyn kets.
> Surely the people is grass, now do they fade like a blossom,
> Surely the people is slain,—it is slain with a slaughter unending.[113]

In these angry words, the modern Hebrew poet-prophet wonders whether the Jewish people will awaken at the trumpet call on the day of redemption. Like Bialik in "City of Slaughter," Sutzkever execrates the victims for their passivity, but follows with his own despair of any redemption in the people and concludes that it can only be found in the grass, in the regenerative powers of nature.[114]

Yet nature too has banished the poet who despairs in a godless universe. In an expression of grief exceeding anything felt by the Romantic poets, the poet bangs his head to feel the pain of his people, but also in despair that in assimilating their suffering to his body he cannot find any comfort, as Jeremiah found in the writing of his lamentations:

> ikh hak mayn sharven on a shtayn un zukh
> in shpliter zaynem trayst far eykh, di letste,
> vayl ikh bin oykh an oys in ayer bukh,
> un mayn zon iz vi ayerer in friling a farkretste.
>
> I hack my skull upon a stone and seek
> In its splinters solace for you, the last,
> For I too am a letter in your book,
> And my sun in spring is like yours, a crippled outcast.[115]

In the book of Exodus, Moses begged God not to destroy the Jewish people after the sin of the Golden Calf but instead to erase him from God's book, the text of the Torah. For his part, the poet cannot deny that he is a letter in the text of Jewish history, in the book of the Jewish people, that he has a responsibility as a poet whose prophetic words fall on deaf ears but must be spoken, as Bialik spoke, as did Isaiah and Jeremiah before him. As such, he shares their fate: his sun too has faded, the "leprous outcast" of spring—the spring that the teacher Mira desperately wanted the children to dream of as their future—but what future, concludes the poet, can there be if their corruption and hypocrisy, the people's failure to react to their destruction, prevent words of consolation?

Magun's capture decided the question of whether to stay in the ghetto, and on September 12, 1943, together with his wife Freydke, Sutzkever fled to join the partisans fighting in the woods, exchanging cultural resistance for a gun and feeling that, given the passivity of the ghetto population, no more could be done to save those left behind. Shortly afterward, the Germans liquidated the ghetto.

Poetry preserved Sutzkever's determination to live, but he believed it also had the power to save his life. In March 1944, when he was fighting alongside the partisans in the forests, it did save him in his perilous crossing of a minefield: he kept the rhythm of a tune in his head as he stepped through this field of death until he was safe.[116] Relating how he found his wife, who was lost in the swamps after they fled from the Germans, by beating a stone against a tree, he declared: "When he is completely anguished and despairing, the poet grabs some word or other and begins to beat with the word and with his head and with his heart against a deaf wall, and then it happens, in a blessed moment, when he is still lying there in despair, that his poem emerges out of the wilderness."[117] Freydke had gone to find a gold ring she lost, and its sparkle by which Sutzkever recognized her serves Sutzkever's Holocaust poetics as a trope for what brings poetry to life, however bloodied and frightening is the vision. The preoccupation with the word which Sutzkever demonstrates in his poems from the ghetto and from the forests shows just how much he conceived the self-reflexive writing of verse as a resistance to the annihilation of Yiddish and of poetry itself, but also how much he created a counter-poetics of the Holocaust that rescued a semblance of humanity from the inhumanity that was consuming his world in flames.

Excavating a Language of Humanity

Like his almost-exact contemporary Sutzkever, the Polish poet Czesław Miłosz voiced resistance to the genocide of the Jews through his poetry and watched the destruction of the ghetto with a disturbingly fascinated gaze. His language, like Sutzkever's, is terse in its distanced yet unflinching documentation of immediate horror. Both poets were modernists in their description of nature. Miłosz was brought up in a Polish-speaking Catholic family in Lithuania and saw at first hand the turmoil of war and ethnic hatred. He is often called an optimistic catastrophist. Miłosz wrote as a bystander, not as a victim slated for extinction, yet he too was aware that his poetry was all he had with which to resist complicity with evil. Miłosz's "Campo di Fiori" appeared anonymously in the underground anthology *Z otchłani* (From the depths), alongside Mieczysław Jastrun's "Tu także jak w Jeruzalem" ("Here too, as in Jerusalem"), which likewise evoked Christian martyrdom.

It is not poetry that rings false, according to Miłosz, but a romanticized vision of humanity and nature, of innocence and tranquility as natural states. Miłosz's language touches the raw nerve of writing poetry during the Holocaust. He writes in "Biedny chrześcijanin patrzy na Getto" ("A Poor Christian Looks at the Ghetto," 1943):

> *Pszczoły obudowują czerwoną wątrobę*
> *Mrówki obudowują czarną kość*
> Rozpoczyna się rodzieranie, deptanie jedwabi,
> Rozpoczyna się tłuczenie szkła, drzewa, miedzi, niklu, srebra, pian
> Gipsowych, blach, strun, trąbek, liści, kul, kryształów—
> Pyk! Fosforyczny ogień z żółtych ścian
> Pochłania ludzkie i zwierzęce włosie.[118]
> Bees build around red liver,
> Ants build around black bone.
> It has begun: the tearing, the trampling on silks,
> It has begun: the breaking of glass, wood, copper, nickel, silver, foam
> Of gypsum, iron sheets, violin strings, trumpets, leaves, balls, crystals.
> Poof! Phosphorescent fire from yellow walls
> Engulfs animal and human hair.[119]

This poem, published in Miłosz's collection *Ocalenie* (*Salvation*) in 1945, witnesses the Warsaw Ghetto uprising in April 1943. The poetic voice of the self-styled "Jew of the New Testament" is aware he may be numbered among the accomplices of death. Miłosz attempts to find a language of complete dehumanization, of utter destruction, to create a poetry that can imagine nature without human beings, where the human body has been erased and where the organs of the corpses are waste material for building. That construction is also a destruction: the deported Jews' belongings are sorted into materials for salvage. The plundering by Polish scavengers among the ruins of the ghetto has begun.

The appropriation of the Jews' goods by neighbors or the German authorities was a stage in the Jews' systematic dispossession and dehumanization as they were herded into ghettos and onto cattle cars. Things were generally what Hitler's victims related to as the objects that displaced their identity in a narrative of deportation and annihilation.[120] The metonymic reduction of the Jews to the things they once possessed and that are burning in the Warsaw Ghetto recalls Szlengel's poem "Rzeczy" ("Things," written some time in 1942–3), which in a compression of the history of the Warsaw Ghetto animates the belongings of their former Jewish owners (we will return to this poem in Chapter 5). Similarly, Sutzkever's "A vogn shikh" ("A Cartload of Shoes," Vilna Ghetto, January 1, 1943) asks what happened to the bodies and feet of the Jews who once wore the shoes in the pile (one of whom was the poet's mother) that is now being taken away to Berlin. As in the "burnt pearls," the shoes are a synecdoche for the disembodied Jews killed at Ponar. The detachment of the synecdoche from its referent, the dead Jews, works in both these poems by Szlengel and Sutzkever to denature the language of reification in the process of deamination and decimation.

Zuzanna Ginczanka, pen name of Zuzanna Polina Gincburg (1917–45), a remarkable young Polish Jewish poet who published modernist verse between the wars, does something similar when she writes in "Non omnis moriar" (a reworking of Horace's monumental *Ode* 3.30) that not all of her will die when she is taken away by the Gestapo—the things that remain will be sorted and pilfered:

Niech wiec rzeczy żydowskie twoja dłoń wyszpera,
Chominowo, lwowianko, dzielna żono szpicla,
Donosicielko chyża, matko folksdojczera.
Tobie, twoim niech służą, bo po cóż by obcym.
Bliscy moi—nie lutnia to, nie puste imię.[121]
So let your hands rummage through Jewish things,
You, Chomin's wife from Lvov, you mother of a volksdeutscher.
May these things be useful to you and yours,
For, dear ones, I leave no name, no song.[122]

Naming her blackmailer who gave away her hiding-place in Lwów, Ginczanka taunts her betrayers to make good use of the "Jewish things" which, unlike Miłosz's poem, acquire a strange lyricism. The poem ends with a mocking hope that her possessions will be transfigured in the hands of her denouncers into an indictment:

Kłęby włosia końskiego i morskiego siana,
Chmury rozprutych poduszek i obłoki pierzyn
Do rąk im przylgną, w skrzydła zmienią ręce obie;
To krew moja pakuły z puchem zlepi świeżym
I uskrzydlonych nagle w anioły przemieni.[123]
Clumps of horsehair, bunches of sea hay,
Clouds of fresh down from pillows and quilts,
Glued on by my blood, will turn their arms into wings,
Transfigure the birds of prey into angels.[124]

The poem is modeled on "Testament Mój" ("My Testament," 1839–40) by the Romantic Polish poet Juliusz Słowacki yet adds the bitter irony that the poet will not only leave no heritage but also no name (Ginczanka was arrested a second time when hiding in Kraków and was executed shortly before the end of the war). Unlike Horace's trope of poetry as an immortal monument, Ginczanka cannot be sure of a trusted reader or that her poem will be read at all and leaves the things of which she is dispossessed as a poetic testament of her annihilation as well as a testimony presented at the Chomins' trial after the war.[125]

Miłosz's mysterious "guardian mole" tunneling through the corpses, by contrast, can recognize the human by the tell-tale "luminous vapor" that distinguishes the ashes of each individual.[126] It is this underground mole, a miner of souls but also a spy and a bearer of conscience, who rescues the human from the decomposition effected by the language of the poem itself. The poet is therefore rightly afraid that the patriarchal mole, who has been reading the "great book of the species" (presumably the Bible), might in his moral accounting find him guilty as one of the helpers of death, one of the uncircumcised waiting two thousand years for the Christian messiah who has betrayed the universal ethics of his faith. The identification of the poet as a "poor Christian," not with the suffering of the victims but with the complicity of bystanders, is a silent indictment not so much of the failure of Poles to feel compassion for their murdered Jewish neighbors as of the failure of the poet himself to do anything to save or redeem the victims.

In "Campo di Fiori" (1943) Miłosz watches the carefree crowds on the merry-go-round as the ghetto burns and challenges the poetics of the heroic, of the beautiful, of the humane. The poet draws a parallel with the carnival atmosphere at the burning of the sixteenth-century heretic Giordano Bruno:

> Czasem wiatr z domów płonących
> Przynosił czarne latawce,
> Łapali płatki w powietrzu
> Jadący na karuzeli.
> Rozwiewał suknie dziewczynom
> Ten wiatr od domów płonących,
> Śmiały się tłumy wesołe
> W czas pięknej warszawskiej niedzieli.[127]
> At times wind from the burning
> would drift dark kites along
> and riders on the carousel
> caught flakes in midair.
> This same hot wind
> blew open the skirts of the girls,
> and the crowds were laughing
> on a beautiful Warsaw Sunday.[128]

The merrymakers are not touched by the ashes blowing in their faces from the burning houses of the Jews, yet the extinction of the Jews' "strange tongue" must affect the poet's tongue if he is to remain a Christian. He must speak the ancient language of martyrdom (not necessarily the language of the Jews) in order to restore the language of poetry itself. The crowd is quite indifferent to the destruction of the ghetto; in fact, the charred "flakes" and the wind blowing from the fire destroying the ghetto only add to the fun of a fairground on a beautiful spring Sunday in Warsaw. In a Lacanian reading, Tomasz Żukowski, however, suggests that both of these poems by Miłosz are linked by the same complicity in watching the burning victims who are thereby excluded from the community.[129] It is murderous indifference that both Miłosz's "Campo di Fiori" and Mieczysław Jastrun's "Here too, as in Jerusalem" attack from a Christian perspective; Jastrun draws a parallel with the early Christians who were thrown to the wolves, although he also compares the wall of the Warsaw Ghetto with the Wailing Wall in Jerusalem, which is the remnant of the destroyed Temple, to express utter destruction and hopelessness. Nevertheless the poet looks to the dawn of resurrection.[130]

Miłosz saw himself as a witness to the Holocaust and spoke out openly against Polish anti-Semitism and complicity before and after the Kielce pogrom in 1946, though he does not seem to have actively saved Jews like the Polish Catholic writer Zofia Kossak who, despite her anti-Semitic views, protested the treatment of Jews.[131] Of the few Polish responses to the Warsaw Ghetto Uprising, Miłosz's poem, like the novella *Wielki Tydzień* (*Holy Week*) by Jerzy Andrzejewski (written in 1943 and published in a considerably revised form in 1945), draws on Catholic humanism. Yet although Andrzejewski shows a spectrum of responses, from indifference and sympathy to anti-Semitic xenophobia, his central protagonist, Jan Malecki, first takes in his Jewish former lover Irena, then abandons her to her fate when she returns to the burning ghetto after a neighbor exposes her. Miłosz, on the other hand, voices the engaged observer who bears the Jews' suffering as a cross. Moreover, the timing of the Warsaw Ghetto Uprising in Holy Week in Andrzejewski's novella suggests a crucifixion, in which the Poles regard the suffering of the Jews as a cross, yet they blame the Jews for the war and some stubbornly stick to their fervent belief that the Germans are solving the Poles' Jewish problem and getting rid of the Christ-killers. In any event, Easter brings no resurrection in this novella. Both writers pointed to the complicity of the witnesses, but while Miłosz believed in a personal sense of moral commitment to other human beings, Andrzejewski saw the collapse of Catholic existentialism.[132]

Miłosz's poetic testimony goes beyond horror to an indictment of moral complicity and the vanity of human lives. Jan Błoński later suggested that Miłosz was addressing Poles' denial of their moral duty to face the truth of what happened in Poland under German occupation.[133] Yet, the poet concludes, this is not the point. The martyrdom of both Giordano Bruno and of Warsaw's Jews is a call for the poet to find the "language of an ancient planet" ("język dawnej planety") so that one day after many years have passed on a new Campo di Fiori rage will kindle at a poet's word ("Na nowym Campo di Fiori/Bunt wznieci słowo poety").[134] This supports Błoński's reading of the poem "Przedmowa" ("Dedication," 1945) as a call for a combative poetry: the poet asks "Czym jest poezja, która nie ocala/ Narodów ani ludzi?" ("What is poetry which does not save/Nations or people?"), but the poet answers this rhetorical question with a resignation to official lies and drunkards' singing. Salvation, the poet is saying, can be found only in the recognition of the salutary aim of good poetry.[135] The poet could not save his friend, but he places his book of poems figuratively on his grave to placate the ghosts of the dead.[136] This was written after the crushing of the Warsaw Uprising in 1944 and the subjugation of Poland by the Kremlin. In the ruins of Warsaw and after the complete destruction of the Jews, Miłosz does not believe in poetry driven by ideology. The twentieth century has demonstrated the fragility of civilization and culture: "What surrounds us, here and now, is not guaranteed. It could just as well not exist—and so man constructs poetry out of the remnants found in ruins."[137]

In the Marxist critic Terry Eagleton's reassessment of Adorno's *Negative Dialectics*, Auschwitz did not invalidate the aesthetic project, even if its terms of reference were permanently tainted by fascism and mass culture, but it did change the aesthetics of pleasure. The body signified suffering, not pleasure: the body was condemned to a living death beyond endurance. A global history of humanity would now stretch from the slingshot to the atom bomb as one story of scarcity and oppression, a fable of permanent catastrophe.[138] This skeletal vision is recognizable from Samuel Beckett's existential landscapes and from post-Nietzschean concepts of permanent destruction. It attempts to recover in the erasure of the body that we saw in Sutzkever and Miłosz a site for the aesthetic, but also (as we will see in the next chapter) for the subject erased by the act of genocide.

It Is Always after Disaster

Is any of this new? Haven't prophets and poets down the ages subverted poetic metaphor in order to force us into an awareness of extremity and atrocity, of the ineffable and the unspeakable? Modernity in particular revealed a violence that was unprecedented in human experience. Paul Fussell in his seminal book on the writing of the First World War remarks how literature and real life intersect. It is as if the figural has become literal and the literal language can only be read figuratively. As Henry James understood on the outbreak of the First World War in 1914, the descent into bloodshed and death reversed the myth of the Age of Progress. Indeed, historiographical attempts to impose some continuity and order could not hide the lack of any rationality in the conduct of the war, which apart from two major battles, if that is what they can be called, was characterized by the stalemate of trench warfare, of suicidal attempts to decide the conflict, which remained largely unchanged for over four years of stalemate, interrupted by unsuccessful assaults by each side which cost thousands of casualties among the infantry.[139] Siegfried Sassoon's reading of Hardy's *Tess of the d'Ubervilles* in the trenches is just one of Fussell's examples of the intersection of literature and life as the war took on fantastic and surreal aspects, exacerbated by the assumptions behind the class system which alienated a conscript army. However, the loss of innocence that marked the experience of trench warfare and gas attacks allowed few hints of redemption in a relentless and ceaseless war of attrition,[140] in which millions were maimed and mutilated for no justified cause. This made sacrifice, one of the common tropes of patriotic devotion to king and country, sound ironic. Wilfred Owen's response to Rupert Brooke's "The Soldier" was constrained by the diction of Georgian poetry in "Dulce et Decorum Pro Patria Mori," but it undermined the aesthetics of patriotic poetry. Indeed, his description (in a letter to Osbert Sitwell) of preparing the Christ-soldier for his daily crucifixion allows little idea of redemption.[141] Literature did sustain men on the front (even if their readings of familiar texts were ironical), but the literature that came out of the new Dantean inferno contradicted the ideology behind existing poetic forms. Fussell assesses attempts to describe modern trench warfare "factually" as failures because conventional rhetoric and clichés were inadequate to communicate to those who were not there the full horror of the experience. It is not that there was no language, but it required a Joyce to invent an idiom and style appropriate for an unending sequence of events that had no meaning and defeated attempts to admit causality.[142]

Nevertheless, we do not get a sense of the crack in Western epistemology or a challenge to established cosmology until we come to Wilfred Owen's "Futility" (1918) with its anti-theology of hopeless despair. Celan faced an even emptier universe, apparently devoid of a creator of Owen's primeval clay, and addressed his "Psalm" (1961) to "Niemand" ("Nobody"):

Niemand knetet uns wieder aus Erde und Lehm,
niemand bespricht unseren Staub.
Niemand.
Gelobt seist du, Niemand.
Dir zulieb wollen
wir blühn.
Dir
entgegen.[143]

> No one kneads us again out of earth and clay,
> no one incants our dust.
> No one.
>
> Blessèd art thou, No One.
> In thy sight would
> we bloom.
> In thy
> spite.[144]

It is tempting to read this reference to an anti-creation in which the clay is not kneaded into life (as John Felstiner does) as a reference to the universal post-apocalypse after the destruction of the Holocaust.[145] Yet Trakl too concluded his depiction of damnation and death with a silent malignant universe in the second version of his "Psalm." What is remarkable about Celan's poem, however, is that out of the despair at the absence of the Creator he seeks the word which will give speech to the unspeakable Name. Here the meaning of "Niemandsrose" (Nobody's rose) in the poem is not to be sought in the kabbalistic or Christian traditions but in the Heideggerian sense of individuation through transcendence which makes possible human speech in the void.[146]

Like Celan, Sutzkever was not religious (though tutored in Jewish tradition), yet he feels the need to pray to an absent deity in the ghetto. However, his prayer too is no less heartfelt because it is beyond despair in an empty universe where the poet has lost his speech, his words. This is what he writes in "Glust zikh mir tsu ton a tefiloh" ("I Long to Say a Prayer," Vilna Ghetto, January 17, 1942)"

> efshar zol ikh betn bay a shtern. 'fraynd mayn vayter,
> kh'hob mayn vort farloyrn, kum un zay im a farbayter'!
> oykh der guter shtern
> vet es nit derhern.
> Perhaps I'll pray to a star: 'Hear, my distant friend,
> I have lost my word; oh, come and take its place!'
> But even the good star
> will not hear my prayer.[147]

The poet feels impelled to "make a prayer" (*ton a tefiloh*), rather than the traditional *davenen*, just as in his prewar Siberian cycle Sutzkever spoke of making a prayer to the snow in his pantheistic recollection of childhood in nature's *shtibel* (small synagogue).[148] Yet without an addressee, the poet is left to babble senselessly till daybreak. To write amid annihilation is to hold on to the possibility of an addressee, not the God of Israel, but a surviving readership who will redeem those senseless words into meaning.[149]

When it became apparent after the liberation of Vilna that the dead were not coming back, Sutzkever wrote in "Tkhiyas hamesim" ("Resurrection," Moscow, 1945) that he looked for the Messiah's shofar to celebrate the new age of freedom, but the dead reject the Divine promises of redemption as false. Now the people have (as we saw in "The Last") become dry grass, mown down in a final slaughter, the poet can only speak in the *grozshprakh* ("grass-language") of the dead, which has replaced the Hebrew of Isaiah and Bialik with a secular Yiddish in the deserted ruins of the city on a forsaken, contaminated earth.[150] On the other hand, the macabre vision of the Jew who lives in a cemetery in "Der keverkind" ("The Grave Child") does offer a hope that a child will be born, if not as a savior, at least to continue Jewish life in the future, a resurrection enacted in poetry, not in theology.

First World War poets sought a language to express the unspeakable violence of modernity in order to protest the stupidity of war so that it might not happen again. In *Heart of Darkness* Joseph Conrad had given a glimpse into knowledge of inhuman horror in the heart of Europe's own darkness. However, Holocaust poets were writing when there was no hope for humanity or any hope to preserve a trace of their existence and tell the world what they experienced. They floundered to find words that could attest to the unbelievable, something which only they knew and understood but which was impossible to tell others. If there was ever a delusion of a stable universe with shared assumptions of universal values, there was now a *before* and an *after* that drew the line between the familiar and relatively safe prewar world and the real, unspeakable present of unimaginable horror. Close scrutiny of the poetry of Celan, Sutzkever, and Miłosz reveals just how much they owe to their poetic heritage and yet how radical was their revision of that heritage in their responses to catastrophe. When everything has changed and all values have been destroyed, the concept and practice of poetry can no longer remain the same. Innocence has been lost, and the familiar poems from the past accrue new dark meanings.

3

Writing Nothing: Negation and Subjectivity in the Holocaust Poetry of Paul Celan and Dan Pagis

Daniel Feldman

Nothing Can Be Said

Nothing, it often seems, remains to be written about Paul Celan's elliptical poems or, more broadly, about literary representation of the event unnamed in his poetry, the Holocaust. The voluminous scholarship on the poetics of ineffability so often associated with the poetry of Celan appears to leave nothing more to say about the subject.[1] Critical discourse tends to be self-conscious, anxious about having nothing new to offer regarding Celan and his poetics, especially in connection with the Holocaust; some lament, like Ecclesiastes, that there is nothing new to say about Celan under the desiccative sun of Holocaust literary criticism. Perhaps, however, it is the search for something new, rather than for nothing that is futile. "How can one write nothing?" asks Jacques Derrida in his influential landmark essay "Shibboleth for Paul Celan" (1986). In this meditation on the poet's esoteric style and the "all-consuming" unnamed historical event, Derrida circumscribes Celan's "circumcised" words[2] and insightfully links "the question of Nothing and the meaning of being in Celan."[3] Derrida's reading of Celan suggests that it is precisely the writing of nothing—the paradoxical inscription of nothing in language—that continues to be revelatory and new about Celan and his gnostic form of evoking the *Shoah*. For if the "question of Nothing" is indeed tied to the "meaning of being" in Celan's poetry, then by saying nothing and making silence audible the witness-author creates a radically subversive negative poetics of the Holocaust. Through his lyrical transcription of the absence that evokes the survivor's negative subjectivity, Celan inverts the poles of conventional affirmation and negation. Moreover, this proposition of a negative subjectivity challenges prevailing ontologies, in particular Heidegger's category of reified *Dasein*.

This chapter addresses Celan's writing of nothing by putting the poet in conversation with Heidegger,[4] who disputes Celan's inscription of substantive nothing, and with Israeli author Dan Pagis, who affirms it. The analysis first ties nullification in speech to cancellation of self in Celan and aims to understand his articulation of a form of subjectivity reconfigured by the Holocaust as negative presence. In Celan, the "apophatic" or negative form of subjectivity establishes selfhood through the poet's repudiation of who he is and emphatic declaration of what he is not. It is expressed in Celan as "nothing I am," a paradoxical subjectivity that insists both on its negation and existence. Celan's project of depicting negative subjectivity informs his broader purpose of engendering a negative poetics of the Holocaust. This claim will elucidate Celan's conception of negation by tracing an important distinction between Celan's and Heidegger's ontologies of nothing. For Heidegger, nothing is nothing more than negation; for Celan, however, nothing may itself be negated to attest, subversively, to that negation's substantive reality. This dispute, however, is not merely a debate of metaphysical abstraction between the poet and the philosopher but indicative of a deeper fault line in poetic representation of the Holocaust. By reading a similar structure of negated subjectivity in the verse of Hebrew poet Dan Pagis, a survivor with a similar heritage and personal background to Celan's in their native Bukovina—he was born in Radautz (Rădăuți), a small town near Czernowitz, I demonstrate the centrality of converting negation into articulated presence in survivors' literary responses to the Holocaust, an unspeakable atrocity about which it may have been more expedient, if impossible, simply to say nothing at all.

Ultimately, this chapter posits that by emphatically saying nothing, Celan and Pagis pioneer a new poetics of the Holocaust that instantiates what Derrida calls the shibboleth-like "insignificant difference as the condition of meaning."[5] In the language of witness of Celan and Pagis nothing is more important than voicing nothing. Their poems evince the difficulty of what it entails for a survivor to exist as a subject after genocide. Accordingly, Derrida's question is still germane: In the wake of the catastrophe of the Holocaust, what does it mean to write nothing and to equate nothing with being? Poetry by Celan and Pagis articulating nothing, testifying for no one, and emerging from nowhere underscores the sibylline significance of writing the Holocaust not only for representation of trauma, but also for how the

Holocaust reformulates subjectivity altogether by giving subjects reduced to nothing continued existence as coherent, living beings. In this reading of Celan and Pagis, nothing is new. That is to say, what is new is pointing to the equivocal nothing at the heart of their writing.

Celan: Noting Nothing

Derrida's unanswered question about the possibility of writing nothing, of composing a nothing notation, comes in response to Celan's exhortation in "Einem, der vor der Tür stand" ("To One Who Stood before the Door"), published in the 1963 collection *Niemandsrose* (*No-One's Rose*), "schreib das lebendige/Nichts ins Gemüt" ("write the living/Nothing on his soul").[6] In accentuating this line, Derrida asks whether an inscription of nothing leaves a mark. Critics have long read Celan's recurring allusions to a rhetorical void at the heart (or inscribed on the heart) of his work as a metaphorical absence. Typical is Lacoue-Labarthe's Heideggerian interpretation of "the experience of nothingness" in Celan as "the *Riß*, or tear, of being."[7] Adorno similarly glosses Celan's negative aesthetic as an existential, soundless encryption of ineffable trauma: "Celan's poems articulate unspeakable horror by being silent, thus turning their truth content into a negative quality."[8] To be sure, Celan's poetry is sheathed in negativity and frequently references a linguistic vacuum; in "Engführung" ("Stretto") he writes: "Wir/taten ein Schweigen darüber," ("We/decked it in silence").[9] That mute skin is usually read as an incommunicable trope. Aris Fioretos, whose Derrida-influenced essay on Celan is suggestively titled "Nothing: History and Materiality in Celan," claims that nothingness is inscribed but never articulated in Celan's poetry.[10] For Fioretos, Derrida's essay on Celan "points to a way of approaching nothingness" through a bifurcation of language into its constituent elements of speech and text.[11] The ever-laconic Celan, according to Fioretos, privileges the written over the oral strand in language's double helix. The gratuitous punctuation and nonverbal typographical signs incised into Celan's poems can be read but never interpreted or spoken. These symbolic written traces function, in Fioretos's view, "as the material inscription of [Celan's] unspeakability, bereft of the semantic dignity which always goes along with speech."[12] Like other prominent theoretically oriented interpreters of Celan, Fioretos assumes a textual priority in Celan's work: "Nothingness is irreducibly linked to writing in a way which has little to do with the free sonorous sway of language magic."[13]

Fioretos is right that for Celan "nothing is paradoxically transcribed in the text," but he and others who consider the blank voids in Celan's poetry to be purely figural go too far in claiming that "nothing resists articulation."[14] Celan writes that his poetry transcribes a "lebendiges Nichts," a *living* absence that is in fact a frequent lexical presence in his texts.[15] Rather than resisting articulation, negative keywords such as "nothing," "no one," "never," and "nowhere" echo sonorously throughout Celan's poems as enunciated lyrics, *pace* Derrida, as shibboleths, keywords whose difference is literally null. Nothing is paradoxically written, read, and heard everywhere in Celan's oeuvre. Contrary to metaphorical readings of absence in Celan, this "nothing" is actually articulated in his poetry. Indeed, Celan's general penchant for negation, possibly the most commonly noted leitmotif of his writing, is not only a conceptual trope, but a linguistic device that negates itself. The resulting nullified apophatic expression forms the foundation for a new post-Holocaust subjectivity accessed through the survivor's obscure shibboleths of being, the incongruous and nearly incommunicable sensation of having lived through one's own death. Celan's negative poetics give voice to the survivor's vertiginous experience of the impossible becoming possible, of non-being mingling with being, of nothing in fact existing.

To convey that paradoxical form of personal ontology, Celan does not necessarily disdain the spoken in favor of the written. Instead, he doubles the paradox of writing nothing with the riddle of saying nothing. While Fioretos claims that Celan's reticent poetry is "neither audible nor transcribable,"[16] Celan talks volubly and pervasively about "Mundvoll Schweigen" ("Mouthfuls of silence")[17] and other intrinsically dialogic phenomena both enabling and inhibiting speech, such as the grille of speech ("Sprachgitter"), turns of breath ("Atemwende"), and shadow-speech ("Schatten spricht") that signify and obstruct meaning. Furthermore, among Celan's most frequently sounded words is "nichts" ("nothing)." Celan's poems are as preoccupied with the hazards of spoken address as they are with the efficacy of written exchange. Both modalities, however, are threatened by a poetics of absence and silence that voices nothing and writes without visible trace. Celan transcribes what is "Ungeschriebenes, zu/Sprache verhärtet" ("Unwritten, hardened/into speech"), as he states in "À la pointe acérée"; this is a language so condensed, the poem continues, that it ineluctably "legt/einen Himmel frei" ("sets/a heaven free").[18] By hardening into emancipatory speech the insoluble contradictions that drove his thought, Celan expresses the terrible dilemma of a survivor living and writing after the Holocaust, a something-as-nothing and nothing-as-something duality that underlies his poetry. Throughout it all, stands Derrida's question: What does it mean to write nothing—for nothing to be written? A similar question arrests interpreters of this poem: What does it mean to read silences as audible or blanks as legible? My claim is that negation and nothing must be read as literal rather than as solely figural in Celan's (and Pagis's) poetry. Indeed, Celan indicates that apprehending the presence of a lack is crucial to his work.

Celan's outlook, in "Wirk nicht voraus" ("Do Not Work Ahead," 1967), is "durchgründet vom Nichts" ("deep-grounded by Nothingness")[19] in both logic and lyric. Nothingness, he writes in a poem aptly titled "Das

Nichts" ("The Nothingness," 1969), "gathers us in—/sets a seal."[20] That vacant seal serves as an emblem on all his work. Nothing plays dice ("Nichts erwürfelt"),[21] so that all of existence is contingent on chancy communication.[22] Yet that negative imprint has, in general, been curiously overlooked in the copious commentaries on Celan. Anne Carson is one of the few anglophone critics to have noticed that "words for 'no,' 'not,' 'never,' 'nowhere,' 'nobody,' 'nothing' dominate" Celan's poems.[23] Carson notes that for Celan the archetypal "poet of nothingness" is Mallarmé, whom Celan frequently evoked early in his career.[24] Geoffrey Hartman draws a similar analogy between Celan and his adoption of "a Mallarmean and totally nonconfessional language of witness."[25] By contrast, Wolosky, while taking note of Celan's affinity for Mallarmé, associates Celan's *via negativa* with the work of Beckett, the author of *Texts for Nothing*.[26]

In German criticism, a few critics have tracked Celan's poetics of negativity.[27] Peter Paul Schwarz called it in the 1960s Celan's "Revolte des Nichts."[28] Yet there is little focus on Celan's apophasis as an affirmation of subjectivity radically altered by the Holocaust. More common is the diametrically opposed approach influenced by Continental philosophy and exemplified by critics such as Szondi, Janz, Menninghaus, Hamacher, and Ziarek, the last of whom cites Hamacher, and, employing a double negative, writes, "Celan's language not only does not invert nothingness into being but rather converts 'its literary being, compositionally and semantically, into nothing.'"[29] I argue for a different reading. By consistently writing and saying nothing, Celan concomitantly asserts and negates himself. For to say or write nothing is simultaneously to convey and withhold meaning. It is to state a denial and to deny any statement. Composing a poetics of nothing, then, allows Celan both to speak and to remain mute; it frees him to engage in the "dialectic of absence and presence that is implicit in negation," a dialectic that exquisitely accommodates Celan's own stance of personal immanence and referential opacity in his poetry.[30] Paul Celan evanescently emerges and just as quickly disappears in his work as an invisible "I" or oblique subject addressing a more apparent and immediate "you" or other. For Celan, writing nothing in nobody's voice is the ideal poetic mode. It reduces subjectivity to a cryptic password and speech to a form of spare silence.

Through this act of linguistic subtraction, the economical poet excises all dross from his texts, even as he doubles the lack. "Nichts,/nichts ist verloren" ("Nothing,/nothing is lost"), he writes in "Stretto."[31] The uncharacteristic redundancy is one of double reduction. If "nothing, nothing is lost," is anything missing? The insistence on negation negating itself suggests a poetic idiom approaching the fringe of language's communicability and finally transcending that limit. The poem points "to what lies beyond language" by gesturing "toward both the nothing which is not (the silencing of language) and the nothing out of which language can come forth."[32] "Nothing lost," in other words, might compute as something gained. Thus, Fioretos reads the double void as canceling itself out: "The first solitary *Nichts* posits the lack which the second *nichts* assures us is not lost."[33] Felstiner similarly reads the double negative as adding up to produce a positive. "Possibly 'Nothing' itself, our lack of traces and signs, is now gone, thanks to this poem," he says.[34] Celan's "nothing is lost" is nevertheless no mere hermeneutic riddle; rather, the doubled negative is a clue to a lost syntactical thread that Celan traces throughout his labyrinthine language. For "nothing, nothing is lost" typifies Celan's unconventional use of pronominal negatives as substantive entities. Celan's contradictory language habitually twists and turns in on itself as it converts terms of negation into unconventional syntactical subjects. For instance, three times in "Stretto" Celan repeats, "Nirgends/fragt es nach dir—/ [...] /Nirgends/fragt es nach dir—/ [...] /Nirgends/fragt—" ("Nowhere/asked after you—/ [...] /Nowhere/asked after you/ [...] /Nowhere/asked—").[35] Nowhere's insistent asking draws our attention to the fact that throughout the poem subjects are not entities but absences: "Keines/erwachte" ("Not one awoke"), "keine/Rauchseele steigt" ("No chimney soul rises").[36] Nowhere asks, no one rises, but the negative concord (which is precluded in normative German) is never resolved in this deracinated view from nowhere: "Der Ort, wo sie lagen, er hat/einen Namen—er hat/keinen" ("The place where they lay it has/a name—it has/none").[37]

The repeated negation in the tightening spatial void of "Stretto"—"nowhere [...] nowhere"—evokes the recurring contradiction of "Niemandes Stimme, wieder" ("Nobody's voice, again") in "Ein Auge, Offen" ("An Eye, Open," 1958)[38]—or the syntactical antinomy of "the nothing," "das Nichts," strangely denominated successively with a (the?) definite article in "Mandorla":

In der Mandel—was steht in der Mandel?
Das Nichts.
Es steht das Nichts in der Mandel.
Das steht es und steht.
Im Nichts—wer steht da?[39]

In the almond—what stands in the almond?
The Nothing.
In the almond stands the Nothing.
There it stands and stands.
In the Nothing—who stands there?[40]

Felstiner flags the anomalous article appended to nothing: "What 'stands' in the almond is not *nichts* ('nothing') but *das Nichts*, 'Nothingness" or 'the Nothing.'"[41] Felstiner further observes that Celan likely gleaned the unusual formulation from Heidegger: In 1952 Celan underlined the phrase "How stands it with the Nothing?" ("Wie steht es um das Nichts?") in his copy of Heidegger's "Was ist Metaphysik?", a connection discussed below.[42] The definite article of "the Nothing" in "Mandorla" makes nothing paradoxically concrete. Moreover, one may ask whether this named nothing, "das Nichts," refers to a specific and consistent subject that perdures over the course of Celan's work. Is "the Nothing" in "Mandorla" (1961) identical with "the living Nothing" in "To One Who Stood Before the Door"? Is it the same Nothing that appears in the poem "The Nothingness" or that surfs the tide in "Matière de Bretagne" ("das Nichts/rollt seine Meere [...] das Nichts, seine Meere," "the Nothing/rolls its seas [...] the Nothing, its seas")?[43] "Nothing" and related negative terms in innumerable other Celan poems blot out the positive pronouns that typically orient dialogic utterances. But such is the genocidal logic of the context of "Stretto," of deportation or displacement into "the terrain/ with the unmistakable trace."[44] Negation cancels individual agency in this negative poetic space while pronouns investing subjects with personal autonomy run scarce. Thus, when the third of the repeated "nowheres" in "Stretto" briefly gives way to an efflorescence of "I" and "you," the change is astonishing:

>   Nirgends
>   fragt es—
> Ich bin, ich,
> ich lag zwischen euch, ich war
> offen, war
> hörbar, ich tickte euch zu, euer Atem
> gehorchte, ich
> bin es noch immer, ihr
> schlaft ja.[45]

>   Nowhere
>   asked—
> I'm the one, I,
> I lay between you, I was
> open, was
> audible, I ticked toward you, your breath
> obeyed, I
> am still the one, and
> you're sleeping.[46]

Suddenly "out of nowhere,"[47] here, at the heart of the poem, an "I" maniacally asserts its presence to a somnolent and heedless "you." The effect, however, is short-lived. The pronominal resurgence is quickly covered up by a return not only to negative poetics but to something even darker, the ghastly residue of individuals fatally caught in the conflagration of the camp:

>   Deckte es
> zu—wer?
> Kam, kam.
> Kam ein Wort, kam,
> kam durch die Nacht,
> wollt leuchten, wollt leuchten.
> Asche.
> Asche, Asche.[48]

>   Covered it up
>   who?
> Came, came.
> Came a word, came,
> came through the night,
> would glisten, would glisten.
> Ashes.
> Ashes, ashes.[49]

What ultimately comes through the straits in "Stretto" is no statement at all—"no 'I,' 'you,' 'they,' or 'we,' but a single word: Ashes."[50] Less than nothing survives the cataclysm; "I," "you," "nothing lost"—all is burned to a cinder, leaving only "Ashes/Ashes, ashes."

A consequence of Celan's prolific use of negative pronouns in lieu of positive pronominal terms is to make rhetorical apophasis take the place of cataphatic speech. That is, negation in Celan plays the discursive role usually reserved for affirmation of the subject. Warped by the repeated weight of that dark word denoting the horrific residue of the catastrophe that "came,/came through the night," speech reverses sense: ashes glisten, negation affirms, and silence speaks. In Celan's post-Holocaust poetics, the poet inverts or suspends the regular polarity of language. Celan's "grammatical suspension," Derrida observes, suggests that nothing and no one "are neither positive nor negative."[51] Moreover, the rhetorical inversion carries theological resonance, for Celan writes on behalf of "Für-niemand-und-Nichts-Stehn" ("Stand-for-no-one-and-Nothing").[52] The effect is to transform adamant negations into enigmatic assertions and anchor them in a bizarre new reality. Nothing and no one emerge as the uncanny protagonists in this new order.

We see this again in the memorable and much-quoted lines from "Aschenglorie" ("Ashglory") in Celan's collection *Atemwende* (*Breathturn*, 1967), "Niemand/zeugt für den/Zeugen" ("No one/witnesses for the/witness"), to which we will return in the afterword.[53] In this breathtaking turn of language, "no one" is elevated to a central position in the poet's testimonial pantheon. But is testimony delivered by "no one" transmitted or blocked? The question is akin to Celan's fundamental uncertainty whether saying "nothing" makes a sound. "Assertion and negation, personification and blind force"[54] strike a fragile equipoise in this verse tenuously set on the ambiguous fulcrum of "no one" bearing witness for the anonymous witness. "No one" may be either the repudiation or affirmation of the possibility of witnessing. Furthermore, according to Wolosky, negation here is endowed with a creative force or, at least, the force of a creator.[55] The poem heretically insinuates negative theology by apophatically invoking an apathetic "No-one-and-Nothing" divinity who silently testifies to His people's destruction. Indeed, a negatively defined (or grotesquely divined) godhead could be Celan's incorporeal subject, but the text may adumbrate something bolder still by suggesting, as Hartman writes, that "the invisible may be Celan himself, who aspires to the most reticent self-presence" by vanishing into his text.[56] If "Niemand" (nobody) is a proper name for the poetic subject and not God, then rather than resorting to an iconoclastic *via negativa*, the poet might be proposing a revolutionary *vita negativa*, a life lived as no one. In Hartman's words, "A self-effacing Celan could be saying: 'I am Nobody, yet must validate the idea of witness by my poems.'"[57] In this case, the invisible nobody reappears as the central somebody of the text.

A blasphemous appeal to both no one and nothing also distinguishes one of Celan's best-known poems "Psalm" (1961), the same year as "Mandorla." The poem exponentially raises genocidal obliteration by history to the power of sacrilegious new heights:

Niemand knetet uns wieder aus Erde und Lehm,
niemand bespricht unsern Staub.
Niemand.
Gelobt seist du, Niemand.[58]

No one molds us again out of earth and clay,
no one incants our dust.
No one.
Blessed art thou, No One.[59]

Who is praised in this unholy psalm? No one. "Sie lobten nicht Gott" ("They did not praise God"), Celan writes in another poem, "Es war Erde in ihnen"[60] ("There Was Earth Inside Them," 1959).[61] Instead, "sie gruben und hörten nichts mehr" ("they dug and heard nothing more").[62] Nullified prayer gives way to a listened-to silence. In "Psalm," a numinous but negated "No one" is accorded acrid benediction. Where no one is blessed, hypostatized nothing follows close behind. Early in the poem, "Niemand," "No one," repeats in multiple forms, including the enigmatic and resonant "Niemandsrose" ("No-One's Rose"). The poem then pivots from irreverent negative theology to assertion of inscrutable subjectivity:

Ein Nichts
waren wir, sind wir, werden
wir bleiben, blühend:
die Nichts-, die
Niemandsrose.[63]

A Nothing
we were, are, and ever
shall be, blooming:
the Nothing-, the
No-One's-Rose.[64]

First the nebulous negation—"A Nothing"—and then the equally baffling assertion: "We were, are, and ever shall be." One hears overtones of the biblical statement of divine ontology, "eheye asher eheye" ("I am what I am" in Exodus 3:4), meaning, we do exist! But we exist solely as "Ein Nichts," as non-being or nothing. There is no syntactical coherence to the crucial phrase, "A Nothing we were, are, shall be." We are—nothing. The gulf between "we were" and "we were nothing" is slight, seemingly trivial, but that insignificant difference situates meaning in the text. As Derrida postulates, nothing makes all the difference.[65] A silent turn of breath, or *Atemwende*, across the line breaks radically transforms this verse from a despondent admission of absence to an ecstatic profession of paradoxical survival: we exist, but as nothing. By eliding this ephemeral breathturn and reading across the caesura one produces a couplet whose constituent parts contradict. Such enjambment born of absurd negation speaks for Celan's revolutionary new paradigm. The prosody encapsulates Celan's poetics: One line tapering off into silence is enjambed with the unexpected continuation of a verse that had been seemingly extinguished and reduced to nothing. The enjambed line extends poetic life beyond the void of negated space. The line breaks of Celan's poetry recapitulate the broken lives of survivors.

For Celan, such lyrical enjambment turning line by line from the nothingness at the end of one verse to the breath sustained at the start of the next line animates his conception of poetry, especially in contrast to the inexorable finality of prose: "Prose line to the end/poem line—/the omitted," he writes with a brusque Dickinsonian em-dash exemplifying his negation of end-stopped verse.[66] "Lyric poetry—/torn-offness," he continues, as if lyricism and nullification were synonymous. Poetry, Celan says, should literally take one's breath away. "He who catching his breath between two lines of poetry looks around for comma or conjunction, misses out," he writes.[67] In his "Meridian" speech Celan suggests that poetry itself can be a kind of breathturn: "Dichtung: das kann eine Atemwende bedeuten. Wer weiß, vielleicht legt die Dichtung den Weg—auch den Weg der Kunst—um einer solchen Atemwende willen zurück" ("Poetry: that can mean a breathturn.

Who knows, perhaps poetry travels this route—also the route of art—for the sake of such a breathturn?").[68] With reference to the entirety of Celan's corpus, Ziarek declares, "*Atemwende*, this turning of breath, is a breath-turning, breath-taking reversal of the poetic paradigm."[69] In "Psalm," the breathless joining of "Ein Nichts" with "waren wir" confounds ordinary sense and innovates a radically new poetic idiom by forcing the reader to integrate two antithetical claims into an unconventional affirmative whole that bursts all bounds of linguistic logic.

In turn, the compound paradox "A none we were" represents an a-non(e)-ymous genocidal experience that violates the limits of rational comprehension. How, logically, can one speak of having been none? *No one* can utter this impossible phrase. But according to Celan, that is precisely the point: "No one" *can* voice these words devoid of normative meaning. The survivor-poet speaks on behalf of himself and fellow victimized subjects, no ones (or "No-one-roses") who, in the same ethereal line-broken breath, bear witness to their antithetical experience by proclaiming, "I am" and "I am not." "We are none" is the victims' strange shibboleth, a paradoxical and multivalent claim that encodes the dense, contradictory ramifications of what it means to pass over the abyss of constative meaning into the domain of the victim, particularly one who survives the calamity and outlives their own death. For the survivor, "I am" is an absurd, impossible claim. Personal integration belongs to no one who endured the Shoah. Mass atrocity leaves "no one," no "I" in its wake, because genocidal terror, especially in its Nazi form, assaults "the very idea of selfhood" and baffles the lyricist's "investment in voicing subjectivity."[70] Genocide is an event without a subject.[71]

For Arendt the Nazis' most diabolical offense was the creation of a totalitarian reality in which "the killing of man's individuality" was so effective as to prove that "henceforth nothing belonged to him and he belonged to no one. His death merely set a seal on the fact that he had never existed."[72] A genocidal world in which nothing belongs to the victims and they belong to no one—to *niemand* and *nichts*—so thoroughly contradicts personal identity that to reckon with it the survivor-poet is compelled to invent a new grammar not only replete with neologisms but rooted in non-subjectivity. "Nothing we were" coheres in this postlapsarian idiolect as an identifier for the victims who were, are, and ever shall be contradictions, no ones who existed as non-subjects or negated subjects but still regard themselves as "nothing that is" suspended between existence and annihilation.

Heidegger: Nothing Nihilates

Celan's idiosyncratic poetics of negativity and idiosyncratic model of being and nothingness challenge preeminent ontological theories of his time. In particular, his verse offers a perspective that we may term Being-after-death in a way that controverts Heidegger's concept of Being-toward-death (Sein-zum-Tode). Instead of linking the ultimate value of Being to knowledge of one's own inevitable death, as Heidegger does, Celan ties his complex notion of existence to recognition of having tenuously survived his own death. "Wir waren tot und konnten atmen" ("we were dead and could breathe"), he writes in an early postwar poem "Erinnerung an Frankreich," ("Memory of France," 1948),[73] succinctly framing the survivors' stupefaction at still being alive despite sensing that they had been annihilated in the cataclysm. While Heidegger claims that Being-toward-death demonstrates "the possibility of the absolute impossibility of *Dasein*" and solidifies the exclusive *Jemeinigkeit* relationship between existence and one's "ownmost potentiality-of-being,"[74] Being-after-death in Celan irrevocably splits apart the poet's faith in the possibility of cohering as a subject after annihilation. For Celan, as opposed to Heidegger, the certainty of eventual death does not produce meaning; astonishment at inexplicable survival does. Consequently, much of Celan's work is an attempt to articulate the self after its own near-extirpation, an elucidation of the survivor's paradoxical sense of Being-after-death. For example, his pseudo-prayer poems denying ecclesiastic adulation establish his speakers on the far side of a mortal divide by paraphrasing Psalm 115:17, "The dead will not praise the Lord."[75] His entire purpose, he famously says in his 1958 Bremen address (as we have mentioned in the previous chapter), is to square his survival as a German-speaking Jewish poet with the "tausend Finsternisse todbringender Rede" ("thousand darknesses of deathbringing speech"), specifically German speech, by going "mit seinem Dasein zur Sprache geht, wirklichkeitswund und Wirklichkeit suchend" ("with his very being to language, stricken by and seeking reality").[76]

Writing against the shadow of a historical menace that showed "the individual [to be] fungible and replaceable under the liquidator's boots," as Adorno said,[77] Celan recasts personal existence as an open question. While Heidegger argues that the human subject becomes intelligible through a triumphant affirmation of its own selfhood in declarative language—"Who then is man? He who must affirm what he is. To affirm means to declare... Man *is* he who he *is*, precisely in the affirmation of his own existence"[78]— Celan throws the subject's very existence in the wake of disaster into doubt. "Es ist,/ich weiß es, nicht wahr,/daß wir lebten" ("it is,/I know, not true/that we lived"), he writes in "Soviel Gestirne" ("So Many Constellations").[79] Celan writes not attestations of existence but tergiversations of absence. He pens "das hundert-/züngige Mein-/gedicht, das Genicht" ("the hundred-/tongued lie-/poem, the noem").[80] Celan's "das Genicht" blends "Gedicht" ("poem") with "nicht" (nothing) in a neologism which translators have rendered as "noem" to indicate Celan's aesthetic, an equivocal poetry of nothing.

Where Heidegger sees the ineluctable individuality of one's own death, the *Jemeinigkeit* of inevitable death, as making Dasein ever more "non-relational" and "essentially disclosed to itself,"[81] Celan discerns an inexorable sense of murky alienation from oneself and one's fate. The existential ambiguity of whether he in fact survived undermines any definitive statement about being. The relevant question to pose, Adorno suggests in an oft-cited statement that partially retracts his initial dictum about poetry after Auschwitz (itself partly prompted by Celan's verse, as discussed in Chapter 2), is not whether art is possible after the Holocaust, but whether subjectivity is:

> Darum mag falsch gewesen sein, nach Auschwitz ließe kein Gedicht mehr sich schreiben. Nicht falsch aber ist die minder kulturelle Frage, ob nach Auschwitz noch sich leben lasse, ob vollends es dürfe, wer zufällig entrann und rechtens hätte umgebracht werden müssen.[82]

> It may have been wrong to say that after Auschwitz you could no longer write poems. But it is not wrong to raise the less cultural question of whether after Auschwitz you can go on living—especially whether one who accidentally escaped, one who by rights should have been killed, may go on living.[83]

Celan evokes precisely this quandary not merely to offer the dead poetic prosopopoeia but rather to express another subject, a foreign self, or "befremdetes Ich," within.[84] Throughout his literary corpus, as Celan says in "The Meridian," he attempts to locate "den Ort, wo das Fremde war, den Ort, wo die Person sich freizusetzen vermochte, als ein—befremdetes—Ich"[85] ("the place where the strangeness was, the place where a person was able to set himself free as an—estranged—I"[86]). The subject's liberation, in Celan's view, lies in its capacity to endure through an other—or in nothing. *Contra* Sartre, whose own existentialist treatment of Heidegger's ontology led him to conclude in *Being and Nothingness* (*L'Être et le néant*) that nothingness describes an absurd void enclosing existence, Celan reconciles existence and nothingness. In Celan, being and nothingness do not contradict each other. On the contrary, nothingness is a mode of being, perhaps the sole mode available to someone who has veritably experienced his own death. "Ein Nichts waren wir"("A nothing we were"), Celan affirms, forsaking logic and grammar. But as Beckett says, "Being is not syntactical."[87] What there is, in Celan's eccentric ontology, is nothing.

The apparently sophistic question of whether someone or something can be nothing, as in "A nothing we were," or if nothing can indeed be something sharply divides Celan and Heidegger. Can we speak of the nothing that is not there or the nothing that is? Heidegger intimates the former, Celan the latter. The distinction suggests a sophomoric game of casuistic metaphysics, but elucidating that negative nicety is precisely what Heidegger plays out in

"Was ist Metaphysik?" ("What is Metaphysics?"), his inaugural lecture at the University of Freiburg in 1929:

> Wie steht es um das Nichts? [...] Was ist das Nichts? Schon der erste Anlauf zu dieser Frage zeigt etwas Ungewöhnliches. In diesem Fragen setzen wir im Vorhinein das Nichts als etwas an, das so und so "ist"—als ein Seiendes. Davon ist es aber doch gerade schlechthin unterschieden. Das Fragen nach dem Nichts—was und wie es, das Nichts, sei—verkehrt das Befragte in sein Gegenteil. Die Frage beraubt sich selbst ihres eigenes Gegenstandes. Dementsprechend ist auch jede Antwort auf diese Frage von Hause aus unmöglich. Denn sie bewegt sich notwendig in der Form: das Nichts "ist" das und das. Frage und Antwort sind im Hinblick auf das Nichts gleicherweise in sich widersinnig.[88]

> How is it with the nothing? [...] What is the nothing? Our very first approach to this question has something unusual about it. In our asking we posit the nothing in advance as something that "is" such and such; we posit it as a being. But that is exactly what it is distinguished from. Interrogating the nothing—asking what and how it, the nothing, is—turns what is interrogated into its opposite. The question deprives itself of its own object. Accordingly, every answer to this question is also impossible from the start. For it necessarily assumes the form: the nothing "is" this or that. With regard to the nothing, question and answer alike are inherently absurd.[89]

Nothingness cannot be investigated because it cannot be, Heidegger states. Little (or nothing) can intelligently be said of what nothing is, because "[n]othingness is the complete negation of the totality of beings."[90] "Das Nichts selber nichtet," he insists ("the nothing itself nihilates").[91] Heidegger's analysis of nothing as lack induces him to ask what he calls "die Grundfrage der Metaphysik, "the fundamental question of phenomenology": "Warum ist überhaupt Seiendes und nicht vielmehr Nichts?" ("Why are there beings at all, and why not rather nothing?").[92]

In his copy of this under-appreciated intertext in his dialogue with Heidegger, Celan underlined Heidegger's initial, confounding question of negative existence, "Wie steht es um das Nichts?" (literally "How does it stand about the Nothing?"). But despite adopting some of Heidegger's categories and formulations, particularly the emphasis of "*the* nothing," Celan strikes a line diametrically opposed to Heidegger. Far from accepting Heidegger's conclusion that a substantive nothing is "von Hause aus unmöglich" ("impossible from the start") and "in sich widersinnig" ("inherently absurd"), Celan perceives an abundance of nothing, absence which he posits as the core of his ontology. For Celan, nothing exists.

Of the many constellations of knowing and being that Heidegger explores, "What is Metaphysics?" best illustrates what separates him from Celan. A response from Celan comes in "Soviel Gestirne" ("So Many Constellations"). The poem's closing lines vacillate between multiple modalities of knowing and conjugations of *wissen* before locating the insuperable gap of existence:

ich weiß,
ich weiß und du weißt, wir wußten,
wir wußten nicht, wir
waren ja da und nicht dort,
und zuweilen, wenn
nur das Nichts zwischen uns stand, fanden
wir ganz zueinander.[93]

I know,
I know and you know, we knew
we did not know, we
were there and not there,
and at times when
only the Nothing stood between us, we
found our way to each other.[94]

The speaker stumbles for an epistemic foothold—"I know,/I know and you know, we knew/we did not know"—and settles on the ultimate uncertainty: "Nothing stood between us." Subjectivity is rendered uncertain; only nothing, "nur das Nichts," exists between us. For Heidegger, this constitutes logical impossibility. But literally nothing stands between him and Celan. In specific, nothing as a substantive entity radically sets them apart. Derrida's maxim again obtains: seemingly invisible distinctions produce significant difference.

"Nothing" was to drive a wedge between Heidegger and Celan throughout their relationship. Scholarly consensus typically aligns Celan with Heidegger. Lacoue-Labarthe, Szondi, Hamacher, and Ziarek reflect the orthodox reading. Lacoue-Labarthe leads this interpretive trend: "Celan's poetry goes beyond an unreserved recognition of Heidegger; I think one can assert that it is, in its entirety, a dialogue with Heidegger's thought."[95] Nevertheless, any encounter Celan's work stages with Heideggerian metaphysics occurs under the sign of an event that the philosopher could never bring himself to name: Heidegger said *nothing* about the Holocaust or his support for the Nazi regime. Celan, like others, held out hope for a heartfelt "word to come in the heart" from the venerated thinker about his political past, "von einer Hoffnung, heute,/auf eines Denkenden/kommendes/Wort/im Herzen", as Celan wrote in "Todtnauberg," a poem about his sole visit with Heidegger in 1967.[96] Like others, Celan hoped in vain; Heidegger was virtually silent on the issue. His reticence, unlike Celan's, makes no sound.

Nothing comes of Heidegger's obdurate nothing, but Celan used the occasion of his confrontation with Heidegger and his failed attempt to elicit a word of contrition or justification in Todtnauberg to produce a poem proposing an alternate version of "there-being," "Da-sein," Heidegger's signature concept. Named after a place and set "in the hut" ("in der/Hütte") of the austere philosopher, "Todtnauberg" responds to Heidegger's silence by locating the poet's own subjectivity not in a dwelling place but in writing: "In das Buch/—wessen Namen nahms auf/vor dem meinen?" ("Into the book/—whose name did it take in/before mine?")."[97] The dissemination of identity into material text considers what it means for one textually to be there, inhering "in the scribed lines" ("geschriebene Zeile") of a guest book. If language is, as Heidegger says, "the house of being," then Celan unsettles the thinker in both his philosophical and physical redoubt by leaving him speechless. Celan trespasses the borders of Heidegger's metaphysical refuge by instigating, as Levinas says, "a most clumsy intrusion in the famous 'language that speaks,' the famous '*die Sprache spricht*': entrance of the beggar into 'the house of being.'"[98] Dwelling in normative German language, Heidegger is rooted in an originary home; Celan, by contrast, tunnels with his fractured neologisms to a "Wortlandschaft," a no-place exile located nowhere.[99] He sings, "O einer, o keiner, o niemand, o du:/Wohin gings, da's nirgendhin ging?" ("O one, O none, O no one, O you:/Where did it go, then, making for nowhere?")[100] He asks, "Im Nichts—wer steht da?" ("In the Nothing—who stands there?"). For Celan, nowhere is a destination, nothing a place. If in Heidegger's view nothing nihilates and language is the dwelling house of being, then that home has no room for Celan. To Celan, nothing is the root of being as well as a place of absurd communion, an absent void where the deposed "king stands" in the apophatic glory of an empty aureole in "Mandorla" and "a breath goes blindly between there and not-there" in the myriad equivocations of "So Many Constellations." Heidegger's language is a capacious house for coherent and logical subjectivity, but it offers no sanctuary for Celan and his notion of nothing that is.

Pagis: Mistaking Nothing

Celan is not the only writer who seems to be excluded from Heidegger's logocentric house of being. Dan Pagis, who is both a Hebrew author and Holocaust survivor, is doubly barred. Linguistically, Hebrew affords Pagis no means of clearly asserting personal ontology: he cannot write "I am," since Hebrew, like other Semitic languages, offers no copula. In Hebrew, there simply is no "is." Dorota Glowacka notes that Hebrew's lack of a copula verb would make it an unwelcome nomad in Heidegger's phenomenology: "The elision of the copula (of the verb 'to be') in the Hebrew language indicates a displacement of Hebrew from 'the house of Being.'"[101] As a result, Pagis has literally nothing at his disposal to say that he exists. But Pagis is also philosophically predisposed to challenge Heidegger's notion of ontological presence and to affirm Celan's model of substantive absence, for he, like Celan, is skeptical about his coherence as a subject overshadowed by traumatic memory. In his poetry on the Holocaust, Pagis exploits the absent copula as well as other linguistic instabilities and aporias in his language to broach an existential paradox reflecting his own sense of self shaped by negation. Pagis locates personal existence in absence and subjectivity in nothing. Furthermore, his verse depends on inscribed erasures. Missing words, letters, and selves haunt Pagis's writing. More critically for the purposes of our analysis of a Holocaust poetics of negated subjectivity, Pagis's poetry confirms that the patterns of negation and apophatic subjectivity innovated by Celan are not limited to Celan's own work or exclusively offered in opposition to Heidegger but are instead indicative of patterns and ideas informing poetry about the Holocaust more generally, especially verse written by survivors. Not only are Pagis and Celan alike in their technique of setting negation against itself, but they also share a similar cultural background. Although Pagis was a decade younger than Celan and still a child when the Holocaust began, both grew up in German-speaking assimilated Jewish homes in the cosmopolitan milieu of Bukovina, a densely Jewish and exceptionally polyglot enclave of prewar Romania.[102] Raised to revere the literary culture of the former Austro-Hungarian Empire, Pagis and Celan were also briefly exposed to new trends in Hebrew and Zionist thought. When the fascists took power in Romania, both survived harrowing internment in camps and experienced the death of most of their family and fellow deportees. As poets they further resemble each other in reconceiving the poetic self by deploying in verse a strategy of enunciating nothingness. Each does this in a subversive use of language: Pagis in Israel through the ironies and associations of modern Hebrew, a new mother tongue in which he expressed his disjunction with the past; Celan from France (after a brief, unhappy sojourn in Austria, the only time he lived in a German-speaking land) through a reclamation and radical revision of his *Muttersprache*, German.[103]

Unlike Celan, however, Pagis takes nothing for granted. Nothing, he assumes, constitutes the negated core of the survivor's subjectivity and the crux of his message, but Pagis also doubts the successful reception of his words. Instead, Pagis believes that mistakes will confound his speech. Fear of error, misreading, and failed communication bedevil his verse, turning his quest for a sympathetic reader into a bold attempt to cross the abyss of voicing nothing. His best-known poem "Katuv be'iparon" ("Written in Pencil in the Sealed Railway Car") stages this desperate hope to reach a reader, even as it erases any substantive statement. The poem poses as found poetry, perhaps the breathless dying words of a victim scribbling her last testament in a cattle car. The poem begins with reference to a place that is in fact no-place, a transport en route to hell:

Kan bamishloakh hazeh
Ani khavah
'im hevel bni
im tiru et bni hagadol
Kayin ben adam
tagidu lo sheani [104]

here in this transport
I am Eve
with Abel my son
if you see my other son
Cain son of Adam
tell him that I [105]

Of Eve's message to her son Cain, which she requests the reader to convey, the sole word that survives is "I," the Hebrew attestation of self, "ani." The "I" statements at the start and end of this brief poem enunciate an imperiled self that makes an address but does not rely on its reception to constitute subjectivity amidst self-negating circumstances. Scholars take note of an implicit circularity in the poem that loops the truncated final "I" back to the opening "here," creating a cyclical text whose end leads back to its beginning Ouroboros-like in an endless appeal that compensates for the zero copula by placing the elided verb in the middle: "if you see Cain tell him that I/[am] here in this transport."[106] Completing the circuit uncovers what Eve might have hoped to impart, but her terse statement as constituted already offers powerful ethical resonance in its two keywords, "ani" ("I") and "kan" ("here"). An unspoken nothing joins the terms: together, the loop reads, "I [am] here." Susan Gubar argues that the missing copular link signifies the "abrogation of humanism's faith in autonomous subjectivity."[107] But by marking her presence in text, the speaker audaciously claims subjectivity, albeit one vitiated by impending doom and recorded in the "soon-to-fade ephemeral erasability"[108] of "'iparon" (pencil), from the same etymology as "'afar" (dust). The disparity between the evanescence of Eve's writing and the finality of her fate in the sealed freight car is already insinuated in the liturgical overtones of the poem's title, which draws on a central refrain of the High Holidays service: "On New Year's Day the decree is written; on the Day of Atonement it is sealed." If the speaker's desperate promulgation of self occurs under the threat of erasure to both body and text, her claim to be "here" must be understood as an attempt to inhere in an elusive, traveling deathtrap located nowhere fixed as well as in writing that is impermanent and predominantly left unsaid. The poem thus constitutes a special case of what Amir Eshel calls "the perspective of poetic presence,"[109] since in this text immanence is intimated in words unwritten, in a missing message, in readers reading nothing.

"Hamisdar" ("Roll Call") likewise emerges from the abysm of an untraceable "here":

> Hu 'omed, roke'a me'at bemagafav,
> meshafshef et yadav: kar lo beruakh haboker,
> malakh kharutz she'amal ve'alah bedargah.
> Pit'om nidmeh lo sheshagah: kulo ein'ayim
> hu khozer umoneh bapinkas hapatuakh
> et hagufim hammekhakim lo baribu'a
> makhaneh belev makhaneh: rak ani
> eineni, eineni, ani ta'ut,
> mekhabeh maher et 'einai, mokhek et tsili.
> Lo ekhsar, ana. Hakheshbon ya'aleh
> bil'adai: kan le'olam.[110]

> He stands, stamps a little in his boots,
> rubs his hands. He's cold in the morning breeze;
> a diligent angel, who worked hard for his promotions.
> Suddenly he thinks he's made a mistake: all eyes,
> he counts again in the open notebook
> all the bodies waiting for him in the square,
> camp within a camp: only I
> am not, I am not there, I am a mistake,
> turn off my eyes, quickly, erase my shadow.
> I shall not want. The sum will be all right
> without me: here forever.[111]

The poem's scenario is motivated by the possibility that the concentration camp roll call has been tabulated in error, that a mistake has entered into the counting of the condemned. The juxtaposition of the vernacular "ani ta'ut," ("I am a mistake") against the biblical undercurrent of "lo ekhsar," "I shall not want," from the opening of Psalm 23 ("The Lord is my shepherd, I shall not want"), underscores the profound absurdity of the victims' fate. As the demonic roll call master counts and re-counts his prisoners, the speaker protests, "I am a mistake,/turn off my eyes, quickly, erase my shadow." The error lies not in the cruel roll call, a means of accounting for the absence or presence of the speaker and other prisoners, but in the situation itself. "I" should not be here, eyed at by a sadistic officer, the speaker contends. His ordeal is a wretched farce. Closer scrutiny, however, reveals that he is hardly there at all.

If the roll call is designed to surveil the presence of dehumanized prisoners, the speaker subverts the procedure by absenting himself from the objectifying scene. In preserving the felicitous play between specular "eyes" and the many "I's" in the text, Stephen Mitchell's translation suggests how the puns on "eyni" (my eye), "ani" (I), and "eyneni" (I am not) rub out the "I" addressing the reader. This poem about seeing oneself transformed first into an object of surveillance, oppression, and then annihilated into nothing repeatedly and insistently asserts "I." In this ocular exchange, the demonic roll call master's cold gaze destroys the speaker's subjectivity and turns the camp prisoners into counted objects so that numbers replace names. Countering the officer's nullifying notebook with a startling admission of self-negation, the speaker absents himself from the poetic frame ("I/am not, I am not there") before locating himself anew, confident that the sum will tally "without me: here forever." Like the dizzying "wir/waren ja da und nicht dort" ("we were there and not-there") in Celan's "Soviel Gestirne" ("So Many Constellations"), "Roll Call" defies any fixed deictic orientation. Both "not there" and "here forever," the speaker simultaneously inhabits the camp's terrestrial space and secretes himself into some amorphous cosmic beyond; he inheres in the poetic presence of a textual "kan," here, but also aspires to be deleted from the lethal Nazi ledger and thus permanently blotted out. Writing is arbitrary, erasure permanent, yet this poem speaking from nowhere aims to have it both ways: it concurrently insists on immanence and absence, "I am" and "I am not."

As with Celan's "Psalm," a perfunctory reading of "Roll Call" elides the poem's crucial caesura between "I am" and "not" and hence misses the tension of the enjambed "I am" sliding into its opposite: "I/am not." The fourfold repetition of "I am," "I am," "I am," "I shall," gives way with nearly imperceptible subtlety to the plaintive abnegation of "I am not," "I am not," "I am a mistake," "I shall not," challenging the reader to pause in the fleeting stutter between subjectivity and its erasure. Furthermore, subversion of subjectivity and dissolving of deixis are integrally related. By untethering the speaker from an embodied subject position, the text renders it impossible to locate the final "here." Deixis depends on proprioception (the sensation of physically inhabiting space),[112] but the collapse of the speaker's capacity for material integration reduces presence in this text to incorporeal immanence as either ethereal writing or intangible remnant of the dystopian inferno.

Pagis follows "Roll Call" with other poems in which speakers aver that they are nothing by attesting to existential or semantic error. "'Akevot" ("Footprints"), for instance, states, "It's true, I was a mistake, forgotten in the sealed car... But I didn't know I was alive."[113] "Otobiografiya" ("Autobiography") obliterates the speaker in an endless cycle of archaic, serial fratricide: "I died with the first blow and was buried among the rocks of the field... My brother invented murder, my parents invented grief, I invented silence."[114] Perhaps the most emphatic act of self-eradication comes in "Pe lesatan" ("An Opening for Satan"), a poem that introduces an apparently illogical phrase: "I was guillotined." A necromantic voice speaks from beyond the grave while still contributing to the evolution of language:

Keshe'amad lifnei hagilyotinah
amar Danton: "hapo'el legalyet
(hapo'al hekhadash hazeh)
mugbal bintiyah bizman veguf,
ki lo aspik lomar bizman avar
'gulyatiti.'"
Mishpat kharif vekhad, aval tamim.
Hinneh ani (uveemet eineni meyukhad)
ne'erafti
nitleiti
nisrafti
noreiti
nitvakhti
Nishtakhakhti.
(Mah ani poteakh peh lesatan;
hu od 'alul lehizakher
Shemibekhinah musarit, lefakhot,
beintayim nitsachti.)[115]

When he stood before the guillotine
Danton said: "The verb 'to guillotine'
(our new verb)
is limited in tense and person,
for I cannot say in past tense,
'I was guillotined.'"
A sharp statement, but naive.
For in truth I (I'm no one), I am nobody special, I've been
beheaded
hanged
burned
shot
slaughtered
forgotten.

The innovative phrase "I was guillotined" (a single word in Hebrew, "gulyatiti") carries no syntactical sense, for who can claim to have been guillotined in the past tense? No one can utter this phrase, but Pagis presents the same hermeneutic of logical inversion that we saw in Celan: it is precisely "no one" who can say "I was guillotined." "I am nobody," the speaker claims, echoing the paradoxical figure of "I" (pause) "am not" in

"Roll Call." Nobody says "I was guillotined"—and this is Pagis's intent. "No one" makes these statements. The survivor is an antinomy, a no one who survived by mistake, a subject transformed by genocide into material absence.

Wittgenstein states in the *Tractatus,* "Der Tod ist kein Ereignis des Lebens. Den Tod erlebt man nicht" ("Death is not an event in life: we do not live to experience death").[116] One does not, cannot experience death, logic stipulates. But Holocaust poetry like Pagis's and Celan's reminds us that logic is not relevant to what was done to victims of the Nazi extermination process. "You can't die a thousand times. I can," Pagis writes in "Autobiography."[117] While syntax dictates that the utterance "I am not" is syntactically invalid, a logical error, Celan and Pagis grapple with the validity of "I am." They instead assert, "I am no one."

What, finally, is the character of this "no one?" Pagis's "Edut" ("Testimony") delivers its own affidavit:

Lo lo: hem behekhlet
hayu benei-adam: madim, magafayim.
Eikh lehasbir. Hem nivreu betselem.
Ani hayiti tsel.
Li hayah bore akher. Vehu bekhasdo lo hishir bi mah sheyamut.
Uvarakhti elav, 'aliti kalil, kakhol,
mefuyas, hayiti omer: mitnatsel:
'ashan el 'ashan kol yakhol
sheein lo guf udmut.[118]

No, no: they definitely were human beings: uniforms, boots.
How to explain? They were created in the image.
I was a shade.
A different creator made me.
And he in his grace left nothing of me that would die.
And I fled to him, rose weightless, blue, forgiving,
I would even say: apologizing—
smoke to omnipotent smoke
without body or image.[119]

"Testimony" tells nothing of the poet's personal history; rather, it speaks through an inversion of a traditional Jewish prayer. Instead of ascribing incorporeal existence to God, "eyn lo dmut haguf veyno guf" ("He has neither bodily image or body)," in "Yigdal," a canonical hymn (commonly ascribed to the fifteenth-century Hebrew poet Daniel Ben Yehuda Dayan) enumerating Maimonides's thirteen principles of Jewish faith, Pagis assigns the divine attributes to his murdered Holocaust victim narrator, here shockingly effaced and turned into abominable, inhuman smoke. The speaker exists in a heretical realm of alternate demiurges and permeable mortality: "ani hayiti tsel" ("I was a shade"). Yet the "I" of the poetical voice remains to relate the horror.

Existing in a shadowy realm of phantasmic specters, the wraithlike speaker abjures his own physical form even as he attests to the essential human image of his oppressors. In Hebrew these terms disclose a troubling semantic affinity that the speaker denies sharing with his persecutors: the words "tsel," shade, and "tselem," human image, are nearly carbon copies of each other, save for the physical substance and additional letter *mem* that distinguish the corporeal "tselem" from the crepuscular "tsel." The same combination of phonemes and letters recurs later in the poem scrambled as "mitnatsel" (apologizing). The apologetic note sounds discordant, yet here the compensatory *mem* salvages the word from becoming what the speaker insists he is not, "nitsal," rescued or saved. A "nitsol" is a survivor. In Pagis, the contrite word, "mitnatsel," is finally offered, although only by the dissonant letter *mem* overwriting "nitsal" and canceling the possibility of a survivor as subject. Early in the poem the invisible writing of a missing *mem* dims the inviolate human form of "tselem" into the ghostly shadow of "tsel," while excessive writing later turns rescue, "nitsal," into remorse, "mitnatsel." First invisible letters efface the human image; then superfluous characters mutilate a potential survivor into a rueful, invisible nothing. The other added letter in "mitnatsel," *tav*, combines with *mem* to spell "met," or "dead." "Met-nitsal" means "the survivor has died." Writing seen and unseen conspire to kill subjectivity and transfigure the human form into shadowy smoke that disappears without a trace.

Rescue, as it so often does, arrives unseen in Pagis and Celan, transcribed into language as if by an invisible hand. A return to Celan through his work "Einmal" ("Once"), illumines the dark subject matter of Shoah poetry by saving subjectivity from invisibly dissolving into nothing:

Einmal
da hörte ich ihn,
da wusch er die Welt,
ungesehn, nachtlang,
wirklich.
Eins und Unendlich,
vernichtet,
ichten.
Licht war. Rettung.[120]

Once
I heard him here,
here he washed the world,
unseen, nightlong,

real.
One and Infinite
annihilated
I-ing.
Light was. Rescue.

Worlds collide in this brief primordial poem. Revelation and annihilation, the audible and the unseen, the personal and the cosmic clash and envelop each other in the compact space of this one text. The poem juxtaposes "Einmal" ("Once"), a single isolated moment, against eternity, "Unendlich" ("Infinite"), as well as the rustlings of theophany, "I heard him," against an invisible, dark reality ("ungesehn, nachtlang/wirklich"). Moreover, the rhetoric offers an aural analogue to this disparity through the staccato, monosyllabic "Eins" extended by the long, trisyllabic "Unendlich." Derrida, furthermore, notes that the morpheme "ich," I, of subjectivity surfaces in the text only *once*, although it phonetically hides in the repeated reverberations of "Unendlich," "wirklich," "vernichtet," "ichten," and "Licht."[121] Celan brings these antitheses to a pitched climax in a direct contrast between the ethical extremes of genocide: "vernichtet," exterminated, is placed in tension with "ichten," a neologism meaning "to I." Ziarek reads "to I" as a proximate form of "to annihilate" by subsuming the appropriated other in the ego of the poetic subject[122]; however, I interpret "vernichten" and "ichten" as polar opposites. Stripped of its negative prefix, "vernichtet" ("annihilated") gives way across the line break to "ichten" ("to I-ilate"). Pausing for breath in the enjambed closing caesura of this final poem in Celan's *Breathturn* collection, the reader transforms the ultimate genocidal negation—the object of the Nazi *Vernichtungskrieg*—into a basis for the production of the subject, the inalienable "I." In this way, unconventional language achieves what rational logic could not by negating violent negation to reconstitute essential human subjectivity, denied by genocide.

New words and worlds can yet come into being, as Celan sheds light on the dark recesses of language with his own demiurgic formula "Licht war" ("Light was").[123] While mourning the many unsaved victims, including his own mother, Celan's neologisms nonetheless rescue the self from the nihilistic reign of nothing by extracting the subject, "ich," from the bleak annihilation of "vernichtet." A similar "heliotropic"[124] reading detects how the black dawn of despair already incorporates white milk in "Death Fugue," Celan's most acclaimed poem.[125] In "Once," however, obliteration of all being morphs into the construction of a subject, as the poet rewrites reduction to nothing, "nichtet," as having I-ed, "ichten."

Celan's poem charges readers of poetry with a moral calling. If extreme historic trauma such as the Holocaust destroys the individual subject, then it is the work of genocide literature to "I," to "ichten." The reader's responsibility is to oppose *vernichten* and to engage in a process of *ichten* whereby we restore subjectivity to the victims. To do so one must learn to read between lines, letters, and sounds in order to discern shadowy script and hear silent, sometimes concealed words. Pagis makes clear in his late prose poem "Lemishal Sifruti" ("For a Literary Survey") written shortly before his death, that the task is nothing less than to read nothing with care:

> Atem shoalim keitsad ani kotev. Aval sheyishaer beineinu. Ani notel batsal bashel, sokhet oto, tovel et ha'et bamits vekotev. Zohi deyo setarim metsuyenet: mits habatsal khaser tsev'a (bedomeh ladema'ot shema'aleh habatsal), veakharei shehu mityabesh eino motir shum siman. Hadaf shuv nireh tahor keshehayah. Rak im yikrevu oto el haesh veyilhetu oto, yitgaleh hakatuv, tekhilah behisus, ot po ot sham, ulevasof kedin, kol mishpat umishpat. Ela mah? Et sod haesh ein ish yode'a, umi ykchshod bo, badaf hatahor, shekatuv bo mashehu?[126]

> You ask how I write. Let's just keep it between us! I take a ripe onion, squeeze it, dip my pen in the juice, and write. It makes excellent invisible ink: onion juice is colorless (just like the tears an onion elicits), and leaves no trace after it dries. The page appears as pristine as before. Only if you draw it close to the fire and set it ablaze will the writing reveal itself, first hesitantly, a letter here and a letter there, and then, finally, every sentence. Naturally! No one knows the secret of the fire, and who would suspect the pure page of having anything written on it?

This posthumously published text gives playful expression to the evanescence of Holocaust writing and the charred trace it leaves behind. Though light in tone, the poem, like the fiery script it conceals, smolders with hidden fury. The implied question it answers—how, indeed, can one write after an experience like the Holocaust?—continues to trouble literary criticism, but to the untrained eye, the poet replies, he writes nothing. Like the speakers in aforementioned texts, the text claims to be a nothing; it leaves no apparent trace. Underneath its invisible onion ink, however, to anyone who cares to place the seemingly pristine page in the fiery context of conflagration from which it came, the text reveals its secret words.

Pagis, a scholar of medieval Hebrew poetry as well as a poet, was surely familiar with the midrash and mystical commentaries that characterize the Torah as a script of superimposed flames, "eish shakhor 'al gabei eish lavan" ("black fire upon white fire," Devarim Rabbah Parsha 3; Zohar 3 Parshat Naso 132a). Black script on white parchment reveals only the textual veneer, but the blank void surrounding the words may encode as much as the inscribed text. Pagis's poem affirms that more is written in the white absences and silences around the texts than their black script conveys. In works of consuming passion, like those of Pagis and Celan, a hidden ink envelops the spoken words, giving the writing another layer of intensity; such poetry is indeed written in omnipotent smoke. But by reading the unwritten white nothing around the black script those seeking to pass a poetics of the Holocaust can begin to set these words ablaze. Why, for instance, does the poet in Pagis's "Literary Survey" use an onion? Its translucent juice is not particularly combustible, and though its layered skins reveal additional strata brought to light through the act of peeling. The Hebrew word for onion, "batsal," however, suggests a deeper resonance. "Batsal" includes "tsel," shade, repeating another key term from Pagis's poems "Testimony" and "Roll Call." But this onion veils still darker shades within. For if one learns to read both the black ink and the unvoiced white absence, the text reveals the invisible last letter of "batsal." By adding the letter "mem" to "batsal" it completes "betselem," in the image, as in creation's original human form. Literature written "betselem," in the human image, leaves no obvious mark, but it burns and scorches in resistance to annihilation.

Conclusion: Hear Nothing More

Pagis and Celan explicitly instruct their readers how to read their poems bearing witness to the ineffable. Pagis advises, "Kl'a et kolkha/esof et yadekha, ushma/bekol/hadaf hareyk" ("Shackle your voice/enfold your hands, and listen/to the voice/of the blank page.")[127] "They dug and heard nothing more," writes Celan, establishing a paradigm for his interpreters.[128] Those who dig deeply into these texts learn to hear the written nothing they voice in a negative poetics of articulated absence. This two-toned injunction to read the "blank page" and hear "nothing more" is also a guide for how to read atrocity literature more generally. Despite persistent clichés about unrepresentable trauma, Celan and Pagis demonstrate that what is ineffable may already be written and what is unwritten may somehow be said. Celan wrote, "La poésie ne s'impose plus, elle s'expose" ("poetry no longer imposes, it exposes itself"),[129] and the conscientious reader must read both what is written and what is not.

If this task seems impossible, then that assessment may have comforted Celan, who recognized that his art was following an improbable path. Celan admits in "The Meridian," "diesen unmöglichen Weg, diesen Weg des Unmöglichen" ("I find something that comforts me at having taken, in your presence, this impossible path, this path of the impossible").[130] Levinas doubles the difficulty: Celan's poetry, he says, travels "along the impossible path of the Impossible."[131] By writing nothing, Celan and Pagis run the gauntlet of the impossible. "Sie versucht, den Bereich des Gegebenen und des Möglichen auszumessen" (They "measure the area of the given and the possible"), Celan writes in his own poetic response to a literary survey.[132] Such writing, again in the words of "The Meridian," is "freigesetzt unter dem

Zeichen einer zwar radikalen, aber gleichzeitig auch der ihr von der Sprache gezogenen Grenzen, der ihr von der Sprache erschlossenen Möglichkeiten eingedenk bleibenden Individuation" ("set free under the sign of a radical individuation, which, however, remains mindful [both] of the limits drawn by language, [as well as] the possibilities opened by language").[133] Poetry that articulates nothing expands the boundaries of the possible by testing the limits of literary language.

Celan's last poems, published posthumously, continue the vein of exhorting an idealized other to read nothing: "Du liest/es fordert/der Unsichtbaren den Wind" ("You read,/the Invisible/summons the wind"), we read in "Rebleute" ("Vinegrowers").[134] That summons to make us hear the billowing articulation of nothing demands a sensitivity so acute that it threatens to disappear entirely. But Celan resolutely clings to the hope that his texts would find their way to the intended other and "wash up [...] on heartland," completing the journey from "I" to "you": "Ich hier, ich hier, ich; ich, der ich dir all das sagen kann, sagen hätt können" ("I here, I here, I; I, who can say, could have said, all that to you").[135] By transcribing the stammer of nobody and nothing, Celan situates his poetry in the ghostly "fissure between speech on the page, seemingly so absolute, and an invisible writing that may not be retrievable."[136] Despite the weighty task, retrieve it we can, if we only learn to read with sufficient sensitivity and care to raise subjectivity from the voids of Celan's work: "Hier livitiert/der Schwerste./Hier bin ich" ("Here the heaviest Levi-/tates./Here am I"), he writes in a late poem, "Gedichtzu, gedichtauf" ("Poem-Closed, Poem-Open").[137] "Hier bin ich" ("Here am I") enclosed in words, announces an I whose being is, as Derrida says, "almost nothing."[138] This inscription of self in the writing of nothing is the same fragile articulation of fleeting subjectivity voiced by the negated speakers of Celan's "Psalm," "Stretto," and "Todtnauberg" as well as Pagis's "Written in Pencil," "Roll Call," and "Testimony." Selfhood, for a survivor and poet such as Celan or Pagis, becomes a cryptic shibboleth, a byword that is almost nothing, but which makes all the difference: "I am, I am only cipher commemorating that which will have been consigned to oblivion, destined to become name, for a finite time, the time of a rose, name of nothing, voices of no one."[139] Co-signed as nobody and written under the opening and closing sign of nothing, Celan's late poem finally signals the author's poetic presence and signs his name: "Here am I."

4

Miklós Radnóti: Postcards from a Death March

Efraim Sicher

A Hungarian Poet in Hungarian

If Heinrich Heine emphatically identified himself as "ein deutscher Dichter,"[1] as distinct from a French poet, Radnóti identified exclusively as a Hungarian poet. Unlike Celan, who, as we have seen, was troubled by the strain on the German-Jewish symbiosis during and after the Holocaust, but who could write only in his German mother tongue, Radnóti situated himself entirely in the Hungarian poetic tradition. He rarely refers to Jews or Judaism in his poetry except, significantly, for a comic Christmas ditty on why Heine is banned from German literature (1939).

In his letter refusing to contribute poems to a Jewish yearbook, *Ararát*, Radnóti replied to the editor Aladár Komlós, a prominent Hungarian Jewish scholar and poet, why he did not share his essentialist view of Jewishness:

> I have never denied my Jewishness, to this day I am still "of the Jewish religion" (later I will explain this), but I don't feel Jewish. I was not raised

---

For biographical information about Radnóti, this chapter draws largely on Zsuzsanna Ozsváth's biography, *In the Footsteps of Orpheus: The Life and Times of Miklós Radnóti* (Bloomington: Indiana University Press, 2001) and on Győző Ferencz, "Foreword," in Radnóti, *The Complete Poetry in Hungarian and English*, trans. Gabor Barabas (Jefferson, NC: McFarland, 2014), 1–10. See also Győző Ferencz, *Radnóti Miklós élete és költészete* [The Life and Poetry of Miklós Radnóti] (Budapest: Osiris, 2005). I am grateful to Louise Vasvári and Ilana Rosen for their encouragement, corrections, and invaluable assistance in negotiating the intricacies of the Hungarian language.

in this religion, and I have no need for it, I do not practice it. I consider race, blood ties, roots in the soil, and the ancestral sorrow pulsing through our nerves as nonsense and not the determinants of my "mentality," "spirituality," or "poeticity." Even sociologically, I consider Jewry to be a community created by coercion. Such is my experience. Maybe it isn't so, but that's how I feel, and I cannot live a lie. My Jewishness is an "existential problem" because circumstances, laws, and the world have made it so. It has been forced on me as a problem. Besides that, I am a Hungarian poet.[2]

And despite his homeland denying him, he declared his love for the soil and landscape of his native country:

My "homeland" does not scream at me from the bookshelves: "go to hell stinking Jew," but rather it opens its landscapes up to me; the bush does not entangle me more than others; and the tree does not lift its branches lest I reach its fruit. If I would experience anything of this sort, I would kill myself, because I couldn't live differently than the way I do; and I could neither believe nor think differently than the way I do. I feel the same today, in 1942, after three months of labor service and eleven days of punishment camp (don't laugh at me, I know you lived through the [First World] War, but that was different, it was not humiliating). Banished from literature, where tiny poets who barely reach my ankles are scribbling, I hold in my pocket my useless and unused teacher's certificate, and so it will be in the foreseeable days, months, and years. And if they kill me? That won't make a difference. [...] I don't feel Jewish. Why am I of the Jewish religion just the same? I don't care about religion, race, etc. I believe only in its force of shaping the spirit, but barely so, perhaps not even that. It is hard to explain it, and what makes it even harder is that if I care at all about religion, it is Catholicism.[3]

Radnóti here sees himself unequivocally as a Hungarian poet, who at an early age had determined to become a Hungarian poet in Hungary and in Hungarian, whose poetic vision breathed the Hungarian landscape. He declares that he does not "believe in the 'Jewish writer' or in 'Jewish literature'" and disdains writers who recall their Jewishness only when affected by the anti-Jewish laws. This is the reason why he does not submit his poetry to what he calls "denominational" journals.[4]

Radnóti consistently and persistently stuck to his self-identification as a Hungarian poet even when beaten and incarcerated in forced labor camps. He preserved the traditions and forms of Hungarian poetry. In particular, from the 1930s his poetry draws directly on the classical Eclogues, which since the eighteenth century were adopted by Hungarian poets who wanted to create their own pastoral Arcadia to express their national identity.[5]

As we will see, the bucolic atmosphere of the Virgilian pastoral offered a challenge when adapted to the political context of Europe in the 1930s with the rise of fascism and a new world war on the horizon, when barbarism and anti-Semitic laws overshadowed the poet's fame. Nor can we ignore the impact on Radnóti's poetry of modernism, particularly the French avant-garde (Baudelaire and Verlaine were among his early influences). Although unable as a Jew to get a permanent position, despite a doctorate from Szeged University, Radnóti remained to the end a true Hungarian patriot. In this chapter we will see how Radnóti did not transform his poetics during the Holocaust but viewed his humiliating experiences of persecution and forced labor through the prism of his apocalyptic vision which developed over the years out of his humanist Catholicism and pantheist nature poetry.

Radnóti's conversion to Christianity, together with his wife Fanni, in May 1943 during a short leave from forced labor service, seems to be an act of faith, which goes back to his days at Szeged University.[6] Moreover, it came at a time when it did not completely protect them from anti-Jewish measures and could not make a significant difference to their chances of survival after the German invasion on March 19, 1944, and the subsequent mass deportations to Auschwitz. The priest who converted them was Sándor Sík (himself born of converted Jews), the same leading Piarist and poet who defended Radnóti in his appeal against his indictment for obscenity and blasphemy when in 1931 his second collection of verse was confiscated. Sík, a professor of literature at Szeged University, encouraged and influenced Radnóti over many years. Conversion was not uncommon. In fact, a number of prominent Hungarian Jewish intellectuals rejected their Jewish ancestry and converted from the 1920s onward as a way of reconciling their increasingly marginalized status as Jews with their desire to be accepted in Magyar society, which regarded assimilated Jews as suspect or unwelcome because of their origin. They had little in common with the privileged wealthy Jewish industrialists, many of whom also converted; both groups despised the *Ostjuden*, the unassimilated East European Jews.[7]

True, there were different views among Hungarian Jewish writers about their identity, but they were generally highly assimilated. The majority came from socially upward-mobile secular Jewish families, a generation after Hungary's Jews reaped the benefits of emancipation and economic success as agents of modernization just when Hungary needed entrepreneurs and investors. However, with the collapse of the Austro-Hungarian Empire and the defeat of Béla Kun's communist revolution, Jews who had willingly accepted or inherited Hungarian cultural identity found themselves under attack as aliens and traitors by the powerful far right allied with the Catholic Church. The situation worsened with the depression and social unrest after the Wall Street crash in 1929.[8] Yet Radnóti and the circles in which he lived and wrote, who matured in the aftermath of the First World War, were idealists and saw their future in the professions or in the arts as proponents of reform, whether they followed socialism or Catholic humanism. Conversion granted a delusion of belonging, and, though the first anti-Jewish law of 1939 exempted those who converted before 1919, the high levels of intermarriage did not lead to social acceptance. Indeed, the third anti-Jewish law in 1941 included converts in the racial category of Jews who could not have sexual relations with Gentiles.[9] When he wanted to change his name in 1934 (as many Jews did) from Glatter to Radnóti, after the Hungarian place name of his grandfather's birth, the authorities arbitrarily changed it to Radnóczi.[10] There could, nevertheless, be no hyphenated identity for Radnóti as there was for Aladár Komlós, Károly Pap, and Imre Ámos.[11]

Under Gemini

Radnóti is often linked to a "Jewish fate" by dint of his death in the Holocaust and claimed as a Holocaust poet, sometimes ignoring his previous acclaimed career as a foremost Hungarian poet.[12] Early in his life, however, Radnóti experienced a trauma which affected his poetics and his identity as a poet, an event long before the Holocaust, which left the imprint of the specter of death and personal guilt in his poetry to the end of his life. We read about it in an autobiographical prose fiction, *Under Gemini* (*Ikrek hava*, literally "The snow of twins," 1940),[13] written in 1939 during enactment of new anti-Jewish legislation that reversed Hungarian Jews' emancipation and set social divisions between Jews and Hungarians, including the labor laws that discriminated even further against employment of Jews, curtailing Radnóti's already-restricted income, and that made possible the conscription of Jews to labor brigades, which later sealed Radnóti's own fate. Significantly, the memoir opens with a Proustian memory of a public execution of a Hungarian officer that might have reminded us of the Dreyfus affair if it had not been presented purely as a public spectacle, a display of patriotism from which the narrator remains detached, more concerned with the antics of his precocious younger sister Ági, for whom he has been made responsible that day but who evades him and adventurously sneaks through the crowd to get a better view of the bloody judicial murder. The impassive narrator presents a poetic voice that transcends history and the world war that destroyed the Austro-Hungarian Empire. Radnóti's vision is fixed on the ideals of poetry.

In a return to childhood memory that collapses time, the narrator Miklós tells his wife Fanni how his mother sent him from his uncle Miklós's house in the country to his relatives in Budapest to get a cart to take his dying father to a doctor. After a horrendous journey on foot and by train the child arrives soaked and terrified. After his father's death, he stays with his uncle

Lajos while his sister Ági stays with his mother. The interlocutor, his beloved wife Fanni, shows no surprise at the revelation of the boy's despondency and despair at being abandoned and isolated from his family and familiar surroundings. Her expression of sympathy and identification accentuate the feelings of alienation of the boy in the story, who exhorts his aunt to give him the Frommer pistol he discovered in a drawer in order to wield his power over her and over his own death. In the face of the boy's threatening demand to go home, Uncle Lajos informs him that his mother is really his stepmother and cannot support two children. The boy realizes that it is true that his biological mother died in giving birth to him. Three years later, his aunt reveals that a twin brother also died with his mother in childbirth. These belated tidings fill him with obsessive feelings of guilt about the death of his mother and twin brother, his other self who has died within him, perhaps in order for him to live. "And then the beginning of something about which only poems can be written... would that be when youth began? What years they were! Was it you who remained? Or the other? You killed th-em, you kill-ed th... ".[14] This suffocating thought of self-blame makes death an everlasting presence in his mind. The death of his father is followed by that of his uncle Eduárd, about whom he fondly reminiscences but who tried to bully him into a business career. Then his friend Jean, with whom he had intimate conversations about poetry, is conscripted to the French army and dies in the war. Ági and his stepmother are far away. From death and solitude poetry is born.

The ghost of Radnóti's Gemini-twin inhabited his poetry and plagued him with guilt as if he were Cain who murdered his brother. In a 1937 poem marking his twenty-eighth birthday, which opens his collection *Meredek út* (Steep Road, 1938), Radnóti addresses his mother in self-accusing tones, measuring her twenty-eight years at death against his life, asking whether his life was "worth two dead." He blames his despondent childhood on his mother's abandonment of him and yet this is what has made him the poet he is:

Mögöttem két halott,
előttem a világ,
oly mélyről nőtem én,
mint a haramiák;
oly árván nőtem én,
a mélységből ide,
a pendülő, kemény
szabadság tágas és
szeles tetőire.
Two dead behind me,
before me, the world,
rising from the depths

like a bandit;
an orphaned soul rising
from the murky depths,
to live here, atop the
ringing, unforgiving, vast,
and wind-swept roofs of freedom.[15]

The sense of existential desolation defines his calling as a poet, as we see in "Első ecloga" ("First Eclogue," 1937). Against the background of the Spanish Civil War and the death of Lorca, whom Radnóti admired, the poet tells the shepherd that nobody will take note of a poet's death. It is the poet's fate to write without any surety he will be heard:

> Észre se vettek. S jó, ha a szél a parazsat kotorászva
> tört sorokat lel a máglya helyén s megjegyzi magának.
> Ennyi marad meg majd a kíváncsi utódnak a műből.
> No, no one noticed or took note, except perhaps the wind poking
> through the ashes of his grave that came upon some broken lines of
>   verse
> and committed them to memory, for future generations. (*CPEH* 118)

In answer to the shepherd's inquiry whether he expects any echo of his words, he replies:

> Ágyúdörej közt? Üszkösödő romok, árva faluk közt?
> Írok azért, s úgy élek e kerge világ közepén, mint
> ott az a tölgy él; tudja, kivágják, s rajta fehérlik
> bár a kereszt, mely jelzi, hogy arra fog irtani holnap
> már a favágó,—várja, de addig is új levelet hajt.
> Amidst cannon fire? Charred ruins, orphaned and abandoned towns?
> And yet, this is where I must live and write, in this world gone mad,
> like an ancient oak knowing he'll be cut down, a white cross on his
>   trunk
> marking him for destruction, and come the dawn the
>   lumberjacks will
> come,—but he stands unfazed still growing, sending out new shoots
>   and leaves. (*CPEH* 118–19)

Radnóti's landscape in "First Eclogue" modernizes the Virgilian pastoral to contemporary war and violent conflict, updating Virgil's lines in *Georgics* which serve as an epigraph to the poem: *Quippe ubi fas versum atque nefas: tot bella per orbem, tam multae scelerum facies* ("For here are right and wrong inverted; so many wars overrun the world, so many are the shapes of sin"; *Georgics*, 1:505–06).[16] The poet offers a minimalist hope that the poet's words will endure, yet it is a hope vouched in the natural metaphor of the strong oak that knows it will be cut down but continues to grow and put down roots nonetheless.

Virgil at War

Of course, Virgil was aware of the daunting problem of war in poetry which challenged both poetics *in extremis* and the integrity of the poet, as he noted in "Eclogue 9" (which Radnóti translated in 1938). Doubting the power of singing doves when faced with the might of the eagle, that is the Roman Empire and its ruthless and arbitrary expropriations and evictions, Virgil writes:

>...sed carmina tantum
nostra valent, Lycida, tela inter Martia, quantum
Chaonias dicunt aquila veniente columbas. (Virgil, "Eclogue 9," 11–13)
But our songs have as much power amid the weapons of war,
Lycidas, as they say Chaonian doves have when the eagle comes.[17]

The Irish poet Seamus Heaney has made the case for the versatility of the Eclogues down the ages (including Radnóti and Miłosz) to maintain their self-conscious literary form but also to withstand the onslaught of barbarity.[18] "First Eclogue" was written on the eve of the Spanish Civil War and "Under Gemini" was composed against the background of rearmament and of Hungary's tightening of ties with Nazi Germany, as well as annexation of parts of Slovakia under the Vienna Awards; later, Romania ceded part of Transylvania, reversing Hungary's territorial losses following its humiliating defeat in the First World War. As war was again about to break out, Radnóti had apocalyptic visions straight out of the Christian scriptures of the coming conflagration that would devour woman and child,[19] premonitions of death that seemed to be realized on a daily basis with the eruption of the Second World War. The Soviet invasion of Poland under the Ribbentrop-Molotov pact seemed a betrayal of any remaining ideological hopes in socialism and nauseated Radnóti, who was left disillusioned and depressed.[20]

Zsuzsanna Ozsváth contends that at this time a change came over Radnóti, and his poetry started to conform to patterns of modern Jewish lament for catastrophe.[21] However, it seems to me, on the contrary, that his poetry shows how close he remained to post-Romantic images of the poet's death and to Christian notions of apocalypse, although there are no personal declarations of religious faith in his poetry. His poem "Háborús napló" ("War Diary," January 8, 1936) envisions a hostile world on the brink of disaster in a constant state of war and violence. Over half the poet's life has passed under the shadow of war, and he writes under the glinting knives of powerful foes; he imagines he is mired in quicksand, yet there are rare moments when he writes with resolve. In his dreams he glimpses the pristine source of his poetry in a tranquil, undisturbed nature. The poetic voice addresses the paranoid poet whose imagination pursues the fleeting image of freedom in an ominous, surrealist landscape:

> A világ új háborúba fordul, éhes
> felhő falja föl égen az enyhe kéket,
> s ahogy borul, úgy féltve átkarol s zokog
> fiatal feleséged.
> And as this world careens toward yet another war and
> ravenous clouds devour the blueness of the genial sky,
> your young wife collapses and sobs in the gathering
> gloom as she holds you in a desperate embrace. (*CPEH* 94–5)

The poet's heavy pen moving slowly across the page is scant defense against the morbid forces of a universal destruction. Winter is approaching, and the poetic voice foresees his broken body sinking unnoticed into the wormy earth, which fills his mouth and eyes. Nevertheless, he compares himself to road construction laborers in the mountains who rebuild their flimsy huts every time these collapse and who persevere in their primitive bare existence. Yet he also takes recourse to the simile of a night watchman on a ship who spies land, which represents for some the soul. A dead star awakens at the sound of his voice, and the wind carries it far. However much the poet may be humiliated as an individual, the seer promises him immortality—a recurrent theme in Radnóti's verse of this period.

For all the increasing darkness, the precarious and ill-fated mission of the poet-witness defies tyranny in the name of freedom of poetry, despite its slim chance of survival in a perilous world.[22] As we see in "First Eclogue," April is untrustworthy and delayed under a deceitful sun; later, in "Péntek" ("Friday," May 18, 1941), against the background of arrests and the attack on Yugoslavia which brought bombing raids in its wake, April went mad with frost and ice while the sun went into hiding. "Második Ecloga" ("Second Eclogue," April 27, 1941) is a dialogue not with the shepherd but with a bomber pilot who dreams of his girlfriend as he destroys European cities (as the Germans had bombed Guernica in 1937, an atrocity memorably commemorated by Picasso in an oil canvas admired by Radnóti). To the pilot's question whether there is a place for him in his poetry, the poet responds that he writes, what else can he do?

> Írok, mit is tehetnék. S egy vers milyen veszélyes,
> ha tudnád, egy sor is mily kényes és szeszélyes,

mert bátorság ez is, lásd, a költő ír, a macska
miákol és az eb vonít s a kis halacska—
s a többi...
I write, what else can I do? A poem is dangerous,
and if you only knew how one whimsical, delicate line,
even that takes courage, see, a poet writes, a cat meows
and a dog howls while tiny fish—
but then you know the rest... (*CPEH* 138-9)

The poet repeatedly records his disgust at an amoral world bent on destruction. Yet, he cannot disengage from it for he must witness the miracle of nature and love. To the end, love endures, and Fifi (Fanni) remains his true muse.

Toward Apocalypse

In this cursory glance at Radnóti's poetry, the poet emerges as a figure who clings to a hedonistic, neo-pagan vision of women and love, despite (or because of) the cruelty all around. Premonitions of violent death accompany his poetry from the mid-1930s as he works through the childhood trauma following the death of his father in July 1921 (described in *Under Gemini*), transforming the confessional genre in a highly individualistic voice that resists the anti-Semitic violence he experienced at university and later the attacks on him in the press. In "Hajnaltól Éjfélig" ("From Dawn to Midnight," 1938), for example, he imagines his own burial and wonders if at least his poetry will survive. In the guise of a post-Romantic poet-prophet, he insisted on his own independent identity as a believer in a universalist humanism, while breaking taboos and defying dogma. It is in this perspective that we must approach the poems Radnóti wrote in the labor camps, including the "Picture Postcards" written on the death march that ended his life.

Jews and other religious or political undesirables, such as communists, were liable to military labor service (*munkaszolgálat*) but could not bear arms and had to perform hard labor for the military such as clearing mines and digging anti-tank defenses; some of the conscripts were detailed to factories or railroad construction. Radnóti was first drafted to the labor service on September 5, 1940, and endured three months of brutal torture doing back-breaking manual work designed to beat the men into degradation. On his second call-up in July 1942, which lasted until May 1943, when prominent friends and supporters successfully petitioned for his discharge, he had to wear the yellow Jewish armband. An infected dental abscess caused him agony, and he often despaired, though rarely complained of his mistreatment but continued to write his diary and poems about nature. He regarded his suffering as universal and he blamed the evil system which had taken over Hungary, ignoring popular support for the fascist government and its anti-Jewish measures.[23] When he served again, from June 1944, he wore a white armband to signify he was baptized, though this did little to protect him from routine beatings and arbitrary punishments (which regularly featured hogtying and trussing from poles). The captives were routinely abused and maltreated: although they were, initially, conscripted to perform their patriotic duty for their homeland, in effect they were systematically worked and starved to death. From 1942, Jewish servicemen (many of them intellectuals or prominent members of the community) were sent to the Ukrainian front, from which most of them never returned.[24]

Ozsváth sums up Radnóti's determination to maintain his dignity in his struggle with the state system from the 1930s onward:

> He refused to accept any identity other than that which he chose for himself. Hence he had to keep some distance from the ravages of raw despair or else forfeit his mythical belief in his place in the Hungarian world of letters and jeopardize his creative spark as a poet. [...] He refused to give in, to accept the horrific, the insane, and the grotesque as his lot. He rather chose to live heroically, to suffer or, if need be, to die for his country. This desire was so great and so overarching that it froze in him any inclination to acknowledge his personal agony and shame.[25]

As long as it remained possible, Radnóti continued to write and—to critical acclaim—publish his poetry and translations. The physical and mental suffering could not, however, but affect him, and his sense of foreboding grew. Yet despite the ominous sky above him, the poet holds on to his "I":

> A holdra tajték zúdul, az égen
> sötétzöld savót von a méreg.
> Cigarettát sodrok magamnak,
> lassan, gondosan. Élek.
> The froth dribbles from the moon,
> as a green poison stains the sky.
> I roll myself a cigarette, and slowly,
> cautiously, I begin to live.
> ("Tajtékos Ég" ["Frothy Sky"], June 8, 1940;
> *CPEH* 132–3)

The poet thinks that, as long as he still lives, he can afford to be nonchalant facing a horrendous reality and the prospect of worse to come. Despondency could spell only defeat. He remained, as he wrote in his poem "Nem tudhatom... " ("I cannot know...," January 17, 1944), rooted in Hungarian soil, at home in its natural landscape which he knew intimately; he hoped that when he died, he would sink into its earth:

> Nem tudhatom, hogy másnak e tájék mit jelent,
> nekem szülőházam itt e lángoktól ölelt
> kis ország, messze ringó gyerekkorom világa.
> Belőle nőtem én, mint fatörzsből gyönge ága
> s remélem, testem is majd e földbe süpped el.
> Itthon vagyok.
> I cannot know what this land may mean to others, but
> for me it's my place of birth, smothered in flames, a sacred
> plot of ground, the distant world of my youth where I sprouted
> like a tender branch from the hide of a tree, and I pray
> that my flesh may be interred within this costly earth.
> For here I'm home. (*CPEH* 158–9)

This rootedness comes from a post-romantic belief in the attachment of the poet's cultural identity to his native soil; it resists the history of Hungarian anti-Semitism as well as the ongoing political situation which denied Radnóti any place in Hungarian society. His belief in his universal message to humankind was steadfast in Hungary's darkest hours: he believed that although he was stripped bare, unsure if there was still a protecting angel, his banned words will resound when new walls will be built in the future ("Sem emlék, sem varázslat" ["Neither Memory, Nor Magic"], April 30, 1944; *CPEH* 164–5).

The storm darkened over Radnóti in June 1941 with the German invasion of the Soviet Union and further anti-Jewish decrees, but another kind of storm, that of passion, strained Radnóti's marriage—his adulterous affair with the painter Judit Beck. In "Harmadik ecloga" ("Third Eclogue," June 12, 1941), Radnóti appeals to the pastoral muse to save him from his nightmares of universal destruction and wishes to write about his secret love before he perishes.

> Pásztori Múzsa, segíts! úgy halnak e korban a költők...
> csak ránkomlik az ég, nem jelzi halom porainkat,
> sem nemesivu szép, görög urna nem őrzi, de egy-két
> versünk hogyha marad... szerelemről irhatok én még?
> Pastoral Muse save me! in this senseless age when poets must die...
> I feel the sky is falling, and know no monument shall mark our
> grave nor noble Greek amphora, merely one or two poems, if they
> survive... but shall I write a few lines more about my secret love?
> (*CPEH* 141–2)

None of this stopped Radnóti writing his best lyrics, including passionate love poems for Judit Beck and nature poems during his labor service. The lyricism was no escape from the imminent doom on the horizon, since no doubt news reached him of mass killings of Jews in Ukraine and elsewhere in occupied Europe, deportations and liquidation of ghettos, and maltreatment or shooting of Jews by the Hungarian army. This could not be allowed to stand in the way of his ambitions as Hungary's poet-bard, aspiring, as Zsuzsanna Ozsváth puts it, to the lyre of Orpheus, which allowed him to glide between life and death.[26] Freedom is hibernating in "Száll a Tavasz... Előhang az Eclogákhoz" ("Spring Flies...: Preface to the Eclogues," April 11, 1942), but the advent of spring which Lucretius promised in *De rerum natura* fails to bring any true liberation from the slavery of winter.[27] Death approaches to free the prisoner's body, as human flesh burns in "Egyszer Csak" ("Suddenly," April 20, 1942). Radnóti knew his time was running out.

The Virgilian form is near breaking point. "Negyedik Ecloga" ("Fourth Eclogue," March 15, 1943) was written on the anniversary of the failed Hungarian revolt of 1848, in which the revolutionary poet Sándor Petőfi fell; his "Nemzeti dal" ("National Song") inspired the rebels. Radnóti was writing as a doomed poet of the pastoral, howling in rage, while the responding voice (no longer identified as the pastoral muse) reminds him of his romantic song about the joys of nature—a beetle on his hand or a naked woman stepping out of the river, but expresses the hope that the poet will transcend his earthly existence to shout his protest in the sky above a wrecked world. The poet, a captive in a labor camp, appeals to the unnamed voice of the muse:

> Rabságból ezt se látni már.
> Hegy lettem volna, vagy növény, madár…
> vigasztaló, pillangó gondolat,
> rúnő istenkedés. Segíts szabadság,
> ó hadd leljem meg végre hónomat!
> From my captivity none of this can be seen.
> Had I been but a mountain, a plant, or a bird…
> but then this is a fluttering thought sent to console me,
> a fleeting godhood in the mist. Help me
> let me find my way back home! (*CPEH*, 152–3)

Death and violence were moving uncomfortably close to Radnóti., Apart from the death of the leading Hungarian poet Mihály Babits (1883–1941) and of the painter István Huber Dési (1895–1944), fellow-poet György Bálint was persecuted and imprisoned for his leftist views, then sent to a punitive battalion, and died on the Ukrainian front in January 1943. In "Ötödik ecloga" ("Fifth Eclogue"), written in Bálint's memory on November 21, 1943, Radnóti tries to put off writing about his friend. We hear no corresponding pastoral muse in this fragmentary poetic epistle,[28] but an inner voice urges the poet to summon the spirit of his friend, to make his death in Ukraine real, not a rumor of having gone missing or a delusion that he is walking in the forests. The poet understands that his poetry has the power to do this, but a cold feeling in his ribs freezes him. Ironically, he closes the poem with the fearful hesitation of confronting death so closely:

> Két bordám közt mar feszülő, rossz fajdalom ébred,
> reszket ilyenkor s emlékemben oly élesen élnek
> rég mondott szavaid s úgy érzem testi valódat,
> mint a halottakét—
>   Mégsem tudok írni ma rólad!
> Between my ribs I am gripped by a searing pain, for
> at times like this your memory trembles so vividly in my mind
> that I can still hear your murmured words, and feel you right here,
> as present, and as real, and as true, as the dead-
> And yet, I can no longer write about you, tonight! (*CPEH* 159)

The unwritten obituary, or elegy, which substitutes for both the pastoral and the death of the pastoral, tries unwillingly to come to terms with the terrifying forces which are destroying everything human. The poet acknowledges that there is a danger that writing about the catastrophe might paralyze the poet.

In an untitled poem written on May 19, 1944, Radnóti writes in the first person of the prophet bard and begins each stanza with "I lived on this earth in an age," voicing a poetic indictment of the unspeakable horror perpetrated in front of his eyes. As if answering the unasked question about the poet's ability to describe this, Radnóti declares:

> Oly korban éltem én e földón,
> mikor a költő is csak hallgatott,
> és várta, hogy talán megszólal újra—
> inert méltó átkot itt úgysem mondhatna más,—
> a rettentő szavak tudósa, Esaias.
> I lived in an age on this earth
> when even the poet was silent,
> waiting to find his voice once more—
> and then, there were none left to curse the world,—
> like Isaiah, the master of dreadful words. ("Töredék"
>   ["Fragment"] *CPEH* 166–7)

Isaiah is the only appropriate voice capable of cursing, although in fact the Hebrew prophet who foretold utter destruction spoke of hope and redemption if the people heeded his words. Radnóti evidently felt he could not keep silence, but Ozsváth assures us that in speaking out, although alone and ostracized, Radnóti remains true to the Hungarian tradition of patriotic resistance to all tyranny and oppression, which was central to Radnóti's poetry and identity. Radnóti does not single out the anti-Semitism that personally affected him but deplores the universal ruthless cruelty and unnatural confusion which now rules his world.[29]

Postcards from a Death March

Radnóti left for his third term of labor service the next day, on May 20, 1944, just a few days before his mother and sister were deported to Auschwitz. His wife Fifi took refuge in a convent. The German occupiers found ready assistance from the Hungarian authorities and local police in the round-up and deportation of 437,000 Jews in only five months. Radnóti and other Jewish men conscripted to the labor service, however, were sent to the copper mines in Bor, south-east of Belgrade in occupied Yugoslavia, where they served in 1943–4, as part of an agreement between Hungary and the German army. High-ranking Nazi officials demanded Jewish forced laborers to fill the urgent need for manpower, since the local Serbians were considered untrustworthy. Some three thousand Jewish servicemen were transported to sub-camps bearing German names, from which the men marched long distances every day, barely subsisting on a starvation diet and tormented by the guards who were goaded on by the camp commander, the sadistic and fanatically anti-Semitic Ede Morányi.[30] Radnóti was assigned to Camp Heidenau, in the mountains above Žagubica in eastern Serbia, where he was housed in barracks with other converts, but later had a large yellow star painted on his back like the other Jewish prisoners.[31] Yet throughout his labor service Radnóti refused to be beaten into being a "Jew" and, despite bouts of suicidal depression and fears of insanity, persevered in believing in his self-sacrifice as a loyal Hungarian poet, without complaining of the inhuman conditions and physical exhaustion. The famous poet spoke to his fellow camp inmates and discussed poetry with them. They gathered round him like Plato's students as he helped keep up their morale and humanity and read them some of his own poems.[32] The arduous labor under the supervision of the German Todt Organization and guarded by local armed Hungarian military (Honvéd) involved blasting the rock and clearing heavy stones for the construction of a railway that would transport the badly needed copper from the mines at Bor, which supplied 50 percent of the German army's needs for ore. Radnóti managed to get hold of a small notebook in the prisoners' barter with Serbian peasants who regularly came to the perimeter fence.[33] In it he jotted down poems recording his observations of what was happening around him. This is writing *in extremis* tested to the limits.

The first poem in the Bor Notebook is "Hetedik Ecloga" ("Seventh Eclogue"), dated Lager Heidenau, July 1944 (no sixth eclogue has come down to us, although we might consider "Töredék" ["Fragment"] as its draft). The poem seems to have lost any pretension of a dialogue yet clings to the mythical pastoral form in a world of death and destruction which has banished the poet from Arcadia. Radnóti remains stubbornly consistent with his previous lyrics, keeping strictly to his precise classical meter. There is still love, but it is longing and desire at a distance, through barbed wire. The poet considers the freedom beyond the wire as a dream which sustains the broken bodies of the prisoners who imagine going home—but what, the poet asks, does home mean? Does the home which he left still exist in bombed-out Budapest? And is there a homeland which can still read the traditional hexameters of Hungarian poetry in which he writes? The question bears on the viability of his claimed identity as a Hungarian poet whose homeland has denied him, but also on the possibility of redeeming the ruined terrestrial kingdom of evil described in the previous Eclogues.

The poet answers this question by describing how he writes in far more restricting and constricting conditions than the Hebrew prophets:

Ékezetek nélkül, csak sort sor alá tapogatva,
úgy írom itt a homályban a verset, mint ahogy élek,
vaksin, hernyóként araszolgatván a papíron;
zseblámpát, könyvet, mindent elvettek a *Lager*
őrei s posta se jön, köd száll le csupán barakunkra.
I write without commas [literally, without diacritics], as one line runs
    into another,
like a blind man fumbling in the gathering dark.
Bleary-eyed my hand crawls across the paper like a caterpillar,
my light, my books confiscated by the guards,
living without word or mail as a thick fog settles over our barracks.
    (*CPHE* 167–8)

The camp guards have confiscated flashlights and books, and the mail never comes. Reduced to the barest existence, the poet sees himself as a worm-ridden captive beast besieged by fleas, who shares with the feverish, mutilated bodies of various nationalities (one of whom happens to be a pensive Jew) a single hope for freedom and for a woman's love. He does not think of himself as part of a collective or as a persecuted Jew but as a voice in the wilderness in the fog-covered barracks. He lies awake in a sleepless vigil, tasting in his mouth a half-smoked cigarette instead of the kisses of his beloved, whom he addresses, telling her in the last stanza that when both sleep and death refuse to come, only his beloved can make it possible for him to go on. If there is a tentative hope, as night falls and both their slavery and their lives have shortened by another day, it is the faith in love. These lines might seem trite and clichéd if it were not for the horrific circumstances that made independent thought or human dignity impossible.

The next poem in the Bor Notebook is in fact addressed to the poet's wife, the source of his hope in love, "Levél A Hitveshez" ("Letter to My Wife," Camp Heidenau, August–September 1942). In this poem, written in the silent solitude of a forced labor camp, distanced from his wife by war and mountains, the poet finds a source of resilience in the surrounding natural vegetation but also in memories of his adolescent love. Although his vision of his beloved is darkened by a bomber squadron, and the air raid siren disturbs his thoughts of whether he will see her again and whether she still loves him, the voice of reason gives him a kind of peace despite living as a defenseless prisoner in danger from enemy planes and savage men. This romantic faith in the sustaining power of love and nature underlies "Gyökér" ("Root," Lager Heidenau, August 8, 1944). The poet looks at the world as a root, growing into nature and building the poem as an organic living creature, reminding us of the poetic yearning for a return to the earth in "War Diary"; he will be buried transfixed by roots. He is no longer a flower and lives among vermin, where his poetry was born, with only disdain for the world, but he draws force from the tree weighed down by foliage. It is not that the poet is oblivious to the saw wailing over his head which is cutting down the tree and by extension the poem; rather, the poet transcends the unseen daily atrocities and global destruction through the metaphorical merging of self into nature.

> Virág voltam, gyökér lettem,
> súlyos, sötét föld felettem,
> sorsom elvégeztetett,
> fűrész sír fejem felett.
> I, who was once a flower, have become a root,
> with the heavy earth above me,
> my dark fate fulfilled,
> a saw wailing above my head. (*CPEH*, 169-70)

This rootedness in nature under the ground, safe from destruction, reiterates the repetitive motif we have seen in Radnóti's poetry of his personal, rather than political, sense of belonging to his Hungarian homeland.

Like "Letter to My Wife," "A la recherche...." (Lager Heidenau, August 17, 1944) seeks refuge in Proustian memories of a lost past and recreates the exuberant and inebriating bohemian life the poet once led. Those days of wine and poetry can only be revisited in dreams, and in fact the conscripts keep up their spirits with fantasies of idyllic carefree pleasures in the past.[34] The angel of freedom lies buried with the fallen on the fields of Ukraine, Spain, and Flanders—some of them recruits to war who fulfilled their patriotic duty with clenched teeth and others Hungarian labor servicemen who were selected because they were religious, political, or racial undesirables and were thrown into sealed cattle cars or made to stand unarmed in minefields. All were worn down by war, as were the youthful smiles of the women. A prisoner in the Serbian mountains, the poet summons the spirit of his friends to sip from their glasses in a communion of the dead and the dying.

The voice replacing the Virgilian shepherd in "Nyolcadik Ecloga" ("Eighth Eclogue," Lager Heidenau, August 23, 1944) is the angry voice of the prophet Nahum, the third of the twelve minor prophets of the Bible, who prophesied that divine wrath and vengeance would rain down on the sinful Assyrian city of Nineveh. In the poet's Christian reading of the Hebrew prophet, there are no consoling words for the people or promises of redemption, but the dialogue between the prophet and the poet serves to remind the poet that the prophet's angry words live on and are never more relevant than in the present apocalypse, where, as in ancient Nineveh (which B. S. Adams reads as alluding to Germany),[35] the ugly soul of humankind is laid bare:

> Gyors nemzetek öldösik egymást,
> s mint Ninivé úgy meztelenül le az emberi lélek.
> Mit használtak a szózatok és a falánk, fene sáskák
> zöld felhője mit ért? hisz az ember az állatok alja!
>   Careening nations still annihilate one another,
> and like Nineveh, man's soul has been laid transparent and bare.
> What good are words, or threats of damnation, and what good
>   came of
> green clouds of ravenous locusts? man is still the most debased of all
>   the beasts! (*CPEH* 171–2)

In the new apocalypse, European cities become grotesque infernos, babies are bashed against walls, and girders of buildings collapse. What good then is the prophet's rage? The zealous prophet declares the heavenly kingdom promised by a youthful rabbi, Jesus—the shepherd who has eclipsed Virgil and his pagan false Arcadia.[36] Herein lies the redeeming value of poetry *in extremis*, the power to speak of a higher vision when everything human has been destroyed.[37] Curiously, there is no hint here of the genocide unrolling in Hungary; instead, the destruction is shown to be universal. The poem is implicitly framed in the standard Christian dogma of fulfilling the mission of the prophets and perfecting the religion of the Jews in a universal "nation of Christ" that must prepare for the end of days and the second coming of the Christian messiah, who evidently wins the poet's socialist sympathies as a savior of the poor and oppressed.[38] Acknowledging the affinity of prophets and poets and recognizing the fury in the poet's latest poems, the prophet invites the poet to join him on his mission to witness the destruction and rebuke the populace. The prophet advises the poet to bring his wife along with him on the trek and choose a sturdy walking stick.

However, the trek on which Radnóti was about to embark was not a missionary path but a road of thorns. "Erőltetetti menet" ("Forced March," dated Bor, September 15, 1944), written after the servicemen were evacuated from their camps in the mountains, moves from the universal cosmological overview of the previous poems to searing snapshots of individual pain and suffering. Like Celan, Radnóti turned to the *Nibelungenlied,* choosing for his model Walter von der Vogelweide's Middle High German *Elegie,* a lament for past years that cannot be retrieved, which Radnóti had translated.[39] It reminds us of "A la recherche....," but with the disturbing difference that there can be no looking back, on pain of death, and the return journey leads to an uncertain destination. A prisoner has collapsed on the road and, knowing he will be shot if he goes near the tempting ditch, rises to his feet in the hope that he will manage to get home. The poet first thinks that the man is foolish to believe he can return home when everything has been burnt to the ground, but then the poet wonders if his own home is still there, with his beloved Fanni waiting for him at the gate. The vision of tranquil summer days beckons, and he calls on his fellow prisoner to go no further, not to leave him behind, but to shout: "kiálts ram! s fölkelek!" ("That I may rise and wake!"; *CPEH* 174; cf. Isaiah 60:1; Malachi 4:2; Romans 13:11; Ephesians 5:14). Yet the poet is no Lazarus from the Christian scriptures, and he is relying on the eternity of nature to maintain his deluded moon-struck faith in the resurrection of a past life that has given way to the present daily terror.

The last poems in the Bor notebook are acute observations of what the poet saw on the forced march. They are titled "Picture Postcards" ("Razglednicák," from the Serbo-Croat *razglednica* with an added Hungarian plural ending). In the "Cartes Postales" ("Picture Postcards," 1937), penned during his stay in France, Radnóti summoned the effervescent moment of living while remaining detached from an enchanting scene, but here he dissolves the poetic distance from what we know was affecting him physically and mentally day in day out. The normality of horror intrudes into the pastoral and forces the reader into shocked bewilderment. In "Razglednica" ("Picture Postcard," dated August 30, 1944, in the mountains), which appears before "Forced March" in the notebook, the cannon pounding wildly in Bulgaria signals the coming capitulation to Soviet forces on September 9. Yet the poet does not see Bulgaria's break with the Axis, following that of Romania on August 23, as a source of jubilation that war might be coming to an end and that the defeat of Hungary is not far off. On the contrary, the anthropomorphic rendering of war reflects a malignant and hostile prospect in an apocalyptic landscape. The inhuman chaos of refugees and retreating armies is also a mental blockage that prevents orderly perception of the scene of the apocalyptic horseman that has run out of control.

Te állandó vagy bennem e mozgó zűrzavarban,
tudatom mélyén fénylesz örökre mozdulatlan
s némán, akár az angyal, ha pusztulást csodál,

vagy korhadt fának odván temetkező bogár
And yet among all this madness you still,
in the depths of all my knowing, a brilliant light,
as mute as an angel marveling at the apocalypse,
or a beetle tending to its grave in the hollows of a moldering tree.
   (*CPEH* 173)

Only the addressee, the "you" deep in the poet's consciousness (presumably his lover), provides a stable point that shines in this darkness. Yet the dual perception of the beloved as an overawed angel witnessing the grand carnival of universal death and an insect staging its funeral in a rotted, dying nature does not rule out the parallel uplifting, guiding beacon of love and its accompanying awareness of the minuscule standing of humankind in a decrepit world that is on the verge of a destruction. The muse of love does not stand apart from the prophetic vision of death.

As the Red Army approached, the Germans dismantled operations at Bor. One group of 3,000 men was sent back to Hungary on September 17 on what turned out to be a death march; a number of the servicemen (including Radnóti), who feared that those who stayed behind would be massacred by the Einsatzgruppen, bribed and cajoled the officers to join the first contingent. The second contingent left a few days later and was liberated en route by Tito's partisans. Serbian peasants cared for them until the Russians arrived, and the survivors managed to get back to Hungary via Arad and Temesvár (Timișoara) in Romania.[40] The first group passed Belgrade and stopped briefly in Zimony.[41] On the way, there were mass escapes; however, the march continued through Pancsova (Pančevo), Titel, and Ujvidék (Novi Sad) before it came to Cservenka (Crvenka), where the men were locked in a brick factory. As ethnic Germans and German troops fled the advancing Red Army, Bosnian Waffen SS guards accompanied 800 men (Radnóti among them) to Zambor (Sombor) and then to Szentkirályszabadja. On the night between October 7 and 8, over seven hundred of the Jewish forced laborers who remained in Cservenka were murdered.

Discipline on the forced march was ruthless: anyone trying to gather food from the fields was shot, as were stragglers.[42] In "Razglednica (2)" ("Picture Postcard #2," dated Cservenka, October 6, 1944), Radnóti described the devastation of the Hungarian and German retreat as haystacks and houses burned while frightened Serbian peasants sat by the roadside and silently watched. Yet the exhausted poet can still summon the pastoral shepherdess in a lyricism that, like Celan's but without his deep irony, disturbs us. A conventional optical illusion in the representation of a pastoral landscape forces us into recognition of a brutal reality:

   Itt még vizet fodroz a tóra lepő
   apró pásztorleány
   s felhőt iszik a vízre ráhajolva

a fodros birkanyáj.
But here, the pond ripples gently
as the young shepherdess steps into the water,
and the ruffled sheep bend their heads
to drink in the clouds. (*CPEH* 174)

The violence of war intrudes by means of unspoken contrast into the picture postcard of a tranquil rural scene. The fact that it is viewed by an unidentified and unobtrusive prisoner on a forced march emphasizes further the discord between poetry and what is threatening the pastoral.

"Razglednica (3)" ("Picture Postcard #3," dated Mohács, October 24, 1944) comes closer to registering the observer's own suffering, although the poet stands at a disturbing distance from what is happening to him personally.

Az ökrök száján véres nyál csorog,
az emberek mind véreset vizelnek,
The oxen drool bloody saliva,
the men urinate blood; (*CPEH* 175)

This is poetry as document, a postcard picture of a forced march. The forced march of 500 kilometers from Bor has reduced the men to cattle; the resulting kidney failure is a symptom of their abjection and suffering.[43] Death hangs over them as an immediate reality, not an imminent threat:

a század bűzös, vad csomókban áll.
Fölöttünk fú a förtelmes halál.
the stinking company congregates in ragged groups,
as death rages above. (*CPEH* 175)

The pastoral has apparently succumbed to the stench of rotting human flesh in a grotesque canvas of inescapable death. However, Radnóti's imagery is consistent with the poetics of his previous lyrical poetry, which likewise gives close attention to the earthy details of a sensuous nature, as in the saliva of the calf in the opening title poem of his first collection, *Pogány köszöntő* (Pagan Salute, 1930). In the opening poem of his 1935 collection *Újhold* (New Moon), "Mint a bika" ("Like a Bull," August 22, 1933), for example, we also read of the foaming drool of the bull who represents the animal force of nature,[44] but also the vital strength of the poet's own determination to fight for his principles before he falls, like the bull, fighting:

Igy küzdők én is és igy esem el majd,
s okulásul késő koroknak, csontjaim őrzi a raj.
This is how I will do battle, and how I, too, will fall, and let this
be a lesson for future generations, and let the earth guard my bones.
(*CPEH* 70–1)

That heroic death, like that of Sándor Petőfi in the 1848 Hungarian Uprising, is a persistent motif in Radnóti's poetry, though the background of this 1933 poem is Hitler's rise to power and the increasing authoritarianism of the anti-Semitic Horthy regime. In "Picture Postcard #3," by contrast, there is little sense of this brute strength in the oxen or the poet's resistance, yet the poet's perception of an immortal and relentless nature that will preserve the poet's body and his memory has not changed. There is no glory in battle, as in Thucydides' *History of the Peloponnesian War,* there is no room for pity or tears, but there is something of what Thucydides managed to convey of the utter destruction and total annihilation of plague and war.[45]

On October 8, SS troops on horseback who had overtaken the column of prisoners at Ószivác (Sivac) started shooting at random. A fellow campmate Miklós Lorsi, a café musician from Budapest who managed to keep his violin in the camp, was wounded, and Radnóti tried to help him get up.[46] In "Razglednica (4)" ("Picture Postcard #4," Szentkirályszabadja, October 31, 1944), written on the back of a cod liver oil advertisement, the poet describes how he lay down beside the wounded man and played dead to avoid being shot himself.

> Mellézuhantam, átfordul a teste
> s feszes volt már, mint húr, ha pattan.
> I fell beside him, his body rolled over
> already as stiff as a string about to snap. (*CPEH* 175)

The affiliation of the violin string and the death of his friend indicates something about to snap also in the poet's body. The poet foresees that this is how he too will die, echoing the premonition of death in his self-image of the poet as witness-martyr, a neo-Romantic trope which recurs throughout his work. Punning on a Hungarian proverb *A türelem rózsát teremt,* meaning patience will be rewarded (literally "patience bears roses"),[47] the poet plays dead in order to witness his own imminent death:

> Tarkólövés.—Igy végzed hát te is,—
> súgtam magamnak,—csak feküdj nyugodtan.
> Halált virágzik most a türelem.—
> *Der springt noch auf,*—hangzott fölöttem.
> Sárral kevert vér száradt fülemen.
> Shot in the back of the neck.—"So this is how you, too, will end,"—
> I whispered to myself.—"Just lie still.
> From patience death will bloom."—
> "*Der springt noch auf,*"—I heard someone say above me;
> as mud caked with blood dried upon my ears. (*CPEH* 175)

This time death has touched him very closely, and the voice of the SS officer standing above him is barely heard through the congealed blood covering his own ear. What the SS man actually says ("This one is still moving") could be understood in two ways: he is probably ascertaining whether the shot man needs a bullet to finish him off, but his words can equally allude to the poet, who writes his last poem.[48] The jarring effect of the German words in the Hungarian poem brings home the proximity of death and the poet's identification with the murdered man, whose blood touches his ear, the audial receptacle of prophecy, but which is also a mark of fraternity, mixed with mud or earth, identifying the poet as a corpse fit for burial. The frozen final image leaves the poet in a state of paralysis that represents (as in the "Fifth Eclogue") the inability to express the unspeakable.

If Radnóti expected that the slave laborers would be released on reaching Hungary, he was disappointed to find they were being moved on toward the Austrian border; the Nazis wanted to hold on to their Jewish prisoners and decided to send them to concentration camps in the Reich. The Arrow Cross took over the government on October 15, and the extermination of Hungarian Jewry gathered pace. On October 28, the men were packed into cattle cars and transported to Szentkirályszabadja, where they were handed back to their Hungarian guards from Bor and awaited the other labor battalions, before setting off again on a forced march on November 3. On or about November 9, near Abda, not far from the Austrian border, twenty-one of the weakest prisoners (including Radnóti) who could no longer walk were put in horse-drawn carts by their Hungarian guards under the command of Sergeant András Tálas, who failed to deliver the prisoners to a hospital and shot them instead; they were buried in a mass grave. Tálas was executed for war crimes by the communists in 1947, but after the fall of communism the common grave of those executed by the communist regime was honored by the right-wing Hungarian government as a site of national martyrdom, though under public pressure the name of Tálas was removed from the monument.[49]

In 1946 the bodies of the prisoners were exhumed and Radnóti's corpse was identified. The Bor notebook was found in one of his pockets with the smeared, barely illegible inscription in English and four other languages, asking the finder to forward this notebook, which

> [...] contains the poems of the Hungarian poet Miklós Radnóti, to Mr. Gyula Ortutay, Budapest University Lecturer, Budapest, VII. Horánszky u. 1.I. Thank you in anticipation.[50]

In 1946, Radnóti's widow Fanni published *Tajtékos ég* (Frothy Sky), a collection that included five poems Radnóti entrusted to his friend Sándor Szilai in the camps at Bor and which Szilai published in liberated Romania in October 1944. Later, in 1971, a facsimile of the Bor notebook (*Bor notesz*) was published and became a major part of the canon of Radnóti's verse. Indeed, Radnóti's biographer and translator Győző Ferencz claims that it is Radnóti's last poems found on his body that secured his reputation as a leading Hungarian poet at home and abroad, indeed one of the few Hungarian poets known internationally and ranked with major Anglophone authors— Ferencz compares Radnóti with American confessional poets[51]; George Szires compares his poems with the adaptations of Virgil's eclogues by Louis MacNeice.[52] This might seem paradoxical in view of the stigmatization which the poet suffered as a Jew (in March 1943, for example, he was publicly humiliated by a Hungarian officer). However, his execution joined poetry and biography in a realization of his consistent self-image throughout his poetry of a Hungarian poet-martyr. Nevertheless, he was killed as a Jew, not as a poet. As a Jew he could not be considered a Hungarian poet under the fascists. Under the current right-wing régime, he has been rehabilitated as a Hungarian war poet, but, like a number of Hungarian survivor poets, he is not read or taught in Hungary as a Holocaust victim.[53]

To the end, Radnóti had in mind an addressee—the Hungarian public— and did not lose sight of his muse, his beloved Fanni, who represented his faith in love when death was all around. Yet what can be said about the poetic identity of an author whose existence has been eliminated and whose cultural identity has been rejected? Does the "I" of the poetic voice have any subjecthood in such circumstances? The philosopher Jennifer Anna Gosetti-Ferencei tries to resolve the paradox of a writing self that is condemned to die by turning to Maurice Blanchot's *Writing of Destruction*.[54] Yet Blanchot's notion of the author's self-effacement in a death that is anticipated in disaster depends on resistance to destruction, whereas, as we have seen, Radnóti embraced the poet's death in his poetry long before the Holocaust and inscribed his own death as a martyr-witness before the death march, though not as a Jewish victim, as Sue Vice assumes.[55] Contrary to what Gosetti-Ferencei states, Celan was similarly expecting his death in the labor battalions and only later survived to memorialize the experience in his poetry. Both Radnóti and Celan were writing the disaster as it happened, but it is precisely the reduction of self to the essential voice of the poet who sacrifices himself to guard the truth, a convention of Hungarian poetry, that enables Radnóti to synchronize versification and lyrical form with the reality which denies the poet's existence and destroys the values of poetry. Celan, on the other hand, as we have seen, called on poetic traditions to give new, often ironic, meaning to their use in a horrific reality and in so doing complicated the relationship of the poetic voice with the language in which he wrote, creating a poetics of negativity.[56] In both cases, nevertheless, the poetic voice facing annihilation of self, whether the dehumanizing effect of imprisonment and forced labor or the prospect of imminent execution, expresses a distancing from the self whose effacement is being witnessed. Writing about literary testimony by Holocaust survivors, Dana Amir speaks of the resulting gap between writer and autobiographical self,[57] but the effect is surely all the more disturbing when the gap is unassimilable after the extermination of the author who exists only in the reading experience. Only the poem witnesses the death of the author.

For Radnóti, death was a fulfillment of his writing, and life was a temporary reprieve, not a form of exile as it was for Kafka. It is not in the spirit of the "Penal Colony" that Radnóti writes in his diary in August 1939, "One writes less and less. Yet one writes, not knowing whether it is one's own death sentence one is etching on the paper."[58] Rather, Radnóti was expressing his resistance to his increasing marginalization and eventual silencing under the darkening clouds of fascism and war through his insistence on writing what might be his death sentence. Destruction and death are immanent in nature in Radnóti's poetic universe, not separate or uncertain as for Blanchot; it is an existential reason to write and not a threat to the poetic self. Radnóti's rage is reserved not for the disaster but for what the disaster represents; he transcends the reign of evil in this world in a vision of redemption both in nature and in love.

5

Władysław Szlengel's Ghetto Poems: Writing to the Dead

Daniel Feldman

Writing from the "Other Side"

Poetry written during the Holocaust constitutes not only *poesis in extremis* but also the extremes of poetry. It is literature that exists at the limits of what language can be. The poetry of Władysław Szlengel, the so-called "bard of the Warsaw Ghetto,"[1] exemplifies this distinction. In the last nine months of his life from September 1942 through May 1943 Szlengel wrote poems that aspire to go beyond the conventions of aesthetic speech and to forge in poetry a new form of living, or at least a lasting mark of having lived. Szlengel's verse is the ultimate metonym: poetry not as a metaphor for life but as an extension or condensation of it, the sole surviving sign of having once lived. Szlengel's ghetto poems offer the most immediate expression of what it was like to live at the very edge of the precipice, at the border of near-certain death. There is nothing symbolic in his poetry. Instead, his poems convey concrete, visceral knowledge of massacre and a raw, emotional encounter with unremitting terror shared by nearly all who remained in the ghetto after the decimation of Warsaw Jewry in the *Grossaktion* (Great Deportation) of summer 1942, when between 265,000 and 300,000 ghetto inmates were sent to their deaths in Treblinka. Witnesses who read Szlengel's poems in the ghetto recall the transcendent poignancy of his writing. "These words soaked into my blood with this terrible fear of undeserved death waiting everywhere," ghetto survivor Halina Birenbaum remembers of Szlengel's poems.[2] "They were a living reflection of our feelings, thoughts, needs, pains, and merciless fight for every moment of life," Birenbaum recounts. "The poems still live inside me."[3] Szlengel's texts were read in the ghetto not as art but as a record of bare life lived at the violent extreme of human experience. Written between life and death, Szlengel's poems elide any clear line between the literary and literal.

If Szlengel's "wiersze-dokumenty" ("poem-documents"), as he called his final poetic works,[4] offer an indelible glimpse into the fateful last months of ghetto existence as it subsisted in the shadow of death, his poems also highlight the profound rupture and painful isolation entailed in writing so close to the edge of communicability. Szlengel makes it clear that his late poems could never find their intended audience, because his texts were in fact written for those already dead: "Przeglądam i segreguję wiersze pisane dla tych, których nie ma... To czytałem umarłym"[5] ("I review and arrange poems written for those who are gone... This is what I read to the dead"[6]), he states. He was writing from a place that was effectively severed from the world and addressing a readership that he could scarcely reach. Nevertheless, he yearned to be read—and remembered, especially by non-Jewish Poles whom he could glimpse from his room at the edge of the ghetto through the "okno na tamtą stronę," the "window onto the other side" that he depicts in a poem bearing that title.[7] Like the physical window in his room, Szlengel's poetry is also an aperture offering a privileged, if harrowing, view into another sphere of existence, namely the ghetto's otherworldly realm of constant fear, privation, and terror. This metaphor, however, derives not from the actual text of Szlengel's poem but as an effect from reading his poetry as literary testimony about a destroyed world. To analyze Szlengel's late writing is to engage in a dizzying reversal of the typical process of criticism by which the critic first identifies figural language in the literary text and then hews to definitive precision in interpreting the symbolic order that the text creates. Szlengel eschews figural signification altogether. Bożena Shallcross comments: "Szlengel's metonymy communicates the concrete through the most concrete."[8] Although shorn of metaphor, his writing is so thoroughly suffused with pathos that it ineluctably invites production of symbols by the reader who attempts to frame the poem's field of reference. Szlengel's physical window onto reality thus becomes our metaphorical mirror of reading, as Piotr Kilanowski notes:

> Okno Szlengla jest więc oknem janusowym, usytuowanym na progu światów, pozwalającym autorowi wyjrzeć poza mury getta i pozwalającym nam z tej strony muru, z tej strony historii, z tej strony dzielącego nas metaforycznego murka, zajrzeć do getta.[9]

> Szlengel's window is therefore a Janus window, situated on the threshold of worlds, allowing the author to look beyond the walls of the ghetto and allowing us to look into the ghetto from this side of the wall, from this side of history, from this side of the metaphorical wall separating us.

Rooted in circumstances that required no symbolic intensification, Szlengel's astringent "poem-documents" from "the other side" are beyond metaphor in their own right but rich in sites of interpretative amplification available to the postwar reader.

Whether and how his poems might be read by a postwar audience at all rather than by the murdered Jewish audience for whom he originally wrote them was one of Szlengel's abiding concerns. Speculating or perhaps even dreaming that "dziś, jutro czy za rok"[10] ("today, tomorrow, or in a year") his poems would eventually reach a general Polish audience that was spared the dire fate of the Jews, Szlengel sought to gauge just how alien his writing might strike the uninitiated reader. Vivid as his poems are, he acknowledges that his writing would likely seem opaque, even incomprehensible to anyone who did not experience the anguish, hunger, and fear that he and his fellow inmates in the Warsaw Ghetto knew far too well. He predicted that to the postwar reader his poems might appear "dla niego dalekie, egzotyczne i coraz bardziej oddalone" ("distant, exotic, and increasingly remote for him").[11] "Są wiersze, których czytelnik polski nie 'rozgryzie'" ("These are poems that the Polish reader will not decipher or 'crack'"), he wrote in an apologia addressed "To the Polish Reader."[12] He feared being forgotten but did not relish being remembered only to be misunderstood.

The specter of incommunicability haunted Szlengel. Several of his late poems urgently demand an audience: with God, with the Nazis, with the dead, with future generations, or with his former Polish friends on the other side of the wall. In "Telefon" ("Telephone") he describes sitting in a ghetto office beside one of the ghetto's precious telephones and longing to call "kogoś po tamtej stronie"[13] ("someone on the other side").[14] Access to a phone is not a figurative trope but another historic reference, a special perquisite of Szlengel's ignominious tenure as a member of the ghetto's reviled *Jüdischer Ordnungsdienst*, the Jewish police force.[15] He evidently served in the Jewish police from the time the ghetto was sealed in autumn 1940 until the onset of mass deportations in summer 1942, when he resigned his position in moral abhorrence, a decision he documented in another poem titled "Pożegnanie z czapką" ("Farewell to My Cap").[16] Szlengel, incidentally, is the only member of the force known to have written poetry in the ghetto.[17] The telephone in Szlengel's poem of that name facilitates the author's yearning to project his voice telephonically—literally, to sound his voice from afar—as a means of relieving his cultural solitude behind the ghetto walls. Like poetry, the phone has the potential to spread his words across space by bridging the gap to the other side:

Z sercem rozbitem i chorem,
z myślami o tamtej stronie
siedziałem sobie wieczorem
przy telefonie—[18]

> With a sick and broken heart,
> with all my thoughts on the other side
> I was sitting alone
> next to the telephone.[19]

Yet the tantalizing telephone only frustrates the poet's desire for fellowship and stymies any opportunity for engagement, as the speaker realizes with dismay that he has no one to call. Since the outset of the war, he and his erstwhile non-Jewish friends have been set on radically different paths. Szlengel may possess the necessary means of communication, but he has no interlocutor with whom to share it:

> I nagle myślę: na Boga—
> nie mam właściwie do kogo,
> w roku trzydziestym dziewiątym
> poszedłem inną drogą—
> Rozeszły się nasze drogi,
> przyjaźni ugrzęzły w toni
> i teraz, no proszę—nie mam
> nawet do kogo zadzwonić.[20]
> Suddenly I realize
> my God there is no one I can call.
> In nineteen thirty-nine I followed
> a different road.
> Our paths have parted and all
> the friendships on the other side sank deeply
> out of sight. Now you see
> there is not one I can call.[21]

Even with the exceptional privilege of a phone at his fingertips, Szlengel cannot reach anyone on the outside. Divergent historical fates have put Jews and Poles on opposite sides of a conceptual divide. Instead, he addresses his poetry to those inside the walls.

Szlengel's precocious recognition of the gulf that would make the ghetto experience and his representation of it virtually illegible to anyone who was not there reflects the significance of his poetry as the literary paragon of the *Oyneg Shabbos* archive, the underground documentation project led by Emanuel Ringelblum that preserved many of Szlengel's poems among a wealth of other documents from the Warsaw Ghetto. Although his service in the ghetto police undermined his credibility and disqualified him from active membership in this clandestine archival operation, Szlengel's writing was included in the two tranches of the collection recovered after the Holocaust. The third part of the archive, buried in early April 1943, was never found. It may have included Szlengel's last poems written on the eve of the Ghetto Uprising.

Writing in late January and early February 1943, Szlengel already anticipated the difficulty that the postwar reader would face in comprehending the misery of the ghetto. Despite the postwar reader's epistemological advantage of superior knowledge of what ultimately was to ensue, general understanding of the war's historical course would not necessarily translate into comprehension of what the victims endured. On the contrary, the scale of the atrocities would make the ghetto residents' experience of distress inscrutable to anyone who was not there. His poems, Szengel feared, might present an impenetrable "dżungla, w której niełatwo znajdziecie drogę"[22] ("jungle in which you won't easily find a path").[23] Addressing the postwar reader, Szlengel writes, "Tematyka i rekwizyty są dla was obce i niezrozumiałe, wymagają wielu komentarzy. Są słowa i pointy, których głębie i przeraźliwy smutek poznać można po przygotowaniu, jakie dać może tylko życie za murem i pod pejczem esesmanów"[24] ("The themes and the props are foreign and incomprehensible to you. They require numerous comments. There are words and meanings whose depths and terrible sadness can be recognized only after living behind the wall under the whip of the SS man").[25] Szlengel's recognition that the ghetto wall that physically divided him from his beloved Warsaw also comprised a yawning epistemological chasm that placed him at an impassable extreme from postwar readers epitomizes the insight at the heart of the *Oyneg Shabbos* initiative, as conceived by Ringelblum: counterintuitively, the eviscerating magnitude of the Holocaust meant that it had to be documented immediately and accurately before it was effaced by time.[26] Even amidst the devastation of the Nazi massacre, Ringelblum and Szlengel understood that the enormity of the catastrophe would warp memory and distort perception. Rather than sharpening recollections, time would only exacerbate the problem of representing the Holocaust. In his magisterial history of the *Oyneg Shabbos* archive, Samuel Kassow writes, "Ringelblum understood the need to encourage writing 'from inside the event,' writing that would not be skewed by the distorting lens of retrospective recollection."[27] The logic of the Holocaust demanded that it be portrayed while it occurred, since focusing on the Final Solution's horrifying end would make it virtually impossible to grasp what it felt like while it was in progress. "The 'before' would be erased by the 'after,'" Ringelblum believed.[28] Appreciating literature's potential to preserve the present, Ringelbum insisted that poetry be included in the archive. Szlengel obliged. Motivated by a sense of mission to record the suffocating atmosphere of those desperate days, he wrote with increasing speed and conviction as he redefined himself and his poetics. The war was the terrible catalyst for his best creative work. Only during the genocide was poetry tantamount to life; afterward it would be mere literature.

From Wit to Witness

That the dread and anger felt by the last inhabitants of the Warsaw Ghetto found unexpected voice in the poetry of Władysław Szlengel is startling. A prolific contributor to Polish cabaret and musical theater in the late 1930s, Szlengel was a young Polish-Jewish writer of popular songs and light verse whose prewar life is known only in sketchy terms due to a dearth of surviving documents. He was born in Warsaw (or possibly Łódź, as Ringelblum intimates) likely in 1912 (or 1914). He married a fellow secular Jew whose name is unknown. He does not seem to have had children. Szlengel grew up in Warsaw and closely identified with the city's literary scene associated with the iconoclastic, informal poetics of the interwar *Skamander* group led by Julian Tuwim. Together with his wife he spent the early months of the war in Białystok, where he served as literary director of a regional theater. He apparently participated as a soldier in the failed defense against the Nazi and Soviet invasions of Poland in September 1939 and returned in 1940 to Warsaw, where he moved into a tenement building that was incorporated into the Warsaw Ghetto in November 1940. Until the Great Deportation in summer 1942, Szlengel was widely celebrated in the ghetto as a poetic wit whose well-known sarcastic poems and uproarious cabaret performances offered moments of rare levity and comic relief from the dire circumstances in the ghetto. He was the unparalleled leading jester in an urban jail of unrelenting sorrow. His humorous songs and ditties were performed in the ghetto by cultural luminaries, such as the singer Wiera Gran and pianist Władysław Szpilman. However, his comic genius was expressed most prominently in his role as head writer, host, and star of *Żywy Dziennik* (*Live Journal*), a parodic weekly revue of ghetto life and what Roskies calls the "trendiest news source of the ghetto" presented before ghetto elites at the prestigious Café Sztuka (Art Cafe).[29] The show offered a humorous sendup of ghetto events with performances that continued until days before the Great Deportation. Little of this live comedic work survives, but a representative sample of Szlengel's satirical poems from the pre-deportation period was collected in the first tranche of the *Oyneg Shabbos* archive.

Only after deportations to Treblinka commenced did Szlengel's creative focus shift from comic diversion and sarcastic detachment to desperate documentation and direct engagement. He became the mouthpiece for the ghetto inmates' terrifying experience, borne equally by writer and reader, of living on the threshold of death. Though still acerbic and incisive, his writing changed as he assumed the role of literary witness. Szlengel's surviving poetry from the final months of both his life and the ghetto's existence reflects what victims were saying to themselves. This was a poetics of "absolute metonymic precision"[30] imbued with a "sense of immediacy and urgency."[31] In an essay appraising Szlengel's role as "Der dikhter fun geto," the "bard of the ghetto,"[32] Ringelblum writes:

Zeyne lider geshriben in poylish zenen geven zeyer populer in geto. Zey hobn obgegeben di shtimungen fun geto. Di lider zeyne flegn deklamirt un retsitirt veren oyf farsheydene farveylungen. Zey hobn gevandert fun hant tsu hant in opshriftn oyf mashin oder hectografirte. Nisht gekukt deroyf, vos di lider zeynen kinstlerish geshtanen nisht hoykh, hobn zey aber shtark oysgenumen, gerirt di tsuherer bis trern, veyl zey zeynen geven aktuele, barirt temes, mit velkhe dos geto hot gelebt, gefibert.[33]

His poems written in Polish were very popular in the ghetto. They conveyed the moods of the ghetto. The poems were declaimed and recited on various occasions. They were passed from hand to hand in typed and hectographed copies. Although the poems were artistically mediocre, they were strongly embraced and moved those who heard them to tears, because they were topical, touching on problems that the ghetto lived and feared.[34]

Although Ringelblum did not hold Szlengel's verse in high esteem aesthetically, he did admire the poet's ability to achieve what was most elusive in the *Oyneg Shobbos* archive: faithful depiction of how people "felt as they lost their loved ones, witnessed the destruction of their community, and awaited the probability of a painful death."[35] By accurately conveying the "moods of the ghetto," as Ringelblum put it, Szlengel's lyric verse from late 1942 and early 1943 offers a human record of the unfolding calamity as it was felt in the ghetto during its fateful final months.

Writing during one of the bleakest periods of the Holocaust in Poland, Szlengel sensed this darkly sublime metamorphosis in his art. On July 15, 1942, precisely one week before the start of the Great Deportation, when rumors were already flying about an impending Nazi operation, Szlengel wrote a poem to accompany an invitation to a children's performance issued by Janusz Korczak, the famed pedagogue and children's rights advocate who was also director of the *Dom Sierot,* the ghetto orphanage. Korczak sought to prepare the children under his care for their imminent deaths by staging a play in which they performed a premature death.[36] Various ghetto dignitaries and patrons of the orphanage were asked to attend. The invitation closed with a short poem by Szlengel suggesting that audience members could expect a transcendent artistic experience: "Coś więcej niż tekst—bo nastrój;/ Coś więcej niż emocja—bo przeżycie;/Coś więcej niż aktorzy—bo dzieci"[37] ("Something more than text—because of atmosphere;/Something more than emotion—because of experience;/Something more than actors—because of children"). Doomed children performing the parts of children facing their death were not ordinary actors, and texts written in this desperate atmosphere were hardly poems. The gap between the literary and the literal, the symbolic and the singular was growing smaller as art transmuted into something different under the extreme conditions of the ghetto. Szlengel and his poems would soon become "coś więcej," "something more," than before, but the change did not occur at once, as Szlengel's next poem regarding Korczak indicates.

Three weeks later, when Korczak was ordered to deliver the nearly two hundred children in his orphanage to the *Umschlagplatz,* the assembly point for deportation, Szlengel chronicled the event in a poem titled "Kartka z dziennika 'akcji,'" ("A Page from the *Aktion* Diary"). This self-conscious hybrid of elegiac poem and public diary entry immortalizes the somber procession of Korczak, his staff, and the children, through the streets of the ghetto. The text tries to elicit a shred of redemptive hope from the devastating scene:

> Dziś widziałem Janusza Korczaka,
> Jak szedł z dziećmi w ostatnim pochodzie,
> A dzieci były czyściutko ubrane,
> Jak na spacer niedzielny w ogrodzie.
> [...]
> Pomyślałem w tej chwili zwyczajnej,
> Dla Europy nic przecież niewartej,
> Że on dla nas w historię w tej chwili
> Najpiękniejszą wpisuje tu kartę.[38]
> I saw Janusz Korczak today go
> with his orphans in the last procession.
> In their best clean clothes the children
> walked as if in a park on Sunday.
> [...]
> At this moment, completely ordinary
> and meaningless for Europe, I thought
> that Janusz Korczak is writing
> the most beautiful page of our history.[39]

This was perhaps the last time Szlengel attempted to valorize the Holocaust by mining it for allegorical meaning. When the relentless wave of deportations finally came to an end on Yom Kippur (the Day of Atonement), September 21, 1942, Szlengel, like nearly everyone who remained in the ghetto, understood that nothing could redeem what they had just witnessed. There would be no further attempt to imagine the martyrdom of the dead as gloriously "writing/the most beautiful page of our history." On the contrary, the dwindling number of Jews still alive in the ghetto were urgently called upon to resist however they could, in part by recording the horrific history being written there every day.

In the interregnum of mass murder that prevailed between the end of the Great Deportation in September 1942 and the start of the Ghetto Uprising on April 19, 1943, Szlengel was transformed. John Carpenter writes of

Szlengel: "His sense of irony and satire," always refined, evolved "into something new, very powerful, and tragic. More artistic development, and change, were compressed into the last years of his life than most writers achieve in a lifetime."[40] This change was evident in the cycle of poems that Szlengel compiled in January and early February 1943. Prompted by fears of a renewed wave of liquidations, Szlengel wrote in response to minute perturbations to the ghetto's fragile equilibrium. On January 8, 1943, SS troops raided the brush shop in the Warsaw Ghetto, one of the largest workshops still in operation. The Nazi operation sowed panic throughout the shrunken ghetto. Ten days later, in the early morning of January 18, SS forces again entered the ghetto, this time to conduct a larger roundup of Jews. Having survived the terror of the previous year's massive deportations, the remaining ghetto inhabitants reacted with immediate alarm and action. Many hid. Some fought back. A small group of young Jews brazenly killed several German officers, marking the first organized acts of armed resistance in the ghetto. The events of that fortnight in January 1943 shifted the course of history in the Warsaw Ghetto by setting it on a path toward armed Jewish rebellion, a campaign embraced by most of the remaining ghetto inhabitants.[41] They well understood what awaited them. The brief reprieve they had enjoyed since the pause of the previous year's mass deportations was over: the Germans intended to resume deportations from the ghetto in order to kill off the last remnant of what had once been the largest Jewish community in Europe. The remaining 60,000 ghetto residents were the traumatized and bereaved last inhabitants of an enclosed city within a city that had once numbered up to 450,000 Jews. These last residents had eluded years of devastating disease, deprivation, and death. Yet they knew what lay in store. They were not survivors; they were next.

Szlengel prepared for the end by hastily compiling a volume of poems that would constitute his final testament and enduring masterpiece. He recognized that his time was limited: "Czas najwyższy uporządkować papiery"[42] ("It is high time I arranged my papers").[43] He prefaced the collection with a poetic essay titled "Co czytałem umarłym" ("What I Read to the Dead") in which he elucidates his motivations with a sense of ethical responsibility that far transcends conventional aesthetic preoccupations: "Nie chcę zostawiać tylko cyfr dla statystyki, chcę przyszłą historię wzbogacić (złe słowo) w przyczynki, dokumenty i ilustracje"[44] ("I don't want to leave just numbers for statistics, I want to enrich [wrong word] future history with small additions, documents, and illustrations").[45] In order to go beyond sterile statistics, Szlengel wrote "poem-documents" that bear witness to the "współlokatorzy, sąsiedzi, przyjaciele, towarzysze dyskusji, często mimowolni współtwórcy tego, co ten tom zawiera"[46] ("roommates, neighbors, friends, companion in discussions, often involuntary co-authors of the contents of this volume")[47] who were the poems' intended audience. All of them are gone, deported in the latest Nazi raid. "Towarzysze mojej wędrówki odeszli, a wiersze stały się w przeciągu jednej godziny wierszami, które czytałem umarłym"[48] ("The companions of my journey have passed away, and within the span of a single hour the poems became poems that I read to the dead").[49]

He fulfills his pledge to humanize his murdered companions by naming them and offering brief sketches of each one. Even as he confronts the historical futility of his effort, he says that he owes it to his friends to bear testimony to their lives:

> Imiona—Ziuta, Asia, Eli, Fania, Sioma, czy to wam coś mówi? Nic. Ludzie. Niepotrzebni. Było takich tysiące. Tysiącami szli na plac, tysiącami byli bici pejczami, odrywani od rodzin, ładowani do wagonów. Gazowani. Nieważni. Statystyka ich nie wymieni, żaden krzyż nie odznaczy. Imiona. Puste dźwięki. Dla mnie to ludzie żywi, bliscy, dotykalni, to życia, które znam, to szmaty zdarzeń, w których byłem. Te tragedie przerastające siłę odczuwań dla mnie ważniejsze od losów Europy.[50]

> The names—Ziuta, Asya, Eli, Fania, Shoma, do they tell you anything? Nothing. People. Not needed. There were thousands of people like that. By thousands they walked to the *Platz*, by thousands they were beaten with whips, torn away from their families, packed into train wagons. Gassed. Unimportant. Statistics won't mention them, no cross will honor them. Names. Empty sounds. For me these people are living, close, palpable, lives that I know, numberless events in which I participated. These tragedies beyond the power of feeling are for me more important than the fate of Europe.[51]

Szlengel was trying to be as specific as possible. The fate of Europe was an abstraction, even a metaphor. His friends and companions in the ghetto, by contrast, were real. With this insight, Szlengel began to search for a poetic style that would preserve the individuality of the victims and oppose the murderous anonymity and meaningless statistics of those "odrywani od rodzin, ładowani do wagonów. Gazowani" ("torn away from their families, packed into train wagons. Gassed"). To Szlengel, the dead were individual personalities with particular identities and narratives. To the Nazis, however, they were faceless numbers, metaphorical representatives of a malignant threat to the master race; Jews were not human but symbols in a terrible myth. The Nazis took individuals and turned them into ciphers, impersonal figures in a collective racial conflict. This is the obliterating "substitutive force"[52] of the Holocaust that Szlengel resists through poems focused with total "precision and specificity"[53] on real people and factual things that he depicts metonymically as individual parts of a contiguous whole rather than as metaphorical archetypes in a symbolic order of interchangeable figures.

With time quickly elapsing before what was left of the ghetto would be liquidated, Szlengel diligently pursued his goal of crafting a literary poetics apposite to his dire situation and opposed to the "substitutive" logic of the Nazis. Despite contending with circumstances of incredible adversity, Szlengel anticipates Roman Jakobson's theory of "the twofold character of language" by intuiting a tension between the "two polar figures of speech, metaphor and metonymy."[54] Szlengel acutely grasped the necessity of forging a non-figural form of poetry aligned not with the metaphorical pole of selection and substitution but with the metonymic pole of connection and relationship. His poems insist on the power of metonymy, the hallmark of narrative prose more often than that of verse, to posit kinship between discrete parts of an interrelated whole. In writing that disdains both mathematical and metaphorical figures, Szlengel innovates a poetics that searches for connection and continuity amid conditions of deadly disruption and dissociation. He turns away from the symbolic order of alienating numbers and allegorical substitution to cling to language as a medium of shared meaning and dialogic communication in the hope that his poems might overcome the isolation and separation that threatened to cut him off forever from the literary exchange of experience and emotion.

This is the poetic and ethical force behind Szlengel's final poems. In verse devoid of metaphor, he attempts to salvage his dead friends from the oblivion of anonymous statistics. This was his way of bearing witness to the irreplaceable, non-figural specificity of his companions' lives. He would bequeath them a chance at posterity through the strength of his writing—if only his words could evade oblivion, too. His poems thus stage a desperate contest between memory and erasure reflecting the risk that his poems and the people they evoke might be consigned to amnesia. Fully aware that the Nazi onslaught meant the destruction of individuals and all memory of them, Szlengel sought to create a poetics offering final tribute to "close, palpable lives" retrieved from the sadistic erasure of statistics. Structured by metonymic speech, Szlengel's poems are themselves the surviving metonym, the part that remains of a broader society rich with intrinsic vitality; his texts, buried under the ghetto, stand in for the author and his friends, all of whom were buried without a grave. Szlengel's late poems, including "Rzeczy" ("Things"), "Pomnik" ("A Monument"), "Mała stacja Treblinki" ("Little Station of Treblinka"), "Paszporty" ("Passports"), and "Już czas" ("It is Time") were saved by being hidden under the Warsaw Ghetto in the second part of the *Oyneg Shabbos* archive. Elsewhere he graphically depicts this collective undertaking of ghetto residents burrowing underground—no mere metaphor, as this was literally an underground society, and Szlengel was its preeminent poet excavating poetry from the suffocating mood.

Going Underground

In "What I Read to the Dead" Szlengel documents the ghetto's feverish subterranean activity in advance of the approaching rebellion. Bunkers were prepared, tunnels dug, and life became atavistic as the remaining ghetto residents turned into "zwierzęta ryją prymitywne kretowiska" ("animals burrowing into primitive molehills").[55] This description of the nocturnal excavation inside the ghetto preempts by several months Miłosz's metaphorical "guardian mole slowly boring a tunnel" in "Biedny chrześcijanin patrzy na Getto" ("A Poor Christian Looks at the Ghetto").[56] Szlengel portrays the preparations as an assemblage of supplies:

> Światło, kable podziemne, przebijanie wylotów, znów cegły, sznury, piach... Dużo piachu... Piach... Nary, prycze. Aprowizacja na miesiące.
>
> Przekreśla się elektryczność, wodociągi, wszystko. Dwadzieścia wieków przekreślonych przez pejcz esesmana. Epoka jaskiniowa. Kaganki. Studnie wiejskie. Długa noc. Ludzie wracają pod ziemię.[57]
>
> Lighting, underground cables, tunneling to exits. Again bricks, ropes, sand... Lots of sand... Sand. Stretchers, bunks. Provisions for months.
>
> Electricity, water pipes, everything is ruled out. Twenty centuries struck out by an SS man's whip. The time of the cavemen. Oil lamps. Country wells. A long night. People go back underground.[58]

Szlengel's description offers no metaphors but a series of metonyms portraying the construction of bunkers under the ghetto. Elements of this account draw on pieces of connective material: wire, cables, ropes, pipes. As the ghetto residents build the network of tunnels in which they will live out their final days, Szlengel constructs a connective poetic idiom with which to encompass the oppressive ordeal through its separate parts: privation, anger, grief, death, and resistance. He laments the absurd historic regression by which the last ghetto residents must revert to "the time of the cavemen" living underground, but it was only thanks to such subterranean preservation, particularly the interment of archival papers by the *Oyneg Shabbos* operatives, that most of Szlengel's poems survived.

As documents in the secret *Oyneg Shabbos* archive, Szlengel's poems are themselves part of a larger whole, albeit an anomalous part. Much of the archive consists of reports, diaries, testimonies, and print artifacts documenting ghetto life. Ringelblum harbored an "innate belief that nothing was 'unimportant,'"[59] and therefore, he left instructions to collect literary work, as well, but the bias in the archive unquestionably skewed toward eyewitness testimonies, official documents, and quantitative data.

One of the archive's essayists, Gustawa Jarecka, expressed the position held by many contributors to the project: "Statistics and official proclamations are the fundamental documents of the [Great Deportation]. Written accounts can only provide some additional details about events and specific incidents. But basically nothing is more expressive than statistics!"[60] Jarecka articulated a prevalent distrust of words that was diametrically opposed to Szlengel's skepticism toward statistics: "The desire to write is as strong as the repugnance of words. We hate words because they too often have served as a cover for emptiness or meanness. We despise them for they pale in comparison with the emotion tormenting us."[61] Szlengel had a different view. He never lost his faith in words. He firmly believed "that people who needed poetry, even this poetry, hadn't lost everything yet."[62] Indeed, when everything else had been taken from the victims, language is what remained. Words were all that was left of people who vanished.

Szlengel's faith in poetry as a linguistic testament to his murdered companions' lives is evident in "Rzeczy" ("Things") and "Pomnik" ("A Monument"), two poems in which words stand in for things that in turn stand in for individuals who stand in for all the victims. Both "Things" and "A Monument" exemplify Szlengel's poetics of resisting dehumanization by adhering to a metonymy of vivid memorialization. The chain of relatedness linking word to object to person in these texts recapitulates the capacity of speech to forge connection through the relationship between part and whole as well as between speaker and addressee, signifier and signified, past and present.

"Things" is a litany of sundry household items and possessions that Jews took with them to the Warsaw Ghetto. The "things" are variously expensive and ordinary, utilitarian and frivolous. They are chosen not for their metaphorical value but for their representation of the comprehensive scope of the Jews' prewar lives:

> Z Hożej i Wspólnej, i Marszałkowskiej
> jechały wozy... wozy żydowskie...
> meble, stoły i stołki,
> walizeczki, tobołki,
> kufry, skrzynki i bety,
> garnitury, portrety,
> pościel, garnki, dywany
> i draperie ze ściany.[63]
> From Hoza Street and Marszałkowska
> carts were moving, Jewish carts:
> furniture, tables and chairs,
> suitcases, bundles
> and chests, boxes and bedding,
> suits and portraits,
> pots, linen and wall hangings.[64]

The catalog of possessions brought to the ghetto links the impoverished inmates to the normalcy of their former lives. The metonymy of concrete objects thus creates a continuity of identity against the ruptures of expulsion to the ghetto and the daily struggle there for survival. Nonetheless, the fraught connection to "before" weakens with each successive displacement as the Jews jettison a share of their "things" every time they are squeezed into increasingly cramped sections of the contracting ghetto:

> A ze Śliskiej na Niską
> znów jechało to wszystko.
> Meble, stoły i stołki,
> walizeczki, tobołki.
> Pościel, garnki—psze panów,
> ale już bez dywanów.
> Po platerach ni znaku
> i już nie ma wiśniaków,
> garniturów ni betów,
> i słoików, portretów.
> Już zostały na Śliskiej.[65]
> And from Śliska Street to Niska everything
> all over again went moving:
> Furniture, tables and chairs,
> suitcases and bundles,
> and pots—gents that's it.
> Now there is no carpet
> of silverware not a sign,
> no cherry brandy this time.
> No suits or boots
> or jars or portraits.
> Already all these trifles
> were left behind on Śliska.[66]

As the poem progresses and the ghetto constricts, more objects are abandoned, reflecting the gradual stripping away of the Jews' humanity and the destruction of their lives. The loss of possessions parallels a loss of self and autonomy; the remaining Jews are literally dispossessed both of their property and their right to life. The ghetto decreases, its inhabitants move from one apartment to another, smaller one, and the litany of objects gets shorter as conditions become more desperate. There is no longer space or need for many of the discarded belongings:

> Nie ma mebli i stołków,
> garnków oraz tobołków.
> Zaginęły czajniki,

książki, bety, słoiki.[67]
No furniture or stools,
no jugs or bundles.
Teapots have vanished,
books, boots, storage jars.[68]

Cherished belongings become unnecessary, discarded chattel, just as Nazi ideology deemed their Jewish owners to be expendable and "niepotrzebni" ("not needed"). The indispensability of Szlengel's verse, however, lies in its ability to stand in the way of the Nazi attempt to eliminate belongings and belonging—culminating in denial of the Jews' kinship with humanity—by asserting the persistence of relationship between the victims and their former lives, represented here through the trappings of mundane domesticity, the geography of the Warsaw streetscape, and the language of grief that connects the everyday losses of the ghetto to a profound, evolving tragedy. "Things" offers both an homage to the victims' prewar lives and a monument to the owners' enduring humanity; the victims' suffered the loss of their objects but were never reduced to things. As Shallcross notes, the poem juxtaposes the persistence of abandoned belongings with the Nazi attempt to erase their former owners: "The metonymic suggestiveness of the detritus does not allow the lingering human presence, in its everydayness, to be entirely erased."[69] Language recovers belonging and belongings where the genocide sundered it all.

A similar logic structures "A Monument," a poem in which a Jewish woman is deported to Treblinka while her husband and son are at work in forced labor workshops. The poem opens with an ironic jab at the futility of traditional elegy in the face of pervasive pointless death:

Bohaterom—poematy, rapsody!!!
Bohaterów uczczą potomni,
na cokołach nazwiska ryte
i marmurowy pomnik.
[…]
Zostaną po Wielkich Legendy,
że tacy byli Ogromni,
mit zakrzepnie i—będzie
Pomnik.
A kto wam opowie, Przyszli
nie spiż i nie mitu temat—
że JĄ zabrali—zabili…
i że JEJ nie ma…[70]
To the heroes, poems! Rhapsodies!
Future generations will honor the heroes
with marble monuments,

names engraved on a plinth.
[...]
Legends will be made about the Great Ones—
that they were Gigantic.
Myths will be set in stone, there will be a
Monument.
But you of the future, who will tell you
not the bronze, not the myth—
that they took Her away, they killed Her.
That She is no longer alive.[71]

Heroes are accorded rhapsodies and tributes of art. Enduring monuments of stone speak for the legendary dead. But the death of a single Jew taken from her kitchen as she stood by the stove is deprived such glory; instead, her monument is more modest and concrete:

Na półce milczący,
zimny i martwy Jej garnek.
[...]
Będzie patrzył i nie zapomni...
Tam Matki wystygły garnek
JEJ POMNIK.[72]
On the shelf, silent—
cold and lifeless—stands her pot.
[...]
He will look, and he won't forget:
There, now cold,
stands mother's pot,
HER MONUMENT.[73]

The pot, enshrined only through the poet's word, serves as the sole metonym of the woman's life. The old poetic forms of mythic encomium no longer cohere: the Holocaust, with its incalculable death and gratuitous dehumanization, demanded a new poetics of irony and utilitarian specificity encapsulated in the household object that stands in for the murdered individual. The amalgam of irony and colloquial speech recalls Tuwim's enduring influence over Szlengel,[74] but the poem also reflects the innovation of Szlengel's poetics in eschewing all metaphorical symbolism. The "pot as a solitary material sign is not an empty and abstract item," Shallcross writes; instead, "Szlengel endows the object, which, during the woman's life, embodied nothing more than its use value, with a commemorative function."[75] The poetics of Szlengel's ghetto poetry invests real things, including the most humble objects, with the capacity to take on monumental importance as surrogate relics of martyrdom, since there was nothing else that remained of the dead. To Szlengel, grand gestures were inconceivable, even risible. Objects were all that were left of the victims' lives, and when even the objects were obliterated, only words remained. This is how Szlengel adapted the metonymy of his poetics to total annihilation.

If "A Monument" is a tableau of private anguish, a scene of personal tragedy stripped down to its bare essentials, "Little Station of Treblinka" applies the same poetic technique to the collective fate of Warsaw's Jews. A simple statement of basic facts and spare, unadorned elements, the poem offers an astonishing index of how much Szlengel and the Jews in the ghetto knew or imagined about the destination of the transports and what awaited them there.[76] An obscure rural rail station is portrayed with haunting simplicity:

> A stacja jest maleńka
> i rosną trzy choinki
> i napis jest zwyczajny:
> tu stacja Treblinki.
> I nie ma nawet kasy
> ani bagażowego,
> za milion nie dostaniesz
> biletu powrotnego.[77]
> The station is tiny.
> Three fir trees grow side by side.
> The sign at the front is ordinary—
> this is Treblinka station.
> There isn't even
> a ticket office. No porters.
> No one can buy a return ticket
> even for a million.[78]

The menace of the place is expressed through its spectral absence: "Nie ma... ani" ("there isn't... no"). No one returns from this forlorn place of nothingness. Erasure and silence belie the atrocity that occurred adjacent to this unassuming station. Into this void Szlengel interjects an angry statement of poetic irony and testimonial knowledge. We know, he makes clear:

> I milczy słup stacyjny,
> i milczą trzy choinki,
> i milczy czarny napis,
> że... stacja Treblinki.
> I tylko wisi z dawna
> (reklama w każdym razie)
> zniszczony stary napis:
> Gotujcie na gazie.[79]

> The station tower is silent.
> The three firs are silent.
> The black sign too is silent,
> says only Treblinka station.
> An inscription is still hanging
> Since the old days,
> (an advertisement):
> Gas is best for cooking.[80]

Where nature and the sinister rail siding itself seem to be complicit in maintaining the Nazis' silence about the secret mass murder, Szlengel uses acerbic irony and black humor rooted in prewar speech that is printed on a sign (truth in advertising) to proclaim what he and the ghetto residents incontrovertibly know: Treblinka is where Jews are being gassed to death. The joke, Adam Kowalczyk, argues, is that despite the conspiratorial silence about the gassing—"milczy... milczą... milczy" ("silent... silent... silent")— news of the ghastly murder has always been written there, inscribed on a billboard: "Okrutne jest w tym żarcie Szlengla to, że ostatnią rzeczą, jaką dostrzega podróżujący przed wkroczeniem do obozu koncentracyjnego i na krótki czas przed śmiercią, jest właśnie ten napis, który w błazeński sposób zwiastuje sposób jego uśmiercenia. I to jest właśnie czarny humor Szlengla" ("The cruel thing about Szlengel's joke is that the last thing the traveler notices before entering the concentration camp and shortly before his death is this inscription, which in a clownish way heralds his death. And this is Szlengel's black humor").[81] The joke reveals a horrible knowledge that can only be expressed with contempt.

"Little Station of Treblinka" reflects a category of knowledge without mastery but disabused of delusions. Escapees from Treblinka and other informants had brought eyewitness intelligence about Treblinka back to the Warsaw Ghetto, where it was widely circulated in the months before the uprising, but this knowledge did nothing to assuage the residents' fears.[82] To Szlengel's mind, it only made matters worse. "Najbardziej męczyło to, że wiedzieli, co ich czeka [...].Wiedzą ludzie, wiedzą" ("The worst is that they knew what awaited them [...]. People know, they know"), he wrote.[83] Ringelblum and his colleagues in the *Oyneg Shabbos* operation transcribed and circulated testimony about the Final Solution, aiming to get the facts out to the Jews and the world; Szlengel's purpose was different. His role was not to disseminate knowledge about the killing but to document how that knowledge affected the victims. "What people knew and when, and how news from the outside reached the Jews trapped inside,"[84] is a major concern of historical sociology of the Holocaust, but the poetry of the Holocaust addresses not what people knew but how it felt to know the horrifying truth. Szlengel offers a remarkable account of the painful assimilation of that dark knowledge and he categorically states that they did indeed know:

> Już wiemy wszystko. Jak się stłacza do wagonów, co się mówi i myśli w piwnicy Umschlagplatzu, jak esesmani wywabili pochowanych groźbą użycia gazów, wiemy, jak zabijano, jak zabierano obuwie i palta, jak Szmerling przyjmuje defiladę, znamy ostatnie życzenia bliskich.
> Wiemy.
> Wiemy.[85]
> We already know everything. How they cram the wagons, what people say and think in the cellar of the *Umschlagplatz,* how the SS men lured out the ones who hid with the threat of gassing. We know how they killed, how they took shoes and coats, how Szmerling greets the procession, we know the last wishes of our dear ones.
> We know.
> We know.[86]

Knowledge of one's own death is an order of knowledge unlike any other. Knowing the end before it comes represents a sort of grim clairvoyance usually vouchsafed only to God. A chasm is crossed when one's own imminent death is disclosed to a degree of near certainty. Such knowledge makes one "bogom równi" ("equal of the gods")[87] as Szlengel writes in "Za pięć dwunasta" ("Five to Twelve"). Painful as such knowledge is, it nevertheless freed Szlengel to speak with greater audacity as he assumed the authority to speak for the dead: "Przeklinam za tych, co kląć już nie mogą" ("I curse, for those who cannot curse any longer").[88] Szlengel elevated his level of address to a cosmic or prophetic challenge to God as he sought to move beyond knowledge to action.

Words as Weapons

Two final motifs in Szlengel's ghetto poetry are his willingness to accuse God of dereliction of divinity and to summon the remaining ghetto inhabitants to armed resistance. These themes emerge in several of his last poems in which he emancipates himself from any lingering faith in metaphorical illusions about God, survival, or martyrdom. In "Obrachunek z Bogiem" ("An Account with God"),[89] the speaker encounters God, who appears in the guise of an elderly man from outside the ghetto:

> Miał siwą długą brodę
> I chodził bez opaski...
> Kenkarty wprawdzie nie miał
> Bo przybył prosto z raju

Lecz miał obywatelstwo
Podobno—Urugwaju...
Wyjąłem dużą księgę
A Pan Bóg Watermana.
He had a grey long beard
And he came without an arm band...
He did not possess an ID card,
Because He arrived straight from Paradise,
But He apparently had citizenship—of Uruguay...
I took out a large book
And God, a Waterman pen.[90]

The poet sits with God to compare accounts. God arrives without the mandatory armband of ghetto inmates or the obligatory *Kennkarte* required by the Nazis. Instead, he has something more valuable, if farcical, given the context: citizenship of the neutral state of Uruguay, which potentially granted persecuted Jews refuge. The poet opens his book, perhaps a collection of his own verse, and God takes out a pen. But He has nothing to write. The empty metaphor of God's grace pales in comparison to the realia of the ghetto— armbands, identification cards, passports—and the pathos of what the poet has already composed with his own pen, namely the angry words of the poem. God is a myth; the poet and the ghetto, however, are real. The speaker has seen things that exceed what this rather obtuse old man "with a long beard" and privileged papers from outside the ghetto could possibly know. God cannot feasibly balance accounts with the speaker, who is focused not on divine mercy but on concrete exigencies. He needs a passport, not God. Another poem, "Paszporty" ("Passports"), makes this still more blunt with the anaphora of its plaintive refrain, "Chciałbym mieć paszport Urugwaju... Chciałbym mieć paszport Paragwaju... Chciałbym mieć paszport Costa Rici... Chciałbym mieć paszport Hondurasu... Chciałbym mieć paszport Urugwaju, mieć Costa Rica, Paragwaj, po to, by mieszkać spokojnie w Warszawie" ("I would like to have a passport from Uruguay... I would like to have a passport from Paraguay... I would like to have a passport of Costa Rica ... I would like to have a passport of Honduras... I would like to have a passport from Uruguay, one from Costa Rica, another from Paraguay, in order to live peacefully in Poland").[91] World geography is transmuted into the more pressing need for physical papers, forged or authentic, that hold a dim promise of escape, such as the Honduran passports that Szlengel's fellow Warsaw Ghetto poet, Itzhak Katzenelson, procured for himself and his son, as it turned out to little avail.[92] With God an empty cipher whose pen carries less weight than a counterfeit passport, Szlengel dispenses with any faith in divine intercession.

Heresy and theological derision rise to prophetic pitch in Szlengel's "Już czas" ("It is Time"), a text that indicts God with criminal negligence in a tribunal presided over by the Jewish people. The speaker uses the first-person plural voice to establish God's guilt:

> Mamy już dosyć modlitw i pokut.
> Dzisiaj Ty staniesz przed sądem naszym
> I będziesz czekał pokornie wyroku.
> Rzucim Ci w serce potężnym kamieniem
> Bluźniercze, straszne, krwawe oskarżenie.[93]
> We have had enough of prayers and penance.
> Today You will stand before our tribunal
> And humbly await a verdict.
> We will hurl at Your heart the tremendous stone
> Of a blasphemous, terrible, bloody accusation.[94]

Blasphemously, the speaker calls God to a Job-like reckoning to account for His actions, which are found wanting. The poem then condemns God to the same ghastly fate to which His people have been unjustly sentenced, although God is punished with cause:

> Za męki getta, widma szubienic
> My upodleni, my umęczeni—
> Za śmierć w Treblince, zgięci pod batem,
> Damy zapłatę!! Damy zapłatę!!
> Teraz nie ujdziesz już swego końca!
> [...]
> I kiedy kat Cię popędzi i zmusi,
> Zagna i wepchnie w komorę parową,
> Zamknie za Tobą hermetyczne wieka,
> Gorącą parą zacznie dusić, dusić,
> I będziesz krzyczał, będziesz chciał uciekać—
> Kiedy się skończą już konania męki,
> Zawloką, wrzucą, tam potwornym dołem
> Wyrwą Ci gwiazdy—złote zęby z szczęki—
> A potem spalą.
> I będziesz popiołem.
> For torture in the ghetto and the specter of the gallows,
> For death in Treblinka, bent under the whip,
> We the degraded, we the exhausted,
> We will pay You back! We will pay You back!
> You will no longer escape Your end.
> [...]
> And when the executioner prods You forward,
> Drives and crams You into the steam chamber

> Sealing the hermetic lid behind You,
> The hot steam will begin to suffocate, suffocate
> And You will cry out, You will want to flee.
> When the torture is finished and the agony of death
> They will drag You and cast You into a hideous pit,
> They will tear away Your stars—the gold teeth in Your jaw
> Then burn You.
> And You will be ash.[95]

Incensed by horrific knowledge of the ghetto and Treblinka, the poet reduces God to ash, even less than a concrete artifact of the genocide, but rather its incinerated remainder, the signal and ephemeral vestige of the Holocaust. What is left of God's bond with His people is burned on the pyres of Treblinka. Szlengel's vivid metonymy of contiguity and connection reaches its appalling logical conclusion: the relationship between God and the Jews comes to an end as they share the same horrible fate. Ash is all that remains after the Holocaust has destroyed hope even for a hallowed death.

What is left of language after all hope has been burned and life is reduced to heaps of ash? The charred remainder of speech is illustrated in "Kontratak" ("Counterattack"), a poem that strives to go beyond expressing emotion to inspiring resistance. Galvanized by the first acts of rebellion in the ghetto in January 1943, Szlengel wrote an ecstatic paean to the movement that culminated in the Warsaw Ghetto Uprising. "Counterattack" is a multi-perspectival poem written in several versions for the last ghetto residents living under extreme duress who were at the precipice of taking action intended to claim, as Alexander Donat later called it, "death with dignity and without the slightest hope of victory in life."[96]

"Counterattack" begins with another burning, that of a Nazi officer's empty cigarette box dropped with nonchalant disdain on yet another Jewish corpse:

> Sączyli krew i łzy w piaszczysty grunt,
> a "panowie"
> na trupy
> od niechcenia
> rzucali pudełka—
> Warum sind Juno rund[97]
> Blood and tears oozing into sandy soil
> As "the lords"
> Casually tossed
> On the bodies
> Empty cigarette boxes,
> Warum sind Juno rund[98]

The poetic voice assumes the perspective of the SS killers. Their ennui vis-a-vis the submissiveness of their victims makes the Jews resemble cows easily herded into cattle cars and beaten for sport simply to relieve the tedium. A spent cigarette box printed with the words of a German advertising jingle reflects the vacuous contempt with which the exalted SS killers, described as gods, hold their Jewish prey. Similar to Celan's "Death Fugue,"[99] Szlengel's "Counterattack" uses the language and imagery of Nazi propaganda to mock and subvert the Aryan ideal of the Übermensch: the Nazi officers are so pleased with themselves and satisfied by the ease with which they dispatch their duty that they cannot fathom any shared humanity with their seemingly bovine victims. Writing a year before Celan composed "Death Fugue" and its refrain of "wir trinken" ("we drink"), Szlengel uses the same motif of imbibing to contrast the murderous self-regard of the master from Deutschland against the abject state of the Jews: "Hier/Trinkt man mehr kein Bier/Hier/Hat man mehr kein Mut/Blut/Blut/Blut" ("Here/One drinks no more beer/Here one has no more courage/Blood/Blood/Blood").[100] Nevertheless, the SS officer errs. No longer will the ghetto represent a SS post where German officers could drink to satiety without fear of resistance or need for valor. The Jewish *Untermenschen* are poised to counterattack.

While the poem subversively deploys antisemitic Nazi tropes, Szlengel exhorts the Jews of the ghetto to rise up in armed rebellion:

> Kule pląsają w radosnym rozśpiewie,
> BUNT MIĘSA,
> BUNT MIĘSA,
> BUNT MIĘSA!
> Mięso pluje przez okna granatem,
> Mięso charczy szkarłatnym płomieniem
> I zrębów życia się czepia !
> Bullets are dancing in a joyous burst of song:
> REVOLT OF THE MEAT,
> REVOLT OF THE MEAT,
> REVOLT OF THE MEAT!
> Meat spits grenades out the windows,
> Meat coughs out streams of scarlet flame
> And clings to the edges of life![101]

To the Nazis' disbelief, the cattle, now mere beef, erupt in a paroxysm of violent revolt, which Szlengel calls "BUNT" ("REVOLT"), the same poetic word that Miłosz uses at the end of "Campo di Fiori" when he imagines a renewed rebellion ignited by the poet's word.[102] Faced with Jewish resistance, the SS officers are stunned, some of them fatally so:

> Żandarm się zachwiał w bramie.
> Spojrzał zdziwiony—chwilę stał,
> Pomacał roztrzaskane ramię—
> Nie wierzył.
> A policeman staggered in a gateway,
> Stared in surprise, for a moment stood still
> Touched his shattered shoulder
> Didn't believe it.[103]

Cut down by the first bullets of the ghetto resistance, the SS men die in arrogant incredulity. They are beaten as much by the courage of the Jewish resistance fighters as by their misplaced faith in Nazi racial metaphors and myths. They believed their lordly status and never fathomed that their bovine victims, mere beef in their eyes, could possibly challenge it. Szlengel offers rapturous praise for this "revolt of the meat," which he depicts with uncharacteristically florid terms such as "bullets are dancing in a joyous burst of song" and grenades thrown in "streams of scarlet flame." Yet even this is no conventional metaphor but rather a shared continuum of rebellion: the staccato bullets and pulsing streams of verse become one field of shared resistance. In urging his readers to rise up and fight Szlengel completes the final transformation of his poetic vocation as he turns words into weapons.[104] As we will see in the next chapter, Katzenelson, in his ghetto poems, lamented being unable to fight. Szlengel, however, understood that he could join the fight through his poems. The poetic language of resistance offered a last opportunity to assert a sense of connection as he roused the entire ghetto to join the uprising.

This is indeed what occurred. "Counterattack," itself a counter-text to Szlengel's earlier irony and satire, became the poet's most widely read poem in the ghetto. Halina Birenbaum recalls:

> The last time in the Ghetto I listened to Szlengel's poems with part of my family [...] the poems were recited with passion and inner satisfaction by my younger brother Chilek (20 years old). It was "Counterattack." It was the day before the outburst of the uprising in [the] ghetto, a few hours before going down to the bunker at 3 Mila Street.[105]

"Counterattack" was passed from hand to hand as the ghetto residents took their positions in the bunkers. The poem became part of the uprising. The entire ghetto had become a warfront, and, although he did not wield a gun or bear arms, Szlengel conceived of himself as a central participant in the fighting.

Szlengel did not survive the rebellion. He, his wife, and over 130 other ghetto residents hiding in the bunker of ghetto underground leader Szymon Kac at 36 Świętojerska Street were discovered on May 8, 1943, and were executed the same day. One eyewitness, Leon Naiberg, recalled that Szlengel spent his last days writing poems urging the Jews to continue to fight. Naiberg writes of Szlengel in his diary entry from May 8: "Yesterday evening the poet was still writing his poems in which he praised the heroism of the fighters and mourned the fate of the Jews. But this was the last time [I saw him] because the bunker was captured."[106]

Writing to the dead until he became one of them, Szlengel, the poet of the ghetto, died without surrendering his pen. He had urged his fellow ghetto inmates to fight and reclaim their humanity. In language that posits a final, enduring vindication of shared human dignity, he forged a lasting bond with readers, alive and dead.

6

"Poem in a Bottle": Itzhak Katzenelson's *Song of the Murdered Jewish People*

Daniel Feldman

Writing within History

Whereas Władysław Szlengel was relatively unknown before he rose to literary prominence in the Warsaw Ghetto, Itzhak Katzenelson came to the Warsaw Ghetto as a refugee specifically on account of his preexisting prominence. A major Hebrew and Yiddish poet, playwright, and educator in interwar Poland, Katzenelson fled his home in Łódź shortly after the city became the first large urban center in Poland to fall to German forces in the opening week of the *Blitzkrieg*. Alarmed by rumors that the Nazis were seeking the capture and possibly execution of public leaders in Łódź, including him, Katzenelson quit the city, which meant abandoning the network of educational institutions he directed there and the large extended family that relied on his leadership of the school system. He fled alone to Kraków, and from there to Warsaw, which, at the time, was thought to be a relatively safe haven, where his wife and three sons joined him in January 1940.[1]

In this chapter we will see that what Katzenelson did and wrote in the Warsaw Ghetto and afterward brings into focus what Paul Ricoeur recognized as the key problem of the interconnection between narrativity and time: "Narrativity is the mode of discourse through which the mode of being which we call temporality, or temporal being, is brought to language."[2]

That is to say, our understanding of what happened is essentially a function of how it is narrated, so that our sense of self is grounded in our sense of time. However, as this chapter will make clear, the violent events of the Holocaust made it impossible for Katzenelson and other Jews incarcerated in the ghetto to conceptualize time because one event followed another, turning upside down the previously held precarious perception of what was happening. The breakdown of temporality necessarily strained possibilities of telling the story, let alone understanding it historically, but it also begged questions about the poet's relationship to God and Jewish history.

When the Warsaw Ghetto was enclosed and Katzenelson was incarcerated within it, he immediately became a leader of the ghetto's literary activities. Katzenelson, like his fellow Zionist educator Abraham Lewin, changed literary languages in recognition that writing in the ghetto would be unlike what he had previously published.[3] In order to reach as many readers in the ghetto as he could, Katzenelson reversed his long-standing practice of writing poetry primarily in Hebrew, the language of his ideological affiliations and nationalist hopes, and reverted to writing in Yiddish, the language of the masses. Literature in the ghetto would be a public service as much as an artistic pursuit. Katzenelson was an influential cultural figure who was quickly recognized, Sven-Erik Rose writes, as "the most significant, most prolific, and best-known poet and dramatist" in the ghetto.[4] He became known as "the threnodist of the Holocaust."[5] Unlike Szlengel, however, Katzenelson's earlier record played an important role in determining what he would write during the Holocaust. As we shall see, this became a persistent pattern of his writing early in the ghetto's history which informed what he wrote later in the war while interned in a transit camp in Vittel, France.

For Katzenelson, poem led to poem and text led to text as his writing evolved in a series of creative amplifications and poetic elaborations. Katzenelson's final and most widely read epic poem titled *Dos lid funem oysgehargetn yidishn folk* (*The Song of the Murdered Jewish People*), which he wrote during his detention in Vittel, could not have been composed without earlier works that laid the artistic groundwork for it. In this sense, Katzenelson exemplifies a nascent literary history that developed during the Holocaust itself. By the time he died in the gas chambers in Auschwitz together with his eldest son Tzvi on May 1, 1944, Katzenelson was not the same author he had been in the ghetto two or three years earlier. The Holocaust, after all, was not a single moment but rather a war against the Jews with its own internal and abnormal chronology. The scope of Katzenelson's oeuvre written during the genocide demonstrates the ramifications of that war against the Jews for an evolving literary poetics that shifted under the dynamic conditions of occupation. Katzenelson's literary development during the Holocaust from Warsaw to Vittel, culminating in *The Song of the Murdered Jewish People*, makes this clear.

Katzenelson arrived in the Warsaw Ghetto as an established older man of letters whose pedagogic energy was largely directed toward the ghetto youth. An educator by temperament and training, he was embraced in the ghetto by the left-wing Zionist *Dror Hechalutz* youth movement; its leader Yitzhak (Antek) Zuckerman gave him an important role as a teacher and spiritual leader in the underground Zionist movement.[6] Mordecai Tenenbaum-Tamaroff, who later died leading the uprising in the Białystok Ghetto, wrote that Katzenelson became "like our brother" who shared a "bit of the desperation we were feeling and he would turn that into something that reached the skies and [through poetry] made it eternal."[7] The Dror group accorded Katzenelson special status by disseminating his work through its underground press and preserving many of his writings in its own secret archives, but Katzenelson, perhaps the ghetto's most prolific writer, also won respect across the ideological spectrum. Orphanages staged his plays, private readings of his works were attended by ghetto elites, copies of his poems passed hand to hand,[8] Emanuel Ringelblum's *Oyneg Shabbos* archive collected samples of his work, and, as David Roskies writes, "Virtually everything that he wrote in the ghetto—one-act and full-length plays, epic and lyric poems, literary criticism—he declaimed before a live audience."[9]

Katzenelson's Yiddish play *Iyev: biblishe tragedye in dray aktn (Job: A Biblical Tragedy in Three Acts)*, published by the clandestine Dror press in a limited run of 150 copies on June 22, 1941, the day that Germany declared war on the Soviet Union, was the first and only single-author book composed and printed in its entirety in the Warsaw Ghetto.[10] On the cover was a chiaroscuro illustration by Shloyme Nusboym of Job contorted in pain in a position familiar to ghetto residents who regularly confronted diseased and famished inmates lying on the streets of the ghetto. Roskies and Diamant consider Katzenelson's play "the most ambitious publication of the underground press in the Warsaw Ghetto."[11] Several of Katzenelson's other plays written in the ghetto take up similarly dark themes of theodicy and fantasies of retribution avenging the victims' suffering in dramas that survivors recalled as offering them spiritual succor amid the squalor of the ghetto.[12]

Katzenelson was exceptionally prepared for the monumental challenge of writing a national lyric of elegy, lament, and protest. He arrived in Warsaw in fall 1939 with a wealth of educational and publishing experience accumulated over a lifetime of writing for the Jewish public. Born in 1886, he was raised in Łódź as the scion of a noted Hebraist and hailed in his childhood as a prodigy. He made his debut as a playwright at the age of twelve with a Yiddish play about the Dreyfus Affair. His influence grew as he became a pioneering author of Hebrew poetry, plays, textbooks, and children's books. He also translated into Hebrew a broad range of texts from English, German, and Yiddish. During the Holocaust, Katzenelson embraced his educational vocation as a leader of cultural activity in the ghetto's desperate conditions. Roskies and Diamant describe him as a singular figure in the ghetto:

> From the moment he found refuge in Warsaw, in mid-November 1939, the poet Yitzhak Katzenelson was a man with a mission: he was active in both the Yiddish and Hebrew cultural societies, always declaiming his verse before live audiences, marking literary anniversaries, writing plays for children and grown-ups, and responding to events throughout the Jew-Zone by redefining the meaning of martyrdom.[13]

Yet Katzenelson's prolific original writing in the ghetto did not deter him from looking backward to literary archetypes that guided his response to the unfolding disaster. He found inspiration in two very different models. The first was the literary example of Haim Nahman Bialik, the Zionist and Hebrew poet, only slightly older than Katzenelson. Katzenelson translated Bialik's landmark 1903 poem "'Al hashekhitah" ("Upon the Slaughter") from Hebrew into Yiddish; it was prefaced by a long essay and published in the ghetto in the summer 1940 issue of the underground newspaper *Dror*.[14] Yechiel Szeintuch assesses Katzenelson's emulation and translation of Bialik as an attempt "l'amod b'imut 'im hamavet kenatun hakove'a et tekhushat hakiyum haindividualit vekevutsatit keekhat" ("to oppose the perception of death as a fixed condition that determined the sense of individual as well as collective existence").[15] Katzenelson's other focus was the Bible. He lectured at length and with passion on the pertinence of the Bible, specifically the Hebrew prophets, to the predicament of the Jews in the ghetto. His spellbinding readings of and lectures on the prophets became the stuff of legend vividly recalled by ghetto survivors in their memoirs.[16] This was an integral element in Katzenelson's attempt to use literature to give historical meaning to the grim experience of the ghetto. Roskies and Diamant explain: "Katzenelson organized and presided over public readings of the Hebrew Bible in his own rhymed Yiddish translations, in which he sought to demonstrate that the Prophets had never been more alive, more relevant."[17] The Bible emerged as Katzenelson's primary literary, ideological, and cultural resource. Trying to find moral purpose in an absurd contemporary reality, Shner remarks, Katzenelson's poetry resorts to "biblical language and engages in bitter dialogues with biblical personalities. Sometimes he speaks like a biblical prophet, sometimes he wrestles with the biblical prophets, Jeremiah and Ezekiel."[18] Biblical intertexts afforded him the literary templates he needed to portray his and his fellow ghetto inmates' experiences as enmeshed not in an irrational racial conflict but as a painful new chapter in a broader meta-historical matrix of the Jewish tragedy.

"Woe to You"

Katzenelson's engagement with national themes became more pronounced in 1942 with the onset of the liquidation of urban populations of Polish Jewry and the deportations to extermination camps. Upon learning of the destruction of the Lublin Ghetto and deportation of its residents to Belzec in April 1942, an aggrieved Katzenelson responded with a poem of unmitigated rage. "Vey dir" ("Woe to You") is a text of "white hot" fury that makes no "distinctions between the German perpetrators of the genocide and the German people as a whole" in vehemently condemning all Germans to a litany of curses.[19] In Sven-Erik Rose's interpretation of the poem, "'Vey dir' deserves to be read for the devastatingly brilliant way that it poetically explores some of the experience, including the rage and the search for voice and agency, of people faced with their own individual and collective destruction."[20] Expressed with biblical intensity, the poem unleashes an intense stream of apocalyptic invective that is located in an indeterminate future and lodged at an apostrophized "you." The poem's rage is unvarnished:

> Vey dir, du host a folk farnikht on umbavofent
> Un nit fertaydikte fun keynem hostu farnikht!
> Veys, nit fertaydikte fun keynem veln harb dikh strofn
> Du vest far umbavofente zikh shteln tsum gerikht!
> Woe to you, who have destroyed an unarmed people,
> who have destroyed a people unprotected by anyone.
> I tell you, those who were unprotected will punish you:
> you will be judged by the people without weapons![21]

The general address to an amorphous collective body of cursed Germans summoned by the poet's first-person voice of direct and urgent apostrophe ("I tell you") reflects Katzenelson's emerging poetics in the early years of the ghetto: he assumes a prophetic vantage point of cosmic address clothed in "vey" ("pain") and "veys" ("know") to pronounce the fate of "Du vest" ("you will"), namely what will befall the German "you" in an undefined hereafter. The ultimate retribution will finally come "after the end, as it were, by a solitary mourner, the 'last of the Jews,' in full knowledge of the entire tragic narrative arc of events."[22] Fury acquires a redemptive purpose in this litany of lyric denunciation. Katzenelson embraced the jeremiad mode: Rendered impotent by imprisonment in the ghetto, the poetic speaker turns to poetic malediction and through it seems to have "discovered the cathartic, transformative power of rage."[23] Moreover, questions of specifically to whom and when these curses will be delivered are left productively ambiguous. In this text of righteous anger spoken by a lone speaker who is amalgamated into the collective fate of the Jews, the curses are leveled from an indeterminate temporal point "after" and addressed toward an amorphous German "you"—none of whom could realistically be expected to read this poem written by an incarcerated Jewish poet in Yiddish.

The vast scale of the poem's apostrophe opens new creative possibilities for Katzenelson, as it allows him to construct a poetic tone apposite to his situation in the Holocaust. The constituent elements of the poem—an individual voice speaking in obloquy on behalf of an entire nation of victims and toward a whole nation of foreign perpetrators—raise issues associated with prosopopoeia and the ascription of agency to absent objects and parties. For whom is this text written? To whom does it speak? This Yiddish poem and its grand collective apostrophe was a means of speaking beyond the rupture of poetic address and the evacuation of presence engendered by the genocide. Rose explains: "'Vey dir' dramatizes the dead speaking across the barrier not just of individual death but indeed of genocidal, collective, and cultural death. It struggles against the Nazi project of killing the very language of Yiddish along with its speakers."[24] Undaunted by Nazi lethality, a new poetic voice emerges:

Mir veln shteyn derhargete un kukn,
onkukn aykh shtum in undzer payn;
un kukndik af aykh, aykh shtumerheyt fartsukn,
Mir esn in di beyner aykh zikh ayn.
We, the slain, will stand up and stare at you,
stare at you mutely in our anguish,
and, staring at you, devour you in silence:
we'll eat into your very bones.[25]

This poem, motivated by the liquidation of the Lublin Ghetto, features the not-yet dead poet speaking in spring 1942 on behalf of the already-dead masses.[26] Three months before the onset of the *Grossaktion* (Great Deportation) of summer 1942 that would result in the emptying of most of the Warsaw Ghetto, Katzenelson had already innovated a poetics "spoken by the dead for the dead."[27] Postwar readers, Rose says, intersect with the text "as interlopers of sorts who assume, or usurp, the place of the readers the poem summons."[28] This was an important step forward in the evolution of Katzenelson's poetics of apostrophized lyric as he worked through the problematic challenges of literary address prompted by writing behind closely guarded ghetto walls. In his later poetry, composed after waves of deportation had already killed most of his readers, Katzenelson would again make prolific use of apostrophe to address an array of unreachable interlocutors, including his murdered family, the massacred Jews, the implacable heavens, the empty cattle cars of the transports, and himself, the bereaved figure of the solitary poet. But that progression would play out over nearly two more years of excruciating agony and loss.

A Purgatory Diary

In summer 1942, at the height of the Great Deportation, Katzenelson lost his wife and two of his three sons. Returning to his ghetto apartment one day in August 1942 he discovered that the Jewish ghetto police had taken his wife Hannah, fourteen-year-old son Bentzion, and eleven-year-old son Benjamin to the *Umschlagplatz*, the deportation point to Treblinka. Kassow comments, "The loss shattered Katzenelson and threatened his sanity. He could not keep his thoughts from dwelling on their final agonies as they entered the gas chambers."[29] For months Katzenelson wrote nothing. After the initial act of resistance in January 1943, when Katzenelson issued a stirring call to die fighting like their brethren in the land of Israel, it became apparent that he was too old to fight, and the Dror movement offered him and his surviving son Tzvi sanctuary in a hideout. The local representative of the Joint Distribution Committee (the American aid organization) arranged Honduran passports for them. When the uprising began in April 1943, Katzenelson and his son were smuggled out of the ghetto to a hiding place on the Aryan side. They eventually made their way to the Hotel Polski, where the Nazis concentrated Jews holding international passports and diplomatic papers; it was suspected to be a Gestapo trap. In May 1943 the SS sent all the captive protective-document holders to the Vittel internment camp in France while the Nazi leadership weighed the fate of these potential hostages for exchanges with German nationals held by Allied governments.[30]

Katzenelson was a survivor of the destroyed Warsaw Ghetto but not of the Holocaust, which continued apace. Time had moved on, but the Nazi menace had not gone away, and Katzenelson was at a creative and psychological impasse.[31] The dizzying pace of traumatic events was more than he could bear, and he struggled in May and June 1943 to cope with the colossal personal and collective toll of recent events. In less than a year he had lost most of his family; witnessed the decimation of Warsaw Jewry; seen the Polish Jewish culture he venerated and helped to lead eviscerated; survived the Ghetto Uprising; and skirted death on innumerable harrowing occasions. Katzenelson knew about the camps, the shootings, the gassings, and (in his reckoning) the seven million Jewish dead. The war, however, was nowhere near an end. In the foreign purgatory of Vittel, afflicted by all he had seen and fearful about what was yet to come, Katzenelson tried and initially failed to make sense of what he had endured. On May 22, 1943, soon after arriving in France, he attempted to resume writing, this time in the form of a diary. He began recording his thoughts in a notebook that would come to be known as the *Pinkas Vitel* (*Vittel Diary*).[32] His point of departure was his wife Hannah's deportation the previous year when, Katzenelson wrote, "my real life began to end."[33] With his purpose and intended reader obscure, he started to write in Yiddish and inscribed, "Ikh mit mayn zun Tzvi" ("I with my son Tzvi"),[34] broke off, bracketed the phrase in parentheses, and then switched languages to Hebrew, perhaps as a means of claiming some private distance from the eyes of his neighbors.[35] Trapped in the internment camp with his one remaining son, Katzenelson offered another fitful start by repeating himself with a single Hebrew line that almost exactly anticipates Dan Pagis's later poem "Written in Pencil in the Sealed Railway Car": "Ani im Tzvi bni" ("I with my son Tzvi").[36] He then trailed off and said nothing more. "Overwhelmed by his losses," Roskies and Diamant comment, Katzenelson could find no way forward.[37] Months passed before he wrote again.

It was as if the disruption of chronological temporality froze any possibility of narrative. Present reality offered Katzenelson little opportunity for narrating the past, let alone for imagining a future. Two months of silence elapsed during which Katzenelson wrote nothing. He had fallen out of time and was paralyzed in a vortex of capricious history akin to his tenuous status, marooned in France in a German internment camp, as a dubiously documented Polish Jew of nominal Honduran status. The past was an abyss, the present a trap, and the future a looming peril. He left no record of his thoughts during this period until resuming the diary with new purpose and in Hebrew on July 22, the day before the first anniversary of the start of the Great Deportation of the Warsaw Ghetto. He delved back into the events of the prior year and laid out a rigorously chronological history of the deportations that reconstructed the 1942 massacre in unstinting detail. As Katzenelson retrospectively "backtracked to the slaughter, as if reliving it in real time," Roskies says, the diary became a "chronology of mass murder" written with "fanatical attention to calendrical time."[38] Few comparable texts of retrospective memory were written during the Holocaust, save for Emanuel Ringelblum's diary and ghetto history.[39] In the sequential entries which he continued to write until September 1943, Katzenelson meticulously chronicled the events of his years in the ghetto: he spared no culpable party and reserved special enmity for the Jewish police, describing what he knew of the deportation and killing processes in agonizing detail and reclaiming a measure of psychological order over all he had borne. Katzenelson's "despair is blatant"[40] in these writings as his personal experience and eyewitness testimony meld with the story of the ghetto in vignettes about its inhabitants. This glance backward from 1943 provided the creative outlet that allowed him a poetic way forward. He wrote with iron resolve and a "twofold purpose: to mourn his personal losses and the destruction of his people; and in their name and his own to demand a moral reckoning from the Germans, the Poles, his fellow Jews, and the free world."[41]

Intellectually, the diary also gave Katzenelson a personal chronology with which to order his thoughts and give coherence to his reflections on his creative work. For instance, he writes in the diary that the genesis of "Woe to You," was his ghetto flatmate and friend Hillel Zeitlin's morning prayers. Katzenelson carried a copy of the poem with him over the following two years as it became a marker of time and a touchstone for how associations and resonances changed in the ghetto under the volatile circumstances:

> I had written the curse ["Woe to you"] when Hannah and my two sons were as yet alive. It was written on thin paper, in small letters crowded together. They were the curses that I invoked against this vilest of nations, after they had annihilated the great and holy Jewish community of Lublin. There was not a single survivor. Hillel Zeitlin, of blessed memory, heard these curses some time before the commencement of the massacre of the Jews of Warsaw. About two years ago, when I still had a family, we shared the same house. Now my family is no more. […] Two years later, on the eve of the complete annihilation of the Jewish people, I read out my curse to the old man. Two years ago, Rabbi Hillel had begun the curse but did not express all of it; he could not find the words: 'Oh! Lord of the Universe. It is terrible!' Two years later, this curse had matured within me, and I wrote it down and read it out.[42]

While his world disintegrated and everything fell apart, poetry was the one constant in Katzenelson's life. Literature became a timepiece and a time capsule, something by which to mark the agonizing passing of time and in which to record the ravaging effects of the violence of history. The *Vittel Diary* allowed Katzenelson to perceive this. By reconstructing the past through the diurnal patterns of a daily diary, Katzenelson was at last able to confront the enormity of his suffering and plot a means of writing about it poetically.

The *Vittel Diary* also demonstrates how closely tied Katzenelson's writing in the internment camp is to his literary production and creative experience in the Warsaw Ghetto. The diary mediated his ghetto memories even as reflections on his literary activity in the ghetto constitute much of what he recalls in the diary. In Vittel, Katzenelson was writing his own literary history, one in which he took stock of how the history of the war became the subject of his literature. His prose and poetry were codependent and mutually generative. Without his Hebrew diary or Yiddish poetry, neither would have been written. This relationship continued, as soon after concluding the diary Katzenelson began work on his final masterpiece, *The Song of the Murdered Jewish People*, which was composed from October 1943 through January 1944 and then thoroughly revised before he was deported from Vittel to Auschwitz in April 1944. The diary and poem are inextricably connected, Roskies contends:

> Writing this Hebrew diary allowed Katzenelson to work through the trauma. Three weeks after making his last entry, he began to compose his Yiddish epic poem, *The Song of the Murdered Jewish People*, which took him six months to complete. The poem was dedicated to the memory of

Hannah, his muse, the only source of meaning now that the heavens, in whose poetic mission he had once believed, were silent.[43]

For Katzenelson, the time had long since passed when poetry could endow the murder of his wife and children with sacred meaning, but poetry could still convey his memories of that time, and in *The Song of the Murdered Jewish People* he set out to do just that.

A Last Lament

The Song begins by grappling with the impossibility of writing poetry after witnessing the horrors of the previous year's atrocities:

> Zing! Nem deyn harf in hant, hoyl, oysgehoylt un gring,
> oyf zeyne strunem varf deyne finger shver,
> vi hertser, tseveytikte, dos lid dos letste zing,
> zing fun di letste yidn eyrepes erd.
>
> Vi ken ikh zingen? Vi ken ikh efenen meyn moyl,
> az ikh bin gebliben eyner nor aleyn—
> meyn veyb un meyne ofehlekh—a groyl!
> Mikh groylt a groyl... me veynt! Ikh her veyt a geveyn. [Canto 1, stanzas 1–2][44]
>
> Sing! Take your harp in hand, light, hollow, and curved,
> And throw your fingers hard against its strings
> Like hearts aggrieved, and sing the last song,
> Sing of the last Jews on European soil.
>
> How can I sing? How can I open my mouth
> When I alone am left, all alone—
> My wife and my little chicks—the horror!
> I shudder... There is a cry. I hear weeping from afar.

The opening canto of this poem, dated October 3–5, 1943, presents a colloquy between the poetic speaker and his muse. In a series of six exchanges that continues through the tenth stanza, the poet oscillates between the poetic imperative to take up the lyre and sing, on the one hand, and the impossibility of writing poetry after all that the poet has seen, on the other. In compact internal and end rhymes, the text links "hoyl" (bare), "oysgehoylt" (hollow), "moyl" (mouth), and "groyl" (horror) to summarize the poet's creative crisis: the bare horror of what he has seen leaves the poet's mouth hollow. He cannot speak. The impossibility of art, presented here in a text written in late 1943 in a Nazi internment camp, dramatically anticipates Adorno's attempts to grapple with this problem years later (discussed above). Finally, in the canto's twelfth stanza, the poet resolves his dilemma via a similar return to memory that helped him overcome his prior reticence, when he had been blocked months earlier, and write a diary. The poet summons the dead to aid him in his creative and commemorative mission:

> A veyz zikh mir, meyn falk, baveyz zikh, shtrek di hent,
> aroys fun griber tif un meyln-lang un ongeprapt gedikht,
> shikht unter shikht, mit kalkh bagosn un farbrent,
> aroyf! Aroyf! Shteygt fun di untershter, der tifster shikht!
>
> Kumt ale fun treblinki, fun sovibar, fun oshventshim,
> fun belzhits kumt, kumt fun ponary un fun nokh, fun nokh!
> Mit oygn oyfgerisn, farglivert a geshrey, a gevald un in a shtim,
> fun zumpn kumt, fun blotes eyngezunken tif, fun poyln mokh—
>
> Kumt getrikente, tsemolene, tseribene, kumt, shtelt zikh oys
> in a karohod, a rad a groysn arum mir, eyn groyme reyf—
> Zeydes, babes, tates, mames mit di kinderlekh in shoys—
> kumt beyner yidishe fun prashkes, fun shtuklef zeyf.
>
> Veyzt mir, baveyzt zikh ale mir, kumt ale, kumt,
> ikh vil eykh ale zen, ikh vil eykh ankukn, ikh vil
> oyf meyn folk, meyn osygehargeten, a kuk ton shtum, farshtumt—
> un ikh vel zingen... ya... aher di harf—ikh shpil!⁴⁵

> Show yourselves to me, my people, reveal yourselves, stretch your hands,
> Out of the graves, from the deep miles-long lime-covered ditches,
> Layer under layer, coated, covered, and burned,
> Rise up! Up! Up from the lowest, deepest layer!
>
> Come all from Treblinka, from Sobibor, from Auschwitz,
> From Belzec, from Ponar, and from more, and from more!
> With eyes wide-open, cries frozen, screams still in your throat,
> Come from the swamps, deep sunken marshes, foul muck.
>
> Come, you dried-out ground-up crushed bones. Show yourselves
> In the round, set a circle large around me, one great ring—
> Grandfathers, grandmothers, fathers, mothers with babes in arm—
> Come, Jewish bones, out of powder and bits of soap.
>
> Show yourselves, reveal yourselves to me, come, come you all,
> I wish to see you, to look at you. I want

Silently and mutely to see my people, regard my murdered nation—
And I will sing... yes... Hand me the harp... I will play!

Summoned from Treblinka, Sobibor, Auschwitz, Belzec, Ponar, and other sites of death whose names Katzenelson knows, the dead join forces with the speaker in leaving a final artistic record of their lives. Emerging from the mass graves of the forests and the ash heaps of the camps, the victims confer on the poet the necessary strength to overcome his profound doubts about the viability of verse. *He* will be the one to play the harp and sing, but *they*, his murdered people, standing mutely around him, are the effaced subject that the poem endeavors to restore and make visible: "show yourselves, reveal yourselves," "I wish to see you," the poet says.

Biblical allusions in the opening canto of *The Song* illustrate how Katzenelson's use of scripture had evolved since his Bible readings and lectures in the ghetto. The motif of taking harp in hand to sing a threnody of despair refers to Psalm 137, "By the rivers of Babylon," the dolorous *ur-text* for the *topos* of Jewish exile. Likewise, the summons addressed to "dried-out ground-up crushed bones" that are commanded to assemble in a circle around the speaker recalls the vision of the valley of the dry bones in Ezekiel 37. Once more, Katzenelson's powers of apostrophe extend beyond the limits of life. However, Ezekiel's prophecy is a metaphor of national revival. For Katzenelson, it is a dark expression of the unprecedented scale of the disaster. There are no Jews left in Europe, only the residue of bones. His Yiddish readership has literally been crushed; even their bones were ground up. The Holocaust caused Katzenelson to place ever more fervent faith not in God, but in Jews. The Bible remained relevant for him but no longer as an archetype of how to voice Jewish lament, but rather, for how the poets of the present disaster had exceeded the prophets of the Temple's destruction. In the ghetto, Katzenelson had taught that Jews under Nazi oppression had much to glean from the Bible; in Vittel, he concluded that the Jewish victims of the Holocaust had much to teach the authors of the Bible. This faith in his murdered people became an abiding element of his last writings as the prophets changed from his mentors into addressees of his verse.

Katzenelson writes in the *Vittel Diary* that the Holocaust had elevated the Jews of Europe above the ancient Jews of Israel. In the last year of his life he believed he was writing in a mode which exceeded the prophetic mode that he earlier championed in the ghetto. Prophecy had become common in the ghettos and camps of Nazi Europe, he claims:

The Jews of today are more richly endowed with God's spirit than their ancient ancestors. God is a continuous force within them and had his permanent abode in their midst. If prophetic vision has ceased in Israel, then it has ceased only among individuals. Indeed amongst the Jewish masses of today it is more powerful than ever it was in the days of our forefathers. We are more like unto Isaiah than were the Jews of his own day.[46]

His aim in redeeming Jewish dignity was to demonstrate that the Jews who died in the Holocaust were no less imbued with cultural nobility than generations of Jews past.

In *The Song*, Katzenelson conceived his project as writing an elegy for a great and historic people. The 900-line text is written in fifteen cantos, each of which is dated, titled, and comprised of fifteen quatrain stanzas. Canto six, stanzas eleven and twelve (dated November 2–4, 1943) states that the biblical prophets pale in comparison to the murdered Jews:

> Eyner shvarts-oygik, a blas yingele, nokh nor a yugens,
> er hot dertsaylt a mayseleh, neyn, nit a mayseleh, er hot gebroyzt, er iz gevezen oyfgeregt,
> Yishaya! Du, ah du, host nit geflamt vi er, host nit gehart aza a yidish a tsung.
>
> Er hot geredt a yidish mit lashon kodesh, neyn! S'iz lashon kodesh bloyz!
> harkh, harkh, kuk on di yidish, di oygn zeyne, un dem shtern un vi er hoybt
> dem kop oyf... Yishaya! Bist nit kleyn geven vi er un nisht gevezen azoy groys,
> bist nit gevezen gut azoy, nit emestik azoy, un host Yishaya nit azoy gegloybt!⁴⁷

> A pale, black-eyed boy, just a child,
> told a story. No, not a story, he blazed with excitement.
> Isaiah! You, oh you could not shine as he, you never heard so fine a Yiddish tongue.
>
> He spoke Yiddish with the Holy Tongue! No, it was all the Holy Tongue!
> Hark, hark, look at the Yiddish, on those eyes, and their rising brows.
> The heads erect... Isaiah! You were never so small or as great,
> You were never as good, as truthful, or, Isaiah, as fervent in your faith!

The various strands of Katzenelson's career—Hebrew and Yiddish, youth and art, the ancient Hebrew past and contemporary Jewish culture—come together in this paean to the murdered youth who transcended the greatest of the Hebrew prophets. The Jewish people, Katzenelson suggests, reached their apogee just as they met what he perceived to be their historical end. It was God and "the heavens" that had changed, not the Jews, as the climactic central canto of this tightly structured text makes clear.⁴⁸

Canto nine, stanzas seven through thirteen of the poem, "To the Heavens," dated November 23–26, 1943, replaces God with a new divinity, the dead

Jews themselves. Using the same audacious apostrophe of "Woe is You," Katzenelson addresses the empty heavens:

> Ir kent nit, ir derkent una shoyn nit mer, farvus? Tsi hobn mir zikh den
> azoy gebitn? Azoy geendert zikh? Mir zenen dokh di zelbike di yidn fun amol—
> un besser nokh a sakh... nit ikh! Nit ikh vil tsu mayne nevi'im zikh fargleykhen, nit ikh ken,
> nor di yidn ale, di tsum toyt gefirte, di milyonen mayne oysgehargete da mit amol
>
> Zey zenen beser nokh, mer oysgeliten, oysgelaytert, mer in galus da! A vos bateyt
> a yid a groyser, an amoliker, antkegn kleyn a yetsdikn, a pashuten, a drukhshnitlikhen yid,
> a poyln, lite, in volin, in yedn galus, fun yidn klagt un shrayt,
> a yirmiya aroys, an iyov in yisurim groys, a melekh an ontoyshther mit a koheles lid.
> [...]
> Ir hot keyn got in zikh nit! Efent oyf di toyeren, ir himlen, efent oyf zey brayt,
> un lozt di kinder ale fun mayn oysgehargeten, fun farpaynikten, mayn folk arayn,
> efent oyf zey tsu der groyser himelfart, gants a folk gekraytsikt shver in leyd,
> darf in aykh arayn... a yeder ayner fun di kinder mayne umgebrachte, ken a got zay zayn!⁴⁹

> Do you not know, not recognize us anymore, why?
> Have we changed so much? We are the same Jews of yore—
> And much better, still... Not I! I do not wish to be compared to the prophets, cannot,
> But the Jews, they all can, they who were led to death, the millions of my murdered people.
>
> They are still better, suffered more, more refined by their exile here! What is
> A great Jew of the past next to a simple, average Jew of the present,
> A Polish or Lithuanian Jew, in Volyn or from anywhere in the exile, from every Jew scream the
> Cries of Jeremiah, the tribulations of Job, the king's sad rhymes of Ecclesiastes.
> [...]

You have no God in you! Open the gates, you heavens, open wide,
And let the children of my murdered, suffering people enter.
Open up the great heavenly path, an entire nation has been crucified in pain,
They may enter. Every one of the children of my slaughtered people a God!

To Katzenelson, this last, most tragic page in Jewish history rendered the Bible obsolete and its prophets ordinary mortals. There was no God, but the heavens were the rightful abode of the new, rightful gods, the slaughtered children of the murdered Jewish people.

Here ended the downward spiral of despair in Katzenelson's poetry, from his inspiring play about Job that gave his listeners in the ghetto pride in their suffering to evocation of martyrdom (*kiddush hashem*) in his June 1942 poem, "Dos lid vegn Shloyme Zhelikhovsky" (The Song of Shloyme Zhelikhovsky), based on the execution of ten Jews from the town of Zduńska Wola on the eve of Shavuot 1942, one of many acts of terror or reprisal designed to induce fear and obedience. With random killings in the Warsaw Ghetto, Katzenelson's mood changed and in his address in Hebrew to Warsaw teachers for Pesach 1942 he emphasized that *kiddush hashem* was the sanctification of the Jewish people and it contributed to the meaning of being a Jew. In glorifying the Jews hanging on the gallows in Zduńska Wola, Katzenelson was calling on his readers to sing for the glory of a suffering people, not for the glory of God. It was not from the heavens that wrath was to come, as in the traditional invocation for divine revenge at the Pesach seder table.[50] The Polish-born Israeli historian Efraim Shmueli recalls Katzenelson's address, on the third Pesach in Nazi bondage:

This night, a night of horrors [...] and a first, first night of redemption [...]. In this siege and strait in Warsaw [...], we celebrate the night of our first redemption which today [...] fortifies us, pulsates within us, and animates us with redoubled courage.[51]

At this last supper, Katzenelson was exhorting his listeners not to follow the example of the Marranos who converted to Christianity but to accept their suffering as a tenet of their faith. Katzenelson was a convinced secular Zionist who took active part in the revival of national Jewish culture at the beginning of the century; he knew he and his listeners could not find redemption in the land of Israel, nor could they rise up against their oppressors. God was in hiding (the traditional concept of *hester panim*, invoked so often in the Holocaust), therefore they had to do without divine intercession in history and accept they were doomed, that this was what gave meaning to their identity as Jews. So what consolation was the Hebrew poet giving? Shmueli summarizes:

With what, then, could a Hebrew poet console his people crushed under the burden of suffering, sealed within itself, and the entire space of its world filled with the fear of death? He will break through this siege with his words, in poetry and prose, in enlightenment of thought, so that their suffering will not remain an opaque burden of "those led to slaughter in a muteness of mouth and tongue." Remembering Jewish identity negates the terror of death. In giving utterance to their suffering while becoming fully aware of their being, "our brothers extend their necks to the sword, and we speak today clearly." Speech is the Jew's way of soul-searching, in an evocation of the spirit of Zionist-humanist faith in rebirth. "In our remnants, there is consolation. After our death, before which we are standing, looking it in the face without fear."[52]

This paradoxical theodicy can be seen in Katzenelson's poem about the Radzin rabbi in the train deporting the Jews to their deaths; God too is sitting there among the deported, apparently unable to save them but present among them. Katzenelson wrote "Dos lid vegn Radziner" ("The Song of the Rabbi of Radzin," November 1942–January 1943) after his wife and two of his sons were taken away in August 1942 and he rejected the Jewish tradition of the Ten Martyrs ('Aseret harugei malkhut), of accepting death as an act of faith in God. In the finale of the poem, the rabbi realizes there is nothing left to do except bury the dead, but he hears the lone voice of God crying—in a midrash on Lamentations, God is heard crying for the destruction of the Temple—yet here the rabbi has no words of comfort for God. The divine Presence was likened in the Talmud (Brakhot 3a) to a dove crying in the ruins; however, unlike Bialik's "Levadi" ("Alone"), in Katzenelson's poem there is nobody left to comfort the lonely God of Israel.[53]

If the divine covenant had lapsed, Jewish history had come to an end. The elegy of *The Song* mourns not only Katzenelson's family, his community, and European Jewry, but the end of Jewish history. If Jewish history is at an end, then so must be Jewish literature. Stanza ten of canto fifteen, the final segment of the poem, titled "The End of it All" and dated January 15–17, 1944, imagines a postwar eastern European landscape without Jews or the literary landmarks and legends of Yiddish culture. Alluding to classics of Yiddish literature, Katzenelson addresses his dead readers:

Nit fregt oyf Kasrilivke nit oyf Yehupetz, lozt gemakh!
Zukh nit kayner, nit di Menakhem-Mendels, di Tuvya-Milkhikers, di
    Shloyme-Nogids, di Motke-Ganefs, a nit zukh!
Zey velen dir, vi di neviim deyne, vi Yeshaya, Yirmiya, Yekhezkel, vi
    Hosheya, Amos, fun dem eybiken Tanakh,
aroysveynen azoy fun Bialiken, oroysreden tsu dir fun Sholem-
    Aleikhem, fun Sholem-Asches bukh.[54]

Don't ask there for Kasrilivke or Yehupetz. Don't!
Don't look for Menakhem-Mendels, Tevye the Dairymen, Shloyme-
   Nogeds, or Motke the Thieves. Don't look!
They'll speak to you like your prophets, like Isaiah, Jeremiah, Ezekiel,
   like Hosea, Amos, from the eternal Bible,
Cry out to you from Bialik, address you from Sholem Aleichem,
   Sholem Asch's books.

The poem set a seal on Jewish literary history, on Isaiah and Bialik, Jeremiah and Sholem Aleichem: with *The Song* Katzenelson was joining them in the closed library of Jewish culture. Henceforth Yiddish culture would be known only through its books, not its readers. Katzenelson drew on Ezekiel ironically, in despair that the dry bones would ever live, although in chapter 37 Ezekiel too was addressing the pulverized dry bones of a people which had lost hope in the coming redemption. If, as we saw in Chapter 1, Wiesel clung to his faith in Auschwitz as a living bond to the divine covenant, Katzenelson's *Song* is a cry of existential despair.[55] The poet used to exhort his eager listeners in the Warsaw Ghetto to find strength and solace in the vitality of their venerable literary heritage, but now Katzenelson attempts to bring the Jewish poetic tradition to a close by consigning the great Jewish writers of the past to oblivion. Henceforth no one would look to the biblical prophets or to the Yiddish masters to read about Jewish life. God had abrogated the covenant and the ancient history of the Jews had come to an end. All that remained was to lament what this murdered people left behind. With both audacity and anguish, Katzenelson declared that the final visionaries of Israel were its millions of victims, nearly all of them now dead.

Nonetheless, Katzenelson knew that there were still free Jews alive in the Land of Israel and in the United States and he took steps to ensure that his poem would survive, even if he did not. In the spring of 1944, shortly after completing his poem, Katzenelson learned that Ruth Adler, a German Jew holding British papers guaranteeing her passage and settlement in Mandatory Palestine, had been granted permission to leave Vittel in exchange for German prisoners of war. A copy of *The Song* was sown into the leather handle of her suitcase and dispatched to the Land of Israel, where she delivered it in June 1944 to Katzenelson's relatives Berl Katznelson and Yitzhak Tabenkin, both prominent leaders in the Zionist Labor movement. Itzhak Katzenelson wrote them a letter to accompany his smuggled manuscript in which he acknowledged his grim prospects and expressed his wishes for his final poem:

> Only you and my cousin will read this Lament for our people slain in its entirety, with its infants and its babies in the wombs of their mothers. Do not publish this Lament in its fifteen chapters or print it, as long as the curse of man still rages upon earth. If both of you find it proper and

> necessary that this Lament should be translated into other languages in order that the nations should know what they too have done to us, since they, too, have been used by and helped this abomination of the nations, the Germans, in the murder of our whole people, not only the Lithuanian and Ukrainian murderers… then keep the translations with you as well until the end of the War. I do not believe that I shall live until that day. Begin the publication of the Lament chapter by chapter in the Jewish press, all on the same day. Only after the fifteen chapters have been disseminated should you publish them as a book. Print the Lament with a dedication to the soul of my Hannah and my brother Berl, who were killed with their families and with my whole people, without any grave.[56]

Katzenelson's relatives followed the instructions and ensured that the poem was published, albeit in translation and in limited circulation. After its publication in May 1945, few wanted to read this angry elegy, which did not fit the postwar ethos of heroic resistance or the narrative of hope and rebirth of the Jewish people.[57] Katzenelson's epic poem, with its apostrophe calling upon so many different entities and parties, struggled to address a postwar readership.

Katzenelson did not know if Adler and her suitcase would ever reach Palestine with its concealed copy of *The Song*. Prudently, he made a reserve plan. Together with Miriam Novitch, a fellow inmate at Vittel, Katzenelson buried copies of the manuscript in three sealed glass bottles under a pine tree on the grounds of the Vittel camp.[58] After liberation by the Americans in summer 1944, Novitch recovered the manuscript. She became the curator of the Ghetto Fighters' House Museum, founded in Israel in 1949 as the world's first Holocaust museum. The museum's official name is the Itzhak Katzenelson Holocaust and Jewish Resistance Heritage Museum, Documentation and Study Center. Deported to Auschwitz, where he was murdered on May 1, 1944, together with his son Tzvi and other arrivals from Vittel, Katzenelson did not live to see his legacy honored in a museum bearing his name by citizens of a new Jewish state. But he called to them through his writing—from the silence of beyond.

PART THREE

7

Translating Oral Memory in Ida Fink's "Traces"

Daniel Feldman

A Surviving Voice

Unlike the examples we have seen in the poetry of Szlengel, Katzenelson, and Radnóti of diverse responses to events in real time, the post-Holocaust writing of Ida Fink presents issues of literary testimony we have not yet discussed, including translation and translatability, visualizing and visibility, representation and memory. Fink's short stories measure the temporal distance between the historical moment of the Holocaust and its retrospective depiction after the war. While her autobiographical fiction scrupulously honors the specific context of its grim historical referent, her stories focus not on restoring the past but on the extreme difficulty of doing so. The proposition tested in story after story in Fink's oeuvre is whether the survivor can bridge the gulf between the crucible of the Holocaust and its aftermath. Although written after the war, Fink's stories suggest that the full terror of the genocide can be represented only in a testimonial voice anchored inside the event that transports the narrating speaker and her literary addressees back through the fissures of time and language into the abyss of the Holocaust. Yet this work of chronological analepsis and historical transposition is always doomed to failure. The attempt to speak from within the event and the challenge of achieving it form the ethical and literary poles that charge Fink's writing with artistic force. Her genius is to embrace, on the one hand, the testimonial injunction to recreate the daily atmosphere of fear and chaos during the Holocaust with fidelity, and, on the other hand, the impossibility of ever realizing that goal. Her realistic vignettes aim to reflect the extremes of the genocide; however, faithfully representing such trauma requires Sisyphean feats of linguistic, aesthetic, and historical translation so arduous that they can scarcely succeed. Fink's protagonists cannot help but to try and reclaim the past, usually to little avail. Nevertheless, their preoccupation with the demands of historical, aesthetic, and linguistic translation attest to the ongoing search for a poetics *in extremis* to meet the fundamental quandary of Holocaust representation, especially in narrative fiction written many years after the war.

Born in 1921 in Zbaraż, Poland (contemporary western Ukraine) to a secular Jewish family, Fink wrote autobiographical fiction about her experiences and those of her family in the Holocaust during a long career that spanned her emigration from Poland to Israel in 1957 until her death in 2011; despite living for many decades in Israel, Fink published exclusively in Polish. Using false Aryan identity papers, Fink and her sister escaped the Zbaraż ghetto in 1942 and spent nearly three years passing as non-Jewish Polish forced laborers in Nazi Germany. Although she was an accomplished teenage pianist and an occasional novice poet before the war, she later claimed that during the Holocaust she had no desire to write. Nevertheless, immediately after liberation Fink sought to commit to writing her memory of what she had seen: "Znikła chęć pisania. Przez całą wojnę nie myślałam o tym. Tymczasem ta chęć wróciła zaraz po wojnie, kiedy jeszcze byłam w Niemczech, w obozie Unra" ("The desire to write disappeared. Throughout the war, I didn't think about it. Meanwhile, this desire returned right after the war, when I was still in Germany, in the UNRRA camp").[1] She began writing in a displaced persons (DP) camp run by the United Nations Relief and Rehabilitation Administration near the Black Forest in the months after the war, and her debut publication appeared in late 1945 in the newspaper of the Ettlingen DP camp as an essay marking the first anniversary of the Warsaw Uprising, a year after the fall of the Warsaw Ghetto.[2] By her own admission, Fink's first attempts to bear witness to the genocide were futile and premature. She later recalled, "Nie napisałam ani słowa. Wtedy sobie tłumaczyłam, że miniony czas jest zbyt bliski, a wszystko, co widziałam, zbyt chaotyczne" ("I didn't write a word. I then explained to myself that the past period was too close and everything I saw too chaotic").[3] The imperative to write about the war began to motivate Fink powerfully and immediately only after liberation; the capacity to do so, however, did not return—apart from her early essay in the DP newspaper. Her development into a survivor charged with bearing literary witness to extreme suffering evolved over the course of many years, during which the burden of shouldering this testimonial responsibility gradually became a key motif in her texts.

Fink's writing dwells as much on the experiences of the Holocaust as on the figural translation of those experiences into linguistically encoded memory. Her fiction offers a glimpse into the literary construction of the witness.

Readers of Fink's vignettes about the Holocaust do not see the moment of mass murder in the woods, for example, but the instant when that murder is recalled, confronted, and articulated in the witnesses' memory. Fink's narrator gives voice to survivors becoming witnesses while posing critical questions about that process. How does the witness emerge in and through language? When is testimony blocked by the inadequacy of words? How can literature bear witness at all? Fink's delicate short stories focus meticulous attention on the agony of survivors-cum-witnesses who had to cope with the dual burden of confronting what they endured while struggling to communicate it to others.

The typical Fink character is a chronicler of an alien, virtually unspeakable past who grapples with the difficulty of making this nearly unintelligible past comprehensible to those who did not experience such unspeakable events: "Trudno powiedzieć" ("It's hard to express"), says one protagonist.[4] "Od dawna chciałam opowiedzieć ten czas... Chciałam, lecz nie mogłam, nie umiałam" ("For so long I have wanted to talk about this time... I wanted to, but I couldn't, I didn't know how") says another.[5] Though repulsed by the barbarous crimes they witnessed, these traumatized characters feel compelled to continue watching and speaking in order to transmit what they have seen to others: "Zerwałan się z ziemi, chciałam biec w las, dalej, żeby nie widzieć" ("I jumped and wanted to run into the woods, so I wouldn't have to see") says yet another character, who continues, "A nie pobiegłam. Coś trzymało mnie w miejscu, mówiło: patrz, nie zamykaj oczu. No i patrzyłam" ("But I didn't run. Something kept me there and said to me: 'Watch. Don't shut your eyes.' So I watched").[6] These characters grasp for a language that they can only hope will coalesce into a poetics of memory equal to the historical and moral obligation to preserve privileged knowledge about the life and death of the victims, share it with those who were not there, and transmit it to the future.

Social historians such as Annette Wieviorka offer a chronological account of the various stages in the emergence of the Holocaust survivor as the paradigmatic figure of moral authority in a contemporary "era of witness,"[7] yet Fink's writing indicates just how circular and conflated temporal distinctions can be for the remembering witness. The past, the present, and the future permeate each other in Fink's short stories.[8] The lucidity of her crystalline, precise prose belies the fluidity and confusion of chronology for those who lived through an event that seemed to be outside of sequential time. The *mise-en-scène* of a Fink short story is thus bifurcated between the historical atrocity that the survivor seeks to revisit in the past and the dispatch of his or her testimonial account in the narrative present. Mediation between those two instances of memory, the reconstruction of the past and the complex articulation of it in the present, is the subject of Fink's fiction. Her characters doubly address first the victims for whom they speak and then the listeners to whom they now appeal. Her stories, consequently, are rooted in the genocidal past but directed to the postwar future. Straddling these frames of reference, Fink's protagonists animate texts "which form a connection between the inner and the outer, allowing the reader (the outside) to gain an inside glimpse into the impact of the hiding experience upon ordinary men, women, and children," while concomitantly suggesting the sheer difficulty of sharing such an extreme experience.[9] In light of this narrative pattern, Fink's characters can be construed as translators of memory bearing messages of traumatic experience from one realm to another. Her protagonists shuttle knowledge across the chasm of time and toward vastly divergent historical coordinates. This translation is both figural and literal. For not only must the surviving witnesses in Fink's stories negotiate the vexing problem of making their particular form of anguished memory communicable to people who were spared such torment, but they must also translate their experiences into the foreign idioms and languages of their interlocutors.

Translation is thus foregrounded in the basic form and substance of Fink's fiction. Linguistic translation is a key component of her work. Her acclaimed debut collection of short stories, *Skrawek czasu* (*A Scrap of Time*), first appeared in Hebrew, Dutch, German, and English translation before the Polish original was published by an expatriate press in London in 1987, shortly before the end of the communist period. A 1990 novel, *Podróż* (*The Journey*), was also first published in London. Not until her third book, in 1996, was Fink published in Poland. Her Polish readership has steadily grown in recent decades, but her work is still widely read in translation, particularly in Hebrew and English. Thematically, moreover, translation is closely tied to the testimonial thrust of her fiction. Yet translation and the difficulties of communication also offer challenges in the stories. The memories that Fink's protagonists strive to recover are often polyglot, disparate, and scattered among the welter of tongues spoken in the killing zones, including German, Russian, Yiddish, and Polish. One character recalls the last words he heard his Polish mother speak: "Słyszałem, jak spytała po niemiecku: 'o co chodzi?'" ("I heard her ask in German, 'What's the matter?'").[10] In another story, a young Polish woman attempts to intercede between two German sentries and a terrified Red Army soldier. She begs to speak for the Russian prisoner, but the Germans, whose "loud songs sung in a harsh foreign language" have terrorized the local residents, tersely rebuff the woman's pleas: "Widziałaś już kiedyś, jak to się robi?... Schau mal, das ist so einfach" ("Have you ever seen how it's done?... Schau mal—look, it's so simple"),[11] they say in mixed German and Polish narration before executing their speechless Russian prisoner. German, the language of the occupiers, is hardly a neutral language—one local resident remarks, "Już w szkole nie lubiłam niemieckiego... Powiedz, czy nie miałam racji?" ("I never liked German even in school... Now tell me if I wasn't right?").[12] Yet the status of translation is all the more fraught as an act of survival in some of

Fink's texts. Speaking the wrong language or using the wrong dialect could imperil the life of a Jew living under a false identity. For such individuals, vigilantly flawless and ceaseless translation was a matter of life and death. "Do you know what it means to live in fear, lying, never speaking your own language, or thinking with your own eyes," one survivor importunately asks a companion, beseeching him to fathom the constant strain of living in perpetual translation, phonetically banished under pain of death from speaking one's own language.[13] Fink's only novel, a fictional retelling of her and her sister's ordeal hiding under false papers as slave laborers in Germany, describes a harrowing episode in which the sisters, posing as local Germans, endanger themselves by mistakenly pronouncing the German city "Karlsruhe" as it is written, rather than as "Kahsruh," in the local dialect.[14] Translation in these narratives is a continual struggle for survival. To pass without detection under an assumed identity depends on translating one's language and entire identity into another culture with no margin for error.

Finally, translation plays a phenomenologically significant role in apprehending the scale of the Nazi assault. Grasping at duplicitous terms and stymied by the limitations of any single language, Fink's narrators are ill equipped to translate the unprecedented ruthlessness of the Nazi conspiracy into words at all. Exemplifying Roman Jakobson's theory of linguistic translation, Fink's characters improvise an array of intralingual, interlingual, and intersemiotic mutations of language[15] to explain appalling events that may be mutually *un*translatable between various tongues. The speaker in the title story in *A Scrap of Time*, for example, charts the victims' gradually dawning awareness of the savagery of the Nazi genocidal scheme as an exercise in evolving translation that proceeded from an initial period when "we took the words 'conscription for labor' literally" to a sobering recognition that "the words 'conscription for labor' had nothing to do with a labor camp."[16] That short story begins in its original Polish version with a quotation of "Im wunderschönen Monat Mai" ("In the wondrous month of May"), a classic poem of high Romantic culture by Heine in the original German, but degenerates into an attempt to untangle the twisted meaning of a repellant new German phrase, also left untranslated: "akcja," from "Aktion," is introduced as a semantic substitute for an older Polish term, "łapanka" ("round-up"), a word whose former meaning the Nazis clouded through a campaign of subterfuge and viciousness. As opposed to the broad meaning of the vernacular term "łapanka" ("round-up"), the insidious foreign neologism "akcja" ("action") specifically denotes a round-up of Jews for the purpose of killing them. It is a codeword for killing that defies translation. The nuanced difference in meaning between the Slavic "łapanka" and the Germanic "akcja" is minute but crucial: "Łapanka— nazwę, która z biegiem czasu, z postępem stosowanych środków została zdegradowana (lub wywyższona?), oddzielona od terminu 'akcja' granicą rasy. Łapano na roboty"[17] ("Round-up'—a word that became devalued—

or dignified?—as time passed, as new methods were developed, and 'round up' was distinguished from 'action' by the borderline of race. Round-ups were for forced labor").[18] Older words proved inadequate to describe this new time; novel terms and fresh modes of intercultural competence became necessary when translation from one language to another no longer entailed simply restating common experience with a different syntax and vocabulary, but instead meant adapting to an altogether new, unprecedented reality that rested on the corruption of words. Heine's German of Romantic sentiment was dead and supplanted by the perpetrators' new German that cloaked death in the deceit of euphemisms.[19] The protagonist in Fink's story grapples with finding a Polish idiom that accounts for these diametrically shifts in language use. Her thoughts suggest that the Holocaust marked an epoch in history—and in translation—that called for a new poetics, capable of rendering unprecedented historical experiences in language.

The narrator of "A Scrap of Time" observes that the identity of the linguistic innovator who first imported the German term "Aktion" into Polish as "akcja" is lost to the fog of memory and the degeneration of language— "Nie wiem, kto pierwszy użył tego słowa, ci, którzy działali, czy też ofiary ich działania, ich akcji, kto stworzył zeń termin techniczny," she writes.[20] ("I don't know who used the word first, those who acted or those were the victims of their action; I don't know who created this technical term."[21]) According to this view, translation as a social and linguistic endeavor is distributed, strikingly, among the oppressors and their victims; contact between the two groups may itself be a macabre, lethal form of translation turning murderous idea into horrific deed. Nonetheless, "technical terms" such as "akcja" fail to capture the ethical, social, and human carnage of the genocide. Even as the Holocaust motivates translation and necessitates new terms, it also degrades language ("została zdegradowana") and disrupts the precise exchange of words.

All these themes are vividly encapsulated in Fink's short story "Ślad" ("Traces"), a very brief text that demonstrates Fink's consummate skill in capitalizing on the power of literature to translate nearly unimaginable events in language addressed to contemporary readers. The Polish title, "Ślad," meaning "a trace" or "the trace," as opposed to the plural "Traces" in the title of the English (and Hebrew) translation, refers to the lingering final memory of murdered victims and grim history that a sole surviving witness struggles to put into words. The story meditates on an older survivor's struggle to communicate previously clotted memories that are visual, polyglot, and traumatic to a younger team of interviewers guided by vastly different linguistic and historical associations.

The protagonist is asked by her interlocutors to convey in oral testimony the ineffable backstory behind a wartime photo that appears to portray nothing but a blurry scene of white absence: "Dużo bieli—to śnieg" ("There's a lot of white in it; that's snow").[22] The survivor's memory of the event behind the photo at first appears as inaccessible and fuzzy as the image. However, the photograph, "a copy of a clumsy amateur snapshot,"[23] encodes the searing memory of Jewish children who defied an SS officer's command and died in order to protect their parents. Much is encapsulated in this story. It combines visual media with the spoken word, the articulation of an indescribably harrowing experience, the crossing of generational assumptions, and the bridging of the linguistic divide between languages. This palimpsest of concerns—all bound up with linguistic and literary reconstitution—makes the text a rich site for exploring the central themes of translation in Fink's work. In what follows, I explore the story as a case study of how the literature of witness navigates a course of testimony between media, generations, and linguistic contexts. By mapping the text's narrative structure, I demonstrate how this compact, poignant story serves as a showcase for the many crucial channels of translation that inform Fink's writing and make her work an invaluable illustration of what is at stake when survivors bear traumatic memory across boundaries of time, place, and language.

Speaking the Image

"Traces" focuses on an emotionally wrought moment during the interview between a group of unidentified questioners and the survivor, who is possibly recording her testimony for posterity. In Israel, Fink worked at Yad Vashem in a related capacity as a collector of survivor testimonies. No specific context is given for the interview or the interviewers. Marianne Hirsch assumes that it is an "intergenerational encounter" between a survivor and a group of anonymous questioners, who, "looking for facts and information, have only traces such as the photograph and the woman's halting narrative to go on."[24] Dorota Glowacka, by contrast, reads the story as the staging of a visit by the protagonist "to a place from the past, which in her case is the town that formerly contained a ghetto of which she was the sole survivor."[25] The interview, Glowacka posits, recounts a discussion between the survivor and the town's current residents. Both interpretations suggest that the reported conversation is intergenerational. Both interpretations are plausible. Neither, however, is fully supported by the text. Details regarding the contemporary context for the interview are sketchy, barely perceptible against the reticent blankness of the story. In this respect, there is a resemblance between the lack of identifying details outlining the story's scenario in the narrative present and the paucity of details that might explain the visual referent of the photograph unearthed from the narrative's unexcavated past. We know little about either frame of reference. Both the interview in the literary present and the historical image glimpsed in the photographic past remain shadowy. But conjoining the two is the elderly protagonist at the heart of the story. She, the unnamed witness answering the interviewers' questions and inspecting the blurry historical photo, forges a connection intimately linking these two separate spheres of uncertainty. The survivor can glimpse and remember what others cannot. Her mediation between disparate eras structures the narrative and puts her crucial role translating the trace of the story.

As a visual artifact, the photograph presented to the survivor shows nothing. It is an empty frame of white with vague traces spread across an indistinct field of blurry snow. Remarkably, however, the survivor at once identifies the blank referent: "Yes, of course she recognizes it. Why shouldn't she. That was their last ghetto," the text begins.[26] She sees something in the scene of absence that the young people speaking with her do not. Her perspective, born of harrowing experience, makes visible what remains imperceptible to others: "Of course she recognizes." The indignant, pithy opening words of the story in its Polish original, "Tak, owszem, poznaje"[27] ("Yes, obviously, recognizes"), spoken *in medias res* to the interviewers' unvoiced inquiry about the photo, signal a note of defiant pride or even pique about the integrity of the speaker's memory. Why wouldn't she remember? By what rights ought her reliability as a witness be impeached? The balance of the story undermines the putative umbrage behind that rhetorical question by offering ample justification for why the survivor might not accurately recall her traumatic Holocaust experience. Nevertheless, the survivor's unique ability to visualize the unseen past seems assured beyond doubt. The visual prompt of a blurry white picture merely accentuates the contingent "evidential force" of the photographic medium[28]—evidence (from the Latin "videre," to see) is visible only to the witness who can see across time.

The photo may signify a hidden bond between the past and the present, but it is the survivor who makes that connection legible by translating the photo's faint visual trace into narrative. Without narrative context, the image is devoid of meaning. The survivor, then, possesses a unique ability to recover in language what would otherwise remain unknown. Glowacka comments, "Without the speaker's commentary, no one would even notice the footprints in the picture, or, at best, they would remain inconsequential. They are mute signs."[29] As a translator of mute signs and a storyteller of a visual idiom facing erasure, the survivor is charged with responsibility to remember the forgotten past and to recollect the circumstances behind the vague image. She alone is able to give voice to what appears to be nothing more than an empty frame of Holocaust memory. Glowacka and Ruth Ginsburg comment on a parallel return to a disturbing scene of nothingness at the beginning of Claude Lanzmann's epic documentary *Shoah*. In the opening shot of the film, survivor Simon Srebnik is seen at an empty site that was once the death camp Chełmno. Srebnik walks across a landscape where nearly all identifying trace was erased, "a site of innocent 'nothing,' covering up and silencing an act of annihilation, an act of eradication,"[30] before unequivocally declaring, "Ja, das ist der Platz" ("Yes, this is the place").[31] This empty site of absence signifies meaning only through the survivor's memory. Just as the vacant field resonates only to the surviving witness in Lanzmann's *Shoah*, so too does the blank photograph reveal itself solely to the informed survivor in Fink's "Traces."

This diegetic structure of privileged insight vouchsafed to the traumatized individual but invisible to all others repeats in the text's relationship to its audience. The same dynamic also occurs in *Shoah*, which foregoes historical footage in favor of contemporary video testimony, of the sort being recorded in "Traces." While the survivor in "Traces" sees something in the image that the other characters cannot discern, the reader knows something of the protagonist's mind that the interviewers do not. Unlike the interviewers, who hear only the survivor's halting speech, the reader is made aware of the survivor's internal monologue via a form of composite narrative that mixes direct and indirect discourse. As a result, the reader is made privy not only to the protagonist's directly reported speech, but also to her thoughts, including memories of which the interviewers, eager to draw out precisely those same recollections, remain ignorant. The text juxtaposes these two modes of discourse, but the survivor says far more to herself in silently disclosed free indirect speech than she says out loud to her questioners.

This composite model of revealing the past in a piecemeal manner holds ethical significance since the narrative form reflects a pattern of historical knowledge that publicly conceals but privately reveals, a recurring pattern that applies to both image and text. That is to say, Fink's "Traces" suggests a comparable treatment of the opaque photograph and taciturn witness. The picture divulges little; the speaker expresses almost nothing. But when visually translated by the survivor, the vacant image unlocks a shattering story of death (and, as it happens, disappearance[32]), just as the text's third-person narration gives voice to a roiling memory behind the survivor's fierce reticence. The analogous treatment of image and word as modalities of personal memory is telling. On their own, the photo is insufficient, and the witness's words remain baffling. But together they transform confused questions into coherent narrative in a new poetics of witness. The survivor translates the visual image into snippets of verbal memory and the text then stitches the survivor's fragmented recollections into lucid prose. Placed in complementary relationship, these mixed media of reluctant testimony point to a traumatic event that would be lost to oblivion if not for realization of the sole survivor's increasing desire to share it, to act on a cresting hope finally to "tell how they were all shot" and thereby take comfort in having "some trace of them to be left behind."[33] Without literary translation of ineffable trauma into narrative, all trace of the genocidal past would be lost, except the bits of memory that the surviving witness manages to salvage. As figurative translations of traumatic memory, these forms of inflected testimony guarantee a portion of the historical record in both visual and verbal form.

This reading suggests a notion of photography that is dependent upon human decryption, which runs counter to conventional ideas about the image as evidence. Indeed, in their analyses of "Traces," Marianne Hirsch, Magdalena Marszałek, and Jan Gerstner point to the status of the photograph in the Fink text as a visual icon that attests to a scrap of time permanently frozen. This memory technique constitutes a powerful example of the phenomenon that Hirsch calls "postmemory," the putative remembrance by later generations of past traumatic events that they encounter exclusively through mediated narratives and images.[34] Alluding to Barthes's concept in *La chambre claire* of "ça-a-été," Hirsch draws attention to this picture as the "photographic index par excellence," a mechanical "instrument of historical evidence" that forges a "material connection to an event that was there before the lens" and "illustrates the integral link photographs provide for the second generation, those who in their desire for memory and knowledge are left to track the traces of what was there and no longer is."[35] Viewers endow photography with an aura of historical immediacy that ostensibly transports them to a scene that has long since dissolved into the remote past. The time-bending promise of photography is especially alluring to members of later generations whose tenuous relationship to the past is mediated through the prism of transmitted images and collected stories in "postmemory." While Hirsch acknowledges the false seduction of photography, which "can be extremely frustrating," and notes that without the survivor's verbal elucidation, the photograph in "Traces" "would remain silent,"[36] her characterization of the photo as a mechanical talisman or visual relic conjuring distant events from the vapors of forgotten history belies its practical futility in Fink's story; the photo portrayed in this text shows nothing that could enlighten an uninformed viewer. This eccentrically non-referential image, then, subverts the conventional force of photography as unassailable objective evidence. "Es ist auffallend, wie das fotografische Bild in Ida Finks Erzählung der *evidentia* widerspricht," writes Marszałek[37] ("It is striking how the photographic image in Ida Fink's story contradicts the concept of *evidentia*"). Gerstner adds that as opposed to the typical function of photography as a sturdy buttress for historical evidence, "[D]iese Funktion der Fotografie in Finks Geschichte erschöpft sich darin allerdings nicht"[38] ("This function of photography, however, is not fulfilled in Fink's story.") Indeed, the modality of viewing shifts in Fink's text. Rather than rendering the past visible to latter-day spectators, the vestigial picture in this story demonstrates the opacity of the past, its lack of visibility to anyone who was not there. It portrays not a human subject, but footprints, the ghostly last traces of absent victims. It thus points to the formal limitations of photography, not to its rich potential.

Instead of imparting visual information that would beguile postwar viewers into believing that they have seen a precise mechanical reproduction of what is in fact an unknowable past, the fictional "kopia niezręczna"[39] ("clumsy reproduction") of a wartime photograph in Fink's "Traces" evokes the past by way of appeal to the viewer's affect, rather than intellect. The obscure, empty photo registers not in the eye of the viewer, but "in the very sensations of the body,"[40] in some unseen change in the viewer's bodily affect: "Die Fotografie in der Erzählung Finks adressiert also die mnemonische Kraft des Bildes als Katalysator des Gedächtnisses, als Aktivator der körperlichen Erinnerung"[41] ("Photography in Fink's story accordingly addresses the mnemonic power of the image as a catalyst of memory, as a trigger for bodily remembrance"). Indeed, the narrative indicates that the photo's power lies not in its representational significance but in its capacity to unsettle the protagonist's emotional and physical equilibrium.[42] The survivor reaches for the photo, releases it, holds it again at some length, and then attempts once more to place it physically beyond reach and psychologically out of mind: "I prefer not to remember," she says,[43] suggesting that her memory is not as pristine as she initially professed at the beginning of the text, in defense of her faculties of recollection. Suddenly, however, the protagonist finds herself brought up short by what the photo evokes in her mind. Some emotional change has occurred. Acting on a new impulse, she decides to give voice not to the meager visible image but to what lies behind its opaque veneer by accounting for the hint of indistinct footprints left in the snow—"traces of traces of traces"[44] of people long since gone.

What story is documented by the blank photo? "The picture was taken in February," the survivor recalls. The white is snow. Yet beyond offering generalities—"[T]hat's the ghetto," "[T]his is where they lived"—she recoils from divulging historical detail. "It's hard to express," she hedges, explaining her faltering testimony with some contextual background: "They did such terrible things to us that no one was surprised at anything."[45] She pushes the photo away and seems determined to sever her connection to the past, "I prefer not to be reminded," she says again.[46] The protagonist is unwilling to translate the hazy traces of the past. But the immense gulf between what the innocuous photo shows and what the survivor has to say ("immens ist die Kluft zwischen dem, was das Bild zeigt, und dem, was gesagt wird"[47]) brings her crisis of deliberate amnesia to a head. The protagonist can no longer repress the explosive memory of her "last ghetto"; her memories and her desire to record them for posterity become increasingly acute. After looking at the dissonantly blurry photo once more, she decides to speak clearly of the children, "najstarze miało może siedem lat" ("the oldest might have been seven or so"),[48] who were hidden in the ghetto's *Judenrat* building beside which "ten, który fotografował, stać musiał obok domu" ("the person who took the photograph must have been standing").[49] The photo returns the survivor to the children's plight, as if it were unfolding before her again in the present, substantiating Kotarska's claim about the temporal confusion in Fink's fiction.[50]

The story plays out the narrative in the mind of the last surviving witness. Her memory reveals the final trace of murdered children whom only she recalls. The children, once discovered by the Nazis, were brought before the remaining ghetto residents by an SS officer who attempted to trap the children into betraying their parents: "No, dzieci kochane, teraz niech każde z was podejdzie do swoich rodziców" ("Dear children, now each of you go and run to your parents").[51] The survivor-witness remembers the demonic SS officer entreating the children with cloying civility. The children do not speak, and so the SS man stridently commands one child, "Pokaż, gdzie stoi twoja matka lub ojciec" ("Show me your mother and father!").[52] The child remains heroically mute. The Nazi diabolically perseveres, "Brał po kolei inne dzieci i krzyczał, żeby pokazały rodziców, ale one wszystkie milczały" ("He took the other children one by one and shouted at them to point out their parents, but they were all silent").[53] The children do not accede to his demands to identify their families, and their refusal to expose their parents leads to their deaths. But they are not the only victims. All of the town's Jews, except the protagonist, are eventually murdered. The faint footprints in the snow are the last traces of the doomed. "Ludzi nie ma—ich kroki zostały"[54] ("The people are gone—their footprints remain"[55]), the survivor laconically observes; meanwhile, a maelstrom of memory rages in her mind. Contemplating her status as the last survivor of the ghetto, she leaves behind a final trace of the victims by committing their devastating story to language. She wants "żeby pozostał ślad" ("some trace of them to be left behind").[56] She resolves to speak.

The story might exemplify how Holocaust survivors become witnesses to the traumatic past, except that none of the foregoing memory is shared with the interviewer or interviewers. Her interlocutors are deprived of an answer to their question, "Jakie dzieci? Jaki ślad?" ("What children? What trace?")[57] inquisitively posed in response to the survivor's enigmatic, if indirectly reported, wish that "what she is going to say be written down and preserved forever, because she wants a trace to remain."[58] The interviewers are desperate to cajole the elderly survivor into identifying the spectral footprints and mysterious children. But she does not speak, at least not to them. In a tortuous but poignant echo—or trace—of the original Holocaust incident, the sole surviving witness of that atrocity, now an elderly woman, remains silent in the face of insistent questions asked by apparently younger interrogators. She refuses to disclose what she sees in the photo. "What children?" the interviewers ask, in a haunting echo of the SS man's imperative "Pokaż!"[59] ("Show me").[60] The generations have been inverted: children are responsible for saving parents. Where children once sheltered their parents, now the old are asked to identify the massacred young. The disquieting "trace of those children," as the text says of their traumatic story, is legible only to one who has entered into the text as a reader, just as the import of the sketchy footprints imprinted in the otherwise bleached-out photograph signifies only for the survivor who had been in the ghetto. What is heroism? When should one speak? How does one bear witness to silence? When do words communicate and when do they not? These questions reflect generational assumptions of profound significance about survival, legacy, and the transmission of values. Attending to the demands of the old upon the young and the young upon the old requires another level of translation that moves beyond the static frame of any one time to the shifting perspectives of successive generations linked by traumatic memory.

Transgenerational Translation

The last word of reported dialogue which the survivor says aloud in the story is "dzieci" ("children"). The final word in the survivor's internally narrated, unvoiced discourse is "ślad" ("trace"). In the course of her testimony, from stunned silence at recollecting the horrific fate of the "children" to an overpowering urge to enshrine them for posterity, we can trace some lasting "trace" of them in spoken language. This entails consideration of the claims that generations make upon one another in the shadow of the Holocaust. As a work of fiction, "Traces" is constructed as a chain of intergenerational encounters in which one generation entrusts its hope for the future to the other. As the last representative of the generation that endured the ghetto, the survivor is asked by a group of latter-day investigators to identify an image reproduced from a picture taken by an anonymous "amateur" photographer whose exposure is the only visual record of what occurred in that town. The younger interviewers seek to understand history from their elders. But the survivor is reluctant to delve into the past. Pondering who took the photograph and when ("Kto to fotografował? I kiedy?"[61] ["Who photographed it? And when?"[62]]), she starts ruminating on the strangeness of the photo and the inscrutability of the Gestapo's actions with rambling and confusingly disjointed associations: "Dlaczego nie wiadomo. Taki widać był rozkaz. Stali tam, na dziedzińcu, dopóki nie przywieziono dzieci"[63] ("No one knows why. Apparently those were the orders. They stood in the courtyard until the children were brought").[64] Suddenly, she breaks off.[65] Determined, evidently, to protect her own mind from the taxing tribulations of remembering what the interviewers ask her to recall, the survivor again demurs, saying, "Wolę sobie nie przypominać" ("I prefer not to remember").[66] This motivates her younger listeners' exasperated plea to plunge back into the past and speak of the murdered youngsters—"What children?" The specific memory that these latter-generation interviewers hope to elicit is, significantly, about children, the younger generation of victims whose appearance in the *Judenrat* courtyard at the fevered pitch of the dreadful *Aktion* delayed the execution of the town's Jewish adults. Moreover, the explanation for the delay, as the survivor belatedly puzzles out in her mind, was that before the massacre the children were publicly interrogated by an SS officer intent on forcing them into betraying their parents.

The narrative lays bare the inextricably painful bonds of trauma woven between the generations in this latticework of suffering: in an effort to save the last members of the younger generation, parents imprisoned in the ghetto risked their lives by hiding children in the *Judenrat* building even though, at the time, "children no longer had the right to live."[67] But the parents fail in their doomed mission to safeguard their offspring; instead, the children are horrifically turned into diminutive guardians of their parents, a memory which the elderly survivor struggles to share with her eager young audience. Assumptions of generational responsibility are warped, thwarted, and tortuously twisted in this text. Each generation is determined to protect the other: the parents aim to save the last of their children, the children valiantly try to shelter their parents, the young interviewers seek to preserve the last survivor's testimony, and the elderly survivor—who, with an "indulgent smile, rejects the glass of water they hand her" in a metaphor for her listeners' thirsty imbibing of her words—screens the youthful questioners from the most morbid passages of her memory by imitating the murdered children and maintaining her silence. "They were all silent," the narrator says of the doomed children. The survivor is similarly rendered speechless, at least in the moment encapsulated in the story, by competing obligations to the living and the dead. Caught in a double bind of responsibility both to the child victims of the past and to the students of the future, the speaker at first wordlessly keeps her own counsel about how to bridge the generations before resolving that she, as the last witness, must leave behind a trace of the terrible past.

The story shows the claims of the generations upon one another to be honorable and intense but, ultimately, impossible to fulfill. Parents cannot save their children in a world where children have no right to live, and young children cannot realistically protect their parents—they all die, and the story concludes: "Spokojnym głosem prosi o małą przerwę. Szklankę wody, którą jej podają, odsuwa z pobłażliwym uśmiechem. Po przerwie opowie jak ich wszystkich rozstrzelano"[68] ("In a calm voice she asks for a short break. With an indulgent smile she rejects the glass of water they hand her. After the break she will tell how they were all shot"[69]). Likewise, the earnest young interviewers cannot fully grasp what befell the victims or what the last survivor, their venerable interlocutor, personally witnessed. And as much as the elderly survivor wishes to pay tribute to the murdered children by leaving behind "some trace of them," she cannot rightfully speak for the dead or communicate their plight. The narrative, accordingly, never reaches its conclusion. The story ends with the interview incomplete as the survivor "asks for a short break."[70] In the context of Fink's account, the younger generation never learns from their senior interview subject about the children or how they died. The narrative thus attests to the complicated demands of successive generations to bear witness and the inevitable failure to satisfy that collective duty. Within its brief but comprehensive frame, Fink's text demonstrates the exquisite difficulty of creating a durable chain of ethical responsibility and memorial transmission that extends from one generation to the next. Indeed, the text leaves gaping ruptures in the chain of memory or, as Marszałek calls it, "die semantische Spuren-Kette zum Zeugnis" (the semantic chain tracking testimony).[71] The sundering apart of transgenerational transmission is one of the lasting consequences of the genocide and threatens the viability of a durable poetics of witness: a world in which "children no longer had the right to live" is a world in which testimonial memory cannot help but fracture. Glowacka explains the ineluctable failure of Fink's characters to pass on their testimony, despite their best intentions: "Fink's narrators are constructed as recipients of the stories of others [...] Like the guest speaker of 'Traces,' they have become a precious repository of memory."[72]

"Traces" is a paradigmatic text reflecting the impossibility of shoring up the precarious state of Holocaust memory. Myriad histories and innumerable destinies are lost to the instability of memory that follows in the wake of disaster. The hopelessness of finding a transgenerational perspective outside the space of literature is foregrounded in the text as a challenge that can never be overcome: "The account is passed from speaker to speaker, and the narrator must guard that tenuous passage. At any time, the transmission could be interrupted, and the trace of the victim's extinguished life would disappear irretrievably."[73] Despair at assembling an unassailable chain of transmission surfaces in the survivor's last words as well as in the story's final sentence. The survivor begins to speak of the martyred children but then "breaks off." In the concluding line, she inaudibly recalls in her mind the deadly end to the grim episode with the children but puts off speaking it aloud to the interviewers until after a "break." Will she ever gather the strength to voice her account? The reader cannot know. With the event still unarticulated in speech, the story breaks off.[74] Ginsburg says that this ambivalent conclusion between the past and future imitates the attempt to arrest temporal decay in photography: "Time is frozen in space (the narrative present consistently rendered in the present tense), frozen in a silent photograph, in an untouchable memory, in a long, hesitant, present moment in front of 'nothingness.' It culminates in a future, beyond the text—when 'she,' the woman, will actually tell.'"[75] The photograph, the text, and the survivor linking them remain suspended between past and present, always about to bear witness, never fulfilling or betraying the pledge to translate traumatic memory into speech.

Through Linguistic Straits

Breaking off at the climax of pathos both in the historic account of atrocity and in the contemporary staging of the witness's testimony, the narrative adapts mutable forms of language to reflect the linguistic difficulty of communicating the ineffable. The final line, which discloses what the survivor wants to but cannot say, is delivered with gentle poetic irony in the Polish original. A classically trained musician, Fink spent years polishing and editing her prose, and the melodic quality to this haunting conclusion with its harmonized dyads of sound—"Spokojnym głosem," "[P]o przerwie opowie," "ich wszystkich"[76]—is surely achieved by design. Nor is it by mere chance that again in this coda to a story about what is said or left unsaid the closing lines explicitly intone the word "głos" ("voice"). "In a calm voice," the witness makes her indirectly reported request for a recess, a contrast to the shrill demands of others, particularly the strident shouts of the SS officer. The children's enduring silence in the face of the oppressor speaks to us loudly: "Ale dziecko milczało"[77] ("But the child was silent"[78]). The children courageously kept silent. Then they were all shot dead: "ich wszystkich rozstrzelano"[79] ("they were all shot"[80]). How does one say the unsayable? This passage and, indeed, the entire appalling episode, defies translation into any language. The SS officer presumably interrogates the children in one language, namely German, but the narration reconstructs the event in another language, Polish, although the children's relationship with their parents may have been rooted in still a third vernacular, Yiddish. However, the trace of their silent heroism is equally audible (or inaudible) in every language.

The story ends in silence, both the children's and the survivor's.[81] In response to the mass shooting of innocents, perhaps silence is an infuriating but inevitable response. In another short story in *Scrap of Time*, Fink states, "The silence was horrifying because we knew that there was shooting going on."[82] The constriction of language in the face of atrocity is a commonplace tenet of Holocaust literary criticism, but the masterful innovation of Fink's writing is to expose the workings of that linguistic straitening in the time of the discourse. In her writing, silence is not merely a metaphorical figure, but a narrative device that shows how victims respond in real time to the atrocity they face. Her fiction depicts the surviving witnesses struggling to give voice to what, in the final reckoning, they cannot say. "Traces" shows one such translator of memory tenaciously sticking to her task, even as it overwhelms her.

This constraining of language in Fink's work is hardly figural. In explicating the photo and speaking aloud about the ghetto, the survivor is at a literal loss for words. Her staccato speech is replete with disruptions as she fumbles for the precise phrase: "Takie to... takie... no, trudno powiedzieć"[83] ("Such... such... well, it's hard to express").[84] Similarly, in recalling the children, she wrestles with language before her voice trails off, her faculty of speech reduced to an incoherent stammer by the force of what she seeks to express: "Wcale nie wyglądały na dzieci, tylko jak... ach!...."[85] ("They didn't look like children at all, only like... ach.....").[86] The precise phrase ("like little gray mice") eludes her, occurring to her only shortly thereafter through internal, indirect monologue. The linguistic frailty and cumulative paucity of her articulated speech creates a situation of intralingual translation, in Jakobson's terms. Her occasionally awkward choice of words and frequently confusing statements must be glossed by recourse to other words and explanations in the same language. Indeed, various aspects of her speech ring slightly discordant to the native Polish-speaker's ear. Her rhetorical "Dlaczegóż" ("Why not"), in the opening line, or "Ano tak" ("Yes, surely"),[87] in reply to another of the interviewers' questions, suggest a vaguely archaic, mildly affected form of obsolete Polish that would have been anachronistic by the time Fink published her work. Her unidiomatic speech thus approximates the language of someone no longer using Polish in a contemporary, quotidian context and simulating instead the speech patterns of prewar Polish intelligentsia. That could reflect the status of the narrator, but it may also apply to Fink's own position as an émigré author publishing Polish literature from a long-term Mediterranean exile of over fifty years. The daughter of a bourgeois Polish-Jewish secular family with intellectual and artistic ambitions, Fink's cultural education was abruptly curtailed by the war. The groping for a linguistic register that is natural, idiomatic, and contextual in "Traces" is more than a mere stylistic flourish or fictional pretense. Rather, it signals a lingering trace of foreignness in Fink's language that makes hers a defamiliarizing and unsettling voice in Holocaust literature, a kind of internal translation in Fink's work, even in Polish.

Given its strangely unfamiliar tone and profoundly unsettling subject, Fink's writing is difficult to categorize. Is she an Israeli writer? Her output is all in Polish. Is she a Polish author? Her books were written and originally published abroad, and they focus on a minority population, Jews, and their murder at German hands. Is she a Holocaust author? Perhaps, although her stories, written in a reserved and quiet manner, never make killing manifest and do not address the camps, trains, metropolitan ghettos or any of the typical repertoire of Holocaust iconography. Hovering between identities, Fink confounds attempts at simple classification, sometimes to the consternation of critics. Early in her career, when she was still an unpublished aspiring writer, Fink sent a sample of her short stories to an esteemed Israeli author. After reading Fink's work, the author's reply was sharply dismissive: "Gvirati, kakhah lo kotvim al hashoah" ("Madame, this is not how we write about the Holocaust"), he said, according to her account of the incident.[88] Fink simply did not fit the author's template of an Israeli writer of Holocaust literature. Her ambiguous outsider identity never waned. Neither completely Polish nor Israeli, neither a memoirist nor a fabulist, Fink produced a translational aesthetics of memory that speaks across the margins of time, place, and genre.

In order to reach across those boundaries Fink collaborated with a polyglot coterie of translators who granted her access to a wider reading public, including the Hebrew readers among whom she lived in Israel. Fink maintained especially close ties with two of her translators, Madeline G. Levine, her translator into English for *A Scrap of Time*, and David Weinfeld, her translator into Hebrew. The two were not the first to render Fink's work into their respective languages, and both worked on languages that Fink knew well. But this linguistic affinity helps explain the high level of trust and mutual respect that Fink developed with these translators, as attested in their correspondence, archived in the National Library of Israel.[89] With Levine, for example, Fink maintained a warm and personal correspondence in which she praised the quality of Levine's English translations and explicated obscure Polish words. Levine asked Fink to describe situations mentioned in her texts, and Fink, in turn, corrected Levine's misunderstanding of terms that carried specific connotations during the Holocaust. Sensing that her command of English was strong but not perfect, Fink appears to have trusted her translator to render her work into literary English. Fink had similar faith in her longstanding Hebrew translator, David Weinfeld, who became a confidant and counselor advising Fink on drafts of her stories and the compilation of her books. Fink turned to Weinfeld when unsure of her creative accomplishments, and he counseled her in shaping her literary legacy. He was personally involved in establishing her archive at Israel's National Library in Jerusalem, which includes his original hand-written translations of her stories. Although Fink lived in Israel for more than half a century and conversed fluently in Hebrew, she claimed in interviews that she never mastered literary Hebrew and thus felt indebted to her friend and translator for adapting her words into the written idiom of her adopted country where, despite spending many decades and garnering prestigious awards, she never felt that she fully belonged.[90]

Fink's abiding sense of being alienated from her own experience imbues many of her Holocaust stories, including "Traces," with a tenor of internal foreignness. Like the central protagonist of "Traces," Fink is both an insider to the traumatic past and an impartial witness gazing at the trauma from outside. "Only she could leave that trace, because she alone survived," the narrator tells us about her in "Traces."[91] The same holds true for Fink, who felt that it was her duty to recount memories of which she was the sole custodian. This concluding story of Fink's debut collection describes the only remaining survivor remembering her "last ghetto" ("ostatnie getto"), shrunk to a single alley during its "final stage" ("w ostatnim stadium"), an unusual term that may reflect the interviewers' vocation as professional documenters of the past.[92] Fink's work as a whole indicates a constricting of memory in which entire communities and vast histories would have been consigned to silence if not for the limited memory of solitary witnesses who lack the linguistic breadth or personal fortitude to communicate everything they experienced. Last ghetto, final phase, single street, sole survivor—Fink's writing marks a narrowing of memory through the straits of a testimonial and linguistic bottleneck. This is the poetics of the surviving witness. Her own death, moreover, sets a seal on potential transmission of memory, since any stories which she failed to tell will disappear. Though composed decades ago, Fink's writing embodies the fragile state of Holocaust memory in an era that will soon have no direct recourse to the survivors.

It is a wonder, then, that the survivor manages to speak at all. "Traces" demonstrates Fink's success in articulating silence, in depicting the blank image, in exposing the "negative chronotope"[93] of a nearly forgotten time about to disappear into absence. Her work illustrates the essential role of transmedial translation in decoding the lexical underpinnings of visual evidence, and her writing describes the delicate predicament of trying to transmit memory across a transgenerational chasm: disruptions are an integral part of the story, and foreignness is intrinsic to how the tale is told. When asked to unearth long-forgotten memories that are under risk of erasure or when pressed to provide testimony about events that threaten to fade into silence, Fink's characters still manage to find their voice. They speak the erasure. They shed light on the deafening silence and find that there is, after all that has faded or disappeared, a trace of a "głos" ("voice"). Jaded about that horrific time "when no one was surprised at anything," the protagonist of "Traces" is astonished to find that "her voice sounds amazed."[94] She is shocked by her own surprise: "Dziwi się," "[T]o bardzo dziwne," "[C]iekawe," "[T]o bardzo dziwne"[95] ("She is amazed," "[T]hat's very strange," "[V]ery strange," "[T]hat's very strange"[96]). Fink repeatedly emphasizes the wonderment that the survivor feels in looking afresh at the past. It is "jak gdyby teraz dopiero zrozumiała"[97] ("as if she has just now understood"[98]). Despite the passage of years, new insight can still be forged through a meeting of different generations, the mixing of media, and the encounter between speech and memory at the brink of erasure. Galvanized by language, the unfinished work of the survivor who sees what is invisible to others and the task of the reader who hears what others cannot hear in a new exchange of memory in which linguistic limits and the difficulties of voicing trauma are part of the narrative. The murdered children do not speak, and the photo remains mute. But expressed through the straits of translated memory, Fink's writing continues to communicate after the caesura of the Holocaust.

Postscript

Daniel Feldman and Efraim Sicher

All writing comes after. And we always read *post scriptum*. But during the Holocaust, when historical events accelerated to a vertiginous speed, there was no time to wait, reflect, and make coherent sense of the catastrophe before committing it to writing. As atrocity compounded upon atrocity, there was no clear beginning, middle, or end to the constant agony. There was only a continuous maelstrom of terror in which the victims were constantly caught up in incessant cycles of persecution and deportation, bringing unremitting panic and uncertainty, nearly always *after* some unspeakable event and inevitably *before* something still worse. Remarkably, out of this whirlwind of violence and destruction there emerged a polyglot host of voices, many of them exceptionally eloquent. Though subjected to unfathomable and disorienting turmoil, existing on minimal sustenance, and with barely an inkling of how their private lives had suddenly intersected violently with history, the victims wrote to leave a record of their existence, document what they witnessed, mourn their losses, inspire resistance, and endow their suffering with the dignity of language.

Comprehension is an imprecise criterion to apply to the literature of the Holocaust. The pathos and intensity in the wartime poetry of Sutzkever, Celan, Szlengel, and Katzenelson indicate that during the Holocaust Jewish authors found new ways to portray the disaster in real time. Although these authors experienced the Holocaust piecemeal in a subjective and fragmentary manner, the intensity of their personal ordeals exposed each of them to enough of the massive and heterogeneous event to leave a compelling and authentic record of the Holocaust that endures for posterity; the victims' direct knowledge of the genocide exceeds anything we can understand about what it was like to live through it, despite our more capacious historical perspective. Full comprehension of the Holocaust will likely never come. Nevertheless, the authors presented in this book affirm essential truths about the human need to speak amidst suffering and demonstrate the aesthetic power of literature to turn testimony into art, as well as the density of poetry as a medium of traumatic expression. Our book reveals the startling recognition that some of the most important poetic voices of the Holocaust never survived it.

We have sought to present an interpretive model that integrates literary voices from the Holocaust into critical discussion of the poetics of the genocide. In so doing, we have privileged poetry written during the Holocaust, though we are aware that many of these texts were widely read only in edited form after the war, sometimes long after the death of the author. As such, these messages in a bottle must be read as the words of the dead who bear witness for other victims. The language of testimony is always an idiom of displacement—it exists at a remove from an inaccessible null perspective, the victim's lost point of view to which it bears witness. As such, the literature of witness cannot possibly fulfill its mission, even as it cannot abandon its aims.

More than anyone else, Elie Wiesel accentuated this role of the witness. Witnessing is the dominant mode of the survivors' testimony, essential in order for the world to remember persecution, to resist silence, to prevent recurrence. However, the archetype of a witness to a sublime truth derives originally from Christian scriptures, particularly John's missiological proclamation of the truth of Jesus (μαρτυρεῖτε), itself a figural transformation of the Talmudic *topos* of eyewitness testimony in legal disputes, which is strictly regulated by the judicial principles of Torah law. This is quite different from the biblical notion of *'edut* (testimony) by which, in the final chapters of Deuteronomy, Moses adjures the people of Israel to follow the commandments and charges them with a generational duty to bear witness to the covenant. In Western discourses of victimhood and trauma, by contrast, the survivor-witness has been sacralized for triumphing over adversity.[1]

Celan declared in the final lines of "Aschenglorie" ("Ashglory," 1964): "Niemand/zeugt für den Zeugen,"[2] literally "Nobody" bears witness for the witness. However, this was taken by many to be a call to witness *on behalf of* the witness in a vicarious surrogate voicing of protest at any form of human injustice, as in Canadian American poet-activist Rachel Zolf's *No One's Witness: A Monstrous Poetics* (2021), which extracts these lines from Celan's poem to argue for a queer reading that takes in all instances of human suffering. In her poetry collection *Her Absence, This Wanderer*, Zolf, like Cuban-American writer Achy Obejas in *Boomerang/Bumerán* (2021), is self-consciously aware that appropriation of Holocaust suffering is itself a barbaric act that brings us back to Adorno's dictum about poetry after Auschwitz.[3] Psychoanalysts and Zen Buddhists alike focus on bearing witness to the witness of suffering. We do not have to insist on some demarcation line of authenticity, however, to agree that witnessing in contemporary culture has become detached from any original event or personal narrative of trauma.

In his readings of Celan, partly based on the seminars he gave at the University of California, Irvine in the 1970s, Derrida moved from witnessing to mourning, from testimony to ashes.[4] Commenting on the closing lines of Celan's "Ashglory" Derrida writes:

> Folded or refolded in the simplicity of a singularity, a certain repetition thus assures the minimal and "internal" readability of the poem, in the absence even of a witness, indeed, of a signatory or of anyone who might have some knowledge concerning the historical reference of the poetic legacy.[5]

That is, the poem exists independently of a witness or of anyone who might have knowledge of the history to which it refers. Again, we must contemplate the lack of an addressee in the Holocaust poem. Taking his cue from Murray Krieger, to whom his essay "'A Self-Unsealing Poetic Text': The Poetics and Politics of Witnessing," was originally a tribute,[6] Derrida takes the self-conscious risk of suggesting that a poem bears witness to its own poetics, to its unique inception regardless of generic rules and conventions.[7]

Ashes are what figuratively remain of the final remnant. Insubstantial and spectral, ashes are the residual vestige of a prior incineration testifying to the destruction of the subject.[8] The coupling in Celan's poem of ashes with "glory" ("Aschen-glorie") creates ambiguities which resist hermeneutics and work against the semantics of a legal system that facilitated the burning of millions (a system of false witness). We can never be sure whether Celan means the glory of ashes, or the ashes of glory, or the glory that is in ashes; John Felstiner renders the term as "Ash-Aureole."[9] We cannot know with any certainty whom the poet is apostrophizing or what the poet's relationship is with this entity into whom the poet is "digging." Celan might be addressing a fellow survivor to whom Celan swore fidelity while on a vacation in the Black Sea in 1947 with his Bucharest acquaintance Petre Solomon and others at the time of the first Auschwitz trial. Perhaps now, at the time of the second Auschwitz trials (1963–5), he is recalling that oath. The finality of ash echoes the insistent refrain in "Engführung" ("Stretto"), quoted in Chapter 3, that "Asche" ("ashes") is the word that will endure in language after the existential night of extinguished light and murderous speech passes: "Kam, kam./Kam ein Wort, kam,/kam durch die Nacht,/wollt leuchten, wollt leuchten./Asche./Asche, Asche" ("Came, came./Came a word, came,/came through the night,/would glisten, would glisten./Ashes./Ashes, ashes").[10] What is clear, in both cases, is that the ashes are plural: "They consist in not consisting, in losing all consistence. They have no more existence; they are deprived of any substance that gathers together and is identical to itself, deprived of any self-relation, any power, any ipseity."[11] Derrida admits that the "holocaust" [sic], which he translates etymologically as the "all-burning" (*le brûle tout*), is a revenant that reverberates in the hell of our memory as a clock-date, but it is as unnamable and insubstantial as ashes, as the burnt-out language of Celan's poetry, like the shibboleth, the unpronounceable circumcised and ciphered word.[12]

If we are looking for a philosophy of ashes, we need look no further than *Feu la cendre* (1986; *Cinders*, 1991), Derrida's self-reflexive excursus into philosophical discourse from Plato to Nietzsche and Heidegger that doubles back and parodies his previous writing, deconstructing the language of metaphysics. This polyphonic work revolves around a chance ungrammatical phrase which haunts Derrida, *il y a là cendre* (literally, ashes there are, or there are ashes), yet the title alerts us to the deeper sense of death and mourning in its play on fire (*feu*) and the deceased (*le feu*), inferring a paradoxically impossible discourse after Auschwitz, which remains unnamable. Leaving aside the complex uncertainties of Derrida's meandering meditations, let us merely note his parenthetical definition of the cinder as "(what remains without remaining from the holocaust [sic], from the all-burning, from the incineration the incense [sic])."[13] Writing of the ashes is apparently reduced to the burnt offerings from which no Phoenix will rise, but it is a writing of nothing because, inconceivably, nothing remains of the all-consuming fire/dead. The dialectical question is what trace of the burning of the ashes will be left in the unending struggle between memory and oblivion.[14] For Derrida, as for Lyotard, the Holocaust is an event so extreme that it destroys the record of the event itself.

In his deconstructive readings across languages of Celan's "Ashglory," Derrida acknowledges that we cannot witness what we did not experience and that we can only read what is left of loss after what Maurice Blanchot called the utter-burn of history: the "événement absolu de l'histoire, historiquement daté, cette toute-brûlure où toute l'histoire s'est embrasée, où le mouvement du sens s'est abîmé" ("the absolute event of history, which is a date in history, that utter-burn where all history took fire, where the movement of Meaning was swallowed up").[15] In her reading of Blanchot's "écriture de cendres, écriture du désastre" ("writing of ashes, writing of the disaster"),[16] in *Paroles suffoquées* (1987; *Stifled Words*, 1998), Sarah Kofman turns to Robert Antelme's account of the camps in *L'espèce humaine* (1947; *The Human Race,* 1998) and asks how we cannot speak the erased word when we know that it is an ethical imperative to speak it. This suffocated word (*parole* in French usually refers to a spoken word), which cannot be spoken is what she owes to her father, taken away by French police and deported to Auschwitz, where he was, reportedly, brutally murdered by a *kapo*.

> Parce qu'il était juif, mon père est mort à Auschwitz: comment ne pas le dire? Et comment le dire? Comment parler de ce devant quoi cesse toute

possibilité de parler? De cet évènement, mon absolu, qui communique avec l'absolu de l'histoire—intéressant seulement à ce titre? Parler—il le faut—*sans pouvoir*: sans que le langage trop puissant, souverain, ne vienne maitriser la situation la plus aporétique, l'impouvoir absolu et la détresse même, ne vienne l'enfermer dans la clarté et le bonheur du jour? Et comment ne pas en parler, alors que le vœu de tous ceux qui sont revenus—et il n'est pas revenu—a été de raconter, raconter sans fin, comme si seul un « entretien infini » pouvait être à la mesure du dénuement infini?[17]

Because he was a Jew, my father died in Auschwitz: How can it not be said? And how can it be said? How can one speak of that before which all possibility of speech ceases. Of this event, my absolute, which communicates with the absolute of history, and which is of interest only for this reason. To speak: it is necessary—without (the) power [without being able to do so]: without allowing language, too powerful, sovereign, to master the most aporetic situation, absolute powerlessness and very distress, to enclose it in the clarity and happiness of daylight. And how can one not speak of it, when the wish of all those who returned—and he did not return—has been to tell, to tell endlessly, as if only and "infinite conversation" could match the infinite privation?[18]

In Kofman's reading of Antelme's reference to the asphyxiation of words in *The Human Race*, the words that choke if spoken are also suffocated testimony that demands to be voiced. Yet, following Blanchot, she acknowledges that no genre of story can contain the event of Auschwitz.[19]

Celan's intuition that "Niemand" ("Nobody" as pronoun and proper name) bears witness for the witness can be understood not only as a call to speak for or on behalf of the witness, but also as an acknowledgment that nobody will be able to witness what the victim endured, or, indeed, should be expected to do so.[20] Total destruction, Derrida suggests, negates the possibility of its own witnessing, for the annihilation of witness and words is total: "Ash, this is also the name of what annihilates or threatens to destroy even the possibility of bearing witness to annihilation. Ash is the figure of annihilation without remainder, without memory, or without a readable or decipherable archive."[21] The profane "Nobody" of Celan's heretical "Psalm," for instance, speaks of erasure as a misfortune that transpires in a vacuous universe while Szlengel's Job-like imprecations hurled at the heavens demand that God join the Jewish people by turning into ash. The articulation of erased words, of the untold story, as we saw in Fink's story, which ends before the survivor's tale can be related, if it can ever be told, is contiguous with what remains unsaid. So much has been lost and so many more stories will never be heard that what remains untold dwarfs the few scraps of memory that have come through the inferno of time. Like survivors of the Holocaust, every text that was miraculously rescued from the "all-burning" of the Holocaust is an exception; many more turned into ash.

We end with some thoughts about the loss of manuscripts and of authors. In a 1948 volume of poems titled *Geto un andere lider* (Ghetto and Other Poems), Chava Rosenfarb offers a prologue in which she recounts the book's genesis. She originally wrote the poems in this collection while incarcerated in the Łódź Ghetto, where she was the youngest member of a tight-knit circle of Yiddish poets surrounding Simkha Bunim Shayevich, the most accomplished poet in the ghetto. Rosenfarb informs us that when she was deported to Auschwitz, she took her ghetto poems with her and clutched the papers to her body as she lined up naked before Mengele for the selection. When a *kapo* grabbed her poems and threw them into the mud, she was left utterly dispossessed: "Di lider zeynen geven dos letste, vos men hat mir tsugeroybt" ("The poems were the last thing taken from me").[22] Rosenfarb passed the selection and incredibly received a pencil while in Sasel labor camp, near Hamburg, from a benevolent civilian German overseer. With "no paper to write on, just the pencil," she transcribed her ghetto poems from memory on the "planks of the ceiling" in her barracks above her upper bunk.[23] When she was later deported to Bergen-Belsen, Rosenfarb kept the poems in her head. Those she recalled after liberation were published in the 1948 book.

Rosenfarb's account suggests that her ghetto poems are, like her, survivors of the Holocaust, literary remainders of what she had composed in the ghetto, transcribed in the camp, preserved in her head, and published after liberation—all of it but a tiny fraction of the poetry written by Shayevich and his acolytes in the ghetto. Rosenfarb also says that Shayevich had written an epic poem about the ghetto and that she implored him to bury it. He demurred. His poems, like their author, burned to ash. Apart from two major poems that he wrote in the ghetto and shared with members of the *Judenrat,* leading to their dissemination, the rest of his work from the Holocaust was lost. So was the poetry of other members of his group from the Łódź Ghetto. So were the contents of the third tranche of the *Oyneg Shabbos* archive buried in Warsaw in April 1943, including many of Szlengel's poems that Ringelblum cites but that are not extant. Excavations for the third section of the archive yielded nothing but a few charred pages. The rest was likely incinerated when the ghetto was burned. In the Drohobycz Ghetto, Bruno Schulz apparently wrote several short stories and much of a novel tentatively titled *The Messiah* before he was killed there in 1942; all his Holocaust writings vanished. Much of what was written during the Holocaust turned into ashes without a trace. We will never know how much. We can only be sure that a vast portion of the literature of the

Holocaust was destroyed before it could ever be read. The situation brings to mind the ancient words inscribed in Talmudic tradition that the high priest recited to the Jews assembled two millennia earlier in the court of the Second Temple on the holy Day of Atonement: "More than what I have read before you is written here."[24] Much more than what we have read from the Holocaust was written there in the camps, ghettos, forests, and bunkers of Nazi-occupied Europe.

NOTES

Introduction

1. For a survey and analysis of wartime Jewish writing, see David G. Roskies and Naomi Diamant, *Holocaust Literature: A History and Guide* (Waltham, MA: Brandeis University Press, 2012), 43–74.

2. See, for example, Mary Costanza, *The Living Witness: Art in the Concentration Camps and Ghettos* (New York: Free Press, 1981); Miriam Novitch, et al., eds., *Spiritual Resistance: Art from Concentration Camps, 1940–1945: A Selection of Drawings and Paintings from the Collection of Kibbutz Lohamei Hagetaot, Israel* (Philadelphia: Jewish Publication Society of America, 1981).

3. Koppel S. Pinson, "Simon Dubnow: Historian and Political Philosopher," in *Nationalism and History: Essays on Old and New Judaism*, by Simon Dubnow, ed. Pinson (New York: Atheneum, 1970), 39. See John R. Carpenter, *Wall, Watchtower and Pencil Stub: Writing during World War II* (New York: Skyhorse/Yucca, 2014).

4. Yechiel Szeintuch, "The Corpus of Yiddish and Hebrew Literature from Ghettos and Concentration Camps and Its Relevance for Holocaust Studies," in *Studies in Yiddish Literature and Folklore, Monograph Series* 7 (Jerusalem: Mandel Institute for Jewish Studies, Hebrew University of Jerusalem, 1986), 191.

5. David G. Roskies, "The Holocaust According to the Literary Critics," *Prooftexts* 1 (May 1981): 211.

6. Samuel D. Kassow, *Who Will Write Our History?: Emanuel Ringelblum, the Warsaw Ghetto, and the Oyneg Shabes Archive* (Bloomington: Indiana University Press, 2007).

7. Roskies, "The Jewish Anthological Imagination in the Holocaust, 1940–1945," *Prace Filologiczne: Literaturoznawstwo* 12, no. 15 (2022): 187–91.

8. Milton Teichman, "How Writers Fought Back: Literature from the Nazi Ghettos and Camps," *Judaism* 47, no. 3 (1998): 347.

9. Geoffrey Hartman, "Poetics after the Holocaust," in *The Geoffrey Hartman Reader*, ed. Daniel T. O'Hara (Edinburgh: Edinburgh University Press, 2004), 446–9. For specific cases of reconsideration of poetics *after* the Holocaust, see Gert Hofmann, et al., eds., *German and European Poetics after the Holocaust Crisis and Creativity* (Rochester, NY: Camden House, 2011).

10 James E. Young, *Writing and Rewriting the Holocaust: Narrative and the Consequences of Interpretation* (Bloomington: Indiana University Press, 1988), 16–18.
11 Lewin, diary entry of May 26, 1942, quoted in Amos Goldberg, *Trauma in First Person: Diary Writing during the Holocaust*, trans. Shmuel Sermoneta-Gertel and Avner Greenberg (Bloomington: Indiana University Press, 2017), 37.
12 Goldberg, *Trauma in First Person*, 38–9.
13 Roskies, "Bialik in the Ghettos," *Prooftexts* 25, no. 1 (2005): 103–20.
14 Chaim Kaplan, *Scroll of Agony: The Warsaw Diary of Chaim Kaplan*, ed. and trans. Abraham Katsh (Bloomington: Indiana University Press, 1999), 79.
15 Ibid.
16 Roskies, "Bialik in the Ghettos," 108.
17 Leona Toker, *Gulag Literature and the Literature of Nazi Camps: An Intercontexual Reading* (Bloomington: Indiana University Press, 2019), 178–84.
18 Gebirtig, *S'brent: 1939–1942* (Kraków: Yidishe Historishe Kommisie, 1946); *The Song That Never Died: The Poetry of Mordecai Gebirtig*, trans. S. Simchovitch (Oakville, ON: Mosaic Press, 2001).
19 For example, the Yiddish critic Shmuel Niger's mammoth anthology, *Kidesh hashem* [Martyrdom] (New York: CYCO Bicher-Farlag, 1948); Kadia Molodowsky, ed., *Lider fun khurbn, taf-shin—taf-shin-hey* [Poems of the Holocaust, 1939–45] (Tel Aviv: I. L. Peretz, 1962). Postwar Yiddish songbooks include Shmerke Kaczerginski and H. Leivick, eds., *Lider fun di getos un lagern* [Songs of the Ghettos and Concentration Camps] (New York: CYCO Bicher-Farlag, 1948); Eleanor-Hana Mlotek and Malke Gottlieb, eds., *Mir zeynen do: lider fun di getos un lagern* [We are here: Songs of the Holocaust] (New York: Workmen's Circle, 1984).
20 Included in Kaczerginski and H. Leivick, eds., *Lider fun di getos un lagern;* see Rachmil Bryks, *May God Avenge Their Blood: A Holocaust Memoir Triptych*, trans. Yermiyahu Ahron Taub (Lanham, MD: Lexington Books, 2020), 167.
21 Jerzy Ogórek, "Lokomotywa," in *Poetry of the Holocaust: An Anthology*, ed. Jean Boase-Beier and Marian de Vooght (Todmorden, England: Arc, 2019), 46–8.
22 "Ballad of the White Night," trans. Sarah Traister Moskovitz, https://poetryinhell.org/nature/simkha-shayevitch-balad-of-the-white-night/. Poems from the Ringelblum archive are collected in Agnieszka Żółkiewska and Marek Tuszewicki, eds., *Utwory literackie getta warszawskiego. Archiwum Ringelbluma. Konspiracyjne Archiwum Getta Warszawy*, t. 26 (Warsaw: Jewish Historical Institute, 2017).
23 Goldberg, *Trauma in First Person*.
24 Ibid., 46–50.

25 Lawrence Langer, *Holocaust Testimonies: The Ruins of Memory* (New Haven: Yale University Press, 1991), 39–40.

26 See Zoë Waxman, *Writing the Holocaust: Identity, Testimony, Representation* (Oxford: Oxford University Press, 2006), 7–49; Bret Werb, "Shmerke Kaczerginski: The Partisan-Troubadour," *Polin* no. 20 (2008): 392–412. See also Joseph Leftwich's personal tribute, *Abraham Sutzkever: Partisan Poet* (New York: Thomas Yoseloff, 1971); and the illustrated documentary exhibition on Sutzkever's life, *Avraham Sutzkever: bemloat lo shiv'im*, ed. Avraham Novershtern (Jerusalem: Jewish and National Library, 1983). There is so far no comprehensive study of cultural activity in the large ghettos, but see David G. Roskies, ed., *Voices from the Ghetto* (New Haven: Yale University Press, 2019); Eric J. Sundquist, ed., *Writing in Witness: A Holocaust Reader* (Albany, NY: State University of New York Press, 2019); Eliyana R. Adler, "No Raisins, No Almonds: Singing as Spiritual Resistance to the Holocaust," *Shofar: An Interdisciplinary Journal of Jewish Studies* 24, no. 4 (2006): 50–66; Barbara Engelking and Jacek Leociak, *The Warsaw Ghetto: A Guide to the Perished City*, trans. Emma Harris (New Haven, CT: Yale University Press, 2009); Michał (Michel) Borwicz, *Ecrits des condamnés à mort sous l'occupation nazie (1939–45)*, revised edition (Paris: Gallimard, 1973), 32–42; Adam Gillon, "'Here too, as in Jerusalem': Selected Poems of the Ghetto," *Polish Review* 10, no. 3 (1965): 22–9; see also Amos Goldberg, "The History of the Jews in the Ghettos—a Cultural Perspective," in *The Holocaust and Historical Methodology*, ed. Dan Stone (New York: Berghahn, 2012), 79–100; David G. Roskies, "Jewish Cultural Life in the Vilna Ghetto," in *Lithuania and the Jews: The Holocaust Chapter*, ed. Michael MacQueen, Jürgen Matthäus, and David G. Roskies (Washington, DC: Center for Advanced Holocaust Studies, United States Holocaust Memorial Museum, 2005), https://doi.org/10.7916/D8B85JJK. On German-language poets in Theresienstadt, see Sandra Alfers, "Poetry from the Theresienstadt Transit Camp, 1941–1945," *Rocky Mountain Review* 64, no. 1 (2010): 47–70; H. G. Adler, "Dichtung aus Theresienstadt," in *Fruchtblätter*, ed. Harald Hartung, Walter Heistermann, and Peter M. Stephan (Berlin: Pädagogische Hochschule, 1977), 137–42. On cultural activity in Łódź, see Gila Flam, *Singing for Survival: Songs of the Lodz Ghetto, 1940–1945* (Urbana: University of Illinois Press, 1992); Irene Kohn, "Overlooked and Underanalyzed Source Material on Jewish Life in the Ghettos and Camps: Yossi Wajsblat's *Dos Gezang fun Lodzsher Geto/La Ballade du Ghetto du Lodz*," *Journal of Jewish Identities* 1, no. 2 (2008): 109–20; Jack Woods, "Reading Practices and the Formation of 'Interpretive Communities' in the Łódź Ghetto," *Holocaust Studies* 25, no. 4 (2019): 467–91; Lisa H. Zisman, "A Spark of Freedom: Inherited Recitations of Trauma and Resistance," *TDR: The Drama Review* 65, no. 3 (2021): 8–23.

27 Viktor Ullmann, "Goethe and the Ghetto," in *Spuren zu Viktor Ullmann* (Klagenfurt: Arbos, 1998), 7. See Aaron Kramer, "Creation in a Death Camp," in Kramer, ed., *The Last Lullaby*, 3–14; David Bloch, "Viktor Ullman's Yiddish and Hebrew Vocal Arrangements in the Context of Jewish Music Activity in Terezín," in *Viktor Ullmann: die Referate des Symposions*

anlasslich des 50. Todestags 14.–16. Oktober 1994 in Dornach und ergänzende Studien, ed. Hans-Günter Klein (Hamburg: Von Bockel, 1996), 79–86; Joža Karas, *Music in Terezín, 1941–1945*, 2nd edition (Hillsdale, NY: Pendragon Press, 1963); for a fictionalized account see Josef Bor, *The Terezin Requiem*, trans. Edith Pargeter (London: Heinemann, 1963). On cultural activity in Terezín, see Fanny Malafosse, "Theresienstadt: culture et barbarie," *Tsafon* no. 52 (2006): 153–64. See also Marjorie Lamberti, "Making Art in the Terezin Concentration Camp," *New England Review* 17, no. 4 (1995): 104–11; Janet Blatter and Sybil Milton, *Art of the Holocaust* (New York: Routledge, 1981); Gerald Green, *The Artists of Terezin* (New York: Hawthorne Books, 1969). See also H. G. Adler, *Theresienstadt: Antlitz einer Zwangsgemeinschaft*, 2nd revised edition (Tübingen: J. C. B. Mohr, 1961); Adler, *Theresienstadt 1941–1945: The Face of a Coerced Community*, trans. Belinda Cooper (Cambridge: Cambridge University Press, 2017); Peter Filkins, *H. G. Adler: A Life in Many Worlds* (New York: Oxford University Press, 2019), 103–48; Zdenek Lederer, *Ghetto Theresienstadt* (New York: Howard Fertig, 1983); Anna Hájková, *The Last Ghetto: An Everyday History of Theresienstadt* (New York: Oxford University Press, 2020). On the Theresienstadt poetry of Gertrud Kantorowicz, see Sandra Alfers, "Metafory zániku: smrt jako mezní zkušenost a její poetické vyjádřeni v básni Gertrudy Kantorowiczové 'Das Sterben'," in *Terezínské studie a dokumenty*, ed. Jaroslava Milotová and Anna Hájková (Prague: Institut Terezínské iniciativy, 2006), 40–51: Sigrid Bauschinger, "Gertrud Kantorowicz: Gedichte aus Theresienstadt," *Weimarer Beiträge: Zeitschrift für Literaturwissenschaft, Ästhetik und Kulturwissenschaften* 64, no. 1 (2018): 5–21.

28 Sundquist, "Introduction," in *Writing in Witness: A Holocaust Reader*, ed. Eric J. Sundquist (Albany, NY: State University of New York Press, 2018), xii.

29 Langer, *Holocaust Testimonies*, 44.

30 Ibid., 18.

31 Otto Dov Kulka, *Landscapes of the Metropolis of Death: Reflections on Memory and Imagination*, trans. Ralph Mande (London: Allen Lane, 2013).

32 Langer, *The Holocaust and the Literary Imagination* (New Haven: Yale University Press, 1975), 3.

33 Ibid., 17. See also Sidra DeKoven Ezrahi, *By Words Alone: The Holocaust in Literature* (Chicago: Chicago University Press, 1980), 1–12.

34 Adler quoted in Filkins, *H. G. Adler*, 2–3, 175.

35 Steiner, *Language and Silence: Essays, 1958–1966* (London: Faber, 1967).

36 For instance, Langer, *The Holocaust and the Literary Imagination;* Edward Alexander, *The Resonance of Dust: Essays on Holocaust Literature and Jewish Fate* (Columbus: Ohio State University Press, 1979); Alvin H. Rosenfeld, *A Double Dying: Reflections on Holocaust Literature* (Bloomington: Indiana University Press, 1980); David Patterson, *The Shriek of Silence: A Phenomenology of the Holocaust Novel* (Lexington: University Press of Kentucky, 1992); Ezrahi, *By Words Alone;* Sue Vice, *Holocaust Fiction* (London and New York: Routledge, 2000); Efraim Sicher, *The*

Holocaust Novel (New York: Routledge, 2005); Ruth Franklin, *A Thousand Darknesses: Lies and Truth in Holocaust Fiction* (Oxford and New York: Oxford University Press, 2010).

37 Shoshana Felman and Dori Laub, *Testimony: Crises of Witnessing in Literature, Psychoanalysis, and History* (London and New York: Routledge, 1992).

38 For example, Carolyn Forché, ed., *Against Forgetting: Twentieth-Century Poetry of Witness* (New York: Norton, 1993); and its companion volume Forché and Duncan Wu, eds., *The Poetry of Witness: The English Tradition, 1500–2001* (New York: Norton, 2014). For a critique of Forché's "poetry of witness," see Peter Balakian, *Vise and Shadow: Essays on the Lyric Imagination, Poetry, Art, and Culture* (Chicago: Chicago University Press, 2015), 32–46.

39 Antony Rowland, *Poetry as Testimony: Witness and Memory in Twentieth-Century Poems* (London and New York: Routledge, 2014), 1–7.

40 Carolyn Forché, "Reading the Living Archives: The Witness of Literary Art," *Poetry* 198, no. 2 (May 2011): 167. Emphasis in the original.

41 Borwicz, *Ecrits des condamnés à mort*, 26–7.

42 Ibid., 80–5.

43 Frieda W. Aaron, *Bearing the Unbearable: Yiddish and Polish Poetry in the Ghettos and Concentration Camps* (Albany, NY: State University of New York Press, 1990), 19–20.

44 Bryks, *May God Avenge Their Blood*, 168.

45 Celan, *Gesammelte Werke* (Frankfurt am Main: Suhrkamp, 1983), 3: 186; Celan, *Collected Prose*, trans. Rosmarie Waldrop (Manchester: Carcanet Press, 1986), 34–5. On how the "message in the bottle" creates an addressee in students reading Celan's poetry, see Shoshana Felman and Dori Laub, *Testimony: Crises of Witnessing in Literature, Psychoanalysis, and History* (New York and London: Routledge 1992), 39–40. See also Gisela Dischner, "'Flaschenpost' and 'Wurfholz': Reflections on Paul Celan's Poems and Poetics," in *German and European Poetics after the Holocaust Crisis and Creativity*, ed. Gert Hofmann et al. (Rochester, NY: Camden House, 2011), 35–52; see Chapter 2 below.

46 Tamás Emőd, "Írás a palackban" ("Message in a Bottle"), in *Survivors: Hungarian Jewish Poets of the Holocaust*, ed. Thomas Orszag-Land (Middlesbrough: Smokestack Books, 2014), 29–30.

47 Robert Antelme, "Poetry and the Testimony of the Camps," in *On Robert Antelme's The Human Race: Essays and Commentary*, ed. Daniel Dobbels (Evanston, IL: Northwestern University Press, 2003), 33; first published in *Le patriote résistant* 53 (1948). See Gary D. Mole, "The Poet Remained Alone amidst the Corpses of Words…: The Deportation Poetry of André Ulmann and Maurice Honel," *Critical Survey* 20, no. 2 (2008): 78–87.

48 Alvin H. Rosenfeld, *A Double Dying: Reflections on Holocaust Literature* (Bloomington: Indiana University Press, 1980), 85.

49 Elie Wiesel, "The Holocaust as Literary Inspiration," in *Dimensions of the Holocaust*, ed. Lucy Dawidowicz, D. Rabinowitz, and R. M. Brown (Evanston: Northwestern University Press, 1990), 9.

50 Felman, "Education and Crisis, or the Vicissitudes of Teaching," in Felman and Laub, *Testimony*, 5; emphasis in the original.

51 Felman, "Education and Crisis," 25–40.

52 On the question of literary value, see Borwicz, *Ecrits des condamnés à mort*, 285–7.

53 Joy Ladin, "'After the End of the World': Poetry and the Holocaust," *Michigan Quarterly Review* 45, no. 2 (2006): 284–306.

54 See Sue Vice, "Holocaust Poetry and Testimony," *Critical Survey* 20, no. 2 (2008): 15.

55 Borwicz, *Ecrits des condamnés à mort*, 311–26; Aaron, *Bearing the Unbearable*, 13.

56 Roskies, "Did the Shoah Engender a New Poetics?" in *Eastern European Jewish Literature of the 20th and 21st Centuries: Identity and Poetics*, ed. Klavdia Smola (Munich and Berlin: Verlag Otto Sagner, 2013), 347–63. See also Sven-Erik Rose, "A Poetics of Genocide: The Jewish Dead Confront Their German Murderers in Itzhak Katzenelson's Warsaw Ghetto Poem 'Vey dir'," in *Nexus: Essays in German Jewish Studies*, vol. 5, ed. Ruth von Bernuth, Eric Downing, William Collins Donahue, and Martha B. Helfer (Rochester, NY: Camden House, 2021), 135–63.

57 See Nachman Blumental, *Shmusen vegn den yidisher literatur unter der daytshe okupatsiye* (Buenos Aires: Tsentral farband fun polishe yidn in Argentine, 1966); Ber Mark, *Di umgekumene shrayber fun di getos un lagern un zeyere verk* (Warsaw: Farlag yidish bukh, 1954). Miriam Trinh's groundbreaking analysis of poems from the camps and ghettos found in archives reveals a diversity of linguistic and cultural responses which raise methodological issues ("Hahitnasut bashoah upaneha haravtarbutit beaspleklariyat hashirah haravleshionit megetaot umakhanot" [Shoah Experience and Its Multicultural Aspects as Reflected in Multilingual Poetic Texts from Ghettos and Camps (Yiddish, Polish, German, and Hebrew)], Ph.d. diss., Hebrew University of Jerusalem, 2012, vol. 1.

58 Susan Gubar, "The Long and the Short of Holocaust Verse," *New Literary History* 35, no. 3 (2004): 443–5.

59 Ibid., 450.

60 Susan Gubar, *Poetry after Auschwitz: Remembering What One Never Knew* (Bloomington: Indiana University Press, 2003), 7–8, 146.

61 See Antony Rowland, *Holocaust Poetry* (Edinburgh: Edinburgh University Press 2005); Rowland and Robert Eaglestone, eds., *Critical Survey* 20, no. 2 (2008), special issue on Holocaust Poetry.

62 Boase-Beier, *Translating the Poetry of the Holocaust: Translation, Style and the Reader* (London: Bloomsbury, 2015), 23–32; Boase-Beier and Francis Jones, "Holocaust Poetry and Translation," in *Translating Holocaust Lives*,

ed. Jean Boase-Beier, Peter Davies, Andrea Hammel, and Marion Winters (London and New York: Bloomsbury, 2017), 149–70.

63 Boase-Beier, *Translating the Poetry of the Holocaust*.

64 Saul Noam Zaritt, "Letters without Addresses: Abraham Sutzkever's Late Style," *Geveb*, June 30, 2020, https://ingeveb.org/articles/letters-without-addresses

65 Alan Udoff, "On Poetic Dwelling: Situating Celan and the Holocaust," in *Argumentum e Silentio: International Paul Celan Symposium*, ed. Amy D. Colin (Berlin: De Gruyter, 1987), 320–51.

66 On the shortcomings of some Holocaust anthologies of Holocaust literature see Boas-Beier and Jones, "Holocaust Poetry and Translation"; Roskies, "The Holocaust According to Its Anthologists," *Prooftexts* 17 (1997): 95–113.

67 See Anne-Berenike Rothstein, ed., *Poetik des Überlebens: Kulturproduktion im Konzentrationslager* (Berlin: De Gruyter, 2015); Andrés José Nader, *Traumatic Verses: On Poetry in German from the Concentration Camps, 1933–1945* (Suffolk: Boydell & Brewer, 2007); Sandra Alfers, "The Precariousness of Genre: German-Language Poetry from the Holocaust," *Oxford German Studies* 39, no. 3 (2010): 271–89; Constanze Jaiser, "Benennen und Bewahren: Poetische Zeugnisse aus Konzentrationslagern und ihre Rezeption," in *Poetik des Überlebens*, ed. Anne-Berenike Rothstein (Berlin: De Gruyter Oldenbourg, 2015), 84–102. See also Makana Eyre, *Sing, Memory: The Remarkable Story of the Man Who Saved the Music of the Nazi Camps* (New York: W. W. Norton, 2023).

68 Roskies, ed., *The Literature of Destruction: Jewish Responses to Catastrophe* (Philadelphia: Jewish Publication Society of America, 1989).

69 Edward Alexander, "Patterns of Holocaust Poetry: Representative Voices in Yiddish and Hebrew," in *Argumentum e Silentio: International Paul Celan Symposium*, ed. Amy D. Colin (Berlin: De Gruyter, 1987), 296–319.

70 Among several anthologies of "Holocaust poetry" are Hilda Schiff, ed., *Holocaust Poetry* (London: HarperCollins, 1995); Marguerite M. Striar, ed., *Beyond Lament: Poets of the World Bearing Witness to the Holocaust* (Evanston, IL: Northwestern University Press, 1998); Milton Teichman and Sharon Leder, eds., *Truth and Lamentation: Stories and Poems on the Holocaust* (Urbana: Illinois University Press, 1994).

71 Gubar, *Poetry after Auschwitz*, 56. On multilingual literature during the Holocaust and in its aftermath see Alan Rosen, ed., *Literature of the Holocaust* (Cambridge: Cambridge University Press, 2013).

72 Jan Schwarz, *Survivors and Exiles: Yiddish Culture after the Holocaust* (Detroit: Wayne State University Press, 2015), 5–6.

73 Szeintuch, "The Corpus of Yiddish and Hebrew Literature," 186–207.

74 On the debate over Spielberg's and Lanzmann's competing claims to realism, see for example, Miriam B. Hansen, "'Schindler's List' Is Not 'Shoah': The Second Commandment, Popular Modernism, and Public Memory," *Critical Inquiry* 22, no. 2 (1996): 292–312; Yosefa Loshitzky, "Holocaust Others: Spielberg's 'Schindler's List' versus Lanzmann's 'Shoah'," in

Spielberg's Holocaust: Critical Perspectives on Schindler's List, ed. Loshitzky (Bloomington: Indiana University Press, 1997), 104–18; Gary Weissman, *Fantasies of Witnessing: Postwar Efforts to Experience the Holocaust* (Ithaca: Cornell University Press, 2004).

75 See Toker, *Gulag Literature and the Literature of Nazi Camps,* 10–12.

76 See Naomi Mandel's cautionary remarks on Holocaust fiction in Mandel, *Against the Unspeakable: Complicity, the Holocaust, and Slavery in America* (Charlottesville: University of Virginia Press, 2006). For a consideration of the moral issues in confronting the extreme in concentration camps, see Tzvetan Todorov, *Facing the Extreme: Moral Life in the Concentration Camps* (New York: Holt, 1996). See also Toker, *Gulag Literature and the Literature of Nazi Camps.*

Chapter 1

1 I will refer to Eliezer Vizel (Wiesel), …*Un di velt hot geshvign* (Buenos Aires: Tsentral-farband fun poylishe yidn in Argentine, 1956); Elie Wiesel, *La Nuit* (Paris: Editions de Minuit, 1958); *Night*, trans. Stella Rodway (New York: Hill & Wang, 1960); *Night*, trans. Marion Wiesel (New York: Hill & Wang, 2006); page numbers to *Nuit* and to Stella Rodway's translation, the standard edition used in criticism, will be given in parenthesis.

2 Wiesel later explained that his English was not good enough to check the English translation of *Nuit* and that Marion Wiesel's new translation made a number of corrections and revisions ("Preface to the New Translation," *Night*, trans. Marion Wiesel [New York: Hill & Wang, 2006], xiii).

3 Franklin, *A Thousand Darknesses: Lies and Truth in Holocaust Fiction* (Oxford and New York: Oxford University Press, 2010), 71.

4 Wiesel, *Legends of Our Time* (New York: Avon Books, 1972), viii.

5 Seidman, "Elie Wiesel and the Scandal of Jewish Rage," *Jewish Social Studies* [New Series] 3, no. 1 (Autumn 1996): 1–19. For comparisons between the versions see Susan Rubin Suleiman, "Do Facts Matter in Holocaust Memoirs?" in her *Crises of Memory and the Second World War* (Cambridge, MA: Harvard University Press, 2006), 172–7; Colin Davis, "Reviewing Memory: Wiesel, Testimony and Self-Reading," in *European Memories of the Second World War*, ed. H. Peitsch, C. Burdett, and Claire Gorrara (New York: Berghahn, 1999), 122–30. For a dissenting view, see Ruth Wisse, *The Modern Jewish Canon: A Journey through Language and Culture* (New York: Free Press, 2000), 212–17. Alan Astro weighed into the debate over the factuality of *Night* after the appearance of a new translation by Marion Wiesel with a new preface by Wiesel (2006), engaging critically with Seidman's essay (which has itself become a canonical text), "Revisiting Wiesel's *Night* in Yiddish, French, and English," *Partial Answers* 12, no. 1 (2014): 127–53. On the repercussions of reading the memoir against *Night,* see also Peter Manseau, "Revising Night: Elie Wiesel and the Hazards of Holocaust Theology," *Cross Currents* 56, no. 3

(Fall 2006): 387–99; Gary Weissman, *Fantasies of Witnessing: Postwar Efforts to Experience the Holocaust* (Ithaca, NY: Cornell University Press, 2004), 28–88; Daniel Magilow and Lisa Silverman, *Holocaust Representations in History: An Introduction* (London: Bloomsbury, 2015), 53–62.

6   Jan Schwarz, "The Original Yiddish Text and the Context of *Night*," in *Approaches to Teaching Wiesel's Night*, ed. Alan Rosen (New York: Modern Language Association, 2007), 52–8.

7   See Wiesel, "Preface to the New Translation," xiii.

8   Elie Wiesel, "The Holocaust as Literary Inspiration," in *Dimensions of the Holocaust*, ed. Wiesel, L. Dawidowicz, D. Rabinowitz and R. M. Brown, 2nd ed. (Evanston, IL: Northwestern University Press, 1990), 9.

9   Elie Wiesel, "The Death Train," trans. Moshe Spiegel, in *Anthology of Holocaust Literature*, ed. Jacob Glatstein, Israel Knox, and Samuel Margoshes (Philadelphia: Jewish Publication Society of America, 1969), 6–7; ...*Un di velt hot geshvign*, 210.

10 Lawrence Langer, *The Holocaust and the Literary Imagination* (New Haven, CT: Yale University Press, 1975), 88.

11 Bronislava Volková, *Forms of Exile in Jewish Literature and Thought: Twentieth-Century Central Europe and Migration to America* (Boston: Academic Studies Press, 2021), 68.

12 Ibid., 70.

13 See Wiesel's comment on this in his "Preface to the New Translation," xii–xiii.

14 Hayden White, *Figural Realism: Studies in The Mimesis Effect* (Baltimore, MD: Johns Hopkins University Press, 1999).

15 For a dissenting view of this fake memoir, see Michael Bernard-Donals, "Beyond the Question of Authenticity: Witness and Testimony in the *Fragments* Controversy," in *Witnessing the Disaster: Essays on Representation and the Holocaust*, ed. Michael Bernard-Donals and Richard Gleizer (Madison, WI: University of Wisconsin Press, 2003), 196–217. For discussion of how much authenticity matters in Wilkomirski's and Wiesel's memoirs, see Suleiman, "Do Facts Matter in Holocaust Memoirs?" 159–72; Sue Vice has tried to recategorize Wilkomirski's fake memoir as fiction in *Holocaust Fiction* (London: Routledge, 2000).

16 See Efraim Sicher, *The Holocaust Novel* (London and New York: Routledge, 2005), 79–81; Suleiman, "Do Facts Matter in Holocaust Memoirs?," 163.

17 Elie Wiesel, "Does the Holocaust Lie Beyond the Reach of Art?," in *Against Silence: The Voice and Vision of Elie Wiesel*, ed. Irving Abramson (New York: Holocaust Library, 1985), vol. 2, 126.

18 This was said in the context of being selected for *Ophrah's Book Club*, after the scandal over the exposure of James Frey's autobiography as fictional; Wiesel quoted in Philipp Schweighauser, "Trauma and Utopia: Benjamin, Adorno, and Elie Wiesel's *Night*," in *Haunted Narratives: Life Writing in an Age of Trauma*, ed. Gabriele Rippl (Toronto: University of Toronto Press, 2013), 46. See Franklin, *A Thousand Darknesses*, 69–102. James E. Young

tries to divide *Night* from the novels which followed it by distinguishing between a memoir that records facts and interpretation of the historical and religious meaning of those facts (*Writing and Rewriting the Holocaust: Narrative and the Consequences of Interpretation* [Bloomington: Indiana University Press, 1988], 21).

19 Philippe Lejeune, *On Autobiography*, trans. Katherine Leary (Minneapolis: University of Minnesota Press, 1989). Judith M. Hughes also applies Lejeune's theory in her psychoanalytic study of "literary testimony" but excludes Wiesel because, she says, she cannot identify with a religious Jew (*Witnessing the Holocaust: Six Literary Testimonies* [London and New York: Bloomsbury, 2016], 1–2).

20 See for example, Ellen Fine, *Legacy of Night: The Literary Universe of Elie Wiesel* (Albany: State University of New York Press, 1982); Victoria Nesfield and Philip Smith, eds., *The Struggle for Understanding: Elie Wiesel's Literary Works* (Albany, NY: State University of New York Press, 2019).

21 Mauriac, "Foreword," in Elie Wiesel, *Night*, 10; "Préface," *La Nuit*, 12.

22 Fine, *Legacy of Night*, 32–3. Other scholars besides Fine have adopted the "Lazarean" reading of *Night*; see Griselda Pollock, "The Perpetual Anxiety of Lazarus: The Gaze, the Tomb, the Body in the Shroud," in *Concentrationary Art: Jean Cayrol, the Lazarean and the Everyday in Postwar Film, Literature, Music and the Visual Arts*, ed. Griselda Pollock and Max Silverman (New York: Berghahn, 2019), 108–12.

23 Both essays are republished in Cayrol, "Lazarus among Us," translated by Katie Tidmarsh, in *Concentrationary Art: Jean Cayrol, the Lazarean and the Everyday in Postwar Film, Literature, Music and the Visual Arts*, ed. Griselda Pollock and Max Silverman (New York: Berghahn, 2019), 29–62. See Gary D. Mole, *Beyond the Limit-Experience: French Poetry of the Deportation, 1940–1945* (Bern: Peter Lang, 2002).

24 Josephine Knopp, "Wiesel and the Absurd," *Contemporary Literature* 15, no. 2 (Spring 1974): 212–20; Mary Jean Green, "Witness to the Absurd: Elie Wiesel and the French Existentialists," *Renascence* 29, no. 4 (summer 1977): 170–84.

25 …*Un di velt hot geshvign*, 7; *Against Silence: The Voice and Vision of Elie Wiesel*, ed. Irving Abrahamson (New York: Holocaust Library, 1985), vol. 1, 57.

26 Wiesel, *Against Silence*, vol. 1, 57; …*Un di velt hot geshvign*, 7.

27 Menachem Keren-Kratz, "Between Fiction and Reality: Elie Wiesel's Memoirs," in *The Struggle for Understanding: Elie Wiesel's Literary Works*, ed. Victoria Nesfield and Philip Smith (Albany, NY: State University of New York Press, 2019), 3–24.

28 Daniel R. Schwarz, "The Ethics of Reading Elie Wiesel's *Night*," *Style* 32, no. 2 (1998): 221–2. Daniel Magilow and Lisa Silverman assume Moshe the Beadle was a real person, but turned into a literary figure, "the visionary fool, signaling the literary nature of the book" (*Holocaust Representations in History*, 52). Denis Boak, however, regards Moshe as a "parable" with little grounding in fact ("Elie Wiesel's *La Nuit*, A Reconsideration," *Essays in French Literature* 24 [1987]: 87).

29 Moshe Liberman the *shamash* (beadle) of the Ets Khaim synagogue is mentioned as the sole survivor of the deportation of foreign Jews in the memorial book for Sighet's Jews (Yitzhak Alfassi, Eli Netzer, and Anna Szalai, eds., *The Heart Remembers: Jewish Sighet* [Matan: Association of Former Szighetians in Israel, 2003], 71–2). In the Yiddish memoir, Wiesel describes him in more depth as a Kosover Hasid and a pathetic mendicant who is not listened to, just as prophets of destruction are never listened to (...*Un di velt hot geshvign*, 9–13).

30 Wiesel, *Legends of Our Time,* 105–17.

31 Keren-Kratz, "Between Fiction and Reality," 14–15.

32 Gershom Scholem, *Kabbalah* (New York: Quadrangle, 1974), 166. Here, as elsewhere, Marion Wiesel's translation brings the text in line with the vocabulary of Jewish thought to avoid a Christian interpretation (*Night*, translated by Marion Wiesel [New York: Hill & Wang, 2006], 3).

33 For a discussion of *Night* as a reverse or inverted Bildungsroman see David L. Vanderwerken, "Wiesel's *Night* as Anti-Bildungsroman," *Modern Jewish Studies* 7, no. 4 (1990): 57–63.

34 Randolph L. Braham, *Politics of Genocide: The Holocaust in Hungary*, volume 1 (Boulder, CO: Social Science Monographs and New York: Columbia University Press, 2016), 110–18.

35 Quoted in Efraim Sicher, "The Burden of Memory: The Writing of the Post-Holocaust Generation," in *Breaking Crystal: Writing and Memory after Auschwitz*, ed. Efraim Sicher (Urbana, IL: University of Illinois Press, 1998), 22; the source for this saying is apparently the telegram from Rabbi Shlomo David Halevi Ungar of Nitra, Slovakia, to the American Orthodox Union rabbis' rescue committee which stated: "for those who doubt and ask, there are no answers, for those who do not doubt there are no questions" (Nisson Wolpin, ed., *A Path through Ashes* [New York: Mesorah Publications, 1986], 61–2).

36 Eliezer Berkovits, *Emunah leakhar hashoah* [Faith after the Holocaust], trans. Aviv Meltzer (Jerusalem: Yad vashem, 1987), 62.

37 Babylonian Talmud, Tractate Sanhedrin 88B.

38 Fine, *Legacy of Night,* 28.

39 Emil Fackenheim, "Midrashic Existence after the Holocaust: Reflections Occasioned by the Work of Elie Wiesel," in *Confronting the Holocaust: The Impact of Elie Wiesel*, ed. Alvin Rosenfeld and Irving Greenberg (Bloomington: Indiana University Press, 1978), 109–10.

40 "The Writer and His Universe," *Against Silence*, vol. 2, 62. Marion Wiesel slightly rewords the English translation: "This is where—hanging here from this gallows" (*Night*, translated by Marion Wiesel, 65).

41 *All Rivers Run to the Sea: Memoirs* (New York: Schocken, 1995), 84. See Alan L. Berger, "Faith and God during the Holocaust: Teaching *Night* with the Later Memoirs," in Rosen, ed., *Approaches to Teaching Wiesel's Night*, 46–51.

42 In response to scholars and theologians who have questioned Wiesel's story of putting God on trial in Auschwitz, Wiesel later emphatically confirmed his version (Jenni Frazer, "Wiesel: 'Yes, we really did put God on trial,'" *Jewish Chronicle*, September 19, 2008 https://www.thejc.com/news/uk/wiesel-yes-we-really-did-put-god-on-trial-1.5056). His play, *The Trial of God* (1979), however, is not set in Auschwitz, but in a fictitious Ukrainian village, Shamgorod, in 1649, against the background of the Cossack massacres which wiped out whole communities.

43 In *Legends of Our Time*, Wiesel relates a different version of this episode: the boy quells his rebellious thoughts, and it is Pinkhas, a former head of a Galician yeshiva, who rebels against God by declaring he will not fast, but then fasts in defiance of God and goes to his death laughing (55–61). Marion Wiesel slightly mitigates the effect of a breach of faith when she translates, "Deep inside me, I felt a great void opening" (*Night*, translated by Marion Wiesel, 69).

44 Wiesel, *Legacy of Night*, 19.

45 *All Rivers Run to the Sea*, 73.

46 André Neher, *The Exile of the Word: From the Silence of the Bible to the Silence of Auschwitz* (Philadelphia: Jewish Publication Society of America, 1981), 210–26.

47 *...Un di velt hot geshvign*, 244–5.

Chapter 2

1 Frieda W. Aaron, *Bearing the Unbearable: Yiddish and Polish Poetry in the Ghettos and Concentration Camps* (Albany, NY: State University of New York Press, 1990); David G. Roskies, ed., *Voices from the Ghetto* (New Haven: Yale University Press, 2019).

2 Sue Vice, "Holocaust Poetry and Testimony," *Critical Survey* 20, no. 2 (2008): 7–8.

3 Quoted in Ezrahi, *By Words Alone: The Holocaust in Literature* (Chicago: Chicago University Press, 1980), 21.

4 T. W. Adorno, "Kulturkritik und Gesellschaft," *Gesammelte Schriften*, (Frankfurt am Main: Suhrkamp, 1951), 10:30; Adorno, "Cultural Criticism and Society," *Prisms*, trans. S. M. Weber and S. Weber (Cambridge, MA: MIT Press, 1981), 34.

5 For the postwar debate see J. M. Hoyer, "Flowerless Gardeners: Poetry after Auschwitz," in *Holocaust Literature*, ed. Dorian Stuber (Ipswich, MA: Salem Press, 2016), 182–99.

6 T. W. Adorno, *Negative Dialectics*, trans. E. B. Ashton (New York: Seabury, 1973), 361.

7   For an analysis and critique of Adorno's statements and examples of their misuse or misquotation, see Michael Rothberg, "After Adorno: Culture in the Wake of Catastrophe," *New German Critique* no. 72 (1997): 45–81; M. Tettlebaum, "Nothing Is Meant Quite Literally," in Stuber, ed., *Holocaust Literature*, 200–13. See also Gert Hofmann, "Introduction," in *German and European Poetics after the Holocaust Crisis and Creativity*, ed. Hofmann, et al. (Rochester, NY: Camden House, 2011), 1–16; Berel Lang, *Holocaust Representations: Art within the Limits of History and Ethics* (Baltimore: Johns Hopkins University Press, 2000); Sven Kramer, *Auschwitz im Widerstreit: zur Darstellung der Shoah in Film, Philosophie und Literatur* (Wiesbaden: Deutscher Universitätsverlag, 1999); Stefan Krankenhagen, *Auschwitz darstellen: ästhetische Positionen zwischen Adorno, Spielberg und Walser* (Köln: Böhlau, 2001).

8   George Steiner, *Language and Silence: Essays, 1958–1966* (London: Faber, 1967), 81.

9   Walter Benjamin, "Über den Begriff der Geschichte," *Illuminationen: ausgewählte Schriften* (Frankfurt: Suhrkamp, 1977), 254; Benjamin, "Theses on the Philosophy of History," in *Illuminations*, ed. Hannah Arendt, trans. Harry Zohn (New York: Schocken, 1968), 258.

10 T. W. Adorno, "Engagement," *Gesammelte Schriften*, (Frankfurt: Suhrkamp, 1951), 11:422; Adorno, *Notes to Literature*, vol. 2, trans. S. W. Nicholsen (New York: Columbia University Press, 1992), 87.

11 T. W. Adorno, *Negative Dialektik* (Frankfurt am Main: Suhrkamp, 1966), 355; Adorno, *Negative Dialectics*, 362–3. For German critical responses to Adorno's statements on poetry after Auschwitz, see Moshe Zuckermann, "Zum Begriff der Lyrik bei Adorno," in *In der Sprache der Täter: neue Lektüren deutschsprachiger Nachkriegs- und Gegenwartsliteratur*, ed. Stephan Braese (Wiesbaden: Westdeutscher Verlag, 1998), 31–41; Petra Kiedaisch, ed., *Lyrik nach Auschwitz? Adorno und die Dichter* (Stuttgart: Reclam, 1995).

12 Adorno, *Negative Dialectics*, 363.

13 Jean-Paul Sartre, *What Is Literature?* (New York: Philosophical Library, 1949), 297.

14 Jean-François Lyotard, *Heidegger and "the Jews,"* trans. A. Michel and M. S. Roberts (Minneapolis: University of Minnesota Press, 1990), 43–8.

15 John Zilcosky, "Poetry after Auschwitz? Celan and Adorno Revisited," *Deutsche Vierteljahrsschrift für Literaturwissenschaft und Geistesgeschichte* 79, no. 4 (2005): 670–91. See also Ruven Karr, ed., *Celan und der Holocaust: Neue Beiträge zur Forschung* (Hannover: Wehrhahn, 2018).

16 Gisela Dischner, "'Flaschenpost' and 'Wurfholz': Reflections on Paul Celan's Poems and Poetics," in *German and European Poetics after the Holocaust Crisis and Creativity*, ed. Gert Hofmann, et al. (Rochester, NY: Camden House, 2011), 42–3.

17 For a memoir by a fellow Bukovina poet of ghetto life in Czernowitz and deportations, see Alfred Kittner, *Erinnerungen 1906–1991*, ed. Edith Silbermann (Aachen: Rimbaud, 1996), 55–100.

18 On the Romanian labor battalions, see Dallas Michelbacher, *Jewish Forced Labor in Romania, 1940–1944* (Bloomington: Indiana University Press, 2020).
19 Israel Chalfen, *Paul Celan, eine Biographie seiner Jugend* (Frankfurt: Suhrkamp, 1983), 120–1; *Paul Celan, A Biography of His Youth*, trans. Maximilian Bleyleben (New York: Persea Books, 1991), 159–61; John Felstiner, *Paul Celan: Poet, Survivor, Jew* (New Haven: Yale University Press, 1995), 12–17.
20 On Celan's early poetry, see Hugo Bekker, *Paul Celan: Studies in His Early Poetry* (Amsterdam: Rodopi, 2008); Vivian Liska, *Die Nacht der Hymnen: Paul Celans Gedichte 1938–1944* (Bern: Peter Lang, 1993); Amy Colin, *Paul Celan: Holograms of Darkness* (Bloomington: Indiana University Press, 1991), 53–74.
21 Felstiner, *Paul Celan*, 15.
22 Ibid., 16; Paul Celan, *Die Gedichte*, ed. B. Wiedemann (Berlin: Suhrkamp, 2018), 27.
23 Celan, *Die Gedichte*, 351.
24 Paul Celan, *Selected Poems and Prose of Paul Celan*, trans. John Felstiner (New York: Norton, 2001), 9.
25 Celan, *Die Gedichte*, 351.
26 Celan, *Selected Poems*, 9.
27 Felstiner, *Paul Celan*, 17–21.
28 Celan, *Die Gedichte*, 19.
29 Celan, *Selected Poems*, 15.
30 Accessed February 23, 2021, from the Jewish Music Research Center, Hebrew University of Jerusalem, https://www.jewish-music.huji.ac.il/content/dort-wo-die-zeder-forgotten-zionist-anthem-german. See Edwin Seroussi, "Dort wo die Zeder/Ceder: Jewish-German Lyrical Encounters," in *Die Dynamik kulturellen Wandels. Essays und Analysen*, ed. Jenny Svensson (Münster: LIT Verlag, 2013), 55–71. My translation.
31 Israel Chalfen, *Paul Celan, a Biography of His Youth*, 155–6.
32 Celan, *Die Gedichte*, 19.
33 Celan, *Selected Poems*, 15.
34 Felstiner, *Paul Celan*, 21.
35 Hannah Arendt, "What Remains? The Language Remains: A Conversation with Günter Gaus," trans. John Stambaugh, in Arendt, *Essays in Understanding, 1930–1954: Formation, Exile, and Totalitarianism*, ed. Jerome Kohn (New York: Schocken Books, 1994), 1–23; see Arendt, *What Remains: The Collected Poems of Hannah Arendt*, ed. and trans. Samantha Rose Hill (New York: W. W. Norton, 2023). See also Donatella Di Cesare, *Utopia of Understanding: Between Babel and Auschwitz* (Albany, NY: State University of New York Press, 2012), 99, 108–10.
36 Celan, "Ansprache," *Gesammelte Werke* (Frankfurt am Main: Suhrkamp, 1983), 3: 185–86; Celan, *Collected Prose*, trans. Rosmarie Waldrop (Manchester: Carcanet, 1986), 34.

37 On the context of Romanian surrealism in Celan's early poetry and its bearing on Celan's poetics, see Amy Colin, "Paul Celan's Poetics of Destruction," in *Argumentum e Silentio: International Paul Celan Symposium*, ed. Amy D. Colin (Berlin: De Gruyter, 1987), 157–82; Colin, *Paul Celan*, 74–93; Petre Solomon, *Paul Celan: The Romanian Dimension* (Syracuse: Syracuse University Press, 2008).

38 Quoted in Annette Runte, "Mourning as Remembrance: Writing as Figuration and Defiguration in the Poetry of Rose Ausländer," in *German and European Poetics after the Holocaust Crisis and Creativity*, ed. Gert Hofmann, et al. (Rochester, NY: Camden House, 2011), 70–1.

39 Colin, *Paul Celan*, 31.

40 On the cultural background of Bukovina and its significance for Celan's early life and poetry, see Colin, *Paul Celan*, 3–50. See also Cécile Cordon and Helmut Kusdat, eds., *An der Zeiten Ränder: Czernowitz und die Bukowina: Geschichte, Literatur, Verfolgung, Exil* (Wien: Theodor Kramer Gesellschaft, 2002); Colin, "The Tragic Love for German: Holocaust Poetry from the Bukovina," *Cross Currents* 10 (1991): 73–84; Colin, "Czernowitz/Cernăuți/Chernovtsy/Chernivtsi/Czerniowce: Testing Ground for Peaceful Coexistence in a Plural Society," *Journal of Austrian Studies* 53, no.3 (Fall 2020): 17–44; Martin A. Hainz, "Czernowitz und die Bukowina," in *Handbuch der deutsch-jüdischen Literatur*, ed. Hans Otto Horch (Berlin: De Gruyter, 2016), 362–75; Colin, "Writing from the Margin: German-Jewish Women Poets from the Bukovina," *Studies in Twentieth Century Literature* 21, no. 1 (1997): 9–40; Colin and Corbea-Hoisie, "Celan's Bukovina-Meridians," 5–38; Meyer Weinshel, "Centering the Centerlessness: Czernowitz and the Contiguities of German and Yiddish Modernism," *Journal of Austrian Studies* 53, no. 3 (Fall 2020): 85–95. On the Bucharest circle immediately after the war that centered around Alfred Margul-Sperber (Celan, Moses Rosenkranz, Alfred Kittner, Robert Flinker, Immanuel Weißglas, and Manfred Winkler), see Bianca Rosenthal, "Quellen zum frühen Celan," *Monatshefte* 75, no. 4 (Winter 1983): 393–404.

41 Colin, "The Tragic Love for German," 74.

42 Amy-Diana Colin and Andrei Corbea-Hoisie, "Celan's Bukovina-Meridians," in *Paul Celan Today: A Companion*, ed. Michael Eskin, Karen Leeder, and Marko Pajević (Berlin and Boston: De Gruyter, 2021), 35.

43 Colin, "The Tragic Love for German," 73.

44 Ibid., 77; Colin, *Paul Celan*, 20–30. See Elisabeth Axmann, *Fünf Dichter aus der Bukowina: Alfred Margul Sperber (1898–1967), Rose Ausländer (1901–1988), Moses Rosenkranz (1904–2003), Alfred Kittner (1906–1991), Paul Celan (1920–1970)* (Aachen: Rimbaud, 2007). See Alfred Kittner's camp poems in Kittner, *Der Wolkenreiter: Gedichte, 1925–1945*, ed. Edith Silbermann and Amy Colin (Aachen: Rimbaud, 2004), 56–60; Kittner, *Schattenschrift: Gedichte* (Aachen: Rimbaud, 1988), 35–58.

45 Celan, *Die Gedichte*, 17.

46 Celan, *Selected Poems*, 11.

47 Colin, *Paul Celan*, 47.
48 Felstiner, *Paul Celan*, 25.
49 Celan, *Die Gedichte*, 46.
50 Celan, *Selected Poems*, 31.
51 Heinrich Heine, "Deutschland: Ein Wintermärchen," in *Sämtliche Schriften*, ed. K. Bliegreb (Munich: Carl Hanser Verlag, 1971), 4: 45; Felstiner, *Paul Celan*, 35–7.
52 Chalfen, *Paul Celan*, 133; Chalfen, *Paul Celan, A Biography of His Youth*, 163–4. On Celan's relationship with Ausländer, see Edith Silbermann, ed., *Rose Ausländer—die Sappho der östlichen Landschaft* (Aachen: Rimbaud Verlag, 2003); Helmut Braun, *'Du hast mit deinen Sternen nicht gespart': Rose Ausländer und Paul Celan* (Aachen: Rimbaud Verlag, 2021). Braun reproduces "Ins Leben" on p. 103 and points to a similar metaphor "dunkle Milch" (dark milk) in a poem by another Czernowitz friend of Celan, Alfred Margul-Sperber (105).
53 Arthur Rimbaud, "Les déserts de l'amour," *Poésies: Une saison en enfer, Illuminations* (Paris: Librairie Armand Colin, 1958), 148; my translation.
54 Felstiner, *Paul Celan*, 33.
55 Felman, "Education and Crisis," 40.
56 Jastrun, "Funeral," in Adam Gillon, trans., "'Here too, as in Jerusalem': Selected Poems of the Ghetto," *Polish Review* 10, no. 3 (1965): 31–2.
57 Celan, *Die Gedichte*, 46; Celan, *Selected Poems*, 31.
58 Felstiner, *Paul Celan*, 39.
59 Celan, *Die Gedichte*, 46; *Selected Poems*, 31.
60 Celan, *Selected Poems*, 33.
61 On the history of the two rival muses in German art, see Bonnie Roos, "Anselm Kiefer and the Art of Allusion: Dialectics of the Early 'Margarete' and 'Sulamith' Paintings," *Comparative Literature* 58, no. 1 (Winter 2006): 24–43.
62 Langer, *The Holocaust and the Literary Imagination* (New Haven, CT: Yale University Press, 1975), 10.
63 Available at https://www.youtube.com/watch?v=gVwLqEHDCQE.
64 Georg Trakl, *Dichtungen und Briefe*, ed. W. Killy and H. Szklener (Salzburg: O. Müller, 1970), 32.
65 My translation.
66 Trakl, *Dichtungen und Briefe*, 32; Trakl, *Poems*, my translation.
67 Celan, *Die Gedichte*, 47.
68 Celan quoted in Felstiner, *Paul Celan*, 177; see Colin, *Paul Celan*, 44; Christoph Grube, *"so oder so, es bleibt blau oder braun, das Gedicht:" Aspekte der Trakl-Rezeption Paul Celans* (Würzburg: Königshausen & Neumann, 2013).
69 Colin, *Paul Celan*, 43; Braun, *"Du hast mit deinen Sternen nicht gespart,"* 98–105; Felstiner, *Paul Celan*, 9, 27; Colin, "Immanuel James Weißglas,"

in *Holocaust Literature*, ed. S. Lillian Kremer (London and New York: Routledge, 2003), 2: 1302; Leonard Forster, "Todesfuge: Paul Celan, Immanuel Weissglas and the Psalmist," *German Life and Letters* 39, no. 1 (1985): 1–5; Buck, "Kommentar," 22; Braun, Forster, and Buck reproduce Weißglas's poem. See also the memoir of Celan's friend from Bukovina, Edith Silbermann, *Czernowitz—Stadt der Dichter: Geschichte einer jüdischen Familie aus der Bukowina (1900–1948)*, ed. Amy-Diana Colin (Paderborn: Wilhelm Fink, 2015), 93.

70 See on this, Robert Savage, *Hölderlin after the Catastrophe: Heidegger, Adorno, Brecht* (Rochester, NY: Boydell & Brewer, 2008), 1–5. On Celan's response to Hölderlin's "Andenken," see Savage, *Hölderlin after the Catastrophe*, 20–1; Bernhard Böschenstein, "Celan als Leser Hölderlins und Jean Pauls, in *Argumentum e Silentio*, 183–98.

71 Friedrich Hölderlin, *Sämtliche Werke* (Stuttgart: Cotta, 1953), 2: 205.

72 Friedrich Hölderlin, *Poems and Fragments*, trans. Michael Hamburger, bilingual edition (Cambridge: Cambridge University Press, 1980), 498–9.

73 Felstiner, *Paul Celan*, 287; see Savage, *Hölderlin after the Catastrophe*, 21.

74 Felstiner, *Paul Celan*, 26–30. Felstiner reproduces both the Romanian publication of Celan's poem and a photograph from the Yad Vashem archives of an orchestra in the Janowska camp.

75 See on this dilemma from a psychoanalytical standpoint, Brett Ashley Kaplan, "Pleasure, Memory, and Time Suspension in Holocaust Literature: Celan and Delbo," *Comparative Literature Studies* 38, no. 4 (2001): 310–29.

76 Colin, *Paul Celan*, 46.

77 See Steiner, *Language and Silence*, 95–107.

78 Celan, *Collected Prose*, 35.

79 Ibid., 36.

80 Eric Kligerman, *Sites of the Uncanny: Paul Celan, Specularity and the Visual Arts* (Berlin: Walter de Gruyter, 2007), 139.

81 Adorno quoted in Kligerman, *Sites of the Uncanny*, 140.

82 T. W. Adorno, *Aesthetic Theory*, ed. Gretel Adorno and Rolf Tiedemann, trans. Robert Hullot-Kentor (Minneapolis: University of Minneapolis Press, 1997), 322. We will return to Adorno's reading of Celan in the next chapter.

83 Kligerman, *Sites of the Uncanny*, 140.

84 Celan, "Ansprache anlässlich der Entgegennahme des Literaturpreis der Freien Hansestadt Bremen," in *Gesammelte Werke*, ed. Beda Allemann and Stefan Reichert (Frankfurt am Main: Suhrkamp, 1983), 3: 185–6; Celan, *Collected Prose*, trans. Rosmarie Waldrop (Manchester: Carcanet, 1986), 33–5.

85 Roskies, "Yiddish Writing in the Nazi Ghettos and the Art of the Incommensurate," *Modern Language Studies* 16, no. 1 (1986): 29–30.

86 Roskies, "Yiddish Writing in the Nazi Ghettos," 31.

87 Roskies, *Against the Apocalypse: Responses to Catastrophe in Modern Jewish Culture* (Cambridge, MA: Harvard University Press, 1984), 227–57;

M. Kvietkauskas, "Poetisches Zeugnis: Abraham Sutzkever," in *Vilne, Wilna, Wilno, Vilnius: eine jüdische Topografie zwischen Mythos und Moderne*, ed. E.-V. Kotowski, and J. H. Schoeps (Berlin: Hentrich & Hentrich, 2017), 91–101. On cultural resistance in the Vilna Ghetto, see Herman Kruk, *The Last Days of the Jerusalem of Lithuania: Chronicles from the Vilna Ghetto and the Camps, 1939–1944*, ed. Benjamin Harshav and trans. Barbara Harshav (New Haven, CT: Yale University Press, 2002).

88   Justin Cammy and Marta Figlerowicz, "Translating History into Art: The Influences of Cyprian Kamil Norwid in Abraham Sutzkever's Poetry," *Prooftexts* 27, no. 3 (2007): 427–3; Monika Adamczyk-Garbowska, "'I know who you are, but who I am—you do not know…': Reading Yiddish Writers in a Polish Literary Context," *Shofar* 29, no. 3 (Spring 2011): 99–103.

89   Hannah Pollin-Galay, "Avrom Sutzkever's Art of Testimony: Witnessing with the Poet in the Wartime Soviet Union," *Jewish Social Studies* 21, no. 2 (2015): 4–5; Ruth Wisse, "Introduction: The Ghetto Poems of Abraham Sutzkever," in Sutzkever, *Burnt Pearls: Ghetto Poems of Abraham Sutzkever*, trans. Seymour Maine (Oakville, ON: Mosaic Press, 1981), 1–18; Daniel Kac, *Wilno Jerozolimą było: Rzecz o Abrahamie Sutzkeverze* (Sejny: Pogranicze, 2004), 83–92.

90   Pollin-Galay, "Avrom Sutzkever's Art of Testimony," 5.

91   Pollin-Galay, "The Epic Demands of Postwar Yiddish: Avrom Sutzkever's Geheymshtot (1948)," *East European Jewish Affairs* 48, no. 3 (2018): 332.

92   See Jan Schwarz, "After the Destruction of Jewish Vilna: Avrom Sutzkever's Poetry, Testimony and Cultural Rescue Work, 1944–1946," *East European Jewish Affairs* 35, no. 2 (2005): 209–24.

93   Roskies, "Did the Shoah Engender a New Poetics?" 347–50.

94   Abraham Sutzkever, "My Life and My Poetry," *Zingt alts nokh mayn vort / Still My Word Sings: Lider / Poems*, trans. and ed. Heather Valencia, bilingual edition (Dusseldorf: Dusseldorf University Press, 2017), 45.

95   Abraham Sutzkever, "A tog bay di shturmistn," *Lider fun yam hamoves fun vilner geto, fun vald un vander* (Tel Aviv: Ferlag Bergen-Belsen, 1968), 22–3; Sutzkever, "My Life and My Poetry," 46.

96   Abraham Sutzkever, *From the Vilna Ghetto to Nuremberg*, ed. and trans. Justin Camy (Montreal: McGill-Queen's University Press, 2021), 18–23; Sutzkever, "My Life and My Poetry," 49.

97   Sutzkever, "My Life and My Poetry," 31.

98   Sutzkever, *Lider fun yam hamoves*, 17; *Still My Word Sings*, 92–3.

99   Sutzkever, *Lider fun yam hamoves*, 17; *Still My Word Sings*, 92–3.

100   Sutzkever, *From the Vilna Ghetto to Nuremberg*, 159–60.

101   Sutzkever, "Tsum kind," *Lider fun yam hamoves*, 44–5; *Still My Word Sings*, 96–7.

102   Sutzkever, *Lider fun yam hamoves*, 69; Aaron Kremer, ed., *The Last Lullaby: Poetry from the Holocaust*, trans. Kremer (Syracuse: Syracuse University Press. 1998), 131. "Grins" literally means leaves.

103 Sutzkever, *Lider fun yam hamoves*, 70; *The Last Lullaby*, 132. Sutzkever describes in his memoirs Mira Bernshteyn's exploits and the show she put on in October 1941, to which he was invited (*From the Vilna Ghetto to Nuremberg*, 88–9). She was executed after the liquidation of the ghetto in September 1943.

104 See Aaron, *Bearing Witness*, 110–17.

105 See Michael T. Williamson, "Holocaust Poetry and Literary History: Abraham Sutzkever's Prophetic Mode of Witnessing," *College English Association Critic* 81, no. 2 (2019): 166–7.

106 Sutzkever, *Lider fun yam hamoves*, 79; Roskies, "Did the Shoah Engender a New Poetics?," 347.

107 Sutzkever, *Lider fun yam hamoves*, 55. See David E. Fishman, *The Book Smugglers: Partisans, Poets, and the Race to Save Jewish Treasures from the Nazis* (Lebanon, NH: University of New England Press, 2017), 75–89.

108 Fishman, *The Paper Smugglers*, 99–100. In fact, in November 1942, the Germans took away the lead type and sold it to be melted down in a foundry before being shipped to armaments factories (Sutzkever, *From the Vilna Ghetto to Nuremberg*, 104; Zelig Kalmanovich, diary entry for November 15, 1942, cited in Fishman, *The Book Smugglers*, 71).

109 Roskies, *Against the Apocalypse*, 250.

110 Sutzkever, *Lider fun yam hamoves fun vilner geto*, 94; *Still My Word Sings*, 106–7.

111 Sutzkever, *Lider fun yam hamoves fun vilner geto*, 82; *Still My Word Sings*, 104–5.

112 Aaron, *Bearing the Unbearable*, 34; Roskies, "Did the Shoah Engender a New Poetics?".

113 Haim Nahman Bialik, "Akhen khatsir ha'am," *Kol kitvey bialik* (Tel Aviv: Dvir, 1949), 15; translated by Nina Davis Salaman, in Salaman, *Songs of Many Days* (London: Elkin Matthews, 1923), 54.

114 Roskies, "Bialik in the Ghettos," 115.

115 "Song for the Last," our translation. On the context of this poem, see Roskies and Naomi Diamant, *Holocaust Literature: A History and Guide* (Waltham, MA: Brandeis University Press, 2012), 63.

116 Sutzkever, "My Life and My Poetry," 47.

117 Ibid., 53.

118 Czesław Miłosz, *Poezje*, vol. 1 (Paris: Institut Literacki, 1981–2), 107.

119 Czesław Miłosz, "A Poor Christian Looks at the Ghetto," *The Collected Poems*, 1931–1987, trans. the author with R. Hass and others (New York: Ecco, 1988), 64.

120 John R. Carpenter, *Wall, Watchtower and Pencil Stub: Writing during World War II* (New York: Skyhorse/Yucca, 2014).

121 The manuscript, dating from 1942, was first published in *Odrodzenia* 12 (1946): 5; retrieved from https://ginczanka.de/pl/dodatkowy-material/non-omnis-moriar/ February 28, 2022.
122 Translated by Nancy Kassell and Anita Safran, retrieved from https://agnionline.bu.edu/poetry/non-omnis-moriar February, 28, 2022.
123 https://ginczanka.de/pl/dodatkowy-material/non-omnis-moriar/; retrieved February 28, 2022.
124 https://agnionline.bu.edu/poetry/non-omnis-moriar; retrieved February 28, 2022.
125 Agnieszka Haska, "'I Knew Only One Jewess in Hiding...': Zofia and Marian Chomin's Case," *Zagłada Żydów, Studia i Materiały* no. 4 (2008): 392–407. For a different reading of the poem and a comparison with Szlengel's poem "Things," as well as Rachel Auerbach's essay "Lament rzeczy martwych" (Lament for Dead Things), see Leora Bilsky and Vered Lev Kenaan, "Silent Witnesses: The Testimony of Objects in Holocaust Poetry and Prose," *American Imago* 79, no. 3 (2022): 379–412. See also Bożena Shallcross, *The Holocaust Object in Polish and Polish-Jewish Culture* (Bloomington: Indiana University Press, 2011), 36–52; Natalia Aleksiun and Karolina Szymaniak, "Home as an Uncanny Site of Violence in Polish-Jewish Autobiographical Texts on the Holocaust," *East European Politics and Societies* 37, no. 1 (2023): 229–48.
126 Miłosz claimed he did not know what the mole represented (Shallcross, *The Holocaust Object,* 79–80).
127 Miłosz, *Poezje,* 90–1. The version in the 1944 underground publication reads "Chwytali skrawki" (grasped scraps) instead of "Łapali płatki" (caught flakes) (*Poezja ghetta i podziemia żydowskiego w Polsce* [Ghetto poetry from the Jewish underground in Poland], 2nd edition [New York: Association of Friends of Our Tribune, 1945], 23).
128 Miłosz, *Collected Poems,* 33–4 (slightly revised).
129 Tomasz Żukowski, "Zbiorowa nieświadomość. Czesław Miłosz," *Narracje o Zagładzie* 5 (2019): 44–65. See Shallcross, *The Holocaust Object,* 72–91.
130 Translated by Frieda Aaron in Aaron, *Bearing the Unbearable,* 183.
131 Marek Bernacki, "Memory and Reflection: Czesław Miłosz as a Witness to the Holocaust," *Polish Review* 68, no. 1 (2023): 75–89. See also Sławomir Buryła, "Representing the Warsaw Ghetto in Polish Literature," *Polish Review* 68, no. 1 (2023): 59–74.
132 On Andrzejewski's novella and the exchange of letters between the two writers in Warsaw in 1942–43, see Rachel Feldhay Brenner, *Polish Literature and the Holocaust: Eyewitness Testimonies, 1942–1947* (Evanston: Northwestern University Press, 2019), 75–95; on wartime literary Polish responses to Jewish suffering in the Warsaw Ghetto, see Henryk Grynberg, "The Holocaust in Polish Literature," *Notre Dame English Journal*

11, no. 2 (1979): 115–39; Harriet L. Parmet, "Images of the Jew Focused on in the Translated Polish Works of Tadeusz Borowski, Jerzy Andrzejewski, and Czeslaw Miłosz," *Shofar* 18, no. 3 (2000): 13–26; Shallcross, *The Holocaust Object*, 95–111. For a comparison of Miłosz's poems about the Warsaw Ghetto with the diaries of Polish writers who witnessed its destruction, see Rachel Feldhay Brenner, *The Ethics of Witnessing: The Holocaust in Polish Writers' Diaries from Warsaw, 1939–1945* (Evanston: Northwestern University Press, 2014), 3–23.

133 Jan Błoński, "Biedni Polacy patrzą na Getto," *Tygodnik Powszechny* no. 2 (1987): 42–6; translated as "Poor Poles Look at the Ghetto," *Yad Vashem Studies* 19 (1988): 357–67.
134 Miłosz, *Poezje*, 35.
135 Ibid., 124; Miłosz, *Collected Poems*, 78.
136 Miłosz, *Collected Poems*, 79.
137 Czesław Miłosz, *The Witness of Poetry* (Cambridge, MA: Harvard University Press, 1983), 97.
138 Terry Eagleton, *Ideology of the Aesthetic* (Oxford: Oxford University Press, 1990), 242–62.
139 Paul Fussell, *The Great War and Modern Memory* (Oxford: Oxford University Press, 1975), 8–9.
140 Ibid., 18–19.
141 Quoted, ibid., 119.
142 Ibid., 169–74.
143 Celan, *Die Gedichte*, 136.
144 Celan, *Selected Poems and Prose*, 157. On Celan's negative theology in this poem, see Adam Lipszyc, "The Stylus and the Almond: Negative Literary Theologies in Paul Celan," in *Negative Theology as Jewish Modernity*, ed. Michael Fagenblat (Bloomington: Indiana University Press, 2017), 304–21.
145 Felstiner, *Paul Celan*, 168. For multiple interpretations of this poem see Vivian Liska, "Paul Celan, the Last Psalmist," in *Psalms in/on Jerusalem*, ed. Ilana Pardes and Ophir Münz-Manor (Berlin: De Gruyter, 2019), 143–52.
146 Dischner, "'Flaschenpost' and 'Wurfholz,'" 45–6.
147 Sutzkever, *Lider fun yam hamoves*, 21; *Still My Word Sings*, 94, 95.
148 Sutzkever, "Shneementsh," in *The Full Pomegranate: Poems of Avrom Sutzkever*, trans. Richard J. Fein (Albany, NY: State University of New York, 2019), 30–1.
149 See Roskies, *Against the Apocalypse*, 237–8.
150 Sutzkever, *Lider fun yam hamoves*, 357–8. See Williamson, "Holocaust Poetry and Literary History," 164–5.

Chapter 3

1. See Yiftakh Ben Aharon, *Dialog derekh ha'ayin: heyalmut kefetakh el heakher beshirat paul tselan* (Tel Aviv: Resling, 2020); Marc Redfield, *Shibboleth: Judges, Derrida, Celan* (New York: Fordham University Press, 2020); Antti Salminen, "Meridian Zero: Nothings of Celan and Heidegger Compared," *Angelaki: Journal of Theoretical Humanities* 17, no. 3 (2012): 75–84; Galili Shahar, *Haeuven yehamilah: 'al shirat paul tselan* (Jerusalem: Mossad Bialik, 2019); Shane Weller, *Language and Negativity in European Modernism* (Cambridge, UK: Cambridge University Press, 2019).
2. Jacques Derrida, "Shibboleth for Paul Celan," trans. Joshua Wilner, in *Word Traces: Readings of Paul Celan*, ed. Aris Fioretos (Baltimore: Johns Hopkins University Press, 1994), 3–74.
3. Derrida, "Shibboleth for Paul Celan," 67.
4. For examples of the vast body of criticism on the relationship between Heidegger and Celan, see Florian Grosser and Nassima Sahraoui, eds., *Heidegger in the Literary World: Variations on Poetic Thinking* (London: Rowman & Littlefield, 2021); Hagi Kenaan, "Celan and Heidegger at the Mountain of Death: Listening to Hope," *Journal of the British Society for Phenomenology* 52, no. 4 (2021): 352–65; James K. Lyon, *Paul Celan and Martin Heidegger: An Unresolved Conversation, 1951–1970* (Baltimore: Johns Hopkins University Press, 2006); Kristin Rebien, "Dichten, Denken, Lesen: Theories of Reading in Paul Celan and Martin Heidegger," *Germanic Review* 84, no. 1 (2009): 59–83; and Salminen, "Meridian Zero."
5. Derrida, "Shibboleth for Paul Celan," 31.
6. Paul Celan, *Die Gedichte: Neue kommentierte Gesamtausgabe*, ed. Barbara Wiedemann (Berlin: Suhrkamp, 2018), 145; Celan, *Selected Poems and Prose*, trans. John Felstiner (New York: W.W. Norton, 2001), 170–1; Derrida, "Shibboleth for Paul Celan," 65.
7. Quoted in Mark M. Anderson, "The 'Impossibility of Poetry': Celan and Heidegger in France," *New German Critique* 53 (1991): 12.
8. Theodor W. Adorno, *Aesthetic Theory*, trans. Christopher Lenhart (London: Routledge and Kegan Paul, 1984), 400.
9. Celan, *Gedichte*, 118; Celan, *Selected Poems*, 125.
10. Aris Fioretos, "Nothing: History and Materiality in Celan," in *Word Traces: Readings of Paul Celan*, ed. Aris Fioretos (Baltimore: Johns Hopkins University Press, 1994), 329.
11. Ibid., 321.
12. Ibid., 329.
13. Ibid., 321. See also Marlies Janz, *Vom Engagement absoluter Poesie: zur Lyrik und Ästhetik Paul Celans* (Frankfurt: Syndikat, 1976); Winfried Menninghaus, *Paul Celan: Magie der Form* (Frankfurt: Suhrkamp, 1980); and Peter Szondi, "Lecture de Strette: essai sur la poesie de Paul Celan," *Critique* 288 (1971): 387–420.

14 Fioretos, "Nothing," 332.
15 Celan, "Die Niemandrose," *Gedichte*, 145.
16 Fioretos, "Nothing," 329.
17 Celan, "Speech-Grille," *Selected Poems*, 106–7.
18 Celan, "A la pointe acérée," *Gedichte*, 150; my translation.
19 Celan, *Selected Poems*, 324–5.
20 Ibid., 371.
21 Celan, "Atemwende," *Gedichte*, 187.
22 Shira Wolosky, "The Lyric, History, and the Avant-Garde: Theorizing Paul Celan," *Poetics Today* 22, no. 3 (2001): 656–9.
23 Anne Carson, *Economy of the Unlost* (Princeton: Princeton University Press, 1999), 9. On Celan's poetics of negativity, see also Shira Wolosky, *Language Mysticism: The Negative Way of Language in Eliot, Beckett, and Celan* (Stanford: Stanford University Press, 1995), 6; Weller, *Language and Negativity*, 158–86.
24 Carson, *Economy of the Unlost*, 141.
25 Geoffrey Hartman, *The Longest Shadow: In the Aftermath of the Holocaust* (Bloomington: Indiana University Press, 1996), 164.
26 Wolosky, *Language Mysticism*, 4–6.
27 See Margrit Schärer, *Negationen im Werke Paul Celans* (Zürich: Juris, 1976).
28 Peter Paul Schwarz, *Totengedächtnis und dialogische Polarität in der Lyrik Paul Celans* (Düsseldorf: Schwann, 1966), 55.
29 Krzysztof Ziarek, *Inflected Language: Toward a Hermeneutics of Nearness— Heidegger, Levinas, Stevens, Celan* (Albany: SUNY Press, 1994), 142.
30 Carson, *Economy of the Unlost*, 114.
31 Celan, *Gedichte,* 117; *Selected Poems*, 118–31.
32 Wolosky, *Language Mysticism*, 7, 262.
33 Fioretos, "Nothing," 332.
34 John Felstiner, *Paul Celan: Poet, Survivor, Jew* (New Haven: Yale University Press, 1995), 124.
35 Celan, *Gedichte*, 117; *Selected Poems*, 118–31.
36 Ibid.
37 Ibid.
38 Celan, *Gedichte*, 113; *Selected Poems*, 116–17.
39 Celan, *Gedichte*, 146.
40 Celan, *Selected Poems* 172–3.
41 Felstiner, *Celan*, 180.
42 Ibid., 181.
43 Celan, *Gedichte*, 106; Carson, *Economy of the Unlost*, 4–5.
44 Celan, *Selected Poems*, 119.

45 Celan, *Gedichte*, 118.
46 Celan, *Selected Poems*, 121.
47 Felstiner, *Celan*, 121.
48 Celan, *Gedichte*, 118.
49 Celan, *Selected Poems*, 123.
50 Felstiner, *Celan*, 122.
51 Derrida, "Shibboleth," 43–4.
52 Celan, *Selected Poems*, 236–7.
53 Celan, *Gedichte*, 202. See pp. 198–200 below.
54 Wolosky, "Lyrik," 661.
55 Wolosky, *Language Mysticism*, 236–63.
56 Hartman, *Longest Shadow*, 164.
57 Ibid., 172.
58 Celan, *Gedichte*, 136.
59 Celan, *Selected Poems*, 157. See pp. 75–76 above.
60 Celan, *Gedichte*, 129.
61 Celan, *Selected Poems*, 134.
62 Ibid.
63 Celan, *Gedichte*, 136.
64 Celan, *Selected Poems*, 157.
65 Derrida, "Shibboleth," 31, and Fioretos, "Nothing," 333.
66 Paul Celan, *Microliths They Are, Little Stones: Posthumous Prose*, trans. Pierre Joris (New York: Contra Mundum Press, 2020), 89.
67 Ibid., 90.
68 Paul Celan, *Gesammelte Werke* (Frankfurt: Suhrkamp, 1983), 3:198; Celan, *Collected Prose*, trans. Rosmarie Waldrop (New York: Routledge, 2003), 53.
69 Ziarek, *Inflected Language*, 195.
70 Susan Gubar, "The Long and the Short of Holocaust Verse," *New Literary History* 35, no. 3 (2004): 444.
71 See Shoshana Felman and Dori Laub, *Testimony* (New York: Routledge, 1992), 80–92.
72 Hannah Arendt, *The Origins of Totalitarianism* (Cleveland: Meridian, 1958), 452–4.
73 Celan, *Gedichte*, 40.
74 Martin Heidegger, *Being and Time*, trans. Joan Stambaugh (Albany: SUNY Press, 1996), 251.
75 Felstiner, *Paul Celan*, 151.
76 Celan, *Gesammelte Werke*, 3:186; *Selected Poems*, 396. See also the discussion of this point in chapter 2.

77 Theodor W. Adorno, *Negative Dialectics*, trans. E.B. Ashton (New York: Seabury Press, 1973), 362. For a discussion of this passage see pp. 44–46 above.
78 Martin Heidegger, "Hölderlin and the Essence of Poetry," trans. Douglas Scott, in *Existence and Being* (Chicago: Henry Regnery, 1949), 279.
79 Celan, *Gedichte*, 132.
80 Celan, *Gesammelte Werke*, 2: 31; Carson, *Economy of the Unlost*, 112.
81 Heidegger, *Being and Time*, 40, 251.
82 Theodor W. Adorno, *Negative Dialektik* (Frankfurt: Suhrkamp, 1966), 353.
83 Adorno, *Negative Dialectics*, 362–3, amended.
84 Celan, *Gesammelte Werke*, 3: 195.
85 Ibid.
86 Celan, *Selected Poems*, 407.
87 Ruby Cohn, "Ruby Cohn on the Godot Circle," in *Beckett Remembering, Remembering Beckett*, ed. James Knowlson and Elizabeth Knowlson (London: Bloomsbury, 2006), 129.
88 Martin Heidegger, *Gesamtausgabe* (Frankfurt: Vittorio Klostermann, 1976), 9:108–9.
89 Heidegger, *Pathmarks* (New York: Cambridge University Press, 1998), 84–5.
90 Ibid., 86.
91 Heidegger, *Gesamtausgabe*, 114; *Pathmarks*, 90.
92 Heidegger, *Gesamtausgabe*, 122; *Pathmarks*, 96.
93 Celan, *Gedichte*, 131.
94 My translation.
95 Philippe Lacoue-Labarthe, *Poetry as Experience*, trans. Andrea Tarnowski (Stanford: Stanford University Press, 1999), 33.
96 Celan, *Gedichte*, 286–7; *Selected Poems*, 315.
97 Ibid.
98 Emanuel Levinas, *Proper Names*, trans. Michael B. Smith (London: Athlone Press, 1996), 40.
99 Todd Samuel Presner, "Traveling between Delos and Berlin: Heidegger and Celan on the Topography of 'What Remains'," *German Quarterly* 74, no. 4 (2001): 417–29.
100 Celan, *Gedichte*, 129; *Selected Poems*, 135.
101 Dorota Glowacka, "A Date, a Place, a Name: Jacques Derrida's Holocaust Translations," *CR: The New Centennial Review* 7, no. 2 (2007): 136. Heidegger explains his complex investment in the significance of copular verbs in *The Basic Problems of Phenomenology*, rev. ed. (Bloomington: Indiana University Press, 1982), 177ff. Adorno outlines his disagreement with Heidegger's conception of the copula in *Negative Dialectics*, 101.

102 See pp. 52–53 above for a description of the prewar cultural milieu of Bukovina.
103 For more on this heritage, see Sidra DeKoven Ezrahi, *Booking Passage: Exile and Homecoming in the Modern Jewish Imagination* (Berkeley: University of California Press, 2000), 157–78; Marianne Hirsch and Leo Spitzer, *Ghosts of Home: The Afterlife of Czernowitz in Jewish Memory* (Berkeley: University of California Press, 2010).
104 Dan Pagis, *Kol hashirim* (Jerusalem: Hakibbutz hameukhad and Mossad Bialik, 1991), 135.
105 Dan Pagis, *Variable Directions*, trans. Stephen Mitchell (San Francisco: North Point Press, 1989), 29, amended.
106 On the poem's circularity see Wendy Zierler, "Footprints, Traces, Memories: The Operation of Memory in Dan Pagis' 'Aqebot,'" *Judaism* 41, no. 4 (1992): 325; Ezrahi, *Booking Passage*, 84; and Gubar, "The Long and the Short," 448.
107 Gubar, "The Long and the Short," 448.
108 Ibid.
109 Amir Eshel, "Eternal Present: Poetic Figuration and Cultural Memory in the Poetry of Yehuda Amichai, Dan Pagis, and Tuvia Rübner," *Jewish Social Studies* 7, no. 1 (2000): 143.
110 Pagis, *Kol Hashirim*, 136.
111 Pagis, *Variable Directions*, 32, amended.
112 Kaja Silverman, *The Threshold of the Visible World* (New York: Routledge, 1996), 14.
113 Pagis, *Variable Directions*, 36, 39.
114 Ibid., 5.
115 Pagis, *Kol Hashirim*, 269. My translation.
116 Ludwig Wittgenstein, *Tractatus Logico-Philosophicus*, Side-by-Side-by-Side Edition, translated by Frank Ramsey, C.K. Ogden, David Pears, and Brian McGuinness, University of Massachusetts, accessed November 15, 2022, https://people.umass.edu/klement/tlp/tlp.html#p6.4311.
117 Pagis, *Variable Directions*, 5.
118 Pagis, *Kol Hashirim*, 137.
119 Pagis, *Variable Directions*, 33, amended.
120 Celan, *Gedichte*, 218. My translation.
121 Derrida, "Shibboleth," 44.
122 Ziarek, *Inflected Language*, 166.
123 Celan, *Gedichte*, 218.
124 Hartman, *Longest Shadow*, 164.
125 Ezrahi, *Booking Passage*, 145.
126 Pagis, *Kol hashirim*, 308.
127 Ibid., 228.

128 Celan, *Selected Poems*, 134.
129 Celan, *Gesammelte Werke*, 3: 181.
130 Celan, *Gesammelte Werke*, 3: 202; *Selected Poems*, 413.
131 Levinas, *Proper Names*, 46.
132 Celan, *Gesammelte Werke*, 3: 167; Celan, *Collected Prose*, 16.
133 Celan, *Gesammelte Werke*, 3: 197; *Selected Poems*, 409.
134 Celan, *Gedichte*, 577; *Selected Poems*, 377.
135 Celan, *Gesammelte Werke*, 3: 186, 173; *Selected Poems*, 400.
136 Hartman, *Longest Shadow*, 164.
137 Celan, *Gedichte*, 524; *Selected Poems*, 391.
138 Derrida, "Shibboleth," 44.
139 Ibid.

Chapter 4

1 Heine, *Buch der Lieder* (Hamburg: Hoffmann und Campe, 1827), 192.
2 Radnóti, *Napló* (Budapest: Magvető, 1989), 210–11; translated by Alan Campbell in András Gerő, *The Jewish Criterion in Hungary* (Boulder, CO: Social Science Monographs, 2007), 84–5; revised by the author and Ilana Rosen.
3 *Napló*, 211; *The Jewish Criterion in Hungary*, 84.
4 *Napló*, 212; *The Jewish Criterion in Hungary*, 85. Radnóti's widow maintained this refusal to permit publication of his poems in a Jewish journal to the day of her death in 2014, even when a Hungarian Jewish journal issued a special issue on the poet's centenary; see Janos Kőbányai, "(Nyílt) Levél Radnóti Miklós feleségének" [(Open) Letter to Miklós Radnóti's Wife], *Múlt és Jövő* 4 (2009): 7–12. See also Ozsváth, *In the Footsteps of Orpheus*, 189.
5 See László Takács, "The Eclogues of Miklós Radnóti: A Twentieth-Century Vergil," *Acta Antiqua Academiae Scientiarum Hungaricae* 53, nos. 2–3 (2013): 311–22. For a detailed comparative analysis of Radnóti's eclogues, see B. S. Adams, "The Eclogues of Miklós Radnóti," *Slavonic and East European Review* 43, no. 101 (1965): 390–9, and Géfin L. Kemenes, "The Pastoral Muse: The Vergilian Intertext of Miklós Radnóti's Eclogues," *Hungarian Studies* 11 (1996): 45–57.
6 As Radnóti himself testified, *Napló*, 211; Gerő, *The Jewish Criterion in Hungary*, 84.
7 Ozsváth, *In the Footsteps of Orpheus*, 36–9.
8 On the treatment of the Jews and the anti-Semitic policies of the Hungarian government in the interwar years and during the Holocaust, see Raphael Patai, *The Jews of Hungary: History, Culture, Psychology* (Detroit: Wayne State University Press,1996), 458–596; Nathaniel Katzburg, *Hungary and*

the Jews: Policy and Legislation 1920–1943 (Ramat Gan: Bar-Ilan University Press,1981).

9   In 1941, the Jews numbered 725,007 or 4.94 percent of the Hungarian population; there were 100,000 converts or Christians of Jewish origin who were identified as Jews under the racial laws then in effect, of whom, 62,350 lived in Budapest (Randolph L. Braham, *Politics of Genocide: The Holocaust in Hungary*, volume 1 [Boulder, CO: Social Science Monographs and New York: Columbia University Press, 2016], 87–9).

10 Ferencz, "The Poetry of Miklós Radnóti": 7.

11 See Gerő, *The Jewish Criterion in Hungary*; Susan Rubin Suleiman and Éva Forgács, "Introduction," in *Contemporary Jewish Writing in Hungary: An Anthology*, ed. Susan Rubin Suleiman and Éva Forgács (Lincoln, NB: University of Nebraska Press, 2003), xxx; Mihály Szegedy-Maszák, "Radnóti Miklós és a Holocaust Irodalma," [Miklós Radnóti and Holocaust Literature], in *A határ és a határolt: Töprengések a magyar-zsidó irodalom létformáiról* [The Border and the Bounded: Reflections on the Forms of Hungarian-Jewish Literature], ed. Petra Török (Budapest: Országos Rabbiképző Intézet, 1997), 207–29.

12 See Mihály Szegedy-Maszák, "National and International Implications in Radnóti's Poetry," *Hungarian Quarterly* 4 (1996): 13–28; Szegedy-Maszák, "Radnóti Miklós és a Holocaust Irodalma," 207–29.

13 Radnóti, *Ikrek hava. Napló a gyerekkorról* (Budapest: Magyar Helikon, 1973); "Under Gemini: A Diary about Childhood," in *Under Gemini: A Prose Memoir and Selected Poetry*, trans. Kenneth and Zita McRobbie and Jascha Kessler (Budapest: Corvina Kiadó, 1985), 19–59.

14 "Under Gemini," 58–9.

15 Radnóti, "Huszonnyolc év" ("Twenty-Eight Years"), *Miklós Radnóti: The Complete Poetry in Hungarian and English*, trans. Gabor Barabas (Jefferson, NC: McFarland, 2014), 102. All further references to Radnóti's poems will be to this edition and will be given in parenthesis.

16 English translation by H. Rushton Fairclough, *Eclogues, Georgics, Aeneid I–VI*, revised edition (London: Heinemann, 1935), 1: 134–5.

17 Quoted and translated in Takács, "The Eclogues of Miklós Radnóti": 322.

18 Seamus Heaney, "Eclogues 'In Extremis': On the Staying Power of Pastoral," *Proceedings of the Royal Irish Academy, Section C,* Vol.103C (1) (2003): 1–12.

19 Ozsváth, *In the Footsteps of Orpheus*, 141–2.

20 Ibid., 145–6.

21 Zsuzsanna Ozsváth, "Visions of Catastrophe in the Poetry of Miklós Radnóti," *CLCWeb: Comparative Literature and Culture* 11, no. 1 (2009): https://doi.org/10.7771/1481-4374.1414.

22 For a comparison of these modernist tropes in Radnóti and Celan, see Zsuzsanna Ozsváth, "Radnóti, Celan, and Aesthetic Shifts in Central European Holocaust Poetry," in *Comparative Central European Culture*, ed.

Steven Tötösy de Zepetnek (Lafayette, IN: Purdue University Press, 2002), 51–70; https://doi.org/10.2307/j.ctt6wq7hx.6.
23 Ozsváth, *In the Footsteps of Orpheus*, 177–8.
24 Ilana Rosen, "Soldiers or Slaves?: Narratives of Survivors of the Hungarian Army's Labor Service in World War II and the Holocaust," *Dapim—Studies on the Shoah* 26 (2012): 95–123.
25 Ozsváth, *In the Footsteps of Orpheus*, 152.
26 Ozsváth, *In the Footsteps of Orpheus*, 164.
27 Takács, "The Eclogues of Miklós Radnóti," 317.
28 Ibid., 218.
29 Ozsváth, *In the Footsteps of Orpheus*, 199.
30 Ferenc Andai, *In the Hour of Fate and Danger*, trans. Marietta Morry and Lynda Muir (Toronto: Azrieli Foundation, 2020), 9–15. Andai provides a valuable first-hand account of conscription to the labor brigades, including his acquaintance in Camp Haidenau with Radnóti and others. See also the witness accounts of the labor camps at Bor in Szita Szabolcs, *Kényszermunka, erőltetett menet, tömeghalál: túlélő bori munkaszolgálatosok visszaemlékezései, 1943–1944* [Forced labor, forced march: Recollections of Bor forced laborers surviving mass death, 1943–44] (Budapest: Makkabi Kiadó, 2004); translated into Hebrew as *Bor, sipuro shel makhane le'avodot kfiyah, 1943–1944: mivkhar 'eduyot* (Jerusalem: Yad vashem, 2015); Zvi Erez, "Jews for Copper: Jewish-Hungarian Labor Service Companies in Bor," *Yad Vashem Studies* 28 (2000): 243–86; see also Randolph L. Braham, *The Hungarian Labor Service System, 1939–45* (Boulder, CO: East European Quarterly, 1977); Braham, *Politics of Genocide*, 1:333–428.
31 Andai, *In the Hour of Fate and Danger*, 25.
32 Ibid., 2, 26–8, 31–2, 34, 38–40, 45.
33 Ibid., 25.
34 Ibid., 30.
35 Adams, "The Eclogues of Miklós Radnóti," 398.
36 Takács, "The Eclogues of Miklós Radnóti," 319–20.
37 Heaney, "Eclogues in Extremis'," 12.
38 Emery George, *The Poetry of Miklós Radnóti: A Comparative Study* (New York: Karz-Cohl, 1986), 509.
39 George, *The Poetry of Miklós Radnóti*, 206–12, 499.
40 Andai, *In the Hour of Fate and Danger*, 47–93.
41 For a reconstruction of Radnóti's gruesome and grueling journey on foot and in cattle cars across Serbia and Hungary from September 17 to November 9, 1944, see Ozsváth, *In the Footsteps of Orpheus*, 212–22. On the Hungarian labor brigades at Bor in 1943–4 and the death march, see Tamás Csapody, *Bori Munkaszolgálatosok: Fejezetek a Bori Munkaszolgálat Történetéből* [The Forced Laborers of Bor: Chapters from the History of the Forced Laborers of Bor] (Budapest: Vince Kiadó, 2011); Csapody, "Bor

Forced Labor Service as Reflected in Diaries," *Hungarian Historical Review* 9, no. 3 (2020): 391–407; Csapody, *Bortól Szombathelyig: tanulmányok a bori munkaszolgálatról és a bori munkaszolgálatosok részleges névlistája* (Budapest: Zrínyi Kiadó, 2014); Csapody, "A bori munkaszolgálat helyszínei: történelmi mementó és ipari örökség" [Sites of the Forced Labor Camp in Bor, Serbia: Historical Mementos and Industrial Heritage], in *Örökség, történelem, társadalom Rendi társadalom—polgári társadalom 32. A Hajnal István Kör—Társadalomtörténeti Egyesület 2018. évi, szentendrei konferenciájának tanulmánykötete* (Budapest: Hajnal István Kör—Társadalomtörténeti Egyesület, 2020), 341–65.

42 Caroline Mezger, "The 1944 Crvenka Massacre and the Potentials of Postwar Testimony," *Holocaust Studies* 26, no. 4 (2019): 417–41; see also the witness accounts in Szabolcs, *Kényszermunka, erőltetett menet;* and see Braham, *The Hungarian Labor Service System, 1939–45*, 57.

43 See Ozsváth, *In the Footsteps of Orpheus*, 239–5; Vice, "Holocaust Poetry and Testimony," *Critical Survey* 20, no. 2 (2008): 9.

44 See Győző Ferencz, "The Poetry of Miklós Radnóti," *Hungarian Quarterly* 50, no. 195 (2009): 5–6.

45 For a different reading of "Picture Postcard #3," see George, *The Poetry of Miklós Radnóti*, 506.

46 Ábel Kőszegi, *Töredék. Radnóti Miklós utolsó hónapjainak krónikája* [Fragment: Chronicle of Miklós Radnóti's Last Months] (Budapest: Szépirodalma, 1972), 49, quoted in translation in Radnóti, *The Complete Poetry*, ed. and trans. Emery George (Ann Arbor: Ardis, 1980), 392.

47 Ozsváth, *In the Footsteps of Orpheus*, 218. See Vice, "Holocaust Poetry and Testimony," *Critical Survey* 20, no. 2 (2008): 10–11.

48 See Ferencz, "Foreword," in Radnóti, *The Complete Poetry in Hungarian and English*, 10.

49 Csapody, *Bori Munkaszolgálatosok*, 216–19, 227–30.

50 Miklós Radnóti, *Bori notesz* [Bor Notebook] (Budapest: Helikon, 1970), 13; Radnóti, *Camp Notebook. Bori notesz*, bilingual English / Hungarian edition, trans. Francis R. Jones, 2nd edition (Todmorden, England: Arc Publications, 2019), 22–3.

51 Ferencz, "The Poetry of Miklós Radnóti," 7.

52 Szires, "Introduction," in *Camp Notebook*, 15.

53 Thomas Ország-Land, "About Poetry and the Holocaust," in *Survivors: Hungarian Jewish Poets of the Holocaust*, ed. Thomas Ország-Land (Middlesborough: Smokestack Books, 2014), 10–16.

54 Jennifer Anna Gosetti-Ferencei, "Radnóti, Blanchot, and the (Un)writing of Disaster," *CLCWeb: Comparative Literature and Culture* 17, no. 2 (2015): https://doi.org/10.7771/1481-4374.2435

55 Vice, "Holocaust Poetry and Testimony," 7.

56 Szegedy-Maszák, "National and International Implications in Radnóti's Poetry," 16.

Chapter 5

1. Emanuel Ringelblum, "Vladislav shlengel: der dikhter fun geto," *Kesovim fun geto* (Tel Aviv: Y. L Peretz, 1985), 2: 189–93; Bożena Shallcross, *The Holocaust Object in Polish and Polish-Jewish Culture* (Bloomington: Indiana University Press, 2011), 20; John and Bogdana Carpenter, "Introduction to the Work of Wladyslaw Szlengel," *Manhattan Review* 15, no. 2 (2012–13): 11.
2. Halina Birenbaum, "Słowo, które nie ginie nigdy," *Nowiny Kurier*, October 21, 1983; "The Word Which Never Gets Lost," translated by Edyta Gawron and Ada Holtzman, http://www.zchor.org/szlengel/szlengel.htm.
3. Ibid.
4. Władysław Szlengel, *Co czytałem umarłym*, Fundacja Nowoczesna Polska edition (Warsaw: Państwowy Instytut Wydawniczy, 1979), 2.
5. Szlengel, *Co czytałem umarłym*, 9.
6. Władysław Szlengel, "What I Read to the Dead," trans. John and Bogdana Carpenter, *Manhattan Review* 15, no. 2 (2012–13): 25, amended.
7. Szlengel, *Co czytałem umarłym*, 35.
8. Shallcross, *The Holocaust Object*, 19.
9. Piotr Kilanowski, "Przy sublokatorskim oknie. O 'Oknie na tamtą stronę' Władysława Szlengla," *Polonistyka Innowacje* 13 (2021): 27.
10. Szlengel, *Co czytałem umarłym*, 9.
11. Ibid; Szlengel, "To the Polish Reader," trans. John and Bogdana Carpenter, *Manhattan Review* 16, no. 1 (2013–14): 28.
12. Szlengel, *Co czytałem umarłym*, 10; "To the Polish Reader," 29.
13. Szlengel, *Co czytałem umarłym*, 10.
14. Władysław Szlengel, "Telephone," trans. John and Bogdana Carpenter, *Manhattan Review* 15, no. 2 (2012–13): 28.
15. Samuel D. Kassow, *Who Will Write Our History?: Emanuel Ringelblum, the Warsaw Ghetto, and the Oyneg Shabes Archive* (Bloomington: Indiana University Press, 2007), 316, 462.
16. Szlengel, *Co czytałem umarłym*, 66–9.
17. Katarzyna Person, *Warsaw Ghetto Police: The Jewish Order Service during the Nazi Occupation*, trans. Zygmunt Nowak-Soliński (Ithaca: Cornell University Press, 2021), 130.
18. Szlengel, *Co czytałem umarłym*, 10.

Note 57 and 58 from previous chapter:

57. Dana Amir, *Bearing Witness to the Witness: A Psychoanalytical Perspective on Four Modes of Traumatic Testimony* (London and New York: Routledge, 2019), 3–4.
58. Quoted in translation in Ozsváth, *In the Footsteps of Orpheus*, 143.

19 Szlengel, "Telephone," 28.
20 Szlengel, *Co czytałem umarłym*, 10.
21 Szlengel, "Telephone," 28.
22 Szlengel, *Co czytałem umarłym*, 10.
23 Szlengel, "To the Polish Reader," 28.
24 Szlengel, *Co czytałem umarłym*, 10.
25 Szlengel, "To the Polish Reader," 28.
26 Kassow, *Who Will Write Our History?*, 13.
27 Ibid.
28 Ibid., 14.
29 David Roskies, *Voices from the Warsaw Ghetto: Writing Our History* (New Haven: Yale University Press, 2019), 25.
30 Naomi Diamant and David Roskies, *Holocaust Literature: A History and Guide* (Waltham, MA: Brandeis University Press, 2013), 67.
31 Shallcross, *The Holocaust Object*, 19.
32 Ringelblum, *Kesovim fun geto*, 2: 189.
33 Ibid.
34 Kassow, *Who Will Write Our History?*, 462, amended.
35 Ibid., 311–12.
36 Daniel Feldman, "Honoring the Child's Right to Respect: Janusz Korczak as Holocaust Educator," *The Lion and the Unicorn* 40, no. 2 (2016): 140.
37 "Zaproszenie na przedstawienie w Domu Sierot Janusza Korczaka," July 18, 1942, ARG I 352, Ringelblum Archive, vol. 2, document 45, 302, Jewish Historical Institute, Warsaw. https://cbj.jhi.pl/documents/745314/1.
38 Szlengel, *Co czytałem umarłym*, 50.
39 Władysław Szlengel, "A Page from the 'Aktion' Diary," trans. John and Bogdana Carpenter, *Manhattan Review* 17, no. 2 (2016–17): 31–2.
40 John Carpenter, "Burial, Location, Excavation: The Hiding and Discovery of Wladyslaw Szlengel's Poems," *Manhattan Review* 16, no. 1 (2013–14): 7–8.
41 Kassow, *Who Will Write Our History?*, 356; Roskies, *Voices from the Warsaw Ghetto*, xv.
42 Szlengel, *Co czytałem umarłym*, 2.
43 Szlengel, "What I Read to the Dead," 13.
44 Szlengel, *Co czytałem umarłym*, 2.
45 Szlengel, "What I Read to the Dead," 13.
46 Szlengel, *Co czytałem umarłym*, 3.
47 Szlengel, 'What I Read to the Dead," 14.
48 Szlengel, *Co czytałem umarłym*, 2.
49 Szlengel, "What I Read to the Dead," 14.

50 Szlengel, *Co czytałem umarłym*, 7.
51 Szlengel, "What I Read to the Dead," 20–1.
52 Shallcross, *The Holocaust Object*, 17.
53 Ibid., 19.
54 Roman Jakobson, "Two Aspects of Language and Two Types of Aphasic Disturbances," in *Selected Writings, Volume II: Word and Language* (Berlin: De Gruyter Mouton, 1971), 242, 250.
55 Szlengel, *Co czytałem umarłym*, 5; "What I Read to the Dead," 17.
56 See pp. 70–74 above for a discussion of Miłosz's poem.
57 Szlengel, *Co czytałem umarłym*, 9.
58 Szlengel, "What I Read to the Dead," 25.
59 Kassow, *Who Will Write Our History?*, 12.
60 Quoted in ibid., 308.
61 Ibid., 6.
62 Ibid., 316.
63 Szlengel, *Co czytałem umarłym*, 27.
64 Władysław Szlengel, "Things," translated by John and Bogdana Carpenter, *Chicago Review* 52, nos. 2–4 (2006): 283.
65 Szlengel, *Co czytałem umarłym*, 27.
66 Szlengel, "Things," 283.
67 Szlengel, *Co czytałem umarłym*, 28.
68 Szlengel, "Things," 284.
69 Shallcross, *The Holocaust Object*, 22.
70 Szlengel, *Co czytałem umarłym*, 12–13.
71 Szlengel, "A Monument," translated by John and Bogdana Carpenter, *Manhattan Review* 16, no. 1 (2013–14): 21.
72 Szlengel, *Co czytałem umarłym*, 14.
73 Szlengel, "A Monument," 23.
74 Frieda W. Aaron, *Bearing the Unbearable: Yiddish and Polish Poetry in the Ghettos and Concentration Camps* (Albany: State University of New York Press, 1990), 41; Ruth Shenfeld, "Władysław Szlengel veshirato begeto varsha," *Gal-Ed* 10 (1987): 248.
75 *The Holocaust Object*, 23.
76 For the testimony of escapees from Treblinka and the efforts to publicize the truth about the extermination camp, see Kassow, *Who Will Write Our History?*, 108–11. See also Alexander Donat, *The Death Camp Treblinka: A Documentary* (New York: Holocaust Library, 1979); Witold Chrostowski, *Extermination Camp Treblinka* (London: Vallentine Mitchell, 2004); Chris Webb and Michal Chocholatý, *The Treblinka Death Camp: History, Biographies, Remembrance* (Stuttgart: Ibidem, 2014).

77 Szlengel, *Co czytałem umarłym*, 23–4.
78 Szlengel, "The Little Railway Station at Treblinka," trans. John and Bogdana Carpenter, *Manhattan Review* 15, no. 2 (2012–13): 21.
79 Szlengel, *Co czytałem umarłym*, 24.
80 Szlengel, "The Little Railway Station," 21.
81 For more on Szlengel's comedic technique in this poem, see Adam Kowalczyk, "Czarny humor w twórczości Władysława Szlengla ze szczególnym uwzględnieniem wiersza 'Mała stacja Treblinki,'" *Annales Universitatis Paedagogicae Cracoviensis. Studia Historicolitteraria* 15 (2015): 127–8.
82 Kassow, *Who Will Write Our History?*, 173, 311.
83 Szlengel, *Co czytałem umarłym*, 3, 4; "What I Read to the Dead," 15, 16.
84 Kassow, *Who Will Write Our History?*, 320.
85 Szlengel, *Co czytałem umarłym*, 8.
86 Szlengel, "What I Read to the Dead," 24.
87 Szlengel, *Co czytałem umarłym*, 41; "Five to Twelve," trans. John and Bogdana Carpenter, *Manhattan Review* 15, no. 2 (2012–13): 37.
88 Ibid.
89 Władysław Szlengel, poems, translated by Andrew Kobos, edited by Halina Birenbaum, http://www.zchor.org/szlengel/poems.htm.
90 Ibid.
91 Szlengel, *Co czytałem umarłym*, 33; "Passports," trans. John and Bogdana Carpenter, *Manhattan Review* 17, no. 2 (2016–17): 27.
92 See Chapter 6 below.
93 Szlengel, *Co czytałem umarłym*, 55.
94 "It is Time," trans. John and Bogdana Carpenter, *Manhattan Review* 15, no. 2 (2012–13): 32.
95 Szlengel, *Co czytałem umarłym*, 56; "It is Time," 32–3.
96 Quoted in Aaron, *Bearing the Unbearable*, 146.
97 Szlengel, *Co czytałem umarłym*, 59.
98 Władysław Szlengel, "Counterattack," trans. John and Bogdana Carpenter, *Chicago Review* 52, nos. 2–4 (2006): 218–19.
99 See Chapter 2.
100 Szlengel, *Co czytałem umarłym*, 60–1; "Counterattack," 220–1.
101 Ibid.
102 Miłosz, *Poezje*, vol. 1 (Paris: Institut Literacki, 1981–2), 35. See p. 74 above.
103 Szlengel, *Co czytałem umarłym*, 60; "Counterattack," 219.
104 Shenfeld, "Władysław Szlengel veshirato begeto varsha," 277.
105 Birenbaum, "The Word Which Never Gets Lost," zchor.org.
106 Quoted in Kassow, *Who Will Write Our History?*, 323–4.

Chapter 6

1. Moshe Shner, *Janusz Korczak and Yitzhak Katzenelson: Two Educators in the Abysses of History* (Berlin: Walter de Gruyter, 2021), 156–7.
2. Paul Ricoeur, "The Human Experience of Time and Narrative," in *A Ricoeur Reader: Reflection and Imagination*, ed. Mario J. Valdés (Toronto: University of Toronto Press, 1991), 99.
3. David G. Roskies and Naomi Diamant, *Holocaust Literature: A History and Guide* (Waltham, MA: Brandeis University Press, 2012), 71.
4. Sven-Erik Rose, "A Poetics of Genocide: The Jewish Dead Confront Their German Murderers in Itzhak Katzenelson's Warsaw Ghetto Poem 'Vey dir'," in *Nexus: Essays in German Jewish Studies*, vol. 5, ed. Ruth von Bernuth, Eric Downing, William Collins Donahue, and Martha B. Helfer (Rochester, NY: Camden House, 2021), 139.
5. Shner, *Janusz Korczak and Yitzhak Katzenelson*, 155.
6. Samuel D. Kassow, *Who Will Write Our History?: Emanuel Ringelblum, the Warsaw Ghetto, and the Oyneg Shabes Archive* (Bloomington: Indiana University Press, 2007), 326. For Katzenelson's previous standing as a Hebrew educator and beloved children's author, see Shner, *Janusz Korczak and Yitzhak Katzenelson*, 155–6.
7. Quoted in translation in Kassow, *Who Will Write Our History?*, 324–5.
8. Ibid., 324.
9. David G. Roskies, ed., *Voices from the Warsaw Ghetto: Writing Our History* (New Haven: Yale University Press, 2019), 16. See also Yechiel Szeintuch, *Ktavim shenitslu migeto varshe umimakhane vitel* (Jerusalem: Magnes, 1990), 71–3.
10. Roskies and Diamant, *Holocaust Literature*, 58.
11. Ibid.
12. Moshe Shner, "Down the Ladder of Despair: The Holocaust Legacy of Itzhak Katzenelson," *Scripta Judaica Cracoviensia* 15 (2017): 87.
13. Roskies and Diamant, *Holocaust Literature*, 203.
14. David G. Roskies, "Did the Shoah Engender a New Poetics?," in *Eastern European Jewish Literature of the 20th and 21st Centuries: Identity and Poetics*, ed. Klavdia Smola (Munich and Berlin: Verlag Otto Sagner, 2013), 351.
15. Szeintuch, *Ktavim shenitslu*, 42.
16. Kassow, *Who Will Write Our History?*, 324.
17. Roskies and Diamant, *Holocaust Literature*, 58.
18. Shner, "Down the Ladder of Despair," 85.
19. Rose, "A Poetics of Genocide," 144.
20. Ibid., 140.
21. Quoted in Rose, "A Poetics of Genocide," 142.

22 Rose, "A Poetics of Genocide," 141.
23 Roskies, "Did the Shoah Engender?" 352.
24 "A Poetics of Genocide," 152.
25 Ibid.
26 Ibid., 157.
27 Ibid.
28 Ibid.
29 Kassow, *Who Will Write Our History?*, 325.
30 Ibid., 326; Rose, "A Poetics of Genocide," 141; Shner, *Janusz Korczak and Yitzhak Katzenelson*, 161, 190.
31 Kassow, *Who Will Write Our History?*, 325.
32 Roskies and Diamant, *Holocaust Literature*, 71.
33 Quoted in ibid.
34 Itzhak Katzenelson, *Vittel Diary*, trans. Myer Cohen (Lohamei Haghetaot: Ghetto Fighters' House and Hakibbutz hameukhad, 1980), 43.
35 Andrzej Pawelec and Magdalena Joanna Sitarz, "Itzhak Katzenelson's *Dos lid funem oysgehargetn yidishn folk* in Translation: The First Four Decades," *Scripta Judaica Cracoviensia* 15 (2017): 75. See also Roskies, "Did the Shoah Engender?," 357.
36 Katzenelson, *Vittel Diary*, 43.
37 Roskies and Diamant, *Holocaust Literature*, 203.
38 Roskies, "Did the Shoah Engender?," 356–7.
39 See Kassow, *Who Will Write Our History?*, 332.
40 Shner, "Down the Ladder of Despair," 84.
41 Roskies and Diamant, *Holocaust Literature*, 203.
42 Katzenelson, *Vittel Diary*, 246–7.
43 Roskies and Diamant, *Holocaust Literature*, 204.
44 Itzhak Katzenelson, *Dos lid funem oyseghargetn yidishn folk* (Tel Aviv: Hakibbutz hameukhad, 1964), 17. My translation.
45 Katzenelson, *Dos lid*, 20.
46 Katzenelson, *Vittel Diary*, 124.
47 Katzenelson, *Dos lid*, 39.
48 David G. Roskies, ed., *The Literature of Destruction: Jewish Responses to Catastrophe* (Philadelphia: Jewish Publication Society, 1988), 517.
49 Katzenelson, *Dos lid*, 51–2.
50 Shner, *Janusz Korczak and Yitzhak Katzenelson*, 176–80.
51 Efraim Shmueli, *The Last Generation of Jews in Poland* (Boston: Academic Studies Press, 2021), 210–11.
52 Shmueli, *The Last Generation*, 210–11.

53 Shner, *Janusz Korczak and Yitzhak Katzenelson*, 182–9.
54 Katzenelson, *Dos lid*, 75.
55 Shner, *Janusz Korczak and Yitzhak Katzenelson*, 204.
56 Quoted in Pawelec and Sitarz, "Itzhak Katzenelson's 'Dos lid fun oysgehartent idishn folk' in Translation," 74.
57 Shner, *Janusz Korczak and Yitzhak Katzenelson*, 172.
58 Pawelec and Sitarz, "Itzhak Katzenelson's 'Dos lid fun oysgehartent idishn folk' in Translation," 77.

Chapter 7

1 Quoted in Justyna Sobolewska, "Piszę szeptem—rozmowa z Idą Fink," *Gazeta Wyborcza*, May 12, 2003, 14.
2 Bartłomiej Krupa, "Obóz dla dipisów—literackie zapisy doświadczenia życia 'pomiędzy'," *Acta Universitatis Lodziensis. Folia Litteraria Polonica* 42 (2017): 151.
3 Quoted in Sobolewska, "Piszę szeptem," 14.
4 Ida Fink, *Wiosna 1941* (Warsaw: WAB, 2013), 196; *A Scrap of Time and Other Stories*, trans. Madeline Levine and Francine Prose (Evanston: Northwestern University Press, 1995), 135.
5 Fink, *Skrawek czasu* (London: Aneks, 1987), 8; *A Scrap of Time*, 3.
6 Fink, *Wiosna*, 108; *A Scrap of Time*, 19.
7 Annette Wieviorka, *The Era of the Witness* (Ithaca: Cornell University Press, 2006).
8 Ewelina Kotarska, "Doświadczanie czasu w twórczości Idy Fink," *Acta Universitatis Lodziensis. Folia Litteraria Polonica* 13 (2010): 281–3.
9 Ellen Fine, "An Eye on a Scrap of the World: Ida Fink's Witnesses," in *Jewish American and Holocaust Literature*, ed. Alan Berger and Gloria Cronin (Albany: State University of New York Press, 2004), 33.
10 Fink, *Wiosna*, 62; *Scrap of Time*, 126.
11 Ida Fink, *Odpływający ogród*, 25; *Traces*, trans. Philip Boehm and Francine Prose (New York: Henry Holt, 1998), 15.
12 Fink, *Odpływający ogród*, 20; *Traces*, 10.
13 Fink, *Scrap of Time*, 60.
14 Ida Fink, *The Journey*, trans. Joanna Weschler and Francine Prose (New York: Farrar, Strauss, and Giroux, 1992), 218.
15 Roman Jakobson, "On Linguistic Aspects of Translation," in *On Translation*, ed. Reuben Brower (Cambridge: Harvard University Press, 1959), 233.
16 Fink, *Scrap of Time*, 5, 8.

17 Fink, *Skrawek czasu*, 8.
18 Fink, *Scrap of Time*, 4.
19 See the discussion in Chapter 2 of the Nazis' language, which coopted and abused the German of the German Romantics.
20 Fink, *Skrawek czasu*, 8.
21 Fink, *Scrap of Time*, 4.
22 Fink, *Wiosna*, 195; *Scrap of Time*, 135.
23 Ibid.
24 Marianne Hirsch, *The Generation of Postmemory* (New York: Columbia University Press, 2012), 109, 111.
25 Dorota Glowacka, *Disappearing Traces: Holocaust Testimonials, Ethics, and Aesthetics* (Seattle: University of Washington Press, 2012), 142.
26 Fink, *Scrap of Time*, 135.
27 Fink, *Skrawek czasu*, 100.
28 Hirsch, *Postmemory*, 110, quoting Roland Barthes in *La chambre claire* (*Camera Lucida*, 1980). Compare the discussion of photographic evidence in Magdalena Marszałek, "Fotografie und literarisches Zeugnis: Zur Thematisierung der Fotografie im testimonialen Erzählen (Ida Fink, Jaroslaw Marek Rymkiewicz)," *Poetica* 42, no. 1 (2010): 177–9.
29 Glowacka, *Disappearing Traces*, 143.
30 Ruth Ginsburg, "Ida Fink's Scraps and Traces: Forms of Space and the Chronotope of Trauma Narratives," *Partial Answers* 4, no. 2 (2006): 205. Glowacka, *Disappearing Traces*, 134.
31 Quoted ibid.
32 Ginsburg, "Forms of Space," 206.
33 Fink, *Scrap of Time*, 137.
34 Hirsch, *Postmemory*, 111–12. Marszałek, "Fotografie," 182–4. Jan Gerstner, *Das andere Gedächtnis: Fotografie in der Literatur des 20. Jahrhunderts* (Bielefeld: Transcript Verlag, 2013), 245–7.
35 Hirsch, *Postmemory*, 110–11.
36 Ibid., 111, 112.
37 Marszałek, "Fotografie," 184.
38 Gerstner, *Das andere Gedächtnis*, 246.
39 Fink, *Skrawek czasu*, 100.
40 Hirsch, *Postmemory*, 111.
41 Marszałek, "Fotografie," 184.
42 Ibid., 183.
43 Fink, *Scrap of Time*, 136.
44 Glowacka, *Disappearing Traces*, 134, quoting Lanzmann.

45 Fink, *Scrap of Time*, 135.
46 Ibid., 136.
47 Marszałek, "Fotografie," 183–4.
48 Fink, *Wiosna*, 197; *Scrap of Time*, 137.
49 Fink, *Wiosna*, 196; *Scrap of Time*, 135.
50 Kotarska, "Doświadczanie czasu," 299–303.
51 Fink, *Wiosna*, 197; *Scrap of Time*, 137.
52 Fink, *Wiosna*, 198; *Scrap of Time*, 137.
53 Ibid.
54 Fink, *Skrawek czasu*, 100.
55 Fink, *Scrap of Time*, 136.
56 Ibid., 137.
57 Fink, *Wiosna*, 197; *Scrap of Time*, 136.
58 Ibid.
59 Fink, *Skrawek czasu*, 101.
60 Fink, *Scrap of Time*, 137.
61 Fink, *Skrawek czasu*, 100.
62 Fink, *Scrap of Time*, 136.
63 Fink, *Skrawek czasu*, 100.
64 Fink, *Scrap of Time*, 136.
65 Ibid.
66 Fink, *Wiosna*, 196; *Scrap of Time*, 136.
67 Fink, *Scrap of Time*, 137.
68 Fink, *Skrawek czasu*, 101.
69 Fink, *Scrap of Time*, 137.
70 Ibid.
71 Marszałek, "Fotografie," 184.
72 Glowacka, *Disappearing Traces*, 145.
73 Ibid., 146.
74 Fink, *Scrap of Time*, 137.
75 Ginsburg, "Forms of Space," 216.
76 Fink, *Skrawek czasu*, 101.
77 Ibid.
78 Fink, *Scrap of Time*, 137.
79 Fink, *Skrawek czasu*, 101.
80 Fink, *Scrap of Time*, 137.
81 See Glowacka, *Disappearing Traces*, 151.
82 Fink, *Traces*, 32.

83 Fink, *Skrawek czasu*, 100. Ellipses in the original.
84 Fink, *Scrap of Time*, 135.
85 Fink, *Skrawek czasu*, 101. Ellipses in the original.
86 Fink, *Scrap of Time*, 137.
87 Fink, *Skrawek czasu*, 100. My thanks to Anne-Marie Novak for noting these linguistic discrepancies.
88 Shiri Lev-Ari, "Gevirati, kakhah lo kotvim 'al hashoah," *Haaretz*, October 20, 2007, and Sobolewska, "Piszę szeptem," 14.
89 See "Correspondence," Ida Fink Archive, National Library of Israel, Jerusalem.
90 Sobolewska, "Piszę szeptem," 14.
91 Fink, *Scrap of Time*, 137.
92 Fink, *Skrawek czasu*, 100, 101; Fink, *Scrap of Time*, 135, 136.
93 Ginsburg, "Forms of Space," 216.
94 Fink, *Scrap of Time*, 135.
95 Fink, *Skrawek czasu*, 100.
96 Fink, *Scrap of Time*, 135–6.
97 Fink, *Skrawek czasu*, 100.
98 Fink, *Scrap of Time*, 136.

Postscript

1 See the discussion of "witnessing" in survivor testimony in James E. Young, *Writing and Rewriting the Holocaust: Narrative and the Consequences of Interpretation* (Bloomington: Indiana University Press, 1988), 19–22.
2 Paul Celan, *Die Gedichte* (Frankfurt am Main: Suhrkamp, 2018), 202.
3 Rachel Zolf, *Social Poesis: The Poetry of Rachel Zolf*, ed. Heather Milne (Waterloo, ON: Wilfrid Laurier University Press, 2019), 5. See Ulli Baer, ed., *»Niemand zeugt für den Zeugen«. Erinnerungskultur nach der Shoa* (Frankfurt am Main: Suhrkamp, 2000).
4 Jacques Derrida, *Sovereignties in Question: The Poetics of Paul Celan*, ed. Thomas Dutoit and Outi Pasanen (New York: Fordham University Press, 2005).
5 Derrida, *Sovereignties in Question*, 32.
6 Derrida, "'A Self-Unsealing Poetic Text': The Poetics and Politics of Witnessing,'" trans. Rachel Bowlby, in *Revenge of the Aesthetic: The Place of Literature in Theory Today*, ed. Michael Clark (Berkeley: University of California Press, 2000), 180–207, newly translated in *Sovereignties in Question*, 65–96.
7 Derrida, *Sovereignties in Question*, 65.

8 Ibid., 42–3.
9 Celan, *Selected Poems and Prose*, trans. John Felstiner (New York: Norton,2001), 261.
10 Celan, *Selected Poems and Prose*, 122–3.
11 Derrida, *Sovereignties in Question,* 93.
12 Ibid., 46–7.
13 Derrida, *Cinders*, translated by Ned Lukacher (Minneapolis: University of Minnesota Press, 2014), 25. For an analysis of the relation of Derrida's writing to the Holocaust, see David Michael Levin, "Cinders, Traces, Shadows on the Page: The Holocaust in Derrida's Writing," *International Philosophical Quarterly* 43, no. 3 (2003): 269–88; Robert Eaglestone, "Derrida and the Holocaust: A Commentary on the Philosophy of Cinders," *Angelaki: Journal of Theoretical Humanities* 7, no. 2 (2002): 27–38; Gil Anidjar, "The All-Burning: Derrida's Holocaust (Le brûle-tout: l'Holocauste de Derrida)," *Rue Descartes* nos. 89–90 (2016): 204–11. See also Robert Eaglestone, *The Holocaust and the Postmodern* (Oxford: Oxford University Press, 2004).
14 Derrida, *Cinders*, 43.
15 Maurice Blanchot, *L'écriture du désastre* (Paris: Gallimard, 1980), 180; *The Writing of the Disaster*, trans. Ann Smock (Lincoln, NB: University of Nebraska Press, 1995), 47.
16 Kofman, *Paroles suffoquées* (Paris Editions Galilée, 1987), 15.
17 Ibid., 15–16.
18 Kofman, *Smothered Words*, trans. Madeleine Dobie (Evanston: Northwestern University Press, 1998), 9–10.
19 Kofman, *Paroles suffoquées*, 21–2; *Smothered Words,* 14–15.
20 Derrida, *Sovereignties in Question*, 87–90.
21 Ibid., 68.
22 Chava Rosenfarb, *Geto un andere lider—oykh fragmentn fun a tog bukh* (Montreal: Hershman, 1948), x; see Rosenfarb, *Confessions of a Yiddish Writer and Other Essays*, ed. Goldie Morgentaler (Montreal: McGill-Queen's University Press, 2019), 6–7.
23 Jeff Sharlet, *Sweet Heaven When I Die: Faith, Faithlessness, and the Country In Between* (New York: Norton, 2011), 135–6.
24 Mishnah Yoma 7:1.

BIBLIOGRAPHY

Primary Sources

Adler, H. G. *Theresienstadt: Antlitz einer Zwangsgemeinschaft*. 2nd revised edition. Tübingen: Mohr, 1961.
Adler, H. G. "Dichtung aus Theresienstadt." In *Fruchtblätter: Freundesgabe für Alfred Kelletat*, edited by Harald Hartung, Walter Heistermann, and Peter M. Stephan, 137–42. Berlin: Pädagogische Hochschule, 1977.
Adler, H. G. *Theresienstadt 1941–1945: The Face of a Coerced Community*. Translated by Belinda Cooper. Cambridge, UK: Cambridge University Press, 2017.
Apenszlak, Jacob, ed. *Poezja ghetta z podziemia żydowskiego w Polsce*. 2nd ed. New York: Association of Friends of Our Tribune, 1945. Reprinted from *Z otchłani: Poezja*. Warsaw: Wydawnictwo Żydowskiego Komitetu Narodowego, 1944.
Ausländer, Rose. *Gesammelte Werke*. 7 vols. Frankfurt am Main: S. Fischer, 1984–1990.
Ausländer, Rose. *Grüne Mutter Bukowina: ausgewählte Gedichte und Prosa*. Aachen: Rimbaud, 2004.
Ausländer, Rose. *While I Am Drawing Breath*. Translated by Jean Boase-Beier and Anthony Vivis. Todmorden, UK: Arc, 2014.
Axmann, Elisabeth, ed. *Fünf Dichter aus der Bukowina: Alfred Margul Sperber (1898–1967), Rose Ausländer (1901–1988), Moses Rosenkranz (1904–2003), Alfred Kittner (1906–1991), Paul Celan (1920–1970)*. Aachen: Rimbaud, 2007.
Bartoszewski, Władysław, ed. *Tryptyk polsko-żydowski*. Warsaw: Rada Ochrony Pamięci Walk i Męczeństwa, 2003.
Boase-Beier, Jean, and Marian de Vooght, eds. *Poetry of the Holocaust: An Anthology*. Todmorden, UK: Arc, 2019.
Borwicz, Michał M. *Literatura w obozie*. Kraków: Regional Jewish Historical Commission in Kraków, 1946.
Borwicz, Michał M. *Ze smiercią na ty*. Warsaw: Wiedza, 1946.
Borwicz, Michał M. *Pieśń ujdzie cało: antologia wierszy o żydach pod okupacją niemiecką*. Warsaw: Central Jewish Historical Commission in Poland, 1947.
Bryks, Rachmil. *Geto Fabrik 76/Ghetto Factory 76: Poem*. Translated by Theodor Primack and Eugen Kullman. Bilingual edition. New York: Bloch, 1967.
Bryks, Rachmil. *May God Avenge Their Blood: A Holocaust Memoir Triptych*. Translated by Yermiyahu Ahron Taub. Lanham, MD: Lexington Books, 2020.
Celan, Paul. *Gesammelte Werke*. Edited by Beda Allemann and Klaus Reichert. Five vols. Frankfurt am Main: Surhkamp, 1983.
Celan, Paul. *Todesfuge*. Rimbaud: Aachen, 1999.

Celan, Paul. *Selected Poems and Prose*. Translated by John Felstiner. Bilingual edition. New York: W. W. Norton, 2001.
Celan, Paul. *Collected Prose*. Translated by Rosmarie Waldrop. Manchester: Carcanet, 1986; New York: Routledge, 2003.
Celan, Paul. *Die Gedichte: Neue kommentierte Gesamtausgabe*. Edited by Barbara Wiedemann. Berlin: Suhrkamp, 2018.
Celan, Paul. *Memory Rose into Threshold Speech: The Collected Earlier Poetry*. Translated by Pierre Joris. New York: Farrar, Straus, Giroux, 2020.
Celan, Paul. *Microliths They Are, Little Stones: Posthumous Prose*. Translated by Pierre Joris. New York: Contra Mundum Press, 2020.
Colin, Amy D., ed. *Paul Celan—Edith Silbermann: Zeugnisse einer Freundschaft: Gedichte, Briefwechsel, Erinnerungen*. Paderborn: Wilhelm Fink, 2010.
Fink, Ida. *A Scrap of Time*. Translated by Madeline Levine. New York: Pantheon, 1987.
Fink, Ida. *Skrawek czasu*. London: Aneks, 1987.
Fink, Ida. *The Journey*. Translated by Joanna Weschler and Francine Prose. New York: Farrar, Strauss, and Giroux, 1992.
Fink, Ida. *Traces*. Translated by Philip Boehm and Francine Prose. New York: Henry Holt, 1997.
Fink, Ida. *Odpływający ogród*. Warsaw: WAB, 2002.
Fink, Ida. *Wiosna 1941*. Warsaw: WAB, 2013.
Forché, Carolyn, ed. *Against Forgetting: Twentieth-Century Poetry of Witness*. New York: Norton, 1993.
Gebirtig, Mordecai. *S'brent: 1939–1942*. Kraków: Central Jewish Historical Commission in Poland, 1946.
Gebirtig, Mordecai. *The Song That Never Died: The Poetry of Mordecai Gebirtig*. Translated by S. Simchovitch. Oakville, ON: Mosaic, 2001.
Gillon, Adam, ed. and trans. "'Here too, as in Jerusalem': Selected Poems of the Ghetto." *Polish Review* 10, no. 3 (1965): 22–42.
Gömörim, George, and Mari Gömöri, eds. *I Lived on This Earth: Hungarian Poets on the Holocaust*. London: Alba, 2012.
Heiser, Dorothea, and Stuart Taberner, eds. *My Shadow in Dachau: Poems by Victims and Survivors of the Concentration Camp*. Rochester: Camden House, 2014.
Kaczerginski, Szmerke. *Dos gezang fun vilner geto*. Paris: Vilner Farband in Frankraykh, 1947.
Kaczerginski, Szmerke, and H. Leivick, eds. *Lider fun di ghettos un lagern*. New York: CYCO, 1948.
Kantorowicz, Gertrud. *Verse aus Theresienstadt*. Privately published, 1948.
Katzenelson, Itzhak. *Dos lid funem oysgehargetn yidishn folk*. Paris: ABC, 1945.
Katzenelson, Itzhak. *Elegy*. Translated by Rose Freeman-Ishill. Berkeley Heights, NJ: Oriole, 1948.
Katzenelson, Itzhak. *Dos lid funem oysgehargetn yidishn folk*. Tel Aviv: Hakibbutz hameukhad, 1964.
Katzenelson, Itzhak. *The Song of the Murdered Jewish People*. Translated by Noah H. Rosenbloom. Tel Aviv: Hakibbutz hameukhad, 1980.
Katzenelson, Itzhak. *Vittel Diary*. Translated by M. Cohen. Kibbutz Lokhamei. Hagetaot: Ghetto Fighters' House and Hakibbutz hameukhad, 1980.

Katzenelson, Itzhak. *Yidishe geṭo-ksovim varshe, 1940–1943*. Edited by Yechiel Szeintuch. Kibbutz Lokhamei Hagetaot: Ghetto Fighters' House and Hakibbutz hameukhad, 1984.

Kittner, Alfred. *Erinnerungen 1906–1991*. Edited by Edith Silbermann. Aachen: Rimbaud, 1996.

Kittner, Alfred. *Schattenschrift: Gedichte*. Aachen: Rimbaud, 1998.

Kittner, Alfred. *Der Wolkenreiter: Gedichte, 1925–1945*. Edited by Edith Silbermann and Amy Colin. Aachen: Rimbaud, 2004.

Kittner, Alfred, and Amy D. Colin, eds. *Versunkene Dichtung der Bukowina: eine Anthologie deutschsprachiger Lyrik*. Munich: Fink, 1994.

Kolmar, Gertrud. *Dark Soliloquy: The Selected Poems of Gertrud Kolmar*. Translated by Henry A. Smith. New York: Seabury, 1975.

Kolmar, Gertrud. *Weibliches Bildnis: sämtliche Gedichte*. Munich: Deutsches Taschenbuch, 1987.

Kolmar, Gertrud. *The Shimmering Crystal: Poems from "Das Lyrische Werk."* Translated by Elizabeth Spencer. London: Millennium, 1995.

Kolmar, Gertrud. *Leben und Werk. Zeit und Tod*. Frankfurt am Main: S. Fischer 2008.

Kremer, Aaron, ed. *The Last Lullaby: Poetry from the Holocaust*. Syracuse: Syracuse University Press, 1998.

Miłosz, Czesław. *Poezje*. Paris: Instytut Literacki, 1982.

Miłosz, Czesław. *The Witness of Poetry*. Cambridge, MA: Harvard University Press, 1983.

Miłosz, Czesław. *The Collected Poems, 1931–1987*. New York: Ecco, 1990.

Molodowski, Kadia, ed. *Lider fun khurbn, taf-shin—taf-shin-hey*. Tel Aviv: I. L. Peretz, 1962.

Moskovitz, Sarah Traister, ed. *Poetry in Hell: Yiddish Poetry in the Ringelblum Archives*. https://poetryinhell.org/.

Niger, Samuel Charney, ed. *Kidesh hashem*. New York: CYCO, 1948.

Ország-Land, Thomas, ed. and trans. *Survivors: Hungarian Jewish Poets of the Holocaust*. Middlesbrough, UK: Smokestack, 2015.

Pagis, Dan. *Variable Directions*. Translated by Stephen Mitchell. San Francisco: North Point Press, 1989.

Pagis, Dan. *Kol hashirim*. Jerusalem: Hakibbutz hameukhad and Mossad Bialik, 1991.

Radnóti, Miklós. *Bori notesz*. Budapest: Helikon, 1971.

Radnoti, Miklós. *The Witness: Selected Poems*. Translated by Thomas Orszag-Land. Market Drayton: Tern, 1977.

Radnóti, Miklós. *Under Gemini: A Prose Memoir and Selected Poetry*. Translated by Kenneth McRobbie, Zita McRobbie, and Jascha Kessler. Budapest: Corvina, 1985.

Radnóti, Miklós. *Foamy Sky: The Major Poems of Miklós Radnóti*. Edited and translated by Zsuzsanna Ozsváth and Frederick Turner. Princeton: Princeton University Press, 1992.

Radnóti, Miklós. *The Complete Poetry in Hungarian and English*. Translated by Gábor Barabas. Jefferson, NC: McFarland, 2014.

Radnóti, Miklós. *Napló, 1935–1946*. Budapest: Jaffa, 2014.

Radnóti, Miklós. *Camp Notebook. Bori notesz.* Translated by Francis R. Jones. Bilingual edition. Todmorden, UK: Arc, 2019.
Radnoti, Miklós. *Letters to My Love: Holocaust Poetry for Our Time.* Edited and translated by Thomas Ország-Land. No place of publication: Penniless Press, 2019.
Ringelblum, Emanuel. *Kesovim fun geto.* 2 vols. Tel Aviv: Y. L. Peretz, 1985.
Rosenfarb, Chava. *Di balade fun nekhtiken vald.* London: Narod, 1947.
Rosenfarb, Chava. *Dos lid fun dem yidishn kelner abram.* London: Moshe Oved, 1948.
Rosenfarb, Chava. *Geto un andere lider oykh fragmenṭn fun a tog bukh.* Montreal: Hershman, 1948.
Rosenfarb, Chava. *Aroys fun ganeydn.* Tel Aviv: Y. L. Peretz, 1965.
Rosenfarb, Chava. *Exile at Last: Selected Poems.* Edited by Goldie Morgentaler. Toronto: Guernica, 2013.
Roskies, David G., ed. *The Literature of Destruction: Jewish Responses to Catastrophe.* Philadelphia: Jewish Publication Society, 1988.
Roskies, David G., ed. *Voices from the Warsaw Ghetto: Writing Our History.* New Haven: Yale University Press, 2019.
Silbermann, Edith. *Begegnung mit Paul Celan: Erinnerung und Interpretation.* Aachen: Rimbaud, 1993.
Silbermann, Edith, ed. *Rose Ausländer—die Sappho der östlichen Landschaft: eine Anthologie.* Aachen: Rimbaud, 2003.
Silbermann, Edith. *Czernowitz—Stadt der Dichter: Geschichte einer jüdischen Familie aus der Bukowina (1900–1948).* Edited by Amy-Diana Colin. Paderborn: Wilhelm Fink, 2015.
Sundquist, Eric J., ed. *Writing in Witness: A Holocaust Reader.* Albany, NY: State University of New York Press, 2019.
Sutzkever, Abraham. *Selected Poetry and Prose.* Berkeley: University of California Press, 1991.
Sutzkever, Abraham. *The Full Pomegranate: Poems of Avrom Sutzkever.* Translated by Richard J. Fein. Albany, NY: State University of New York, 2019.
Sutzkever, Avrom. *Di festung: lider un poemes geshribn in vilner geto un in vald, 1941–1944.* New York: Ikuf, 1945.
Sutzkever, Avrom. *Fun vilner geto.* Moscow: Der Emes, 1945.
Sutzkever, Avrom. *Geheymshtot: poeme.* Tel Aviv: Akhdut, 1948.
Sutzkever, Avrom. *Poetishe verk.* Two vols. Tel Aviv: Yovel komitet, 1963.
Sutzkever, Avrom. *Burnt Pearls: Ghetto Poems of Abraham Sutzkever.* Translated by Seymour Mayne. Oakville, ON: Mosaic, 1981.
Sutzkever, Avrom. *Zingt alts nokh mayn vort/Still My Word Sings: Lider/Poems.* Bilingual edition. Translated and edited by Heather Valencia. Dusseldorf: Dusseldorf University Press, 2017; Berlin: De Gruyter, 2021.
Sutzkever, Abraham. *From the Vilna Ghetto to Nuremberg.* Edited and translated by Justin Cammy. Montreal: McGill-Queen's University Press, 2021.
Szlengel, Władysław. "Poems, 1943." Edited by Halina Birenbaum. Translated by Andrew Kobos. http://www.zchor.org/szlengel/poems.htm.
Szlengel, Władysław. *Co czytałem umarłym: wiersze getta warszawskiego.* Warsaw: Państwowy Instytut Wydawniczy, 1979.

Szlengel, Władysław. "'Things' and 'Counterattack'." Translated by John and Bogdana Carpenter. *Chicago Review* 52, nos. 2–4 (2006): 283–91.
Szlengel, Władysław. "What I Read to the Dead"; "Around Warsaw;" "Telephone"; "The Little Railway Station at Treblinka"; "It Is Time"; "Waterman"; "Five to Twelve"; "Two Deaths"; "Doorbells." Translated by John and Bogdana Carpenter. *Manhattan Review* 15, no. 2 (2012–13): 13–41.
Szlengel, Władysław. "Two Men in the Snow"; "A Window onto the Other Side"; "The Last Legend About the Golem"; "A Monument"; "On That Day"; "Afterword"; "To the Polish Reader." Translated by John and Bogdana Carpenter. *Manhattan Review* 16, no. 1 (2013–14): 14–29.
Szlengel, Władysław. "The Feast of Tabernacles"; "Do Not Buy New Calendars"; "Passports"; "Conversation with a Child"; "A Page from the *Aktion* Diary"; "Bread." Translated by John and Bogdana Carpenter. *Manhattan Review* 17, no. 2 (2016–17): 23–36.
Weißglas, Immanuel. *Aschenzeit: gesammelte Gedichte*. Aachen: Rimbaud, 1994.
Weißglas, Immanuel. "*Der Tod ein deutscher Meister*": *Immanuel Weißglas frühe Gedichte*. Edited by Heinrich Detering. Aachen: Rimbaud, 2013.
Wiesel, Elie [Eliezer Vizel]. …*Un di velt hot geshvign*. Buenos Aires: Tsentralfarband fun poylishe yidn in Argentine, 1956.
Wiesel, Elie. *La Nuit*. Paris: Editions de Minuit, 1958.
Wiesel, Elie. *Night*. Translated by Stella Rodway. New York: Hill & Wang, 1960.
Wiesel, Elie. "The Death Train." Translated by Moshe Spiegel. In *Anthology of Holocaust Literature*, edited by Jacob Glatstein, Israel Knox, and Samuel Margoshes, 6–7. Philadelphia: Jewish Publication Society of America, 1969.
Wiesel, Elie. *Legends of Our Time*. New York: Avon Books, 1972.
Wiesel, Elie. "Does the Holocaust Lie beyond the Reach of Art?" *New York Times*, April 17, 1983.
Wiesel, Elie. "The Holocaust as Literary Inspiration." In *Dimensions of the Holocaust*, edited by Elie Wiesel, Lucy Dawidowicz, Dorothea Rabinowitz, and Robert M. Brown, 5–23. Evanston, IL: Northwestern University Press, 1990.
Wiesel, Elie. *All Rivers Run to the Sea*: *Memoirs*. New York: Schocken, 1995.
Wiesel, Elie. *Night*. Translated by Marion Wiesel. New York: Hill & Wang, 2006.
Żółkiewska, Agnieszka and Marek Tuszewicki, eds. *Utwory literackie getta warszawskiego. Archiwum Ringelbluma. Konspiracyjne Archiwum Getta Warszawy*, t. 26. Warsaw: Jewish Historical Institute, 2017.

INDEX

Aaron, Frieda W. 9, 12, 65, 67
Abda (Hungary) 18, 128
Abel 96
Abraham (patriarch) 34, 37
The Accident (Wiesel) 29
"An Account with God" (Szlengel) 149
Adam 96
Adams, B. S. 123
Aden (Yemen) 40
Adler, H. G. 7, 51
Adler, Ruth 173–4
Adorno, T. W. 16–17, 20, 44–7, 54, 59–60, 74, 81, 90–1, 166, 198
Aesthetic Theory (Adorno) 59–60
Akselrod, Avrom 4
"À la pointe acérée" (Celan) 82
"À la recherche..." (Radnóti) 122, 124
Alexander, Edward 14
All Rivers Run to the Sea (Wiesel) 25, 37
"Alone" (Bialik) 172
Amir, Dana 129
Amos 172–3
Ámos, Imre 110
...And the World Was Silent (Wiesel) 16, 25, 26–7, 30–1, 39. *See also, Night*
Andrzejewski, Andrzej 73
Antelme, Robert 10–11, 200–1
Antonescu, Ion 47
Appelfeld, Aharon 52
Arad (Romania) 125
Ararát (journal) 107
Arendt, Hannah 51, 89
Aristotle 2, 44
Asch, Sholem 173
"Ashglory" (Celan) 86–7, 198–9

"Aspen Tree" (Celan) 53
Auschwitz–Birkenau 2, 4–7, 13, 16, 20, 29, 33–6, 39, 43–7, 57–60, 74, 91, 109, 120, 158, 165, 167–8, 173–4, 198–202
Ausländer, Rose 52–4, 57
Austria 6, 52, 56, 95, 128
"Autobiography" (Pagis) 98

Babits, Mihály 118
Babylon 7, 67, 168
Bach, Johann Sebastian 55–6
Bálint, György 118
"Ballad of the White Night" (Shayevich) 5
Barthes, Roland 186
Bataille, George 21
Baudelaire, Charles 109
Beck, Judit 117–18
Beckett, Samuel 74, 83, 91
"Before My Burning" (Sutzkever). *See* "The Circus"
Being and Nothingness (Sartre) 91
Belgrade (Beograd) 120, 125
Belzec (Bełżec, Poland) 161, 167–8
Benjamin, Walter 46
Berdichev (Ukraine) 30
Berlin 71
Bernshteyn, Mira 64–5, 69
Bessarabia 47
Bialik, Haim Nahman 3–4, 60, 68–9, 77, 160, 172–3
Białystok (Poland) 136, 159
Birenbaum, Halina 131, 154
The Birth of Tragedy (Nietzsche) 2
"Black Flakes" (Celan) 49–51, 53.
Blanchot, Maurice 129–30, 200–1
Błoński, Jan 73–4

Boase-Beier, Jean 13–14
Boomerang (Obejas) 198
Bor (Serbia) 18, 120–2, 124–6, 128
Bor Notebook (Radnóti) 121–2, 124, 128
Borwicz, Michał (Maksymilian Boruchowicz) 9, 12, 15
Bosnia 125
Breathturn (Celan) 86, 102
Bremen (Germany) 9, 51–2, 60, 90
Brentano, Clemens 58
Brooke, Rupert 75
Bruno, Giordano 72–3
Bryks, Rachmil 9
Bucharest 54, 199
Buchenwald concentration camp (Germany) 26, 30, 35, 38–9, 45
Büchner, Georg 11
Budapest 33, 110, 121, 127–8
Buenos Aires 16, 25
Bukovina 47, 52–3, 57, 60, 80, 95
Bulgaria 124
Buna-Monowitz labor camp (Poland) 37–8, 40
"Burnt Pearls" (Sutzkever) 67, 71

Cain 3, 96, 111
Camera Lucida (Barthes) 186
"Campo di Fiori" (Miłosz) 70, 72–4, 153
Camus, Albert 11, 29–30
Carpenter, John R. 138
Carson, Anne 83
"A Cartload of Shoes" (Sutzkever) 71
Cayrol, Jean 30
Celan, Paul (Antschel) 9–10, 12, 14–20, 43, 47–60, 61, 75–77, 79–105, 107, 124–5, 129, 153, 197–201
Chalfen, Israel 54
Chełmno (death camp, Poland) 184
Chomin, Marian 71–2
Chomin, Zofia 71–2
Cinders (Derrida) 200
"The Circus" (Sutzkever) 62
Colin, Amy D. 52–3
"Come Sweet Death" (Bach) 55
Conrad, Joseph 77

Costa Rica 150
"Counterattack" (Szlengel) 152–4
Critical Survey (journal) 13
"Crown of Thorns" (Celan) 48
Cservenka (Crvenka, Serbia) 125
"Cultural Criticism and Society" (Adorno) 44
Czernowitz (Cernăuți; now Chernivtsi, Ukraine) 47–8, 53–4, 57–8, 80

Dante, Alighieri 7, 67, 75
Danton, Georges Jacques 99
"Darkness" (Celan) 47–8
Dawn (Wiesel) 29
Dayan, Daniel Ben Yehuda 100
"Death Camp" (Klepfisz) 12
"Death Fugue" (Celan) 12, 54–7, 58–9, 102, 153
Death Tango (Bianco) 58–9
"Dedication" (Miłosz) 74
Defoe, Daniel 27
de Gaulle, Charles 29
De rerum natura (Lucretius) 118
Derrida, Jacques 79–82, 86, 88, 93, 102, 105, 199–201
Dési, István Huber 118
Deuteronomy 11, 198
de Vooght, Marian 14
Diamant, Naomi 159–60, 164
Dickinson, Emily 88
Donat, Alexander 152
"Do Not Work Ahead" (Celan) 82
Dostoevsky, Fyodor Mikhailovich 7, 11
Dresden 51
Dreyfus, Alfred 110, 159
Drohobycz (Drohobych, Ukraine) 202
Dror (underground periodical) 4, 159–60
Dubnow, Simon 1
"Dulce et Decorum Pro Patria Mori" (Owen) 75

Eaglestone, Robert 13
Eagleton, Terry 74
Ecclesiastes 79, 170
"Eclogues" (Virgil) 108, 113, 118, 121, 129

Editions de Minuit (publisher) 25
Egypt 33, 66
Eich, Günther 57
Eichmann, Adolf 33
"Eighth Eclogue" (Radnóti) 123
Einaudi (publisher) 26
Elegie (von der Vogelweide) 124
"Eleh ezkera" 65
Elijah 38
Emőd, Tamás 10
The Emperor of Atlantis (Ullmann and Kien) 6
Eshel, Amir 97
Esther 35
Ettlingen DP camp (Germany) 178
Eve 96
"An Eye, Open" (Celan) 84
Ezekiel 160, 168, 173
Ezrahi, Sidra Dekoven 44

Fackenheim, Emil 35
"Farewell to My Cap" (Szlengel) 133
Faust (Goethe) 56
Felman, Shoshana 8, 11, 55
Felstiner, John 51, 53–5, 57–8, 76, 84, 199
Ferencz, Győző 128–9
"Fifth Eclogue" (Radnóti) 118, 128
Fine, Ellen 30, 37
Fink, Ida 13, 20–1, 177–95, 201
Fioretos, Aris 81–2, 84
"First Eclogue" (Radnóti) 112–14
Five Chimneys (Lengyel) 40
"Five to Twelve" (Szlengel) 149
Flanders (Belgium) 122
"Footprints" (Pagis) 98
"Forced March" (Radnóti) 124
"For a Literary Survey" (Pagis) 103–4
Forché, Carolyn 8
The Fortress (Sutzkever) 61
"Fourth Eclogue" (Radnóti) 118
"Fragment" (Radnóti) 119, 121
Fragments (Wilkomirski) 28
France 18–19, 29, 32, 57–8, 90, 95, 124, 158, 163–4
Frankfurt am Main 45
Franklin, Phyllis 25–6
Freiburg 92
"Friday" (Radnóti) 114

"From Dawn to Midnight" (Radnóti) 115
Frommer, Rudolf 111
"Frothy Sky" (Radnóti) 116, 128
Frye, Northrop 65
"Funeral" (Jastrun) 55
Fussell, Paul 74–5
"Futility" (Owen) 75

Gaus, Gunther 51
Gebirtig, Mordecai 4
George, Stefan 56
Georgics (Virgil) 112
Germany 33, 38, 54–7, 113, 123, 159, 178, 181
Gerstein, Yankev 64
Gerstner, Jan 186
Geto Fabrik 76 (Bryks) 9
Ghetto and Other Poems (Rosenfarb) 202
Ghetto Fighters' House Museum (Israel) 20, 174
Ginczanka, Zuzanna (Gincburg) 71–2
Ginsburg, Ruth 184, 191
Glatter, Ági 110
Gleiwitz (Gliwice, Poland) 38
Glick, Hirsh 4
Glowacka, Dorota 94, 183–4, 191
Goethe, Johann Wolfgang von 6, 45, 47, 53, 56
Goldberg, Amos 5
Goldfeld, David 53
Goll, Yvonne 57
Gong, Alfred 53
Gosetti-Ferencei, Jennifer Anna 129
Gradowski, Zalman 2
"Grains of Wheat" (Sutzkever) 66
Gran, Wiera 136
"The Grave Child" (Sutzkever) 77
"Grodek" (Trakl) 56
Gubar, Susan 13–14, 96
Guernica (Spain) 114
Gyor (Hungary) 18

Hamacher, Werner 83, 93
Haman 35
Hardy, Thomas 75
Hartman, Geoffrey 2, 83, 87

INDEX

Hatikvah (Imber) 50
"He" (Weißglas) 57
Heaney, Seamus 113
Heart of Darkness (Conrad) 77
Heidegger, Martin 18, 76, 80–1, 84–5, 89–95, 200
Heine, Heinrich 54, 107, 181–2
Her Absence, This Wanderer (Zolf) 198
"Here Too, As in Jerusalem" (Jastrun) 70, 73
Hirsch, Marianne 183, 186
History of the Peloponnesian War (Thucydides) 127
Hitler, Adolf 6, 45, 51, 70, 127
Hölderlin, Friedrich 57–8
The Holocaust Kingdom (Rousset) 40
Holocaust Poetry (Rowland) 13
"Holocaust Poetry" (Rowland and Eaglestone) 13
Holy Week (Andrzejewski) 73
Honduras 150
Honel, Maurice 10
Horace 71–2
Horánszky (Hungary) 128
Horthy, Miklós 32, 127
Hosea 173
House of the Dead (Dostoevsky) 7
The Human Race (Antelme) 200–1
Hungary 18, 32–3, 108–9, 113, 116–18, 120, 123–5, 128–9

"I Cannot Know ..." (Radnóti) 117
If This Is a Man (Levi) 7, 26
"I Lie in a Coffin" (Sutzkever) 62, 67
"I Long to Say a Prayer" (Sutzkever) 76
The Inferno (Dante) 7, 67, 75
"In the City of Slaughter" (Bialik) 3–4, 68
"In the Wondrous Month of May" (Heine) 181
"Into Life" (Ausländer) 54
Isaac (patriarch) 3, 29, 37
Isaiah 60, 68–9, 77, 119, 124, 168–9, 173
Ishmael 37
Israel, Land of 11, 19, 20–1, 29–30, 32, 36–7, 44, 50, 52, 76, 80, 95, 163, 168, 171–4, 178, 183, 193–4, 198
"It is Time" (Szlengel) 141, 150
"I with My Son Tzvi" (Katzenelson) 163–4

Jacob (patriarch) 50, 54
Jakobson, Roman 141, 181, 193
James, Henry 74
Janowska concentration camp 9, 59
Janz, Marlies 83
Jarecka, Gustawa 143
Jastrun, Mieczysław (Moshe Agatstein) 4, 15, 55, 70, 73
Jens, Walter 57
Jeremiah 4, 28, 54, 68–9, 160, 170, 173
Jerusalem 28, 54, 70, 73, 194
Jesus of Nazareth 29–30, 123, 198
"The Jewess" (Kolmar) 4
Job 4, 30, 34–7, 60, 151, 159, 170–1, 201
Job (Katzenelson) 4, 159
John (apostle) 30, 198
Journal of a Plague Year (Defoe) 27
The Journey (Fink) 180
Joyce, James 75

Kabbalah 31–2
Kac, Szymon 154
Kaczerginski, Shmaryahu 4, 6
Kafka, Franz 7, 130
Kaplan, Chaim 3
Karlsruhe (Germany) 181
Kassow, Samuel 135, 163
Katzenelson, Benjamin 163, 165
Katzenelson, Bentzion 163, 165
Katzenelson, Hannah 163, 165–6, 174
Katzenelson, Itzhak 4, 10, 13, 19–20, 43, 150, 154, 157–74, 177, 197
Katzenelson, Tzvi 158, 163–4, 174
Katznelson, Berl 173–4
Ka-Tsetnik (pseudonym of Yehiel Dinur, born Yehiel Feiner) 13
Kazin, Alfred 35
Keren-Kratz, Menachem 31–2
Khmelnitsky, Bohdan 21, 50
Kielce (Poland) 73
Kien, Peter 6

Kilanowski, Piotr 132
Kishinev (now Chişinău, Moldova) 3
Kittner, Alfred 53, 57
Klemperer, Viktor 51
Klepfisz, Irena 12
Kligerman, Eric 59
Kofman, Sarah 200–1
Kolitz, Zvi 30
Kolmar, Gertrud (pseudonym of Gertrud Käthe Chodziesner) 4
"Kol Nidre" (Sutzkever) 65
Komlós, Aladár 107, 110
Korczak, Janusz 19, 137–8
Kosinski, Jerzy 28
Kossak, Zofia 73
Kotarska, Ewelina 188
Kott, Jan 15
Kovner, Abba 6, 16
Kowalczyk, Adam 148
Kraków (Poland) 4, 72, 157
Kremer, Aaron 14
Krieger, Murray 199
Kulka, Otto Dov 7
Kun, Béla 109

Lacan, Jacques 73
Lackner, Ruth 48
Lacoue-Labarthe, Philippe 81, 93
Ladin, Joy 12
Lamentations (Jeremiah) 4, 68, 172
Landscapes of the Metropolis of Death (Kulka) 7
Langer, Lawrence 5, 7, 27, 56
Language and Silence (Steiner) 7, 45
The Language of the Third Reich (Klemperer) 51
Lengyel, Olga 40
Lanzmann, Claude 21, 184–5
Lasker-Schüler, Else 51
The Last Lullaby (Kremer) 14
"Latrine" (Eich) 57
Laub, Dori 8
"Lazarean Literature" (Cayrol) 30
"Lazarus among Us" (Cayrol) 30
Lazarus of Bethany 30, 124
"The Lead Plates of Romm's Printing House" (Sutzkever) 66
Legends of Our Time (Wiesel) 26, 31

Leiner, Shmuel Shlomo (Radziner Rebbe) 172
Lejeune, John A. 28
Lekert, Hirsh 64
"Lekh-Lekho" (Shayevich) 2
"Letter to My Wife" (Radnóti) 122
Levi, Primo 7, 26
Levi-Yitskhak of Berdichev 30
Levinas, Emmanuel 8, 31, 94, 104
Levine, Madeline G. 194
Lewin, Abraham 3, 158
"Like a Bull" (Radnóti) 126
Linden, Jérôme 25
Literari (magazine) 54
The Literature of Destruction (Roskies) 14
"A Little Flower" (Sutzkever) 64
"Little Station of Treblinka" (Szlengel) 19, 141, 147–8
Live Journal (Szlengel) 136
Łódź 1, 9, 136, 157, 159, 202
London 28, 66, 180
Lorca, Federico García 112
Lorsi, Miklós 127
The Lost Melody (Ring) 31
Lublin 58, 161–2, 165
Lucretius 118
Lvov (Lwów; L'viv, Ukraine) 9, 59, 71
Lyotard, Jean-François 47, 200

Maccabees 4, 50
MacNeice, Louis 129
Magun, Liza 67, 69
Maimonides (Moshe ben Maimon) 100
Majdanek concentration camp (Poland) 28, 64
Mallarmé, Stéphane 56, 83
Mandatory Palestine. *See* Israel, Land of
Mandelstam, Osip 60
"Mandorla" (Celan) 84–5, 87, 94
Manger, Itzik 52
Mann, Mendel 44
Margul-Sperber, Alfred 53
Marranos 171
Marszałek, Magdalena 186, 191
"Matière de Bretagne" (Celan) 85
Mauriac, François 29–30, 32, 35

Meditations on Metaphysics (Adorno) 59
"Memory of France" (Celan) 90
Mengele, Josef 202
Menninghaus, Winfried 83
"Meridian" (Celan) 11, 88–9, 91, 104
The Messiah (Schulz) 202
Miłosz, Czesław 10, 15–17, 43, 69–74, 77, 113, 142, 153
"Mira the Teacher" (Sutzkever) 64–5
Mitchell, Stephen 98
"Mnemosyne" (Hölderlin) 58
Mohács (Hungary) 126
"A Monument" (Szlengel) 19, 141, 143, 145, 147
Morányi, Ede 120
Moses 11, 68, 198
"Mother". *See* "Black Flakes" (Celan)
"My Testament" (Słowacki) 72

Nahum 123
Naiberg, Leon 155
"National Song" (Petőfi) 118
"Nearness of Graves" (Celan) 53, 59
Negative Dialectics (Adorno) 46–7, 74
Neher, André 37
"Neither Memory, Nor Magic" (Radnóti) 117
"Never Say This Is Your Last Road" (Glick) 4
New Moon (Radnóti) 126
Nibelungenlied 53, 124
Nietzsche, Friedrich 2, 35, 74, 200
Night (Wiesel) 4, 13, 16, 25–40
Night and Fog (Resnais) 26, 30
Nineveh 123
"Nocturne" (Celan) 48
"Non omnis moriar" (Ginczanka) 71
No-One's Rose (Celan) 81, 87–8
No One's Witness: A Monstrous Poetics (Zolf) 198
Norwid, Cyprian Kamil 61
"Nothing: History and Materiality in Celan" (Fioretos) 81
"The Nothingness" (Celan) 82–5
Novitch, Miriam 174
Nusboym, Shloyme 159

Obejas, Achy 198
Ofn pripetchik (Warshawsky) 4
"Once" (Celan) 101–2
"An Opening for Satan" (Pagis) 98–9
Ortutay, Gyula 128
Ószivác (Sivac, Serbia) 127
"Our Shtetl Is Burning" (Gebirtig) 4
Out of the Depths (underground anthology) 15, 55
Owen, Wilfred 75
Oyneg Shabbos (Ringelblum) 1, 5–6, 134–6, 141–2, 148, 159, 202
Ozick, Cynthia 49
Ozsváth, Zsuzsanna 113, 116, 118–19

Pagan Salute (Radnóti) 126
"A Page from the *Aktion* Diary" (Szlengel) 19, 138
Pagis, Dan 10, 17–18, 52, 79–82, 94–105, 164
A Painted Bird (Kosinski) 28
Pancsova (Pančevo, Serbia) 125
Pap, Károly 110
Papirosen (Yablokoff) 61
Paraguay 150
Paris 29, 32, 40, 59
"Passports" (Szlengel) 141, 150
"Penal Colony" (Radnóti) 130
Peretz, Y. L. 60, 65–66
Perlman, Hillel ("Monsieur Chouchani") 31
Petliura, Symon 50
Petőfi, Sándor 118, 127
Pforr, Franz 56
Picasso, Pablo 114
Picture Postcards (Radnóti) 10, 18, 115, 124
The Plague (Camus) 29
Plato 120, 200
"Poem–Closed, Poem–Open" (Celan) 105
Poems from the Ghetto (Sutzkever) 61, 69
Poetry of the Holocaust (Boase-Beier and de Vooght) 14, 52
"A Poor Christian Looks at the Ghetto" (Miłosz) 70, 142

Poland 9–10, 15, 31, 33, 67, 73–4, 113, 136–7, 150, 157, 178, 180
Pollin-Galay, Hannah 61
Ponar (Ponary, Lithuania) 4, 6, 63, 67, 71, 167–8
Popovici, Tristan 48
"Postcards from France" (Radnóti) 18
Proust, Marcel 110, 122
"Psalm" (Celan) 75, 87, 89, 98, 105, 201
"Psalm" (Trakl) 57, 76
Psalms 90, 97, 168

"Quiet, Quiet" (Kaczerginski) 4

Radautz (Rădăuți, Romania) 80
Radnóti, Fanni (Fifi) 109–11, 115, 120, 124, 128–9
Radnóti, Miklós (Glatter) 10, 15, 18, 43, 107–30, 177
Radzin (Poland) 172
The Rainbow (Ausländer) 54
Ravitch, Melech 66
"Remembrance" (Hölderlin) 57–8
Resnais, Alain 26, 30
"Resurrection" (Sutzkever) 77
Ricoeur, Paul 157
Riga 1
Rilke, Rainer Maria 45, 56
Rimbaud, Arthur 54–5, 56
Ring, Yechezkel 31
Ringelblum, Emanuel 1, 5–6, 134–7, 142, 148, 159, 164, 202
Rodway, Stella 25
"Roll Call" (Pagis) 97–8, 99–100, 104–5
Roman Empire 113
Romania 14, 31–2, 47–8, 52–3, 58, 95, 113, 124–5, 128
"Root" (Radnóti) 122
Rose, Sven-Erik 158, 161
Rosenfarb, Chava 202
Rosenfeld, Alvin 11
Rosenkranz, Moses 53
Roskies, David G. 1, 3, 13–14, 60–1, 67, 136, 159–60, 164–5
Rousset, David 22, 40
Rowland, Anthony 8, 13

Russia 47–8, 58, 64–5, 125, 180
"Russian Spring" (Celan) 53

Sachs, Nelly 11, 16, 51
Salvation (Miłosz) 70
The Sand from the Urns (Celan) 58
Sarah (matriarch) 37
Sartre, Jean-Paul 30, 46–7, 91
Sasel labor camp (Germany) 202
Sassoon, Siegfried 75
Schiller, Johann Christoph Friedrich von 6
Schindler's List (Spielberg) 21
Schreyer, Isaac 53
Schulz, Bruno 202
Schwartz, Maurice 66
Schwarz, Daniel R. 31
Schwarz, Jan 15
Schwarz, Peter Paul 83
A Scrap of Time (Fink) 180–2, 192, 194
"Second Eclogue" (Radnóti) 114
Secret City (Sutzkever) 61
Seidman, Naomi 26
"'A Self-Unsealing Poetic Text'" (Krieger) 199
Serbia 18, 114, 120, 123, 125
"Seventh Eclogue" (Radnóti) 121
Shakespeare, William 48
Shallcross, Bożena 132, 145–6
"The Shawl" (Ozick) 49–50
Shayevich, Simkha Bunim 5
"Shibboleth for Paul Celan" (Derrida) 79
Shmueli, Efraim 171
Shner, Moshe 160
Shoah (Lanzmann) 21, 184–5
Sholem Aleichem (Solomon Rabinovich) 31, 64, 172–3
Shulamit 56
Shulamite and Maria (Pforr) 56
Siberia 47, 63, 76
Sighet (Sziget, Hungary; Sighetu Marmatiei, Romania) 31–3
Sík, Sándor 109
"The Silesian Weavers" (Heine) 54
Simonov, Konstantin 58
Sitwell, Osbert 75
Slovakia 113

INDEX

Słowacki, Juliusz 72
Sobibor extermination camp (Poland) 167–8
Sodom 34
"The Soldier" (Brooke) 75
Solomon, Petre 58, 199
"So Many Constellations" (Celan) 90, 93–4, 98
"Song for the Last Ones" (Sutzkever) 68
"Song of a Jewish Poet in 1943" (Sutzkever) 66
Song of Songs 56
"Song of the Cedar" (Feld) 50
Song of the Murdered Jewish People (Katzenelson) 10, 19, 157–8, 166–74
"The Song of the Rabbi of Radzin" (Katzenelson) 172
"The Song of Shloyme Zhelikhovsky" (Katzenelson) 171
Soviet Union 4, 117, 159. See also Russia
Spain 122
Spiegel, Isaiah 1
Spielberg, Steven 21
"Spring Flies…" (Radnóti) 118
"Spring 1942" (Shayevich) 2
Srebnik, Simon 184
Steep Road (Radnóti) 111
Steiner, George 7, 12, 45, 56, 59
Stifled Words (Kofman) 200
"Stretto" (Celan) 81, 83–6, 105, 199
"Suddenly" (Radnóti) 118
Sundquist, Eric 7
"Surely, the People Is Grass" (Bialik) 68
Survivors and Exiles (Schwarz) 15
Sutzkever, Abraham (Avrom) 2, 5–6, 10, 13–14, 16–17, 43, 61–9, 71, 74, 76–7, 197
Sutzkever, Freydke 69
"Spring Flies …" (Radnóti) 118
Szeged (Hungary) 109
Szeintuch, Yechiel 1, 15, 160
Szentkirályszabadja (Hungary) 125, 127–8
Szilai, Sándor 128
Szires, George 129

Szlengel, Władysław 10, 18–20, 43, 71, 131–55, 157–8, 177, 197, 201–2
Szmerling, Mieczysław 149
Szondi, Léopold 83, 93
Szpilman, Władysław 136

Tăbăreşti (Romania) 48
Tabenkin, Yitzhak 173
Tálas, András 128
Teichman, Milton 2
"Telephone" (Szlengel) 133–4
Temesvár (Timişoara, Romania) 125
Tenenbaum–Tamaroff, Mordecai 159
Terence 21
Tess of the d'Ubervilles (Hardy) 75
"Testimony" (Pagis) 100–01
Texts for Nothing I (Beckett) 83
Theresienstadt (Terezín) 6–7, 14, 51
"There Was Earth inside Them" (Celan) 12, 87
"Things" (Szlengel) 71, 141, 143–5
"Third Eclogue" (Radnóti) 117
The Thirteen Principles of Jewish Faith (Maimonides) 100
"The Three Gifts" (Peretz) 65
Thucydides 127
Titel (Serbia) 125
Tito, Josip Broz 125
"Todtnauberg" (Celan) 93–4, 105
Toker, Leona 4
Tolstoy, Leo 28
"To One Who Stood Before the Door" (Celan) 81, 85
"To the Polish Reader" (Szlengel) 133
"Traces" (Fink) 20, 177–95
Tractatus (Wittgenstein) 100
"The Train Engine" (Tuwim) 5
Trakl, Georg 56–7, 76
Transnistria 47, 53
Transylvania 32, 113
Treblinka extermination camp (Poland) 19, 131, 136, 141, 145, 147–8, 151–2, 163, 167–8
Tristan and Isolde (Wagner) 56
Turgenev, Ivan Sergeyevich 62
A Turmoil in Heaven (Ring) 31
Tuwim, Julian 4, 15, 136, 146

Udoff, Alan 14
Ujvidék (Novi Sad, Serbia) 125
Ukraine 15, 21, 47, 49, 53, 118–19, 122, 178
Ullmann, Viktor 6
Under Gemini (Radnóti) 110, 113, 115
United States 15, 173
"Upon the Slaughter" (Bialik) 160
Uruguay 150

Verlaine, Paul 56, 109
Vice, Sue 43, 129
Vienna 32, 113
Vilna (Wiłno; Vilnius, Lithuania) 2, 5–6, 17, 60–77
"Vinegrowers" (Celan) 105
Virgil 109, 112–13, 118, 123, 129
Vittel (France) 19–20, 158, 163, 165, 168, 173–4
The Vittel Diary (Katzenelson) 20, 163, 165, 168
Volková, Bronislava 27
Volyn 170
von der Vogelweide, Walter 124

Wagner, Richard 56
"War Diary" (Radnóti) 113, 122
War and Peace (Tolstoy) 28
Warsaw 1, 3–4, 6, 10, 15, 17–19, 70–4, 131–36, 139, 141, 143, 145, 147–8, 150, 152, 157–60, 162–5, 171, 173, 178, 202
We, the Polish Jews (Tuwim) 15
Weißglas, Immanuel 53, 57
Weimar (Germany) 45
Weinfeld, David 194
"What I Read to the Dead" (Szlengel) 132, 139, 142
"What is Metaphysics?" (Heidegger) 92–3
"What Remains?" (Arendt) 51
White, Hayden 28

Wiesel, Elie 4, 11, 13, 16, 20, 25–40, 173, 198
Wiesel, Marion 25
Wieviorka, Annette 179
Wilkomirski, Binjamin 28
Wilson, Woodrow 7
"Window onto the Other Side" (Szlengel) 132
"Winter" (Celan) 49–50
"The Witching Hour" (Celan) 48
Wittgenstein, Ludwig 100
"Woe to You" (Katzenelson) 161–2, 164–5
Wolosky, Shira 83, 87
The Writing of Destruction (Blanchot) 129
Writings of Those Condemned to Death under the Nazi Occupation, 1939–45 (Borwicz) 9
"Written in Pencil in the Sealed Railway Car" (Pagis) 95, 105, 164

Yad Vashem (Israel) 183
Yedi'ot akhronot (newspaper) 29
"Yigdal" (Dayan) 100
"Yosl Rakover Talks to God" (Kolitz) 30
Young, James E. 3
Yugoslavia. *See* Serbia

Žagubica (Serbia) 120
Zambor (Sombor, Serbia) 125
Zaritt, Saul Noam 14
Zbaraż (Poland; Zbarazh, Ukraine) 178
Zduńska Wola (Poland) 171
Zeitlin, Hillel 164–5
Ziarek, Ewa Plonowska 83, 89, 93, 102
Zimony (Serbia) 125
Zohar 32, 36, 103
Zolf, Rachel 198
Zuckerman, Yitzhak (Antek) 159
Żukowski, Tomasz 73

www.ingramcontent.com/pod-product-compliance
Lightning Source LLC
Chambersburg PA
CBHW070025010526
44117CB00011B/1710